FINANCIAL AND OPERATING PERFORMANCE OF INDIAN AUTOMOBILE INDUSTRY

FINANCIAL AND OPERATING PERFORMANCE OF INDIAN AUTOMOBILE INDUSTRY

A. MANOR SELVI

GYAN

This publication has been financially supported by ICSSR, New Delhi and the responsibility for the facts stated, opinions expresses and conclusions reached is entirely that of the author and ICSSR accepts no responsibility for them.

Consultant:

Professor. R.K. Mishra, Institute of Public Enterprise, Hyderabad has acted as Research consultant on behalf of Indian Social Science Research, New Delhi, for the publication of this work.

Financial and Operating Performance of Indian Automobile Industry

ISBN: 978-81-212-1048-5

Published in 2010 in India by
Gyan Publishing House
23, Main Ansari Road, Darya Ganj
New Delhi-110002
Phones : 23282060, 23261060
Fax : 011-23285914
E-mail: books@gyanbooks.com
Website: www.gyanbooks.com

Laser Type Setting by: Rudra Computer Graphics, Delhi
Printed at : Chawla Offset Printers, Delhi

Contents

Foreword

Finance is the nerve centre and lifeline of any economic activity and is, therefore, omnipresent in every sphere of economic and business life. It plays an extremely crucial role in the continuity and growth of a business. Financial management has been viewed as an integral part of overall management. An enterprise, which commits itself to an activity, requires finance. No business firm can be promoted, established and expanded without adequate financial resources. Success and survival of a business firm depends on how well its finance function is managed. The firm may have abundant resources—human and physical – but if the available funds are not properly utilized for the benefit of the firm, it will come to an early end.

The finance manager has to utilize the available funds for the benefit of the business firm. Every effort should be made to render the finance function as effective as possible. Successful financial management of a business firm is manifested by certain benefits, liked increased profitability, raising share prices, regular dividends to shareholders, attractive remuneration to employees and in short, the all round progress of the company. Financial and Operating performance analysis constitutes the approach to judge the effectiveness of the finance function of the firm.

Dr. A. Manor Selvi has examined the Financial and Operating Performance of Indian Automobile Sector based on the selected automobile companies. This book explains implication of better financial management in the Indian Automobile Industry of the present environment apart from clearly explaining the very subject. This book not only explains exhaustively the theoretical aspects of the subject but also makes it easy to understand its applied aspects.

I congratulate Dr. A. Manor Selvi, for her in-depth study on the subject and coming out with a very concise and precise book. I wish her every success in her entire future endeavour.

Dr. A.Vijayakumar
Associate Professor in Commerce
Erode Arts and Science College
Erode-638009, Tamil Nadu

Preface

The term 'Globalisation' has in fact become the magic term of the recent years. It has attracted the attention of the people both at home and abroad. Indian economy is faced with serious problems in the beginning of 90's—large trade deficits, huge foreign debt, sharp decline in the external value of rupees, low economic efficiency, recession. All the above factors led to fiscal and external imbalances, inflation, chronic unemployment and such other related consequences. Considering the graveness of the situation, the government came with a package of comprehensive economic reforms. It has often been characterised as an attempt to globalize our economy in the sense of its being moved closer to an effective integration with the world economy. Initiated in July 1991, liberalization of trade and free enterprise aims at globalization of Indian economy with a view to improve efficiency of production through infusion of competitiveness amongst the Indian traders and producers.

The Indian Industrial manufacturing sector, which posses a relatively high marginal propensity to save and invest contributes significantly to the eventual achievement of a self-sustaining economy with continued high levels of investment and rapid rate of increase in income and industrial development. Automobile Industry is a major constituent of surface transport. It plays a significant role in the GDP of the country. India has growing market potential for automobiles due to rise in demand. The automobile industry has been identified as a high-focus sector by the Indian government. Adequate incentives have been provided to automobile companies to encourage growth in the sector. The vision of the government is to make India a global hub for the manufacture of automobiles. Therefore, the present study was undertaken for a proper insight in to the Financial and Operating performance of Indian Automobile Industry.

This book contains various aspects of financial and operating performance in the Indian Automobile Industry. Further, in order to cater to the needs of research scholars, teachers and financial executive, the subject matter in the book has been treated in a conceptual-cum-analytical manner. The book is intended to be useful for practicing managers, financial executives working in the service sectors, students of M.Com, MBA, MFC and other banking professional examinations. Further, this book is of special interest of PhD and M.Phil scholars of various universities, colleges and research institutions. The contents of the book may be much useful to researchers pursuing research in the field of working capital management.

I earnestly hope that it would serve its purpose and meet the market needs. However, I would gratefully welcome suggestions and feedback from colleagues, students and practitioners. Any constructive criticism will undoubtedly help us greatly to enhance our research capability. I express our heartfelt gratitude to God Almighty whose blessings guided me in carrying out the research successfully. The work presented in this book could be possible only because of the co-operation, guidance and assistance given by a number of persons and a few institutions. It is difficult to recount them all and I tender due apologies to all those contributions I have not been able to recount. However, I cannot afford not to mention a few.

I am highly obliged to my supervisor and guide Dr. A.Vijayakumar, M.Com., M.Phil., Ph.D., PGDCA, Associate Professor in Commerce, Erode Arts College, Erode for his availability, friendly approach, right direction, qualities of a good mentor which acted as great fillip to me to pursue the research work. I thank him profusely for having spared his precious time for discussion for hours together in computing the task. It was he who inspired me to develop the ideas on original lines and guided me with his new approach and valuable suggestions which have helped me a lot in bringing out the thesis in the present form.

At the outset I wish to register my sincere thanks to Bharathiar University, Coimbatore, the Management of Erode Arts College, to the former Principal-in-charge Mr. P. Ramasamy M.Sc., M.Phil., and to the present Principal Dr. V. Venkateswaran, M.Sc., M.Phil., Ph.D., FCRSI, Erode Arts College, Erode for having provided me an opportunity to pursue my research study during 2005-2007 under full-time programme.

My special thanks go to HOD of Commerce and faculty members of Department of Commerce, Erode Arts College, Erode for offering constant encouragement, extensive help, valuable comments and necessary guidance. I am also thankful to faculty members of other departments, Erode Arts College, Erode for evincing keen interest in my work. I also express my heartfelt thanks to all the non-teaching staffs of Erode Arts College, Erode. I am very grateful to Librarian, Erode Arts College, Erode. Mr. S. Sivakumar Librarian, PSG Institute of Management, Coimbatore and all the librarians of various Universities, Colleges and IFMR (Chennai), the interview with them proved highly beneficial in locating the missing links in the present study.

I also thank Indian Council of Social Science Research, New Delhi for providing financial assistance under Publication of Doctoral theses grant for publishing this work. I also extend my profound thanks to Gyan Publishing House, New Delhi, for giving shape to my ideas by publishing this book in a record time.

I wish to thank Prof. V.M. Antonisamy, Rtd. Professor, who checked and improved my language by correction mistakes in spelling, grammar, punctuation, etc.,.

My sincere thanks are also due to PSG Institute of Management (Learning Resource Centre), Coimbatore and Institute of Financial Management and Research (IFMR) Chennai who have made available to me the books, periodicals and other literature mentioned in this study.

I express my gratitude to my beloved parents, brothers, sisters and friends and all other associates and well wishers, who have extended their strong support, co-operation and encouragement in my life and especially in the thesis work done by me. I also thank SS InfoTech, Erode for their computed job work done neatly and on time.

A. MANOR SELVI

Acknowledgements

The investigator express her heartfelt gratitude to God Almighty whose blessings guided her in carrying out the research successfully.

The work presented in this thesis could be possible only because of the co-operation, guidance and assistance given by a number of persons and a few institutions. It is difficult to recount them all and I tender due apologies to all those whose contributions I have not been able to recount. However, I cannot afford not to mention a few.

I am highly obliged to my supervisor and guide **Dr. A.Vijayakumar, M.Com., M.Phil., Ph.D., PGDCA.,** Reader in Commerce, Erode Arts College, Erode for his availability, friendly approach, right direction, qualities of a good mentor which acted as great fillip to me to pursue the research work. I thank him profusely for having spared his precious time for discussion for hours together in computing the task. It was he who inspired me to develop the ideas on original lines and guided me with his new approach and valuable suggestions which have helped me a lot in bringing out the thesis in the present form.

At the outset I wish to register my sincere thanks to Bharathiar University, Coimbatore, the Management of Erode Arts College, to the former Principal-in-charge **Mr. K. Ramasamy M.Sc., M.Phil.,** and to the present Principal **Dr. V. Venkateswaran, M.Sc., M.Phil., Ph.D., FCRSI** Erode Arts College, Erode for having provided me an opportunity to pursue my research study during 2005-2007 under full-time programme.

My special thanks go to **Dr. M. Balachandran,** HOD of Commerce and faculty members of Department of Commerce, Erode Arts College, Erode for offering constant encouragement, extensive help, valuable comments and necessary guidance.

I am also thankful to faculty members of other departments, Erode Arts College, Erode for envincing keen interest in my work. I also express my heartfelt thanks to all the non-teaching staffs of Erode Arts College, Erode.

I am very grateful to Librarian, Erode Arts College, Erode Mr. S. Sivakumar Librarian, PSG Institute of Management, Coimbatore and all the librarians of various Universities, Colleges and IFMR (Chennai), the interview with them proved highly beneficial in locating the missing links in the present study.

I wish to thank Prof. **V.M. Antonisamy,** Rtd. Professor, who checked and improved my language by correction mistakes in spelling, grammar, punctuation, etc.

My sincere thanks are also due to PSG Institute of Management (Learning Resource Centre), Coimbatore and Institute of Financial Management and Research (IFMR) Chennai who have made available to me the books, periodicals and other literature mentioned in this study.

Special words of thanks are due to the officials of various industries selected for study for providing me with necessary information and materials.

I express my gratitude to my beloved parents, brothers, sisters and friends and all other associates and well wishers, who have extended their strong support, co-operation and encouragement in my life and especially in the thesis work done by me.

I also thank SS InfoTech, Erode for their computed job work done neatly and on time.

A. MANOR SELVI

List of Tables

List of Figures

1

Introduction

Corporate sector in one form or other existed in the ancient past. But, at that time much attention was not paid to it. With the passage of time, the corporate sector has come to play a predominant role in the economic life of almost all countries, irrespective of their ideological moorings. This sector has been recognized as a model and democratic form of business organisation. It occupies a pivotal place not only in the industrially advanced countries, but also in the developing countries like India. The process of industrialization and development of business activity in these countries are interrelated and interdependent. This sector, inturn, operates within the purview of the economic environment, industrial culture and political and social philosophy.

The corporate sector is the backbone of the Indian economy so far as it provides a vital, effective and organised system for the growth of the industrial as well as non-industrial sectors of the economy. The contribution of corporate sector towards the balanced development of various areas of an organised economic activity can easily be seen in the combined efforts of various companies in achieving the goal of industrialisation and increased production. Corporate sectors have short term goals such as improving annual profits and value added as well as long term goals in terms of contribution to national wealth, creation of more employment, building up infrastructural facilities, building up a broad-based and healthy capital structure, operating of essential services, creating export potential and thus participating actively in the overall economic growth of a country and improving the standard of living of its people. Ultimately, the Gross Domestic Product (GDP) and the tax revenue to the Government in the form of both direct and indirect taxes are maximized. The rapid growth of the corporate sector in India and the increasing scale of its operations and investments have turned it into the most dominant form of economic organisation.

The ever increasing importance and role of corporate sector in the economic growth of a country, particularly, in the developing country like India, have attracted several academicians, professional institutions, researchers and administrators to conduct diversified studies in this area. There is the need to study the industries' internal efficiency which ultimately shall determine the overall industrial development in future. The present study is a small endeavor to update our knowledge in this aspect.

Meaning and Concept of Financial Appraisal

Finance is the nerve centure and lifeline of any economic activity and is, therefore, omnipresent in every sphere of economic and business life. It plays an extremely crucial role in the continuity and growth of a business. Financial management has been viewed as an integral part of overall management. An enterprise, which commits itself to an activity, requires finance. No business firm can be promoted, established and expanded without adequate financial resources. Success and survival of a business firm depends on how well its financial function is managed. The firm may have abundant resources-human and physical, but if the available funds are not properly utilized for the benefit of the firm, it will come to an early end. So, the finance manager has to utilize the available funds for the benefit of the business firm. Every effort should be made to render the financial functions as effective as possible. Successful financial management of a business firm is manifested by certain benefits, like increased profitability, raising share prices, regular dividends to shareholders, attractive remuneration to employees and in short, the all round progress of the company. Financial performance analysis constitutes the approach to judge the effectiveness of the financial function of the firm.

Financial analysis is a process of evaluating relationship between various components to obtain a better understanding of a firm's position and performance[1]. It is the process of identifying the financial strength and weaknesses of the firm by properly establishing relationship between the items in the balance sheet and the profit and loss account[2]. Financial analysis is a process of synthesis and intellectual activity. It is a technique of X-raying the financial position as well as the progress of a company. An analysis of financial statement gives a comprehensive understanding of business operations and their impact on the financial health. If the business operations result in profits, the total investment is enhanced, bringing prosperity to shareholders, increasing goodwill and strengthening of credit. On the other hand, if there are losses, capital invested to the extent of loss is lost or dissipated ability to pay creditors and lenders is weakened and the business concern operates under a "handicap".

Need and Aims of Financial Analysis

Financial statement analysis is useful both as a way to anticipate future conditions and more important as a starting point for planning action that will influence future course of events[3]. Analysis of financial statements is an effort to find answer to a variety of practical and important questions such as prospects for future earnings, ability to pay interest, debt maturities and profitability of a sound dividend policy, etc. The main importance of financial analysis is the pin-pointing of the strengths and weaknesses of a business enterprise by regrouping and analysing the figures contained in financial statements. Satisfactory diagnosis can rarely be made on the basis of such information which are included in these financial statements alone because figures are dumb. But, if they are analysed, they get tongue and therefore they help the management and other interested parties in accessing financial adventures of an enterprise.

In any economic society all active participants do become interested in varying degrees in the performance of the business enterprise. Within every commercial enterprise, of whatever size, there are inevitably many different interests to be served[4]. Some of these interest groups include owners, employees, customers, society, government, suppliers and managers. By appraising the performance through financial statement analysis, management may review a company's progress to date and decide upon the course of action to be taken in future. Performance appraisal helps management in the task of planning of operations.

Investors comprising shareholders and debenture holders, have a vital interest in the appraisal of performance of an enterprise. Investors are interested in two things: Firstly, they want the safety of their investment; secondly, the ability of a company to earn profit. They are also interested in a concern whose future is bright. Through performance appraisal they get the information which they need. Creditors are interested in ascertaining whether the company can employ the funds loaned to in such a way that it will be to meet current interest obligations and repay loan when it falls due. They act as magic eye highlighting the credit worthiness of a company. Creditors often appraise the performance of a company before lending the money and supplying the goods. Government regulates economic activities in various spheres. Central and State Government and local authorities are also interested in knowing the performance of a business in order to assess their revenues through various taxes to regulate capital issues and public utility regulations. Employees have an interest in the operating results and the financial strength of a company. The remuneration of workers must be generated from the company's revenues.

Thus, workers wages, to a great extent, depend upon the success of the firm. Labour unions use the performance data as a basis for their demand for increase in wages. The past operating performance of the business as well as its current financial position is often studied to measure the ability of the enterprise to meet new wage commitments. Every business enterprise has its own social responsibility. Although managers, owners, creditors and employees are members of the society and have their respective interest in the business, individuals or groups of individuals apart, the society as a whole has some expectations from the business. So they are all interested in knowing the social performance such as environmental obligations, labours and social welfare, employment generated, regional development etc.,. In addition to the above, news agencies, trade associations, economic and commercial research institutions, members of parliament, members of public accounts committee in respect of government companies are also interested in the results of performance appraisal to know the progress being made in the present position of an industry.

Tools and Techniques for Analysis of Financial Statements

There are many techniques which may be used for analysing financial statements. These techniques may be classified as follows:

(a) Accounting Techniques

(b) Statistical Techniques

(c) Mathematical Techniques

Accounting techniques or tools which may be used for financial analysis are many such as ratio analysis, common-size statement analysis, trend analysis, comparative statement analysis, value added analysis etc. The users pick up the techniques to suit their requirements and also on the basis of data available to them. Further, use of statistical techniques has become a normal phenomenon in any type of analysis. This statistical techniques which are proposed to be used in financial statement analysis consists of measures of central tendency like mean, median, mode, measures of dispersion, like range, mean deviation and standard deviation, correlation and regression analysis, analysis of time service, analysis of variance, chi-square test etc., Further, the use of various mathematical techniques is also made frequently for financial analysis. The mathematical tools generally applied are Programme Evaluation and Review Techniques (PERT), Critical Path Method (CPM), Linear Programming etc. However, in this study various accounting and statistical techniques have been applied for analysing the financial statement. The mathematical techniques could not be applied in the present study for want of necessary data.

Scope of the Study

Financial analysis is the process of determining the operating and financial characteristics of a firm from accounting and financial statements. The goals of such analysis are to determine the efficiencies or performance of firms management as reflected in the financial records and reports. The analyst attempts to measure the firms operating performance, profitability, liquidity, solvency etc. That the business is conduced in a rational and normal way ensuring enough returns to the shareholders to atleast maintain its market value. Keeping in view the interest of investors and the society as a whole, a company's performance can be evaluated broadly on three counts

1. On the basis of its operating achievement
2. On the basis of its financial achievement
3. On the basis of its social achievement

All the above factors have their own importance. Yet an investor, apart from other things first looks to get back sufficient returns on its investment. Therefore financial and operating performance of company stands the most important factor for its evaluation. The study continues itself to the financial and operating performance of selected industries. It excludes non financial areas such as personal and research and development etc., from its purview.

Statement of the Problem

India's manufacturing sector used to account for only about 10 per cent of its GDP in the early 1950s, but currently it accounts for about 19 per cent. The sector was highly protected from any form both internal and external competition over a long period of time and until the early 1990s when the country embraced the new economic policy. Since 1991, the manufacturing sector in the country has been undergoing a wave of liberalization, the main objective of it is to reduce, both external and internal barriers entry. Such a reduction, it was argued, would enhance the competitiveness of the sector and thereby making it more efficient. Since 1992-93, the manufacturing sector has grown at the rate of about 6.9 per cent per annum, though there have been considerable fluctuations in its growth rate. Against this background, it is very important to analyse the performance of manufacturing sector after liberalisation to show how the liberalization has really led to an improvement in the growth performance of the sector.

In India, the automobile industry is one of the largest industry. It is one of the key sectors of the economy. The industry has shown great advances since delicensing and opening up of the sector to Foreign Direct Investment (FDI) in 1991-92. It has deep forward and backward linkages with the rest of the economy, and hence has strong multiflier effect. The automobile industry including manufacture of components is estimated to provide employment directly to some 5 lakhs of people and indirectly to around 50 million people. This results in the automobile industry being the drainer of economic growth and India is keen to use it as a level of accelerated growth in the country. Therefore, the present study is undertaken to make the financial and operating performance of the selected sectors of the Indian automobile industry. The study is undertaken to analyse the growth of automobile industry after liberalization, production trend, sales trend, profitability analysis, financial structure, financial performance, assessment of financial health and Economic Value Added (EVA) analysis of the industry.

Production is considered as the backbone of the manufacturing sector. Production function is considered as the effective tool to satisfy the customers' demand and to operate in an economical and efficient manner. The study of the production performance is important to know the operating level of the business and financial efficiency of the business enterprise. Survival of the business in the present competitive world depends on the quality production and the technological development in the business. Therefore, the present study attempts to study the production trend of the Indian automobile industry after liberalization. Further the analysis of capacity utilisation can significantly provide the production performance of the industry as a whole. Therefore an attempt has also been made to study about the capacity utilisation of the selected sectors of the Indian automobile industry.

Sales is the important component for the development of the business. Sales can be enhanced only by following good sales policy. Due to the pricing policy of the government, the companies have to face some fluctuations in the sales. These fluctuations may lead to increase or decrease the financial risk of the companies. In order to study the sales trends of the automobile industry in India, the present study is carried out.

The efficiency of the business is measured by the amount of profit earned. The greater the profit, the more efficient is the business considered to be. The profit of a business may be measured by studying the profitability of investment in it. Profitability may be defined as the ability of a given investment to earn a return from its use. This ability is referred to as lending power or operating performance of the concerned investment. Profitability is a relative term and its relation with the other factors by which the profit is affected. It is the test of efficiency, powerful motivational factor and the measure of control in any business. Hence, an attempt has been made to study the profitability of Indian automobile industry after liberalisation.

Actually profitability is highly sensitive economic variable which is affected by a host of factors operating through a variety of ways. Some of them affect product prices and quantities; some affect cost of production while others make changes in capital stock, size, market share and growth of the firm. Further, corporate policy relating to various functions will affect profitability. Some of them are relevant in the short run while others have impact in the long run. It is difficult to build a theory of profitability, which accounts for all such factors. Because of these difficulties, it is quite natural to analyse the variation in profitability by taking the partial approach i.e., to find the effect of certain major variables, ignoring the implications of other left out independent variables at a time. The present study is a step towards this direction.

Financial appraisal provides a method for assessing the financial strengths and weaknesses of the Indian automobile industry using financial statements. There are two views of the financial strength of every organisation based on the period of lending i.e, the short term and long term. The short term financial strength relates to the technical solvency of an organization in the near future, while the long-term financial strength depends on the structure that has been imposed in financing more permanent assets requirements. The present study is made to analyse the short-term and long-term financial strength of the Indian automobile industry after liberalization.

The assessment of the corporate financial condition is important to financial analysts worldwide. The ability to discriminate between the weak and the strong, or between those that will fail or prosper, is critical to successful economic development. Bankers, suppliers of trade credit, stockholders, stock exchanges and governmental regulatory bodies, etc., have all a vested interest in appraising the strength of both emerging and established companies. To properly assess financial health, many tools can be brought to bear. Traditional financial ratio analysis is very important, but it can be used in conjunction with other tools. This study will combine ratio analysis with a statistical techniques and discriminate analysis. It will apply a popular model, The Altman's Z Score Model (Altman's, 1968) in order to assess the financial health of selected sectors of the Indian automobile industry.

According to accounting concept, business profit is measured by deducting expenses from income earned during the period. Notably, the accounting concept does not take into account opportunity cost and risk adjusted return on capital employed in the business. In order to overcome limitations of accounting - based measures of financial performance, Stern Steward and Company adopted modified concept of economic profit in 1990 named Economic Value Added (EVA)[5]. EVA as a tool of financial management which enlightens us whether operating profit is enough to cover the cost of capital. Shareholders must earn sufficient returns for the risk they have taken in investing their funds in company's capital. The EVA frame work, which is becoming a more and more admired tool for measuring the financial performance corporates, offers a consistent approach to set goals and measure performance, communicate with investors, evaluate strategies, allocate capital valuing acquisitions and determine incentive bonuses. The recognition of this concept in India is gradually picking up and it is excepted that in the coming years more and more Indian companies will start relying upon this new measure of financial performance. It can be believed that the concept of Economic Value Added, which is reasonably old in the west, appears relatively a new magic portion to Indian corporation and this has basically required the investigators to glimpse through its nuts and bolts particularly to value what EVA is all about in Indian context. This is the reason the present study has made an attempt to analyse emergence of EVA in the selected sectors of the Indian automobile industry.

The liberalization measures culminated in 1990-91 have opened up new business opportunities and allowed the expansion of the existing business similar to that of the corporations depended more on their performance and global competitiveness than on protection. This new situation demands more accurate tools of measuring the performance of the corporate, shareholders, managers, employees, customers, governments and other interested people who want to know whether the performance of the corporation justifies the investment made in them. For them the conventional tools did not provide enough of the required information. So this study aims to build new methods of analysing the performance of the corporations, by taking cases from accounting, statistics, finance and quantitative methods.

Selection of Automobile Industry

Transport sector is the backbone of country's economic growth and development. Transportation throughout the world has made possible an unprecedented level of mobility across the geographical boundaries. The mobility has given many people more options about where to live, and work than they had years ago. Similarly, mobility has broadened the access of business to new markets and more choices by increasing the available pool of resources. From the economic point of view, transportation is a vital factor for steady economic growth and development. The trade facilitated by transportation has been a growing component of national income in all the countries. Studies show that the contribution of transportation in GDP has a positive impact[6]. The structure of the economy also influences the transport system[7] because consumer expenditure on transportation contributes to national economy. Transport sector is equally important for both industrialized and developing economies. Transport sector including water transport, aviation and surface transport are major players of Gross Domestic Product (GDP), which includes the value of all goods and services. Being the largest transport networking in the world, particularly in road transportation, automobile industry plays a significant role in the GDP of the country.

Automobile industry is a major constituent of surface transport. Automobiles as a commodity include passenger cars, commercial vehicles, three wheelers and two wheelers. India has growing market potential for automobiles due to rise in demand. As a result more and more manufacturers are bringing in new forms of the existing product because diffusion of a new product depends upon demand statistics. Automobile manufactures, particularly car manufacturers are attracting buyers with new model shopping to tap growing demand for automobiles. Utility vehicles also posted significant growth. Further, two and three wheelers industries specially the motor cycle segments have shown a steep jump, while the volume growth of all the players has recorded pretty good market share. Therefore, automobile industry has been selected for this study in order to determine its financial and operational performance during the study period. In this study researcher focuses on automobiles such as commercial vehicles, passenger cars and multiutility vehicles and two and three wheelers.

Significance of the Study

Performance appraisal is of special importance in industries and automobile industry is one such industry. From the point of view of the socio-economic development of the country, automobile industry is significant enough in terms of investment and employment. The sales and profitability function in automobile industry differ from that of other industries. Even though many studies in this direction have been conducted, the present one would be of greater significance to many. It would help to understand the pattern and the structure of financial variables of leading companies apart from identifying the financial relationship of companies with their respective industries. The change in the economic policy of the government certainly has got impact on the performance of corporate units in India. A need at the present juncture is therefore felt to study the impact of such changes on the performance of corporate sector and hence the research problem has to be changed to "Financial and Operational Performance of Indian Automobile Industry". This particular topic has been selected for the study because continuous effort has been made to examine the changes that might have occurred in the performance of automobile industry due to the changes in the government policy.

As such, the study is expected to help the corporate management, the financiers, the investors and the government at large, to take valuable decisions at their own. The study has academic relevance too in so far as new theoretical and practical knowledge would be added to the existing stock of knowledge undoubtedly. The present study will act as a masterpiece on the subject for further research and development. There is no study on performance appraisal of Indian automobile industry after liberalization. Therefore, to cover the gaps in the earlier studies, the present study is undertaken to give an insight into the performance of selected sectors of Indian automobile industry. It would also enable shareholders, investors and investment analyst to identify the determinants of corporate performance. Further, it would provide insight to banks, financial institutions and long term lenders to understand the financial capability and effectiveness of the companies. Moreover, it would open up new vistas to the industry association and the Government in understanding the characteristics of the companies for inter and intra firm comparison. It might also help the academic researchers, researchers in securities, industry and company by providing different perspective of the analysis.

References

1. Westons J.F., Eugen F. Brigham, Essentials of Managerial Finance, 9th edition, The Dryden Press.
2. Pandey, I.M. (1986). Financial Management, Vikas Publishing Company, Mumbai, p. 3.
3. Westons J.F., Eugen F. Brigham, Ibid., p.72.
4. Richard M.S. Wilson and Gerard Metugh (1987). Financial Analysis: A managerial introduction (London: Cassell Educational Limited), p. 5.
5. Khustrokhan, H.R., (2002). "Tata Tea Ropes in Stern Stewart & Company to Better EVA", Business Standard, Sep. 17, p.7.
6. ENO Transportation Foundation Inc., Transportation in America, Lansdowne, VA, 1996.
7. Nakicenovic, N. (1991). "Diffusion of Pervasive System: A case of Transport Infrastructures", Technological Forecasting and Social Change, p. 39.

2

Review of Literature

The review of literature guides the researchers for getting better understanding of methodology used, limitation of various available estimation procedures and database, and lucid interpretation and reconciliation of the conflicting results. Besides this, the review of empirical studies explores the avenues for future and present research efforts related to the subject matter. In case of conflicting and unexpected results, the research can take the advantages of knowledge of their researchers simply through the medium of their published works. A number of research studies have been carried out on different aspects of financial appraisal by the researchers, economists and academicians in India and abroad. Different authors have analysed financial performance in different perspectives. A review of these analyses is important in order to develop an approach that can be employed in the context of the study of Indian automobile industry. Therefore, the present chapter reviews the empirical studies related with the different aspects of financial appraisal. The chapter has been divided into four sections.

Section I - presents the review of those studies that have been carried out in the financial performance.

Section II - a review of studies with the profitability analysis has been presented.

Section III - a review of studies with the economic value added analysis has been presented.

Section IV - concentrates on researcher's observations about the research on financial and operating performance of Indian automobile industry.

Section I

Review of Empirical Studies on Financial Performance

George Paul (1985)[1] studied the financial performance of diversified companies in India: A comparative study of diversified and non-diversified companies. The financial performance of 32 relatively matched pairs of diversifying and non-diversifying companies in five Indian industries are compared. The findings indicated that diversifiers generally outperform non-diversifiers on indicators of growth, profitability, safety and market evaluation. However, inter-industry differences in the benefits of diversification indicate that diversification is selectively useful.

Satyanarayana (1986)[2] in his paper entitled 'State Government Enterprises in Andhra Pradesh: An Overview', expressed that so far as government enterprises were concerned, some of the problems related to management of finances which in turn were influenced by their physical as well as operational performance and also by their social obligations. Hence, the efficiency of these enterprises is judged not only by their physical appearance but also by their financial performance.

Mishra (1988)[3] in his study entitled 'Performance Evaluation of Public Enterprises in India', intensively examined the physical/ financial performance of public enterprises. His study demonstrates that public enterprises have fallen behind the expectations and there is a strong school of thought describing the poor performance of public enterprises largely due to the internal factors. This study hold lack of accountability, over-investment, wrong financing and dividend decisions were responsible for poor public enterprise performance.

Rosario G. Manasan, Junaita Amatong and Gil Beltran (1988)[4] have made a study of the public enterprise sector in the Philippines: economic contribution and performance, 1975-1984. The public enterprise sector in the Philippines has grown at a tremendous pace in the last decade. It has contributed a large proportion of gross domestic capital formation but its impact on production, employment and savings is by no means significant. At the same time, estimates of financial profitability ratios and factor productivity measures suggest that the public sector enterprises are generally inefficient.

Chattopadhayay (1989)[5] in 'Central Government Enterprises: An Eighteen years profile', had brought an evaluation work on the performance of Central Government Enterprises covering a period of 18 years from 1969-70 to 1986-87. He presented the criticisms leveled against the performance of public sector enterprises and evaluated that the public sector units do have the potential to record much better results, provided they are run on business lines by maximising the rate of return on capital employed. He has put forward a number of suggestions to improve the working of these units, including the application of principles of sound management.

Sankar, Mishra and Nandagopal (1990)[6] 'A study sponsored by Planning Commission, Government of India', highlighted that the financial performance of state level public enterprises was not satisfactory. The scope of this study was 1981-82 to 1986-87. The analysis of state level public enterprises was conducted at three levels. Firstly, all the state level public enterprises in India were discussed in terms of investments, borrowings,paid-up equity capital, profit/loss position and their growth in numbers as well as distribution in different sectors. Secondly, the status of state level public enterprises was reviewed and, finally, their sector-wise and state-wise positions were analysed. The findings of the study were that the state level public enterprises had a long way to go in order to earn optimum rates of return on investment. About one-third of these enterprises were in the red at the gross margin level, other one-third incurred losses at the operating margin level and about one-third of the enterprises showed small amount of surplus. The study showed that the financial performance was unsound and there was poor record in respect of the finalisation of accounts.

Pant (1991)[7] has sought to identify factors which influence corporate economic performance. Important industrial characteristics which have been used by industrial organization researchers as the determinants of financial performance are concentration, market share, industry growth, research and development expenditure, advertisement intensity, and size of firms in the industry. These characteristics may allow firms to be in a better position to implement their strategies successfully and profitably. Consequently, firms may reflect better performance on account of favourable industrial characteristics.

Jagan Mohan Rao (1993)[8] in 'Financial appraisal of Indian Automotive Tyre Industry' studied the financial appraisal of Indian automotive tyre industry. The study was intended to probe into the financial condition-financial strength and weakness-of the Indian tyre industry. To this end a modest attempt has been made to measure and evaluate the financial performance through inter-company and inter-sectoral analysis over a given period of time (1981-1988). The main findings are that fixed assets utilisation in many of the tyre undertakings was not as productive as expected and inventory was managed fairly well. The tyre industry's overall profit performance was subjected to inconsistency and ineffective.

Kallu Rao (1993)[9] has made a study of inter company financial analysis of tea industry-retrospect and prospect. An attempt has been made in this study to analyse the important variables of tea industry and projected future trends regarding sales and profit for the next 10 year periods, with a view to help the policy makers to take appropriate decisions. Various financial ratios have been calculated for analyzing the financial health of the industry. The forecast of sales and profits of tea manufacturing companies shows that the Indian tea industry has bright prospects. The recent changes in the Indian economic policies will boost up the foreign exchange earnings, which will benefit those companies, which are exporting to hard currency areas.

Pai, Vadivel and Kamala (1995)[10] studied the diversified companies and financial performance: A study. An effort was made to study the relationship between diversified firms and their financial performance. Seven large firms having different products-both related and otherwise-in their portfolio and operating in diverse industries were analyzed. A set of performance measures / ratios was employed to determine the level of financial performance. The results reveal that the diversified firms studied have been healthy financial performance. However, variation in performance from one firm to another has been observed and statistically established.

In RBI study (1995)[11] an attempt was made to study the financial performance of private corporate business sector during the period 1994-95. Of the 1030 companies covered in this study, 925 are non-financial companies and 105 are financial companies. The results of the non-financial and financial companies are also analyzed size-wise apart from the analysis of the consolidated results for the entire sector. The good corporate performance during 1994-95 reflected in major profitability ratios registering distinct improvement in the year under review as compared to the previous year.

Vijayakumar (1996)[12] in 'Assessment of Corporate Liquidity- a discriminant analysis approach' has revealed that the growth rate of sales, leverage, current ratio, operating expenses to sales and vertical integration are the important variables which determine the profitability of companies in the sugar industry. Further, the author has studied the short-term liquidity position in twenty-eight selected sugar factories in co-operative and private sectors. A discriminant analysis has been undertaken to distinguish the good risk companies from poor risk companies based on current and liquidity ratios. Discriminating 'Z' scores have been calculated with the help of discriminant function and according to the 'Z' scores the companies are ranked in the order of liquidity.

Joanne Loundes (1998)[13] in his study examined performance of Australian Government Trading Enterprises:- An overview. Assessing the performance of Government Trading Enterprises (GTEs) has become increasingly important in the context of the push towards privatisation. This paper provides an overview of GTE performance over the 5 years to 1996 using the IBIS Enterprise Database, following the method of analyzing firm performance as outlined by the steering committee (1998). The results indicate that there are large differences in performance across firms, and more particularly, across the industries.

Raj S. Dhankar (1998)[14] has given a new look at the criteria of performance measurement for business enterprises in India-a study of public sector undertakings. The author gives a new model for measuring the performance of a business enterprise in India, wherein, the basis is to compare its actual rate of return with its expected risk adjusted rate of return. Realizing the importance and controversy of public sector in India, an attempt was made to measure the performance of all public sector undertakings, which were started up to 1964 and were in operation until 1983. It is shocking to know that half of them on an average what to talk of making excess returns, have not been able to earn equal to their cost of capital.

Key Sengupta (1998)[15] studied the performance of the fertilizers industry in India. Analysis of cost functions and cobb-douglas production function have been made to study the performance of the industry, the results of which reveal that the industry is subject to the law of increasing costs. The findings get further support from the examination of the production function, which reveals that the average productivity of labour exceeds its marginal productivity. Analysis of shifting cost functions further highlight that the firms belonging to this industry expand capacities, even before fully exploiting the existing capacity conforming to the oligopolistic behavioral tendency of the firms belonging to the fertilizers industry.

Raghunathan and Prabina Das (1999)[16] have made a study of the corporate performance of post-Liberalization. In this study, they analyzed the performance of Indian Manufacturing sector in the last 8 years since liberalization on the parameters of profitability, liquidity, leverage and solvency. While the solvency and profitability ratios were encouraging till 1996 they have been gradually diminishing after that. This problem gets more pronounced when the EVA is calculated which shows that the Indian Manufacturing sector has destroyed wealth, while the MNCs have generated wealth for their shareholders. The study points that poor corporate performance has led to an economic slowdown and not the other way round. Corporate raised funds during the blacken days of equity markets and ended up investing these funds at below their cost of capital. The outcome has been a prolonged economic slowdown.

Juliet D'Souza and William L. Megginson (1999)[17] have studied the financial and operating performance of privatized firms during the 1990s. This study compares the pre and post privatization financial and operating performance of 85 companies from 28 industrialized countries that were privatized through public share offerings for the period from 1990 through 1996. The significant increases in profitability, output, operating efficiency, dividend payments and significant decreases in leverage ratios for the full sample of firms after privatization were noticed. Capital expenditures increase significantly in absolute terms, but not relative to sales. Employment declines, but insignificantly. The findings of the study strongly suggest that privatization yields significant performance improvements.

Rupa Rege Nitsure and Mathew Joseph (1999)[18] in their study entitled, "Liberalisation and the Behaviour of Indian Industry (A Corporate - Sector Analysis based on Capacity Utilisation) examined the impact of economic reform on productive capacity creation and utilization across various industries in the nineties. The results suggest that although substantial achievements occurred initially in creation and utilization of capacities in the various industries, there is significant room for further improvement in utilization. It analyzed the determinants of capacity use such as credit flows, import liberalization, fiscal consolidation and demand conditions, using panel data for 802 firms for the period 1993-98 to suggest an optimum combination of policies that is critical for realizing the unused capacity.

Rajeswari (2000)[19] studied the Liquidity Management of Tamil Nadu Cement Corporation Ltd. Alangulam - A Case Study. It can be concluded from the analysis, the liquidity position of TANCEM is not stable. Regarding liquidity ratios, there was too much of liquidity in the first two years of the study period. A very high degree of liquidity is also bad as idle assets earn nothing and affects profitability. It can be concluded that the liquidity management of TANCEM is poor and is not satisfactory.

Dabasish Sur, Joydeep Biswas and Prasenjit Ganguly (2001)[20] studied the Liquidity Management in Indian Private Sector Enterprises - A case study of Indian Primary Aluminum industry. From the analysis, it may be summarized that the overall performance regarding liquidity management at INDAL was better in terms of efficient utilization of short term funds, whereas HINDALCO was unable to do so. A very high degree of positive correlation between liquidity and profitability in case of both the companies was a notable feature, reflecting the favorable effect of liquidity on profitability.

Aggarwal and Singla (2001)[21] in their study developed a single index of financial performance through the technique of Multiple Discriminant Analysis (MDA), They attempt to identity from among the 11 ratios, used as inputs, those ratios, which are relevant in distinguish between profit making units and loss making units in Indian paper industry. The study indicates that model has correctly classified 82.14 percent of units selected as profit making and loss marking. The study also shows that inventory turnover ratio, interest coverage ratio, net profit to total assets and earning per share are the most important indicators of financial performance. The study also suggests that the results of MDA can be used as predictor of future profitability / sickness.

Joanne Loundes (2001)[22] in the study 'The Financial performance of Australian Government Trading Enterprises Pre- and Post-Reform' revealed that during the 1990's there were several measures introduced to improve the efficiency and financial performance of government trading enterprises in Australia. The purpose of this study was to discover whether there had been any change in the financial performance of government trading enterprises operating in electricity, gas, water, railways and ports industries as a result of these changes. The study reveals that it does not appear to have been a noticeable enhancement in the financial performance of most of this business, although railways have improved slightly, from a low base.

Mark Rogers (2001)[23] in his research the effect of diversification on firm performance analyses the association between diversification and firm performance in a sample of up to 1449 large Australian firms (1994 to 1997). Firm performance is measured by profitability and, for quoted firms, market value. Results from the full sample shows that more focused firms have higher profitability. This result controls for firm specific effects and other determinants of profitability. However, this association is not found in sub-sample regressions for listed firms. This is true both when either profitability or market value is used as a performance measure. The results may indicate that listed firms may be under closer scrutiny and competitive pressures that ensure, on average, that these firms are at their optimal degree of diversification.

Dabasish Sur (2001)[24] studied the Liquidity Management: An overview of four companies in Indian Power Sector. In this study a comparative analysis regarding the liquidity management in Electricity generation and distribution industry has been made for the period 1987-88 to 1996-97. The study reveals that the overall liquidity should be managed in such a way that not only it should not hamper profitability but also its contribution towards increase in profitability should be positive.

Derek Bosworth and Joanne Loundes (2002)[25] in his study entitled the Dynamic performance of Australian Enterprises investigate the interaction of discretionary investments (R&D, capital investment, training and advertising), innovation, productivity and profitability within a dynamic framework of firm performance. A dynamic and closed model of firm performance is set up, and the resulting empirical model is tested as a series of recursive equations, using a four-year balanced panel data set of Australian firms drawn from the Business Longitudinal Survey. The results indicate that current economic profit has an important role to play in enabling firms to invest, and the findings indicate which of these investments are complements and which are substitutes. The study explores the impact of these discretionary investments on innovation and total factor productivity performance. Finally, the impact of past discretionary investments both directly and indirectly (that is, via innovation and productivity performance) on current profitability is examined. Past values of these investments have a significant influence on current profit, effectively closing the model.

Mansur A. Mulla (2002)[26] in 'Use of 'Z' score analysis for evaluation of financial health of textile mills - A case study' has been made an insight into the financial health of Shri Venkatesh Co-operative Textile Mills Ltd., Arunageri of Dharwad District. The 'Z' score analysis has been applied to evaluate the general trend in financial health of a firm over a period by using many of the accounting ratios. From the study it was concluded that the textiles mill under study was just on the verge of financial collapse. On the one hand, current assets declined because of the negative profitability performance, whereas on the other hand, the current liabilities were on the increase because of poor liquidity performance of the mill.

Wolfgang Aussenegg and Ran..o Jelic (2002)[27] examine operating performance of 154 Polish, Hungarian and Czech companies that were fully or partially privatized between January 1990 and December 1998. The study reveals that privatized firms in the sample did not manage to increase profitability, and significantly reduced efficiency and output in the post privatization period. Enterprises privatized through mass privatization programs (Czech SOEs) achieved lower profitability in the post-privatization period compared to their counterparts privatized through case- by - case method. Czech companies have also maintained much higher bank borrowings after privatizations than their polish and Hungarian counterparts. The study further reveals that private sector IPOs underperforms their privatization counterparts in terms of profitability, efficiency, capital investments and output. Finally firm's size does not seem to influence key performance measures in selected countries.

Sudarsana Reddy (2003)[28] studied the Financial Performance of Paper industry in AP. The main objectives set for the study are to evaluate the financing methods and practices to analyze the investment pattern and utilization of fixed assets, to ascertain the working capital condition, to review the profitability performance and to suggest measures to improve the profitability. The data collected have been examined through ratios, trend, common size, comparative financial statement analysis and statistical tests have been applied in appropriate context. The main findings of the study are that A.P. paper industry needs the introduction of additional funds along with restructuring of finances and modernization of technology for better operating performance.

RBI Corporate Studies Division (2003)[29] has made an attempt to study the performance of corporate business sector during the first half of 2002-2003. The results of 146 private companies of various sectors were analyzed on the various parameters of performance. Aggregation and comparison of the results of the first two quarters were done on these performance parameters. It was concluded that the performance of the private sector was better when compared with the first half of the previous year (2001-2002). This was indicated by the following parameters viz., higher sales, reduced interest payments and ultimately improved profitability. Sector-industry wise analysis of performance has been done to highlight those areas where the performance has been better vis-à-vis sectors, which have lagged behind in performance.

Ram Kumar Kakani, Biswatosh Saha and Reddy (2003)[30] attempts to provide an empirical validation of the widely held existing theories on the determinants of firm performance in the Indian context. The study uses financial statements and capital market data of 566 large Indian firms over a time frame of eight years divided into two sub-periods (1992-96 and 1996-2000) and to study Indian firm's financial performance across various dimensions viz., shareholder value, accounting profitability and its components, growth and risk of the sample firms. The study found that size, marketing expenditure and international diversification had a positive relation with a firm's market valuation. The study also found that a firm's ownership compositions, particularly the level of equity ownership by domestic financial institution and dispersed public shareholders, and the leverage of the firm were important factors affecting its financial performance.

Laurent Weill (2004)[31] in his study leverage and corporate performance-a frontier efficiency analysis provides new empirical evidence on a major corporate governance issue: the relationship between leverage and corporate performance. His study provides two major importance's to this literature by applying frontier efficiency techniques to obtain performance measures for companies from several countries (France, Germany and Italy). The study proceeds to regressions of corporate performance on a various set of variables including leverage. The study found mixed evidence depending on the country; while significantly negative in Italy, the relationship between leverage and corporate performance is significantly positive in France and Germany. This tends to support the influence of some institution characteristics on this link.

Petia Topalova (2004)[32] in his study uses firm level data to examine the performance of India's non financial corporate sector since 1989 and evaluate its financial vulnerabilities. The study shows promising trends in liquidity, profitability and leverage of the sector emerged in the early 1990s, they experienced a reversal after 1996. Nevertheless, most indicators were still at comfortable levels, and there is evidence of improvement in 2002. The study also reveals that a number of firms still face problems servicing their debt obligations, posing a risk to lenders. The study of aggregate interest coverage of the corporate sector indicates that potential non-performing loans of the corporate sector remain high. This underscores the need of the corporate sector remain high. This underscores the need for close monitoring of the corporate sector in the future.

Raghunatha Reddy and Padma (2005)[33] in their study, an attempt has been made to study the impact of mergers on corporate performance. It compares the pre and post merger operating performance of the corporations involved in merger to identify their financial characteristics. Empirical research on share price performance suggests that acquiring firm generally earns positive returns prior to announcement, but less than the market portfolio in the post liberalisations period in general and analysis of the pre and post merger operating performance of the acquiring firm.

Santimoy Patra (2005)[34] the impact of liquidity on profitability is analysed in his study considering the case Tata Iron & Steel Company Limited. The study of the impact of liquidity ratios on profitability showed both negative and positive association. Out of seven liquidity ratios selected for this study, four ratios namely current ratio, acid test ratio, current assets to total assets ratio and inventory turnover ratio showed negative correlation with profitability ratio. However, these correlation co-efficient were not statistically significant. The remaining three ratios namely working capital turnover ratio, receivable turnover ratio and cash turnover ratio have shown positive association with the profitability ratio, all of which are statistically significant at 5% level of significance. The result of all the correlation co-efficient is as desirable except correlation co-efficient between inventory turnover ratio and ROI. However this undesirable sign between ITR and ROI is not supported by the multiple regression analysis, which shows the positive association between these two variables. There is increasing profitability which depends upon many factors including liquidity.

Section II

Review of Empirical Studies on Profitability Analysis

See Penerose (1980)[35] revealed that the firms are able to diversify in other markets and hence get released from the constraints. The results of the study by Penerose imply that there is no single optimum firm. A firm could possibly move to any level of profitability. It is also simultaneously recognized that while a firm could grow continuously, all the firms may not grow due to certain constraints of costs and managerial efficiency. Thus, various sizes of firms would continue to exist and firms of different size groups would have different possibility due to the differences in economies of scale. Large size firms can economies due to economies of scale and would be able to have higher rate of profit as compared to smaller firms, which are unable to have internal economies of large-scale production.

Whittington (1980)[36] in 'The Profitability and Size of United Kingdom Companies: 1960-1964' extended his investigation further covering the period from 1960 to 1974 and found that average profitability was largely independent of firm size. The relationship between inter company dispersion of profitability and variability of profits through time tended to decline with firm size. He also found that the average profitability margins and sales/assets ratio did not vary systematically with firm size and also profitability margins of large firms tended to be relatively stable through time whereas their sales/assets ratio did not. Thus, the relative stability through time of the rates of return of large firms was due to relative stability of their profits, rather than the stability of their capacity utilisation. Profitability was not an incentive for large firms to grow at a relatively higher rate.

Asha Jain (1981)[37] in "Price-Cost Margin in Indian Manufacturing industries: An Econometric Analysis" analyzed the price cost margin over time in the 2 digit industries. Price-cost margin was used as a measure of profitability. Cost factors emerged as significant determinants of profitability while the structural variables like concentration ratio, capacity utilization, and growth and capital intensity showed mixed pattern. Results varied among the industries.

Bothwell, Cooley and Hall (1982)[38] in their research "A new view of Market Structure- Performance Debate" used a sample of 156 large U.S Manufacturing firms over a period 1960-67 for determining the relationship between profit rate and other variables like seller concentration, advertising intensity, economics of scale, absolute capital requirements, leverage, profit variability, firm growth, firm size and market share, etc. Positive correlation between seller concentration, market share and growth of demand, business risk, advertisement expenses and profit rate was found. Profit rates were negatively related with the extent of economics and capital requirements.

Gangadhar (1982)[39] in 'Cement Industry-some aspects of profitability' examined and made comment on the profitability of large public limited cement companies in India in order to bring out fluctuations, if any, and to offer possible causes for such fluctuations. The study revealed that the profitability in cement industry has fluctuated very widely with low rate during the period under review. The profit margin in the cement industry has shown declining trend whereas the asset turnover showed an increasing trend. The profit margin accounted to a great extent for lower rate of ROI in the industry as compared to asset turnover.

Rao (1985)[40] in his work entitled 'Impact of Debt-Equity Ratio on Profitability-An Exploratory Study of Engineering Industry', observes if the earning ability i.e., profitability, has any impact on the debt-equity ratio in engineering companies. The study based on the impact of profitability on the debt-equity ratio has revealed a negative association i.e., high debt-equity ratios meant low profitability due to large interest payments, whereas low debt-equity ratio caused high profitability because of low interest payments. The operating efficiency of the firm and reasonable rate of return on owner's capital ultimately depend on the profits earned by it. Thus, profits are necessary to run the firm in a healthy atmosphere of present day cut throat competitions and defend it from business rivalry.

Chalam and Dakshinamurthy (1985)[41] in 'Performance of Public Enterprises in India: Impact of Heavy External Financing', have made a study on the performance of Public Sector Enterprises in India and they have attributed the poor financial performance to the excessive use of external sources in their capital structure. They have evaluated the effects of heavy external finances on net incomes and on short-term liquidity position, in turn affecting the working funds available for successful operation. They have suggested for allowing more private equity participation; increasing the operational efficiency through controlling costs and improving the capacity utilisation and factors such alike.

Deepak Chawola (1986)[42] studied an empirical analysis of the profitability of the Indian man-made fibres industry. This study examines and explains the trends in the profitability of the Indian man-made fibres industry. The relevant data for the study is obtained from 17 firms found in BSE Official Directory for the period 1963-64 to 1977-78. An increase in the excise duty of man-made fibres seems to be associated with the decline in profitability of the industry. Both concentration and vertical integration influence the profitability. However, their impact differs for cellulose and petro-chemical based group of fibres.

Nagarajan and Burthwal (1990)[43] in their research work entitled "profitability and structure: A firm level study of Indian Pharmaceutical Industry", intensively examined the relationship between profitability and structure, using a sample of thirty-eight pharmaceutical firms in India for the period 1970-1982. Two measures of profitability i.e., ratio of net profit to total sales revenue and the ratio of net profits to total assets have been used to find out the determination of profitability. The analysis demonstrated that under the condition of price controls the most significant determinant of the profitability of the firms in this industry is vertical integration. Size and advertising intensity did not appear to be major determinants. This was perhaps due to the inability of firms to translate their market power into prices, because of controls. The coefficient of growth rate of sales was positive and significant, suggesting that factors on the demand side of a firm had a greater impact on profitability than on the supply side.

Conyon and Machin (1991)[44] in 'The Determinants of Profit Margins in U. K. Manufacturing', made an attempt to find the causes of inter-industry variations in profit margins for 90 U.K. Manufacturing Industries over the period 1983 to 1986. Labour-market characteristics (such as trade union coverage and unemployment), import intensity, concentration and capital stock were taken as independent variables. The study revealed that the union coverage and unemployment had a negative impact on profit margins. On the other hand, import intensity, concentration and capital stock were significant in explaining inter-firm variations in profit margins.

Krishnaveni (1991)[45] in her study evaluated the impact of policy changes since 1982-92 on profitability and growth of firms in the industry using Tobin's q as a measure of profitability. The study finds no evidence to show that firms have made supernormal profits. Profitability is found to be explained mainly by age of the firms, vertical integration, diversification and industry policy dummy variables. Important determinants of the growth of firms are found as diversification, industry policy dummy variable, gross retained profits and expansion of capacities. Results also reveal differences in performance between car and non-car sectors as well as within the sectors of the industry.

Chandrasekaran (1993)[46] in 'Determinants of profitability in Cement Industry' has studied the determinants of profitability in cement industry. The objective of this study was to examine determinants of profitability in cement industry. The study aims at drawing inference on impact of policy measures which led to change in price and distribution polices relevant for cement industry. Determinants of profitability are analysed using the technique of ordinary least squares. Based on existing theories and relevant econometric empirical works, variables are selected. The study concluded that efficiency in inventory management and efficient management of current assets were important to improve profitability.

Cleveland and Frederick (1993)[47] in their study 'Profitability, Uncertainty and Firm Size', examines the connections between variations in profit and loss rates among firms in small-firm and large-firm size classes as reflections of uncertainty. They found that, within industries, such variations are particularly great for firms in small-firm size classes, leading to operating policies for small firms best characterized as entrepreneurial. Large firms, in contrast, faced with less uncertainty in earning profit, appear to adopt policies that manifest an emphasis on strategic planning.

Vijayakumar and Venkatachalam (1995)[48] in 'Working Capital and Profitability - An Empirical Analysis' studied the impact of working capital on profitability in sugar industry of Tamil Nadu by selecting a sample of 13 companies; 6 companies in co-operative sector and 7 companies in private sector over the period 1982-83 to 1991-92. They applied simple correlation and multiple regression analysis on working capital and profitability ratios. They concluded through correlation and regression analysis that liquid ratio, inventory turnover ratio, receivables turnover ratio and cash turnover ratio had influenced the profitability of sugar industry in Tamil Nadu.

James Ted McDonald (1997)[49] in the study entitled 'The Determinants of Firm Profitability in Australian Manufacturing' provides new evidence on the determinants of the profitability of Australian manufacturing firms by analyzing a unique firm level data set of firm performance over the period 1983-1993. From estimations based on an adaptation of a standard oligopoly model, econometric results suggest that lagged profitability is a significant determinant of current profit margins, and that industry concentration is positively related to firm profit margin. As well, both union density and real wage inflation are found to be negatively associated with firm profits. Finally, the cyclicality of profit margins depends on industry concentration - firm margins are pro - cyclical in concentrated industries and are counter-cyclical in less concentrated industries.

Sidhu and Gurpreet Bhatia (1998)[50] studied the factors affecting profitability in Indian textile industry. In this study an attempt was made to identify the major determinants of profitability in Indian textile industry with the help of empirical data taken from Bombay Stock Exchange Directory for the year 1983. To find out the factors affecting profitability, regression analysis had been applied. From the analysis, there was no clear-cut relationship between current profitability and capital intensity. The age of the firm was having generally negative but statistically insignificant relationship with current profitability which points towards the fact firms in Indian textile industry are absolute and need modernization.

Kuldip Kaur (1998)[51] studied size, growth and profitability of firms in India. It is in this context that the study of various facets of 235 firms of India has been undertaken, covering the period from 1970-71 to 1989-90. Growth pattern of the firms showed that majority of the firms recorded growth rate from 10 to 20 per cent. Two measures of profitability have been used in the study. First measure is the profitability margin (operating profit as percentage of net sales). Second measure is the profitability rate (gross profit as percentage of net sales). However, the analysis in case of Indian firms showed that there was no systematic tendency for average profitability to increase/ decrease as the size of the firm changed.

Amit Mallick and Debasish Sur (1998)[52] examined the Working capital and profitability: a case study in interrelation. The study explores the correlation between ROI and several ratios relating to working capital management. In this study an effort has been made to make an empirical study of AFT industries Ltd., a tea producing enterprise in Assam for assessing the impact of working capital on profitability by computing simple correlation co-efficient between ROI and each of some selected important ratios relating to working capital management and to test the significance of such coefficients. The study on the inter relation between the selected ratios in the areas of working capital management and profitability of the company revealed both negative and positive association

Simon Feeny and Mark Rogers (1998)[53] in their research work entitled 'profitability in Australian Enterprises' analyses profitability in a sample of large Australian companies over the period 1985 to 1996. Various measures of profitability are used and the paper provides a discussion of the theoretical basis for these measures. The key issues investigated are a comparison of the profitability measures, the distribution of profitability between firms, and the persistence of firm profitability. The results are compared to previous studies on firm profitability.

Vijayakumar (1998)[54] has examined the determinants of corporate size, growth and profitability- the Indian experience. To meet the objectives of the study, Indian public sector industries were selected. The data relating to size, growth and profitability were collected from their annual reports published by the Bureau of Public Enterprises (BPE), Government of India. The study covers the period from 1980-81 to 1995-96. The technique of average, correlation and linear and multiple regression analysis has been used in this study. Inter - industry analysis reveals that the growth is positively and significantly associated with the size in all the industry groups except textiles.

VishnuKanta Purohit (1998)[55] in 'Profitability in Indian Industries: An analysis of firm size and profitability' examined the relation between size and profitability in Indian industries. The study highlights the following two common conclusions. Firstly, though the average profitability of firms does not seem to vary significantly with their size and the variability of profit rates declines with size. Secondly, the average growth rates of firms do not seem to vary significantly with their size but the variability of growth rates only. The study further explores the factors that determine profitability. Besides the size, the model also tests for the impact of age of the firm and growth in sales on profitability at both micro and macro levels. The study concludes that the selected industries and firms have made efforts to increase profitability through various means including increase in size through diversification and moving into higher technology.

Glancey (1998)[56] in his study determinants of growth and profitability in small entrepreneurial firm investigates the relationship between company characteristics including size, age, location and industry group, and profitability and growth. The trade-off between the possibly conflicting objectives of profit and growth is considered primarily from the entrepreneurial rather than the managerial standpoint which previous econometric studies of small firm performance have concentrated on. It is argued that a firm size measure based on employment is more appropriate than one based on sales or assets which previous studies have used. Firm characteristics are found to be of limited value in explaining profitability. However, larger firms are found to grow faster than smaller, and younger firms are found to grow faster than older. There is also some evidence that growth is stronger in urban than in suburban or rural locations.

Agarwal (1999)[57] studied the profitability and growth in Indian Automobile manufacturing industry. The objective of this study is to examine if firms have been making super normal profits since 1975 when price controls were removed. It also evaluates the impact of policy changes since 1981-82 on profitability and growth of firms in the industry using Tobin's Square as a measure of profitability. The study finds no evidence to show that firms have made super normal profits. Profitability is found to be explained mainly by the age of the firms, vertical integration, diversification and industry policy dummy variable. Important determinants of the growth of firms are found as diversification, industry policy dummy variables, gross retained profits and expansion of capacities. Results also reveal differences in performance between car and non-car sectors as well as with in the sectors of the industry.

Soumyendra Kishore Dutta (1999)[58] examined an analysis of profitability trend in the Indian Cotton Mill industry. The disadvantage situations of a large number of mills are reflected in the haphazard movement of the mill sector's profitability ratio. Loss of market share of mill made cotton cloth to synthetic substitutes, burden of unfavorable excise duty, uncertainty in supply of raw cotton, untoward labour legislation, under utilization of capital and high capital cost added to the aforesaid fluctuations in profitability. Lower base of the profitability ratios and the warning financial position of the majority of the mills have left them with resources to undertake renovation and modernization.

Simon Feeny and Mark Rogers (1999)[59] in their research work entitled 'Market Share, Concentration and Diversification in Firm Profitability' review the role of market share, concentration and diversification in firm performance. An empirical analysis of the profitability of 722 Large Australian firms for the period 1993 to 1996 was also undertaken. Using simple regression techniques the analysis suggests that industry concentration (as proxies by the 4-firm concentration ratio) has a positive influence on profitability. The market share of a firm does not appear to have any significant linear association with profitability; however, a non-monotonic relationship is found to be significant.

Govinda Rao and Mohana Rao (1999)[60] in 'Impact of working capital on profitability in cement industry - A Correlation

Analysis', analyse the impact of profitability on working capital in cement industrial units in India. Ten variables on working capital ratios have a close interaction with profitability measures viz., current ratio, debt equity ratio, cash position ratio, working capital turnover ratio, inventory turnover ratio, debtors turnover ratio, cash turnover ratio, current assets turnover ratio and average collection period are selected for analysis. The inter-relationship are to be studied with the help of Karl-Pearson's co-efficient of correlation technique, by arranging the correlation of one variable with each other variable in the form of matrices which are a triangular and symmetrical about the principal diagonal. On overall basis out of 10 variables with PBDIT, 3 variables showed a significant co-efficient and seven exhibited insignificant relationships. Out of the 10 variables, 5 variables showed negative association while the others showed positive relationships.

Mohammed Rafiqul Islam (2000)[61] studied the profitability of Fertilizer Industry in Bangladesh from 1985-86 to 1994-95. The sample included five fertilizer enterprises of the seven fertilizer enterprises in Bangladesh under the control of Bangladesh Chemical Industries Corporation (BCIC). The findings of the study indicate that none of the selected units were consistent and all the units were plagued with declining profits. The study concluded with suggestions for improvement of the profitability of fertilizer industry in Bangladesh.

Simon Feeny (2000)[62] in his research study entitled determinants of profitability: an empirical investigation using Australian tax entities. Using simple regression techniques the analysis suggests that size of entity is positively related to profitability but industry characteristics have limited importance in explaining entity profitability. Concentration, defined at a 4 digit level, is positively and significantly related to entity profitability in 27 per cent of Australian 3 digit industries, while a significant negative association is found in 8 per cent of the industries. There is some evidence that barriers to entry have the positive relationship with entity profitability as dictated by theory when proxies by the industry capital intensity but not when proxies by the minimum efficient scale or industry trademark intensity. There is strong evidence that the market share of an entity has a U-shaped relationship with profitability.

Debashish Rei and Debashish Sur (2001)[63] studied the profitability analysis of Indian food products industry: A case study of Cadbury India Ltd. The study attempts to measure the profitability scenario of Cadbury India Ltd. and analyses the relationship among various profitability ratios and their joint impact using multiple correlation co-efficient and multiple regression method. The study on the inter-relation between the selected ratios regarding the company's position and performance and profitability of the company revealed both negative and positive association.

Vijayakumar (2002)[64] in "Determinants of Profitability-A firm level study of the Sugar Industry of Tamil Nadu", delved into the various determinants of profitability viz., growth rate of sales, vertical integration and leverage. Apart from these three variables, he had selected current ratio, operating expenses to sales ratio and inventory turnover ratio. Econometric models were used to test the various hypotheses relating to profitability with other variables. The researcher noted in his conclusion that efficiency in inventory management and current assets are important to improve the profitability.

Jack Glen, Kevin Lee and Ajit Singh (2002)[65] in their study presents time-series analyses of corporate profitability in seven leading Developing Countries (DCS) using the common methodology as the persistence of profitability (PP) studies and systematically compare the results with those for Advanced Countries (ACS). Surprisingly, both short and long term persistence of profitability for DCS is found to be lower than those for ACS The paper concentrated on economic explanation for these findings. It also reports the results on the persistence of the two components as profitability-capital-output ratios and profit margins. These two raise important general issues of economic interpretation for persistence of profitability (pp) studies, which are outlined.

Vijayakumar (2002)[66] in his study 'Financial appraisal of Salem Co-operative Sugar Mills Ltd, Mohanur' analysed the various aspects of the working of Salem Co-operative Sugar Mills Ltd, Mohanur. Financial appraisal has been studied with respect to profitability, capital structure, fixed assets and working capital. The researcher's main finding is about the Mill's over reliance on external funds which results in interest burden. It is certain that the Mill will have better scope to function in an efficient manner if the owner's funds are increased and the borrowings are reduced.

Vijayakumar and Kadirvel (2003)[67] studied the determinants of profitability of Indian Public Sector Manufacturing Industries-An Econometric analysis. It is evident from the results that age is the strongest determinant of profitability followed by the variables vertical integration, leverage, size, current ratio, inventory turnover ratio, operating expenses to sales ratio and growth rate. The selected variables have both positive and negative contribution in variation of profit rate. In a nutshell, it can be concluded that firms should consider all these possible determinants while considering its profitability.

Vijayakumar and Kadirvel (2003)[68] studied the profitability and size of firm in Indian Minerals and Metals industry. Generally, it is suggested that the larger the firm may be in a position to earn a higher rate of return on its investment than the smaller firm. Similarly, a counter argument is that size breed's inefficiency and hence profitability may decline with size of firms. Thus, they find that some theoretical arguments suggest that profitability should increase with the firm size, others suggest a negative relationship. It is in view of these contradictory suggestions, that it becomes necessary to study the relationship between size and profitability of the firms. For this purpose, Indian public sector minerals and metals industry has been selected. The study reveals that size is found to be significantly associated with the profitability during the study period. It is also evident from the analysis that size is positively associated with the profitability. Thus, larger firm may be in a position to earn higher rate of return on investment through diversification and moving into higher technology.

Zuobao Wei, Oscar Varela, Juleit D' Souza and Kabir Hassan (2003)[69] in 'The financial and operating performance of China's newly privatized firms', examine the pre- and post-privatization financial and operating performance of 208 firms privatized in China during the period 1990-97. The full sample results show significant improvements in real output, real assets and sales efficiency, and significant declines in leverage following privatization, but no significant change in profitability. Further analysis shows that privatized firms experience significant improvements in profitability compared to fully state-owned enterprises during the same period. Firms in which more than 50 per cent voting control is conveyed to private investors via privatization experience significantly greater improvements in profitability, employment, and sales efficiency compared to those that remain under the state's control. Privatization seems to work in China, especially the more private firms become successful operators.

Maninder S. Sarkaria and Shergil (2004)[70] aims to test how market structure may affect performance. The study has employed model consulting determinants of both structure and profits. In order to decompose the variation performance variables like industry effect, seller concentration, market share, capacity utilization, size, leverage, skill, risk, age and capital intensity have been included in the regression models as the determinants as performance. The study results suggest that market share is positively and concentration is negatively related to performance. The industry membership has turned up to be an important determinant of firm growth.

Marcos A. M. Lima and Marcelo Resende (2004)[71] in his work entitled profit margins and business cycles in the Brazilian industry: a panel data study investigates the relationship between profit margins and business cycle in the Brazilian industry during the 1992-1998 period, taking as reference a dynamic panel data model founded around a conjectural variation framework. The empirical results indicate pro-cyclical behavior of profit margins for the aggregate business cycle but are less clear in the case of sector-specific business cycle variables. Among the most robust results, one can highlight the roles of lagged profitability and import intensity and the negligible role of union density.

Bhanu (2005)[72] in his paper the structural adjustment programmes and the new industrial policy adopted by the Indian government has enabled business houses to undertake the programme of expansion either by entering into a new market or through expansion in an existing market. In this context, it is found that in order to expand and grow companies in India they are increasingly resorting to merges and acquisitions. In this regard this study has identified twelve companies and proposes to examine the growth of the merged company's vis-à-vis select one hundred thirty four companies in terms of net fixed assets and paid-up capital for the period 1990-91 to 1997-98. The study also examines the trends in profitability of the merged and selected companies for the above-mentioned period. The study concluded that the merged companies have been more successful and profitability under all the heads examined, were higher for these companies as compared to the select companies.

Section III

Review of Empirical Studies on Economic Value Added (EVA)

Stern (1990)[73] observed that EVA as a performance measure captures the true economic profit of an organization. EVA-based financial management and incentive compensation scheme gives manager better quality information and superior motivation to make decisions that will create the maximum shareholders' wealth in an organization. EVA is a performance measure which is more closely linked to the creation of shareholders' wealth over a period of time. Accordingly, EVA should be made the focal point for financial reporting, planning and decision-making.

Rutledge (1993)[74] supported the concept as such. Economic value added is a phrase used by Stern Stewart & Company to describe the way to measure economic profit. The way to calculate economic profit is to subtract its cost of charge capital from after tax profits. A positive number means that an economic profit exists. Managers today are being swamped by stream of sophisticated new management concepts, each with a fancy name and its own glossary of technical terminology. The latest serving dish of this kind is EVA (Economic Value Added), Sterm Stewart and Co's name for the old friend's economic profit, the old Alfred Marshal concept taught everywhere in micro- economics classes.

Stewart (1994)[75] has expanded that EVA is a powerful new management tool that has gained worldwide recognition as the standard tool of corporate performance. EVA, presents an integrated fremework of financial management and incentive compensation. The adoption of EVA system by more and more companies throughout the world clearly depicts that it provides an integrated decision-making framework, can reform energies and redirect resources to create sustainable value for companies, customers, employees, shareholders and for management.

Ochsner (1995)[76] brought into being that 'Economic Value Added' (EVA) is a performance measure that examines the company's financial results in economic language. It also quantifies the annual constituent of free cash inflows minus total capital expenses This over 50-years old methodology is becoming popular once again because it is not an accounting-based approach, something that many managers have found unreliable. More importantly, EVA technique is making a comeback because they can gauge whether a firm is generating economic returns. This capability satisfies investors that want companies to record such returns. In addition, EVA can be used as a tool for assessing financial performance. This performance measure also has a downside that makes it unacceptable to some managers, who include the fact that EVA uses software in computing financial results, so that managers can not actually know, how performance numbers are derived.

Grant (1996)[77] found that the EVA concept may have everlastingly changed the way real profitability is measured. Pioneered by Stern Stewart Management Services in the 1980s, EVA is a financial tool that focuses on the difference between company's after tax operating profit and its total cost of capital. A survey was conducted that examines the empirical relations between EVA and corporate valuation. Results suggest that EVA significantly bangs the Market Value Added of a firm and that this wealth effect stems from the company's residual return on capital.

Luber (1996)[78] confirmed that MVA is in compliance with the direction of the market. Studies have shown that a company which shows a positive EVA over a period of time will also have an increasing MVA while negative EVA will bring down MVA as the market loses confidence in the competence of a company to ensure a handsome return on the invested capital. The five top most companies as the wealth creators-Coke, GE, Microsoft, Merck and Philip Morris-have strong EVAs and are expected to remain in the top niche in the upcoming years.

Banerjee (1997)[79] has conducted an empirical research to find the superiority of EVA over other traditional financial performance measures. Ten industries have been chosen and each industry is represented by four/five companies. ROI and EVA have been calculated for sample companies and a comparison of both has been undertaken, showing the superiority of EVA over ROI. Indian companies are gradually recognizing the importance of EVA. Some of such companies are Ranbaxy Laboratories, Samtel India Ltd. and Infosys Technologies Ltd.

Bacidore et al., (1997)[80] observed that the operating performance measures are evaluated in the context of shareholder value creation. Economic Value Added performs well in correlation with shareholder value creation. A refinement of Economic Value Added called Refined Economic Value Added, is proposed. This measure is theoretically and empirically superior in measuring a firm's financial performance. They have observed that change in shareholder value can be fittingly depicted by applying market derived cost of capital to market value of company assets/ organization value. They have described the phenomenon with the help of an improved concept termed as Refine Economic Value Added (REVA). This new concept has been defined as:

$$\mathbf{REVA_t = NOPAT_t - K_w\,(MV_{t-1})}$$

Where,

MV_{t-1} = Total market value of the company's assets at the end of the period t-1.

K_w = Weighted average cost of capital.

EVA is an adequate measure of shareholders' value creation but REVA is considered a theortically superior measure for assessing whether a firm's operating performance is adequate from the viewpoint of compensating the firm's financers for the risk to their capital. In a wide-ranging statistical study of both EVA and REVA, it has been demonstrated that REVA statistically outperforms EVA in its ability to predict shareholder value creation.

Burkette and Hedley (1997)[81] explained that the EVA concept can be used to assess organizational performance known as economic profit, it can be applied for profit companies, public sector organizations and non-profit organzations. EVA is being used by these entities in a variety of ways, including as a management communication base, as a measure of corporate and divisional performance, to enlighten management, stockholder interests, and to emphasize the long-term benefits of industrial research and employee training. The profit can be calculated by determining the company's cost of equity capital, the weighted average cost of the firm, the adjusted operating income, the operating income plus back expenses providing a future benefit, assets employed on a book basis, the capital investment and the difference between the readjusted operation and the capital charge.

Dodd and Chen (1997)[82] analyzed that Economic Value Added (EVA) has been acclaimed to the most recent and exciting innovation in company performance measures. Although the popular press reports numerous stories of successful EVA adoption, there has been little empirical evidence supporting the claim that EVA is a useful measure of corporate performance. This study examines the EVA performance of 656 US companies and compares the information usefulness of EVA with accounting earnings and residual income. The authors gave three conclusions from the examination: (i) although improving EVA performance is associated with a higher stock return, the association is not as perfect as claimed by EVA advocates; (ii) EVA is more powerful than traditional measures of accounting profit in explaining stock return; however, accounting earnings are still of significant incremental information value in addition to EVA; and (iii) not only is EVA similar to residual income in concept, they are empirically comparable.

Putnam (1997)[83] pointed out that the investors were bullish on US equities in 1995 and 1996 whereas, 1997 was a much more volatile year. In order to understand this phenomenon a framework of analysis such as EVA is extremely useful. EVA highlights five important factors to analyze the creation of shareholders' value: Net operating profit after tax and before interest, the weighted average cost of capital, investment in the business, the rate of return on investments, and the competitive advantage period.

Tully (1997)[84] brought to book EVA as a method for understanding as to what is happening to the financial performance of an organization. The paper presents the method for calculating EVA and also shows some pictorial presentations of EVAs of several companies like Bajaj Auto, Asian Paints, Procter and Gamble (India) Ltd., Siemens India. It has been concluded that EVA can be a better financial performance evaluation measure than other traditional measures.

Ethiraj (1998)[85] derived that in Indian market many companies are using capital inefficiently and thus destroying value. The tool to measure capital efficacy and economic value is Economic Value Added. Taking EVA as a tool of financial performance HLL and ITC stand at the top of the list. Also important is the relation between EVA and total operating capital employed (assets). This would show how much value the company has generated in relation to the assets it has deployed. It is argued that stock prices move up as a company adopts EVA as an internal performance criterion.

KPMG-BS Study (1998)[86] assessed top 100 companies on EVA, sales, PAT and MVA criteria. The survey has used the BS-1000 list of companies using a composite index comprising sales, profitability and compounded annual growth rate of those companis covering the period 1996-97. Sixty companies have been found able to create positive shareholder value whereas 38 companies have been found to destory it. Accounting numbers have failed to capture shareholder value creation or destruction as per the findings of the study. 24 companies have destroyed shareholder value by reporting negative MVA.

Anand et al., (1999)[87] revealed that EVA, REVA (Refined Ecnomic Value Added) and MVA are better measures of business performance than NOPAT and EPS in terms of shareholders' value creation and competitive advantage of a firm. Since conventional management compensation systems emphasize sales/asset growth at expense of profitability and shareholders' value. Thus, EVA is a measure that shifts focus on an organizational culture of concern for value.

Bao and Bao (1999)[88] revealed the association between EVA and the value of the Indian firms, which are included in the COMPUSAT-Global Vantage database. The results of the study show that the EVA is positively and significantly correlated with the firm value. The results are consistent with the theory in that firms with EVA created value and firms with higher created value have higher stock prices. The study also reveals that explanatory power of EVA is lower than that of earnings and book value of firms under consideration.

Harihar (1999)[89] highlighted some myths regarding EVA. According to the author , Stern and Stewart were not the founders of EVA concept; rather it was first propounded by General Motors in early 1920's. Further, EVA calculations are not simple and need a lot of adjustments in the financial books. The author is also of the view that EVA can not be used for comparison among companies of different industries. The next myth is that EVA figures can be manipulated to suit the needs of management. The last and most dangerous myth discussed is that the high EVA companies are cash rich. For looking at cash adequacy another measure called CVA (Cash Value Added) can be used.

Thenmozhie (1999)[90] explained the concept of EVA and compared it with some other traditional measure of corporate performance viz. ROI, EPS, RONW, ROE, ROCE, etc. He used the coefficient of determination to demonstrate that the traditional measures do not reflect the real value of the shareholders, and thus EVA has to be taken into account to measure the value of shareholders' welath. He has also described the concept of EVA in the Indian scenario with specific reference to companies like NIIT, Hindustan Lever and ITC. Thenmozhie has referred to some of the shortcomings of the concept of EVA but maintains that EVA is a better measure of corporate performance as compared to the traditional measures.

Banerjee (2000)[91] attempted to find out whether Stewart's claim that market value of a company is equal to the discounted value of all future EVAs, holds good in the Indian context or not. For the purpose of the study the researcher selected a sample of 200 companies over a time span of four years (1994-95 to 1997-98). Accorting to him, market value of firm is the function of two components viz., Current Operational Value (COV) and Future Growth Value (FGV). COV is equal to the book value of beginnimg invested capital plus the capitalized value of current year is EVA, where as FGV represents the present value of all future expected future improvements. Based on the analysis of his data he comes to the conclusion that in many cases there is a considerable divergence between MVA and the sum total of COV and FGV.

Parasuram (2000)[92] discussed the EVA position of 14 major public sector banks, 7 new private sector banks, 5 old private sector banks and 2 foreign banks. Among the strength indicators, deposit, return on assets, interest income as a percentage of total assets, interest yield spread as a percentage of total assets and EVA were considered. The study concludes that EVA is an important measure to judge a bank performance in view of the current scenario of banks. EVA has been found to have a high degree of correlation with ROA but not with any of the other measures. It signifies a fact that banks realize the importance of measuring EVA separately even if they do well on other fields.

Thampy and Beheli (2001)[93] studied the economic profits of commercial banks in the public and private sectors during 1990s. It also moves the benchmark of performance of banks from accountintg profits to economic profits and shareholder wealth creation. The study has been restricted to 12 commercial banks consisting of 4 public and 8 private sector banks. The period covered under the study is three years starting from 1995-96 to 1997-98 Beta has been calculated on the basis of daily stock prices data with Bombay Stock Exchanges BSE 200 index returns during Janauary 1, 1997 to March 31, 1998 as the proxy for the market returns. The study shows that the performances of the Indian banks as measured by EVA is not very satisfactory. The results of the study reveal that the commercial banks under consideration have not created any positive EVA due to : (a) banks could be over capitalized and (b) returns are very poor from banking business.

Riceman, et al (2002)[94] argued that the EVA is performance measure that is being used by an increasing number of companies, but academic reserch on EVA is limited . In this study, researchers examined the effect of EVA on the performance of individual managers. Specifically, researchers observed whether managers on EVA-based bonus plans outperform managers on traditional accounting-based bonus plans. The results suggest that managers on EVA bonus plans who understand the EVA concept perform better than managers on traditional bonus plans. However, it is found that the increased in performance results from increased consistency or congruency in the manager's evaluation- reward process rather than from superiority of EVA as a performance measure. It is further established that the effect of EVA bonuses and EVA understanding differs depending on the area of the firm in which the manager is employed. This suggests that EVA may not be an universally appropriate base for reward systems.

Bardia (2002)[95] revealed that the concept of EVA has caught of the fancy of investment analysts recently as an of measuring corporate performance. In a dynamic corporate environment a common investor finds it increasingly difficult to monitor his investments. The method of EVA guides the investors in evaluating the performance of the company and monitoring their investments. It is claimed that EVA is the sole method of accounting properly for various dimensions by which a company's value may be added or lost. In fact, the method emphasizes the quality of earning and not just the quantity. As a matter of number of companies adopting EVA as a tool of performance measurement, is increasing sharply in India.

Costigan and Linda (2002)[96] observed that the EVA is a new measure of performance that is purported to better align managers' incentives to that of the shareholders. Accordingly, firms that experience higher agency conflicts should be more included to use this performance evaluation system. Additionally, the organizational strategy of the firm should ifluence the likelihood of employing EVA. One hundred and fifteen firms were identified as being adopters of EVA. Logisti regression was performed to contrast these firms to a control group of 1,271 non - adopters. The results indicate that firms using EVA exhibit percentage of institutional ownership and a lower percentage of insider ownership than non - adopters. Prospector firms as defined by a higher ratio of research and development to sales tend to use EVA less than defender firms. Accounting adjustments are a focal point of the EVA formulation and the results presented in this study suggest that providing appropriate incentives may be more complex than the developers of EVA imply.

Mangala and Simpy (2002)[97] discussed that maximizing shareholder value had become the new corporate paradigm. Although shareholder's wealth maximization has been recognized by managers and researchers as the ultimate corporate goal, the maximum has gained a new dimension only in the recent years, due to the introduction of the concept of EVA. EVA is the most important driver influencing the market value of a share. So, if the company improves EVA by increasing its return on capital employed and lowering its cost of capital, its market value will increase. The study attempts to study the relationship between EVA and market value among various compaines in India. The EVA of 15 companies among five industries (Fast Moving Consumer Good, Information Tcchnology, Pharma, Automobile, Textile) has been computed. The results of the analysis confirm Stern's hypothesis and conclude that the company's current operational value (COV) is more significant in contributing to a change in market value of shares in Indian context.

Bhata and Dayal BhatNagar (2003)[98] in their study started that EVA cannot be used for comparison among companies of different industries. EVA figures can be manipulated to suit the needs of management. The last and most dangerous myth discussed is that the high EVA companies are cash rich. The author positive EVA figures do not ensure high financial performance. A new variable formed as EVAPRI (Economic Value Added Per Rupee of Investment) has been calculated by dividing the EVA figure by the invested capital of the previous year.

$$\textbf{EVAPRI} = \textbf{EVA}_t / \textbf{Invested Capital}_{(t-1)}$$

It was considered proper to contemplate on a relative measure of EVA so that all companies in an industry could be viewed from a common plat from, while comparing their respective EVA. The above results, industry wise standard deviations for EVA and EVAPRI were also computed. As expected, the distribution for EVAPRI was found to be much less dispersed in all industry groups as compared to EVA.

Section IV

Research Gap

From the above review of empirical works it is clear that different authors have approached financial appraisal in different ways in varying level of analysis. These different approaches helped in the emergence of more and more literature on the subject over time. It gives an idea on extensive and diversed works on financial appraisal. It has been noticed that the studies on financial performance in various sectors provide divergent results relating to the study period over lap or coincide. The main reason for the divergence in the results is the different in the method used for the measurement of factors especially profitability, solvency, liquidity, asset productivity, capital structure and growth rate in the operating performance and social performance. All the studies aimed to analyse the financial performance in Indian Industries with number of factors. Very few studies appeared which used Economic Value Added (EVA) to explore the financial performance of the industries.

From the synoptic appraisal of aforementioned findings on economic value added, it is evidently clear that the concept has originally emerged in the west and later turns out to be time-honoured across the world. Many researchers have applied sophisticated econometric tools for assessing the impact of EVA concept on corporate financial performance. Starting from Stern (1990) to Bhata et al., (2003) it may be revealed that Indian researchers started contributing to this field in 1997. In the beginning, the researcher wrote on the conceptual aspects of EVA but later some empirical studies have also been accomplished. However, as a mater of chance, no study has been conducted at such a colossal extent in India and therefore, to conduct a study of automobilies compaines for the period of 13 years. There is no denying fact that early researcher have made valueable contribution, yet their work had some specific restraints particularly relating to the raw data and its computational course of action. The present study is an attempt to offer a detailed examinaction of the EVA with special reference to Indian automobile industry.

It has been noticed that review of empirical works on profitability gives an idea on extensive and diversed works on profitability. It facilitates to understand the various structural and non-structural variables that determine profitability. It has been noticed that studies on the profitability analysis in various industries used the variables like seller's concentration, advertising intensity, economics of scale, leverage, profit variability, firm growth and size. In the late 1990's, very few studies appeared which used the quantum of sales, return on investment and appropriation of profits to explore the profit variation of the manufacturing industries. Researchers have verified and extended the results over the years.

The survey of the existing literature indicates that so far no specific work has been carried out to examine the financial appraisal of Indian automobile industry after liberalization in the manufacturing sector, although the performance of such a study can not be under estimated. The present study is an attempt in this direction and therefore, aims to enrich the literature of financial performance relating to Indian automobile industry. Further, this study is intended to employ different sophisticated statistical and economic techniques before qualifying any aspects of performance appraisal for wider acceptability and appreciation. The present study is a humble attempt in this regard.

From the above discussion, it is clear that the different authors including economists, financial theorists, management scientists and practicing business executives have approached financial appraisal in different ways and at varying levels of analysis. Though there are various approaches, only a few of them can be considered in this study. The approaches that are included in the study cover analysis of important profitability ratios, analysis of profitability trends, determinants of profitability, analysis of financial position, measuring the long-term and short-term solvency and economic value added analysis in the Indian automobile industry.

References

1. George Paul (1985). Financial performance of Diversified Companies in India: A comparative study of diversified and non-diversified companies, Vikalpa, Vol.10, No.2, pp.179-188.
2. Satyanarayana, J. (1986). State Government Enterprises in Andhra Pradesh: An Overview, in Rao Y. Saraswathy (eds.), Public Enterprises (A State Level Perspective), Delhi: B.R. Publishing Corporations.
3. Mishra, R.K. (1988). Performance Evaluation of Public Enterprises in India, Journal of Institute of Public Enterprises, Vol.6, No.2, pp. 3-23.
4. Rosario G. Manasan, Junaita Amatong and Gil Beltran, (1988). The public enterprise sector in the Philippines: economic contribution and performance: 1975-1984, Public Enterprise, Vol. 8, No. 4, pp. 339-351.
5. Chattopadhayay, P. (March 1989). Central Government Enterprises: An Eighteen Years Profile, Facts for You, Vol. 10, No. 9, pp. 11-19.

6. Sankar T.L, Mishra R.K. and Nandagopal R.N. (1990). State Level Public Enterprises in India: An Overview, Economic and Political Weekly, Bombay, pp.1-37.
7. Pant, L.W. (1991). An Investigation of Industry and Firm Structural characteristics in Corporate Turnaround, Journal of Management Studies, Vol.28, No.12, pp. 623-643.
8. Jagan Mohan Rao, P. (1993). Financial Appraisal of Indian Automotive Tyre Industry, Finance India, Vol.VII, No.3, pp. 683-685.
9. Kallu Rao, P. (1993). Inter Company Financial Analysis of Tea Industry Retrospect and Prospect, Finance India, Vol.VII, No. 3, pp. 587-602.
10. Pai V.S, Vadivel.V and Kamala K.H. (Dec. 1995). "Diversified companies and financial performance: A study, Finance India, Vol.IX, No.4, pp. 977-988.
11. RBI Bulletin (1995). Financial performance of private corporate business sector, Finance India, Vol. IX, No. 4, pp. 901-908.
12. Vijayakumar, A. (1996), Assessment of Corporate Liquidity - A Discriminant Analysis approach, The Management Accountant, Vol. 31, No. 8, pp. 589-591.
13. Joanne Loundes (1998). Performance of Australian Government Trading Enterprises: An overview, Melbourne Institute, Working paper No: 22/98.
14. Raj, S. Dhankar, (1998). A new look at the criteria of performance measurement for business enterprises in India-A study of public sector undertakings, Finance India, Vol. II, No. 1, pp.17-28.
15. Key Sengupta (1998). An empirical exploration of the performance of Fertilizers Industry in India: An econometric analysis, Artha Vijnana, Vol. XL, No. 3, pp. 252-262.
16. Raghunathan V. and Prabina Das, (1999). Corporate Performance: Post- Liberalization, The ICFAI Journal of Applied Finance, Vol. 5, No. 2, pp. 6-29.
17. Juliet D'Souza and William L. Megginson, (1999). Financial and operating performance of privatized firms during the 1990s, The Journal of Finance, Vol. LIV, No.4, pp.1397-1434.
18. Rupa Rege Nitsure and Mathew Joseph, (1999). "Liberalisation and the Behavior of Indian Industry" ABAS International Conference on "Globalisation and Emerging Economics" at Barcelona, Spain, No.14.

19. Rajeswari (2000). Liquidity Management of Tamil Nadu Cement Corporation Ltd, Alangulam- A Case Study, The Management Accountant, Vol.II, No.2, pp. 377-378.
20. Dabasish Sur, Joydeep Biswas and Prasenjit Ganguly, (2001). Liquidity Management in Indian Private Sector Enterprises -A case study of Indian Primary Aluminum industry, Indian Journal of Accounting, Vol. XXXII, pp. 8-14.
21. Aggarwal, N. and Singla, S.K. (2001). How to develop a single index for financial performance, Indian Management, Vol .12, No. 5, pp. 59-62.
22. Joanne Loundes (2001). The Financial Performance of Australian Government Trading Enterprises pre-and post–reform, Melbourne Institute of Applied Economic and Social Research, The University of Melbourne, Working paper No:05./2001
23. Mark Rogers (2001). The Effect of Diversification on Firm Performance, Melbourne Institute of Applied Economic and Social Research, The University of Melbourne, Working Paper No:02/2001.
24. Dabasish Sur (2001). Liquidity Management: An overview of four companies in Indian Power Sector, The Management Accountant, pp. 407-412.
25. Derek Bosworth and Joanne Loundes, (2002). The Dynamic Performance of Australian Enterprises. Melbourne Institute of Applied Economic and Social Research, The university os Melbourne, Working Paper No: 03/2002.
26. Mansur, A. and Mulla, (2002). Use of 'Z' score analysis for evaluation of financial health of textile mills - A case study, Abhigyan, Vol. XIX, No.4, pp.37-40.
27. Wolfgang Aussenegg and Ranko Jelic, (2002). Operating performance of privatized companies in transition economies- the case of Poland, Hungary and the Czech Republic, Research abstract, source: www.ssrn.com.
28. Sudarsana Reddy, G. (2003). Financial Performance of Paper industry in A.P, Finance India, Vol. XVII, No. 3, pp. 1027-1033.
29. RBI Corporate Studies Division (2003). Performance of corporate business sector during the first half of 2002-2003, Finance India, Vol.XVII, No. 3, pp. 987-1002.
30. Ram Kumar Kakani, Biswatosh Saha and Reddy, V.N. (2003). Determinants of financial performance of Indian corporate sector in

the post- liberalization era; An exploratory study, NSE Research Initiative, Paper No: 5, National Stock Exchange of India Limited, pp. 1-38.

31. Laurent Weill (2004). Leverage and corporate performance - A frontier efficiency. University Robert Schuman, instituted detudes politiques, 47 avenue de la Foret-Noire, 67082 Strasbourg cedex, France. e-mail: Laurent. Weill @ urs.G-strasbg.fr.
32. Petia Topalova (2004). Overview of the Indian corporate sector: 1989-2002, IMF Working paper No: WP/04/64, Asia and Pacific Department, pp.1-41.
33. Raghunatha Reddy, D. and Padma, S. (2005). Pre and Post Merger financial performance of selected companies, Indian Journal of Accounting, Vol. XXXV (2), pp. 29 - 38.
34. Santimoy Patra (2005). Liquidity Vs. Profitability, Indian Journal of Accounting, Vol. XXXV(2), pp. 39-43.
35. See Penerose, E.T. (1980). The Theory of Growth of Firm, London: Basil Black Well, Vol .12, pp. 25-36.
36. Whittington, G. (1980). The Profitability and Size of United Kingdom Companies 1960-1964, The Journal of Industrial Economics, Vol.28, pp. 335-342.
37. Asha Jain (1981). Price- Cost Margin in Indian Manufacturing Industries: An Econometric Analysis, Ph.D thesis, IIT, Kanpur.
38. Bothwell, Cooley and Hall, (1982). A New View of Market Structure-Performance Debate, The Journal of Industrial Economics and Statistics, Vol.64, pp.635-645.
39. Gangadhar, V. (1982). Cement Industry-Some Aspects of Profitability, The Management Accountant, p.477.
40. Rao, M.P. (1985). Impact of Debt Equity Ratio on Profitability - An Exploratory Study of Engineering Industry, Lok Udyog, Vol.19 (5), pp. 29-34.
41. Chalam, G.V. and Dakshinamurthy, D. (1985). Performance of Public Enterprises in India: Impact of Heavy External Financing, Public Enterprises, Vol.6, No.2, pp.16-20.
42. Deepak Chawola, (1986). An empirical analysis of the profitability of the Indian man-made fibres industry. Decision, pp.106-115.
43. Nagarajan Burthwal, (1990). Profitability and Structure: A Firm Level Study of Indian Pharmaceutical Industry. The Indian Economic Journal, No.2, Vol. 38, pp.70-84.

44. Conyon, N. and Machin, S. (1991). The Determinants of Profit Margins in U. K.Manufacturing, The Journal of Economics, Vol. 34, No.4, pp. 369-382.

45. Krishnaveni, (1991). Profitability and growth in Indian Automobile manufacturing industry, Indian of Economic Growth, Vol. 26, pp. 81-97.

46. Chandrasekaran, N. (1993). Determinants of profitability in Cement Industry, Decision, Vol. 20, No. 4, pp. 235-244.

47. Cleveland and Frederick, W. (1993). Profitability, Uncertainty and Firm Size, Small Business Economics, Vol. 5, pp. 87-100.

48. Vijayakumar, A. and Venkatachalam, A. (1995). Working Capital and Profitability - An Empirical Analysis, The Management Accountant, Vol . 15, No. 3,pp. 748-750.

49. James Ted McDonald (1997). The Determinants of Firm Profitability in Australian Manufacturing, Applied Economic and Social Research, Melbourne Institute of Applied Economic and Social Research, The University of Melbourne, Working paper No. 17/97.

50. Sidhu H.S. and Gurpreet Bhatia, (1998). Factors affecting in Indian Textile Industry, The Indian Economic Journal, pp.137-143.

51. Kuldip Kaur (1998). Size, Growth and Profitability of Firms in India-An Empirical Investigation. Finance India, Vol. XII, No. 2, pp. 455-457.

52. Amit Mallick and Debasish Sur, (1998). Working Capital and Profitability: A Case Study in Interrelation, The Management Accountant, pp. 805-809.

53. Simon Feeny and Mark Rogers, (1998). Profitability in Australian Enterprises, Melbourne Institute of Applied Economic and Social Research, The University of Melbourne, Working paper No: 21/98.

54. Vijayakumar, A. (1998). Determinants of profitability, Management Accountant, Vol.X, No.4, pp. 925-932.

55. Vishnu Kanta Purohit (1998). Profitability in Indian Industries, New Delhi: Gayatri Publications.

56. Glancey, K. (1998). Determinants of growth and profitability in small entrepreneurial firms, International Journal of Entrepreneurial Behaviour and Research, Vol. 4, No.1, pp.18-27.

57. Agarwal, R.N. (1999). Profitability and Growth in Indian Automobile Manufacturing Industry, Indian Economic Review, Vol. 26, No.1, pp. 81.

58. Soumyendra Kishore Dutta (1999). An Analysis of Profitability trend in the Indian Cotton Mill Industry, Asian Economic Review, Vol. 41, No. 2, pp. 294-307.

59. Simon Feeny and Mark Rogers (1999). Market Share, Concentration and Diversification in Firm Profitability, Melbourne Institute of Applied Economic and Social Research, The University of Melbourne, Working paper No: 20/1999.

60. Govindan Rao, D. and Mohana Rao, P. (1999). Impact of working capital on profitability in cement industry - A correlation analysis, New Delhi: Deep and Deep Publishers.

61. Mohammed Rafiqul Islam (2000). Profitability of Fertilizer Industry in Bangladesh. The Management Accountant, pp. 338-345.

62. Simon Feeny (2000). Determinants of profitability: an empirical investigation using Australian tax entities, Melbourne Institute of Applied Economic and Social Research, The University of Melbourne.

63. Debashish Rei, Debashish Sur, (2001). Profitability Analysis of Indian Food Products Industry: A case study of Cadbury India Ltd, The Management Accountant, Vol. 36, No. 6, pp. 407-412.

64. Vijayakumar, A. (2002). Determinants of Profitability-A Firm Level study of the Sugar Industry of Tamil Nadu, The Management Accountant, pp.458-465.

65. Jack Glen, Kevin Lee and Ajit Singh, (2004). Corporate profitability and the dynamics of competition in emerging markets- A time series analysis, ESRC Center for Business Research, University of Cambridge, Working paper No. 248.

66. Vijayakumar, A. (2002). Financial appraisal of Salem Co-operative Sugar Mills Ltd., Mohanur, in the book Research studies in Commerce and Management, Delhi: Classical Publishing Company, pp. 51-65.

67. Vijayakumar, A. and Kadirve, S. (2003). Determinants of profitability in Indian Public Sector Manufacturing Industries – An Econometric Analysis, The Journal of Institute of Public Enterprises, Vol. 26, pp. 1 - 2.

68. Vijayakumar, A and Kadirvel, S. (2003). Profitability and Size of the firm in Indian Minerals and Metals industry, The Management Accountant, pp. 816-821.

69. Zuobao Wei, Oscar Varela, Juliet D'Souza and Kabir Hassan.M. (2003), The financial and operating performance of China's newly privatized firms, Financial Management, Vol. 32, No. 2, pp. 107-126.

70. Maninder S.Sarkaria, Shergil U.S. (2004). Market Structure and Financial Performance-An Indian Evidence with Enhanced Controls, Ph.D Thesis Submitted to the Guru Nanak Dev University.
71. Marcos A.M.Lima, Marcelo Resende, (2004). Profit margins and business cycles in the Brazilian industry: a panel data study, Taylor and Francis Journal in Applied Economics, pp.923-930.
72. Bhanu, V. (2005). Merged companies-their profitability performance, Indian Journal of Accounting, Vol.XXXV (2), pp. 19-38.
73. Stern and Joel, (1990). One way to build value in your firm, Executive compensation, Financial Executive, pp. 51-54.
74. Rutledge, J. (1993). De-jargoning EVA, Forbes,Vol.152, No. 10,p.148(1).
75. Stewart, G. Bennet, (1994). EVATM Fact and Fantasy, Journal of Applied Corporate Finance, pp. 71-84.
76. Ochsner (1995). Welcome to the new world of Economic Value Added, Compensation and Benefits, Vol.27, No.2, p.30(3).
77. Grant, J. (1996). Foundation of EVA for investment managers: Just in time, EVA, Journal of Financial Management, Vol.23, No.1, p.41(8).
78. Luber, R. B. (1996). Who are the real wealth creators, Fortune, pp.2-3.
79. Banerjee and Ashok, (1997). Economic Value Added (EVA): a better performance measure, The Management Accountant, pp. 86-88.
80. Bacidore, J.M, Boquist, J.A, Miboum, T.T, Thakor, A.V. (1997). The search for the Best Financial Performance Measure, Financial Analysts Journal, pp.11-20.
81. Burkette, G. Hedley, T. (1997). The truth about Economic Value Added, The CPA Journal, No.7, p.46(4).
82. Dodd, James, L, Chen, Shimine, (1997). EVA: A new panacea?, Business and Economic Review, Vol.42, pp. 26-28.
83. Putnam, Bulford (1997). EVA Analysis predicts tough time in US markets, Global Investor, pp. 42-44.
84. Tully, Shawn (1997). Adding value, Business Today, pp. 68-73.
85. Ethiraj, Govindaraj (1998). The EVA feather in the market cap, The Economic Times, p. 1.
86. KPMG-BS. (1998). Corporate India: An Economic Value Scoreboard, The Strategy, pp. 22-25.

87. Anand, Manoj, Garg, Ajay, and Arora, Asha (1999). Economic value added : Business performance measure of shareholder value, The Management Accountant, pp. 351-56.
88. Bao, B.H. and Bao, D.H., (1999). The Association between firm value and Economic Value Added, Indian Accounting Review, Vol.3, No.2, pp. 161-64.
89. Harihar,T.S. (1999). EVA Prorating Myths, Chartered Finance Analyst, pp.8-9.
90. Thenmozhie, M. (1999). Economic value added as a measure of corporate performance, The Indian Journal of Commerce, Vol.52, No.4, pp. 72-85.
91. Banerjee, Ashok (2000). Linkage between Economic Value Added and Market Value : An Analysis, Vikalpa, Vol.25, No.3, pp. 23-36.
92. Parasuram, N.R.(2000). Economic Value Added: Its Computation and Impact on Selected Banking Companies, The ICFAI Journal of Applied Finance, Vol.6, No.4, pp. 171-178.
93. Thampy, A. and Beheli, R (2001). Economic Value Added in Banks, The ICFAI Journal of Applied Finance, Vol.7, No.1, pp 180-189.
94. Riceman, S.S. and Cahan, S.F. (2002). Do Managers Perform Better under EVA Bonus Schemes, Social Science Research Network Electronic Paper Collection, at http://oaoers.ssrb.cin.
95. Bardia, S.C. (2002). Economic Value Added: Overall Consideration, Economic Challenger, pp. 1-7.
96. Costigan, M.H. and Lovata Linda, (2002). Empirical Analysis Adopters of Economic Value Added, Management Accounting Research, Vol. 13, No.2, pp. 40-46.
97. Mangala, Deepa and Joura Simpy, (2002). Linkage between Economic Value Added and Market Value: An Analysis in Indian Context, Indian Management Studies Journal, pp. 55-65.
98. Bhata and Dayal Bhat Nagar, (2003). Economic Value Added for comparison among companies of different industries, The ICFAI Journal of Applied Finance, No.3. Vol. XXII, pp. 36-42.

3

Methodology

In research, the methodology needs to be cautiously designed to capitulate results that are as objective as realistic. An able-bodied comprehensible modus operandi empowers the new-fangled research investigator to re-examine the study milieu. Good methodology follows the standards of the established conventions. For the present study, a number of indispensable inimitabilities of the research methodology skirmishing the application magnitude and research rationalization of each one are defined here in this chapter.

The ensuing paragraphs in this chapter deal with the methodology adopted in selection and analysis of data for this study. It outlines the objective and scope of the study, procedure followed for selection of the sample and the collection of data, classification of the sample and the technique followed in analyzing the data for the period of study. Further, the hypotheses set and limitations of the study have also been dealt herein.

The Problem

The title of the study is "Financial and operating performance of Indian Automobile Industry".

Objectives of the Study

The primary purpose of the present study is to obtain a true insight into the performance of the selected automobile industry in

India. An appraisal of financial and operating performance is made from the accounting point of view to assess the effectiveness of plans, policies and objectives of the industry by measuring the efficiency of the automobile industry under the study, in various areas of operations. For carrying out the study, the following specific objectives have been set.

1. To analyse the trends of production, capacity utilization, sales and market share of the selected sectors of Indian automobile industry.
2. To study the profitability position, trends and determinants of profitability of the selected sectors of Indian automobile industry.
3. To analyse the financial structure, financial position and assessment of financial health of the selected sectors of Indian automobile industry.
4. To offer an economic interpretation to the factors which determine the financial structure of selected sectors of Indian automobile industry.
5. To compute and analyse Economic Value Added (EVA) of the selected sectors of Indian automobile industry.
6. To make suggestions for improvement for successful survival in the competitive business world.

Hypothesis

Hypothesis means the researcher must select from the intricacy of observed events such considerable and pertinent facts that would most effectively elucidate the problem under study. It gives us an idea about indispensable associations, which exist between the different fundamentals within the complexity. Therefore, the hypotheses of the present study are:

1. Hypotheses for Trend Analysis

(i) There is no significant difference between actual production and trend values of production among different years in the selected sectors of Indian automobile industry.

(ii) There is no significant difference between actual sales and trend values of sales among different years in the selected sectors of Indian automobile industry.

2. Hypothesis for Profitability Analysis

(i) There is no significant difference in the mean percentage of profitability ratios between years and between the sectors in Indian automobile industry.

3. Hypotheses for Determinants of Profitability

(i) There is a positive relationship between size and growth rate of assets.

(ii) Profitability is negatively correlated with leverage and current ratio.

(iii) There is a positive relationship between inventory turnover ratio and profitability.

(iv) Fixed assets turnover ratio, vertical integration and past profitability are positively correlated with the profitability.

(v) Profitability is negatively correlated with operating expenses to sales ratio.

4. Hypotheses for Financial Structure Analysis

(i) Financial leverage is independent of industry class.

(ii) Financial leverage is independent of industry size.

(iii) Financial leverage and profitability are independent of each other.

(iv) Financial leverage and operating leverage have got no association between them.

(v) Financial leverage and external financing are independent of each other.

(vi) Financial leverage has got no association with income gearing.

5. Hypothesis for Financial Position Analysis

(i) There is no any significant difference in short term and long term financial ratios between years and between the sectors of Indian Automobile Industry.

The above hypotheses have been taken for the study and they have been tested with the help of Chi-Square Test and 'F' test.

Research Design

It is not possible in practice for an individual research worker to approach all the bits and pieces in the universe. Researcher selects only a small amount of bits and pieces from the universe for the purpose of the study on the basis of stratified sampling. The sample so selected constitutes the sample design for the purpose. A research design is a definite plan for obtaining a sample from a given population. Research design means a sketch or a drawing of a research project's structure. It comprises a series of prior pronouncements that, taken together, provide a roadmap for carrying out a research project. The research design of the present study is outlined hereunder.

Selection of Sample

Keeping in view the scope of the study, it is decided to include all the companies under automobile industry working before or from the year 1991-92 to 2003-04. But, owing to several constraints such as non-availability of financial statements or non-working of a company in a particular year etc., it is compelled to restrict the number of sample companies to 18. Therefore, this study is expost facto based on survey method making a survey of eighteen companies in Indian automobile industry. There are 26 companies operating in the Indian Automobile Industry. The companies under automobile industry are classified into three sectors namely; commercial vehicles, passenger cars and multiutility vehicles and two and three wheelers. The details of the sector with the available

Table 3.1
Total number of companies available in Indian Automobile Industry

Sl.No.	*Sectors*	*Total companies available*	*13 years data available companies*
1.	Commercial Vehicles	5	5
2.	Passenger Cars and Multiutility Vehicles	8	4
3.	Two and Three Wheelers	13	9
	Total	**26**	**18**

Source: Prowess Database, 2004.

Table 3.2
List of sample companies included in the present study

Sl. No.	*Sectors / Companies*	*Year of Incor-poration*	*Ownership*	*Market share (%)*	*Total market share (%)*
	Commercial Vehicles (5)				
1.	Ashok Leyland Ltd.	1956	Hinduja Group	35.62	
2.	Tata Motors Ltd.	1956	Tata Group	34.22	
3.	Bajaj Tempo Ltd.	1958	Firodia Group	11.50	
4.	Eicher Motors Ltd.	1982	Eicher Group	10.65	
5.	Swaraj Mazder Ltd.	1983	State and Private Sector	6.75	**98.74**
	Passenger Cars and Multiutility Vehicles (4)				
6.	Hindustan Motors Ltd.	1942	Birla C.K.Group	8.31	
7.	Mahindra and Mahindra Ltd.	1945	Mahindra and Mahindra	42.17	
8.	Maruti Udyog Ltd.	1981	Private (Foreign)	36.60	
9.	Daewoo Motors India Ltd.	1983	Private (Foreign)	2.68	**89.76**

(Contd.)

(Contd. Table 3.2)

Sl. No.	Sectors / Companies	Year of Incorporation	Ownership	Market share (%)	Total market share (%)
	Two and Three Wheelers (9)				
10.	Bajaj Auto Ltd.	1945	Bajaj Group	18.80	
11.	LML Ltd.	1972	LML Group	11.58	
12.	Maharashtra Scooters Ltd.	1975	Bajaj Group	7.80	
13.	TVS Motor Company Ltd.	1982	T.V.S. Group	12.93	
14.	Kinetic Motor Company Ltd.	1984	Firodia Group	11.75	
15.	Hero Honda Motors Ltd.	1984	Hero (Munsals) Groups	10.54	
16.	Kinetic Engineering Ltd.	1970	Firodia Group	9.72	
17.	Majestic Auto Ltd.	1986	Hero Group	9.04	
18.	Scooters India Ltd.	1972	Central Govt. Commercial Enterprise	7.65	**99.81**

companies of Indian automobile industry are presented in Table 3.1.

For the purpose of the study all the three sectors have been selected. The selected sectors include 26 companies. Out of 26 companies, 5 are under commercial vehicles, 8 under passenger cars and multiutility vehicles and 13 under two and three wheelers sector. Out of 26 companies of the selected sectors, 13 years data is available for 18 companies only. Therefore, all the 18 companies are included in the sample. It accounts for 69.23 per cent of the total companies available in the Indian automobile industry. The selected 18 companies include 5 under commercial vehicles, 4 under passenger cars and multiutility vehicles and 9 under two and three wheeler sectors. List of companies selected included in the present study along with year of incorporation, ownership and its market share is presented in Table 3.2.

It is evident from the Table 3.2 that sample company represents 98.74 percentage of market share in commercial vehicles, 89.76 percentage in passenger cars and multiutility vehicles and 99.81 percentage in two and three wheelers. Thus, the findings based on the occurrence of such representative sample may be presumed to be true representative of automobile industry in the country.

Period of Study

The period 1991-92 to 2003-04 is selected for this study of Indian automobile industry. This 13 years period is chosen in order to have a fairly long, cyclically well balanced period, for which reasonably homogeneous, reliable and upto-date financial data would be available. Further, the span chosen for the study is the period of the beginning of liberalization measures introduced by the Government of India. Hence, the period 1991-92 to 2003-04 is an era of growth of corporate performance in the manufacturing sector, particularly automobile industry and has got genuine economic significance of its own.

Source of Data

The study is mainly based on secondary data. The major source of data analysed and interpreted in this study related to all those companies selected is collected from "PROWESS" database, which is the most reliable on the empowered corporate database of Centre for Monitoring Indian Economy (CMIE). It contains a highly normalized database built on a sound understanding of disclosure in India on around 12,000 companies, which include public, private, co-operative and joint sector companies. The database provides financial statements, ratio analysis, funds flow, cash flow, product profiles, returns and risk on the stock market etc.

Besides prowess database, relevant secondary data have also been collected from BSE Stock Exchange Official Directory, CMIE Publications, Annual Survey of Industry, Business newspapers, Reports on Currency and Finance, Libraries of various Research Institutions, through Internet etc. The study required variety of data; therefore, websites like http://indiainfoline.com, www.indiastat.com and www.google.com have been comprehensively searched.

Data Editing

For this study, major part of data comes from secondary sources. Data has been collected in raw form and then it is made suitable for analysis as per the methodology defined for the purpose.

Selection of Variables

In this study at hand, a number of key financial variables have been identified for the purpose of analysis. The computation of these variables has been made for a period of 13 years. An epigrammatic explanation of the selected variable is outlined below.

Profitability

Return on assets and return on sales are widely used measures of profitability. It is assumed that management may be concerned with effective utilisation of all resources and these two measures could be proper in this line of arguments. The review includes Stkeler (1964), Samuels and Smyth (1968), Neumann, Bobel and Haid (1979), Deepak Chawala (1986), Narayanan and Barthwal (1990), Amit Mallick and Debasish Sur (1998), Agarwal (1999), Mohammed Rafiqul Islam (2000) and Vijayakumar (2002) which provide direct evidence of using return on assets and return on sales as a measure of profitability. The profit rates measured by sales will give a short-term perspective of profitability because sales are annual flows. On the other hand, the return on assets will give us long-term perspective of profitability. In this study, ratio of profit margin on sales is used as dependent variable.

Size

One of the very important structural characteristics of the industry which is commonly used to explain profitability in applied research is the size of the firm. Many researchers have employed firm size as a variable in their study of determinants of profitability. The big firms have been considered to be endowed with certain advantages such as lower costs and higher returns on accounts of access to capital market (Hall and Weiss, 1967)[1] and economies of scale (Sidhu and Bhatia, 1993)[2]. Hence, generally a positive hypothesis is set for size-profitability relationship. The size - profitability relationship is more likely to be curvi-linear and after reaching a certain stage, the advantage of scale economies may cease and beyond that the relationship may even reverse due to the problems of large scale. Due to the expected curvi-linear size performance relationship, size variable is generally employed in long term. Though the positive relationship between size and profitability has been found to be significant, after a point of time, profitability increases at a rate with proposal increase in size. This could arise when (i) other firms in the market follow similar strategies (ii) diseconomies and inefficiency due to in manageable size, and (iii) increased possibility of public criticism of excessive profits as firm becomes larger. Therefore, impact of firm size on profitability can not be determined apriori.

Generally two sizes measures are employed, they are assets and sales turnover. Assets express amount of resources utilised for producing output whereas sales is an output variable. Sales is an annual flow depending upon output produced and sold in the market. Further sales needs to be adjusted for excise payment to more meaningful comparison. Therefore, in this study the log of total assets as the measure of size has been employed.

Leverage

A firm with high leverage ratio represents greater financial risk than a firm with relatively less risk. If competition equalises earnings, then high debt should result in higher return on net worth. It is argued that firms have low debt because they operate in industries with high degree of business risk and thus expect a negative relations between leverage and profitability, it owners are risk averse. It seems that the relationship between leverage and rate of return is indeterminate apriori. In an intra industry study, business risk is assumed to be same and leverage must be a better measure of risk. The debt equity ratio as the measure of leverage has been employed in this study.

Current Ratio

The management of working capital involves decisions about the amount and composition of current assets and how they are financed. Such decisions involve a trade off between solvency and profitability. In inter-firm comparison, the firm with higher current ratio has better liquidity. A high ratio of current assets to current liabilities may be indicative of slack management practices, as it might signal poor credit management in terms of over-extended accounts receivables. A low ratio is also not desirous since there will be an inadequate margin of safety.

Inventory Turnover Ratio

Another variable, which can influence the profitability is the inventory turnover ratio. It is the ratio of sales to inventory which indicates the number of times inventory is replaced during the year. Instead of taking year end stock of inventory, an average of the opening and closing stock of inventory is considered. A high ratio implies good inventory management. But low inventory will adversely affect the ability of a firm to meet customer demand and in turn will affect profitability. On the other hand, a very low inventory turnover ratio signifies excessive inventory or over investment in inventory and high carrying cost. The sign of inventory coefficient is ambiguous.

Fixed Assets Turnover Ratio

Another variable influencing the profitability of the industry is fixed assets turnover ratio which is defined as the ratio of sales to fixed assets. It indicates the relationship between the amount invested in fixed assets and the results in accruing in terms of the sales. It is expected that an increase in this ratio would result in increase in profitability. The capital employed of a firm includes both current and fixed assets. The fixed assets provide the productive base and earning capacity for the firm. But an efficient utilisation of the earning capacity calls for an optimum use of working capital.

Operating Expenses to Sales Ratio

Apart from the above discussed factors operating expenses ratio is included as an explanatory variable in this study. A low operating ratio is by and large a test of operational efficiency. The implication of low operating expenses ratio is that relatively a high percentage share of sales is available for meeting financial liabilities like interest, taxes and dividends. Therefore, a negative relationship is expected with operating expenses and profitability.

Vertical Integration

Firm-specific vertical integration motivated by considerations such as the avoidance of costs incurred in using the market of organize production, government policies and also consideration of market power is an important determinant of profitability. The costs of using the market alternatively known as transaction costs include search cost, cost of drawing up contracts, monitoring costs, etc. In our context government polices assume an important role in determining vertical integration. The degree of vertical integration is sought to be measured by the value added to sales ratio in the analysis. Value added is defined as total sales revenue less costs of purchased inputs, repair charges and customs and excise duty.

Past Profitability

In operational terms it would mean the current level of business success measured in terms of profitability should, to a large extent, depend on the success achieved in the preceding years. The implicit assumption underlying the postulate is that under normal situation a firm in a given year tries to achieve atleast the profitability level of the preceding year. Past profitability of a particular year of a firm has been taken on the profitability in the respective previous year of that firm.

Growth Rate of Assets

The other variable, which is considered, is growth of firm. Growth is essential to a firm even if it is not among the firm's major objectives. The reason is that growth helps in providing the firm finances for attaining its objective by increasing the size of its profit growth, by providing room for initiatives and exercise managerial ability, stimulates managerial efficiency leading to a lower capital output ratio and consequently higher profit rate. It is thus, likely to have positive association with profitability. Growth rate is measured in this study by the ratio of simple growth rate of assets.

Financial Structure

There exists a great deal of controversy regarding the concept of capital structure, financial structure, capitalization and financial-mix. While some prefer to use these terms as synonymous and hence use them interchangeably, others put a distinction between capital structure and financial structure by including only long-term sources of funds (debt and ownership capital) under the former, and all sources of funds (i.e., both long-term and short term) under the latter. Thus, in this study the entire liabilities side of the balance sheet has been considered as financial structure for the purpose of the present study.

Financial Leverage

Financial leverage, expressed as a ratio between total debt to total assets at book value, i.e., D/TA, has been used as the only measure of capital structure in this study. This is the measure which Remmers et al[3] have also used in their study. The reason of accepting this ratio (i.e., total debt to total assets at book value) as financial structure or financial leverage lies with the fact of its conceptual simplicity over other measures and its ability to more completely reflect a firm's total reliance on borrowed capital.

Operating leverage

The traditional measure of operating leverage is the ratio of the percentage change in earnings to the percentage change in sales. Because of lack of a unique measure of operating leverage, some even prefer to calculate it, from the balance sheet data, by dividing net fixed assets by total assets at book value and even by dividing the net fixed assets by average total assets at book value. Operating leverage to be called as degree of operating leverage, has been calculated by dividing the percentage change in average earnings before interest and taxes by the percentage change in average sales.

Mathematically, $$\mathbf{DOL_t} = \frac{[(\mathbf{EBIT_t} - \mathbf{EBIT_{t-1}}) / \mathbf{EBIT_{t-1}}]}{[(\mathbf{SA_t} - \mathbf{SA_{t-1}}) / \mathbf{SA_{t-1}}]}$$

Where,

DOL_t = Degree of operating leverage in time 't'

$EBIT_t$ = Earnings Before Interest and Taxes in year 't'

$EBIT_{t-1}$ = Earnings Before Interest and Taxes in the previous year

SA_t = Sales in year 't'

SA_{t-1} = Sales in previous year

Income Gearing

The ratio of interest to EBIT has been taken as 'income gearing'. Another measure of income gearing, often used in the literature, is the proportion of interest to cash flows. Singh and Hamid[4] have used both of the measures, what they call the 'flow measures of gearing' in their study.

Payout Ratio

The ratio of dividend to profit after tax has been taken as payout ratio.

External Financing

Share capital, borrowings, trade dues and other current liabilities and miscellaneous non-current liabilities, constitute to form the external financing.

Economic Value Added (EVA)

The valued-based performance measure, namely, EVA, introduced by Stern Stewart and company[1] is an incarnation of

Residual Income concept. EVA model is based on the hypothesis that rational investor takes into account just two things; the cash to be generated over the life of a business; and the risk of the cash receipts. Stewart defined 'EVA as an estimation of true economic profit, the amount by which earnings exceed or fall short of required minimum rate of return investors could get by investing in other securities of comparable risk'. It is the net operating profit minus the appropriate charge for the opportunity cost of capital invested in an enterprise (both debt and equity).

Expressed as a formula, EVA for a given period can be written as:

EVA = NOPAT - COST OF CAPITAL EMPLOYED
= NOPAT - WACC x CE

Where,

NOPAT - Net Operating Profit After Taxes but before financing costs

WACC - Weighted Average Cost of Capital; and

CE - Capital Employed

(or)

equivalently, if rate of return is defined as NOPAT / CAPITAL, this turns into a perhaps more revealing formula:

EVA = (RATE OF RETURN - COST OF CAPITAL) X CAPITAL

Where,

RATE OF RETURN	-	NOPAT / CAPITAL
CAPITAL	-	Total balance sheet minus non-interest bearing debt in the beginning of the year.
COST OF CAPITAL	-	[Cost of equity x proportion of equity from capital] + [cost of debt x proportion of debt from capital x (1-tax rate)]

Cost of capital or weighted average cost of capital is the average cost of both equity capital and interest bearing debt.

Cost of debt (K_d)

Cost of debt refers to the average rate of interest the company pays for its debt obligations. Cost of debt (K_d) has been computed as:

K_d = Total interest expenses x (1-Effective tax rate) / Beginning total borrowings

While calculating beginning borrowing all short-term as well as long-term borrowings have to be included as all debts are interest bearing. Therefore, interest paid in the financial year has been considered as total interest expenses.

Cost of Equity (K_e)

To scribble down cost of equity (K_e), Capital Assets Pricing Model (CAPM) has been used. This model holds that firms' equity cost is the composition of risk free rate of return for a stock plus premium representing the volatility of share prices. According to this model, K_e is the shareholders' expected rate of return and this expected rate of return (R_j) is as follows:

$$R_j = R_f + \beta X (R_m - R_f)$$

Where,

R_j = Expected rate of return

R_f = Risk free rate of return,

R_m = Market rate of return, and

β = Sensitivity of the share price in relation to the market index

The interest rate of Government securities has been considered as a proxy for risk free rate of return. The market rate of return has been calculated by using Index Numbers of Security Prices (Bombay Stock Exchange) from year to year (on monthly average basis) base. The yearly return of the index numbers has been computed by using the following formula:

R_m = [(Index number for current year-Index number for previous year) / (Index number of previous year)] x 100

Beta (β) is the risk-free co-efficient which measures the volatility of a given script of a company with respect to volatility of market. It is calculated by comparing return on a share to return in the stock market. Mathematically, beta is the statistical measure of volatility. It is calculated as covariance of daily return on the stock market indices and the return on daily share prices of a particular company, divided by variance of return on daily stock market indices. The Beta co-efficient has been calculated as follows:

$$\beta_j = COV_{im} / \sigma^2_m$$

Where,

β_j = is the Beta of the security in the question

COV_{im} = Stands for co-variance between the return of security and return of market, and

σ^2_m = Stands for the variance of market return

Market Value Added (MVA)

While EVA measures shareholder value addition of firm in terms of its real economic performance, MVA measures market's assessment of firm's value. MVA thus measures value by the management over and above the capital invested in the company by investors.

Market Value Added (MVA) = Market value of company-Capital employed

For a public listed company, its market value is calculated as market value of its equity (number of shares outstanding times their share price) plus book value of debt (since market value of debt is generally not available). Capital employed is effectively the book value of investments in the business madeup of debt and equity.

Effectively, the formula becomes

Market Value Added (MVA) = Market value of equity-Book value of equity

These items have been obtain from balance sheet statement of companies. Data for the market price existing on the close of financial year has been collected from the economic times, CMIE prowess and capitaline databases.

Data Analysis

The financial and statistical analysis approach plays a vital role in the financial environment. To enjoy the benefit of financial and statistical analysis researcher has collected, assembled and correlated the data, classified the data appropriately and condensed them in to a related data series; stated the resultant information in a comprehensive form, text, tables and analysed and interpreted the reported data. The financial and statistical techniques applied in the study are given below:

It is well known that management is concerned with efficient performance, profitability and solvency. For this purpose it has to study certain specific ratios, because, investors look upon certain ratios, which are concerned with an organization's operating and financial performance. For the purpose of this study, researcher has used ratio namely, operating profit margin, net profit margin, return on assets, return on net worth, return on capital employed, earnings per share, dividend per share, dividend payout ratio, current ratio, liquidity ratio, interest coverage ratio, debt equity ratio and fixed assets to net worth ratio.

The role of statistical tools is important in analysing the data and drawing inferences therefrom. In order to derive the open handed results from the information collected through secondary data, various statistical tools like mean, standard deviation, variance, compound annual growth rate, regression, tests of hypotheses both parametric and non-parametric have been accomplished through EXCEL, SX and SPSS softwares. Some of the statistical techniques particularly t-test, Durbin-Watson test, ANOVA, trend analysis and Chi-square test have been used to interpret the sense of mathematical relationship amongst values of different variables so computed in the study.

In the present study regression models have also been used to analyse the influence of independent variables on dependent variables in case of determinants of profitability and financial structure. The hypothesis has been tested separately on the sample. This can be done via the mechanism of the F test and Chi-square test.

Moreover, model recommended on the basis of the findings may prove to be a signpost in the field of corporate finance since the data and information likely to be tested and analysed with the help of latest available quantitative techniques. Furthermore, researchers in particular are a concerned with a change and likely contribution to the field of knowledge by their research so carried out. Similarly, it is expected that the findings of the present study would certainly become an addition to the present knowledge as far as Indian context is concerned. Hence, the scope of the present study is quite wide.

Limitations of the Study

However, there are some limitations of the study, which are generally inherent in all such studies conducted at human being level. The most important among them are:

(i) The study is based on secondary data obtained from the published annual reports and as such its finding depends entirely on the accuracy of such data.

(ii) Non-availability of the required thirteen consecutive year's financial data for the whole period of study has restricted the size of the sample. Therefore, the limitation of the small sample is also prevalent in this study.

(iii) The present study is largely based on ratio analysis which has its own limitations.

(iv) Statistical test used in the study to interpret the analysed data to generalize the findings of the study for the entire population has got their own limitations and result in the analysis is subject to same constraints as are applicable to statistical tools.

(v) The analysis of financial statement of business enterprise gives diagnostic indicators. Researcher being outside external analyst obviously has no access to internal data. Therefore, inside view of the organization cannot be characterized in the study.

(vi) The financial statement does not keep pace with the changing price level.

However, all these limitations, do not, in any way, affect the worth of this research work.

Chapter Scheme

In order to present this research work in a lucid way, it has been divided into eight chapters. The layout of these chapters is delineated below:

Chapter I	is conceptual in nature and has been divided into seven sub-parts, which include introduction, meaning and concept of financial statements, need and aims of financial analysis, tools and techniques of analysis for financial statement, scope of the study, statement of the problem, selection of automobile industry and significance of the study.
Chapter II	presents a brief review of related literatures on the subject.
Chapter III	encompasses the research methodology of the study. This chapter contains thirteen parts that include the problem, objective of the study, hypotheses, research design which includes selection of sample, period of study, sources of data, data editing, selection of variables, data analysis, scope of the study, limitations of the study and chapter scheme.
Chapter IV	brings out analysis of production and sales trend, capacity utilisation, sales and market share of the selected sectors of Indian automobile industry.
Chapter V	is committed to the profitability analysis, profitability trend and determinants of profitability of the selected sectors of Indian automobile industry.
Chapter VI	discusses the financial structure, determinants of financial structure, analysis of financial strength (short-term and long-term) and assessment of financial health using Altman's Z score model of the selected sectors of Indian automobile industry.
Chapter VII	is committed to analyse the Economic Value Added and Market Value Added (MVA) of the selected sectors of Indian automobile industry.

Chapter VIII embodies the summary of conclusions and some workable recommendations for the smooth and efficient functioning of Indian automobile industry.

Towards the end of this research work, comprehensive bibliographies on the subject and some appendices have also been added.

References

1. Hall, M. and Weiss, L. (1967). Firm size and profitability, Review of Economics and Statistics, Vol. 49, pp. 319-331.
2. Sidhu, H.S. and Bhatia G. (1993). Factors affecting profitability in Indian Textile Industry, The Indian Economic Journal, Vol. 41, No. 2, pp. 137-143.
3. Remmers, L., Stonetill, A., Wright, R., and Beakhusen, T, Industry and size as Debt-ratio determinants in manufactuirng internationally, Financial Managmenet, Vol. III, Spring, pp.29-75.
4. Singh, A., and Hamid J, Corporate financial structure in Developing Countries, IFC Technical paper No.1, The World Bank, Washington, D.C.
5. Steward, G.Bennet (1994). EVATM Fact and Fantasy, Journal of Applied Corporate Finance, June 1993, pp. 71-84.

4

Analysis of Production and Sales Trend of Indian Automobiles Industry

Analysis of Production Trend

Production is the activity of making tangible goods. In the economic sense production means both making goods and rendering services that add value to a product even though no physical change has taken place[1]. It covers all the activities of procurement, all action and utilisation of resources such as materials, labour, energy, machinery, etc. Production is one of the most important areas of performance. In business enterprises, production function will be considered to be very effective and useful because it must operate primarily to satisfy customer's demand and it must permit production activities to operate in an economical and efficient manner[2].

Production may be considered as the back bone of the manufacturing business enterprises. The production data of a company may give an idea as to how the company has performed in the year under review as compared to the past or how the company as performed as compared to other companies of the same industry. The production performance of an enterprise can be measured in a number of ways. Production performance of the industry as a whole can be compared with different years; also the comparison can be done in between the competitive industries. For appraising the production performance of individual companies, production in different years can be compared and inter-company comparison between companies under study may be more meaningful for this purpose. The analysis of capacity utilisation can also significantly prove the production performance of a company or of the industries as a whole. All these techniques have been adopted to appraise the production performance of the automobile industry in the present chapter.

An attempt has also been made to estimate trend co-efficients for production of automobiles in India during the study period by fitting a linear regression model. The liner model fitted is as follows.

$$P = \alpha + \beta t + e$$

where P is rate of production, t is the time and α and β are the parameters [intercept and co-efficients respectively] and e is the error term. To test whether the difference between actual production and estimated production was significant or not, the following hypothesis is framed and tested.

H_o - **There is no significant difference between actual production and the trend values of production among different years.**

(or)

H_a - **There is significant difference between actual production and the trend values of production among different years.**

The automobile industry makes more range of product such as commercial vehicles, passenger cars and multiutility vehicles, three wheelers and two-wheelers. Table 4.1 shows the annual production of automobiles in India from the year 1991-92 to 2003-04. The variations of production of various products have also been computed taking the production data of 1991-92 as the base 100. Further, product-wise dispersion in production of Indian automobile

Table 4.1

Annual production of automobile in India

(1991-92 to 2003-04)

(in thousands)

Year	*Commercial Vehicles*	*Passenger Cars*	*Multi-utility Vehicles*	*Three Wheelers*	*Two-Wheelers*		
					Scooter	*Motor Cycle*	*Moped*
1991-92	144.6 (100)	166.2 (100)	39.6 (100)	79.7 (100)	947.1 (100)	403.9 (100)	408.4 (100)
1992-93	128.0 (89)	163.2 (98)	42.8 (108)	69.4 (87)	854.9 (90)	366.1 (91)	393.2 (96)
1993-94	140.0 (97)	215.5 (130)	55.2 (139)	92.4 (116)	860.8 (91)	466.7 (116)	439.2 (108)
1994-95	193.8 (134)	270.6 (163)	49.5 (125)	150.2 (188)	1287.5 (136)	646.8 (160)	511.6 (125)
1995-96	256.6 (177)	348.2 (210)	66.7 (168)	176.4 (221)	1224.9 (129)	809.1 (200)	622.0 (152)

(Contd.)

(Contd. Table 4.1)

Year	Commercial Vehicles	Passenger Cars	Multi-utility Vehicles	Three Wheelers	Two-Wheelers Scooter	Two-Wheelers Motor Cycle	Two-Wheelers Moped
1996-97	300.0 (207)	411.1 (247)	82.6 (209)	221.6 (278)	1312.9 (139)	988.2 (245)	678.1 (166)
1997-98	229.0 (158)	401.0 (241)	79.6 (201)	234.9 (295)	1279.5 (135)	1126.0 (279)	667.2 (163)
1998-99	135.8 (94)	390.7 (235)	114.8 (290)	209.0 (262)	1315.0 (139)	1387.3 (343)	672.2 (165)
1999-00	181.6 (126)	577.2 (347)	121.0 (306)	205.5 (258)	1259.4 (133)	1794.1 (444)	724.5 (177)

(Contd.)

(Contd. Table 4.1)

Year	*Commercial Vehicles*	*Passenger Cars*	*Multi-utility Vehicles*	*Three Wheelers*	*Two-Wheelers*		
					Scooter	*Motor Cycle*	*Moped*
2000-01	151.9 (105)	504.7 (304)	122.0 (308)	203.2 (255)	879.7 (93)	2183.8 (541)	695.0 (170)
2001-02	159.0 (110)	500.3 (301)	114.0 (288)	212.7 (267)	937.5 (99)	2906.3 (720)	427.5 (105)
2002-03	210.6 (146)	557.7 (336)	161.1 (407)	271.2 (340)	850.1 (90)	3914.6 (969)	344.7 (84)
2003-04	281.9 (195)	592.3 (356)	143.7 (363)	286.4 (359)	878.2 (93)	3849.2 (953)	366.4 (90)
Mean	**193.34**	**392.21**	**91.74**	**185.58**	**1067.88**	**1603.24**	**534.62**
CV	**0.30**	**0.39**	**0.44**	**0.37**	**0.19**	**0.78**	**0.27**
CAGR	**2.63**	**11.00**	**11.80**	**10.40**	**-0.67**	**21.00**	**-0.10**

Figures in brackets are indices.
Source: CMIE Database

industry over the study period is achieved through estimation of mean, co-efficient of variation and compound annual growth rate. The estimates are also presented in Table 4.1.

Commercial Vehicles

The production of commercial vehicle for the period of study has been shown in Table 4.1. The production of commercial vehicle mark fluctuating trend throughout the study period. In the year 1991-92, the production was 144.6 thousands which decreased to 128 thousands in 1992-93 showing a decrease of 11 per cent in the indices. This was due to an account of power shortage and the problem of industrial relations. The production increased considerably in the next four years has reached 300 thousands at the indices of 207. But again in 2000-01, there was a decrease in production of commercial vehicles. In the last three years the production increased continuously and it reached 281.9 thousands at the indices of 195 in 2003-04. The mean value of production of commercial vehicle was 193.43 thousands. The compound annual growth rate of production of commercial vehicles was positive which worked out as 2.63 per cent during the study period. The co-efficient of variation (0.30) indicates that the production of commercial vehicles moderatively fluctuated during the study period.

The results of estimates of trend co-efficients for production of commercial vehicles are presented in Table 4.2. It is clear from the table that the difference between the actual production and trend values of production of commercial vehicles was significant as the calculated value chi-square 189.17 was higher than the table value of chi-square at 5 per cent level of significance and the null-hypothesis was rejected while the alternative hypothesis was accepted.

Passenger Cars and Multiutility Vehicles

The annual production of passenger cars and multiutility vehicles has been shown in Table 4.1. The production of passenger cars and multiutility vehicles, showed a fluctuating trend throughout the study period. The production of passenger cars was 166.2 thousands in 1991-92 which increased to 577.2 thousands in 1999-2000 depicting a rice of indices of 347 but in the next two years it declined, as it was 500.3 thousands in the year 2001-02 at the indices of 301. The production of passenger cars increased sharply in the last two years of the period of study. The production of multiutility vehicles was 39.6 thousands in 1991-92, which increased to 122 thousands in the year 2000-01 making in the increase of 208 per cent in the indices. But in the next year the production of multiutility vehicles declined to 114 thousands in the year 2001-02. The production of multiutility vehicles increased in the next year has reached 161.1 thousands in the year 2002-03 but again it came down marginally to 143.7 thousands in the year 2003-04 at the indices of 363.

The mean values of production of passenger cars and multiutility vehicles were 392.21 thousands and 91.74 thousands respectively during the study period. Both have positive compound annual growth rate of production which worked out as 11 per cent and 11.80 per cent. The CV value (0.39 and 0.44) indicates that the production of passenger cars and multiutility vehicles moderately fluctuated during the study period.

The results of estimates of trend co-efficient for production of passenger cars and multiutility vehicles presented in Table 4.2 show that the difference between actual production and trend values of production of passenger cars was significant whereas the difference between the actual production and trend values of production of multiutility vehicles was not significant as for the chi-square value. Thus the null hypothesis was rejected in case of passenger cars while the null hypothesis was accepted in case of multiutility vehicles.

Two and Three Wheelers

It is evident from the Table 4.1 that the production of three wheelers registered an increasing trend up to the year 1997-98. It was 79.7 thousands in 1991-92 which increased very sharply to 234.9 in 1997-98 making a rise of 195 per cent over the period. But in the next three years it declined as it was 203.2 thousands at the indices of 255 in the year 2000-01. The production of three wheelers again increased continuously in the next three years as it reached 286.4 thousands in the year 2003-04. Among the production of two wheelers, the production of motor cycle registered increasing trend

Table 4.2

Estimates of trend co-efficients for production of automobile in India (1991-92 to 2003-04)

S. No.	Type	$P = \alpha + \beta t + e$				Calculated value of Chi-square
		α	β	R^2	F Value	
1.	Commercial Vehicles	159.79 (4.71)	4.79 (1.12)	0.10	1.26	189.17
2.	Passenger Cars	130.35 (4.82)	37.41 (10.98)*	0.92	120.66	58.51
3.	Multiutility Vehicles	22.14 (3.33)	9.94 (11.86)*	0.93	140.55	14.36
4.	Three Wheelers	72.70 (3.98)	16.13 (7.00)*	0.82	49.06	64.26
5.	Scooters	117.61 (8.88)	-7.10 (-0.45)	0.02	0.20	471.09
6.	Motor Cycles	-518.02 (-1.97)	303.04 (9.13)*	0.88	83.43	269.64
7.	Moped	526.62 (5.97)	1.14 (0.10)	0.01	0.01	461.97

*-Significant at 5 percent level; Table value of Chi-square (0.05)=21.0 with df=12

Source: Computed

Table 4.3

Projections for production of automobile in India (in thousands)

Year	*Commercial Vehicles*	*Passenger Cars*	*Multi-utility Vehicles*	*Three Wheelers*	*Two Wheelers*		
					Scooter	*Motor Cycle*	*Moped*
2007-08	241.2	766.3	191.1	346.9	996.9	4633.6	546.0
2008-09	246.0	803.7	201.1	363.0	989.8	4936.7	547.1
2009-10	250.8	841.1	211.0	379.2	982.7	5239.7	548.3
2010-11	255.6	878.6	220.9	395.3	968.5	5542.8	549.7
2011-12	260.4	916.0	230.9	411.4	961.4	5845.8	550.6

Source: Computed

whereas the production of scooters and moped registered fluctuating trend throughout the period of study from 1991-92 to 2003-04. The mean value of production of three wheelers during the study period was 185.58 thousands. The mean value of production of scooters, motor cycle and moped were 1067.88 thousands 1603.24 thousands and 534.62 thousands respectively during the study period. It is observed from the CV value that the production of scooter experienced relatively stable variation, production of three wheelers and moped experienced moderately fluctuating variation and the production of motor cycle experienced erratical fluctuation during the study period. The compound annual growth rate of scooters and moped was negative whereas three wheelers and motor cycle, it was positive during the study period.

It is clear from the Table 4.2 that the difference between actual production and trend values of production was significant in three wheelers, scooters, motor cycles and moped as the calculated value chi-square in all these cases was higher than the table value of chi-square at 5 per cent level of significance and the null hypothesis was rejected while the alternative hypothesis was accepted.

Production of Automobiles in India-Projections

The projections obtained for production of commercial vehicles, passenger cars and multiutility vehicles and two and three wheelers by linear growth models listed in Table 4.3 shows that passenger cars have growing good market potential. Table 4.3 indicates that the commercial vehicles, multiutility vehicles and three wheelers are growing marginally. The table also illustrates that motor cycles have fast emerging growing market in confirm that between two wheelers motor cycles are being preferred over scooters and moped. Finding also points out that by the year 2012 A.D, motor cycle may have more than 80 per cent market share replacing scooters and mopeds.

From the above analysis the linear model of time trend of production has proved to be a "good fit" in case of passenger cars, multiutility vehicles, three-wheelers and motor cycles this is revealed from the value of R^2 the co-efficient of determination. The value of R^2 varied from 0.01 for moped, 0.02 for scooters, 0.10 for commercial vehicles, 0.82 for three wheelers, 0.88 for motor cycle,

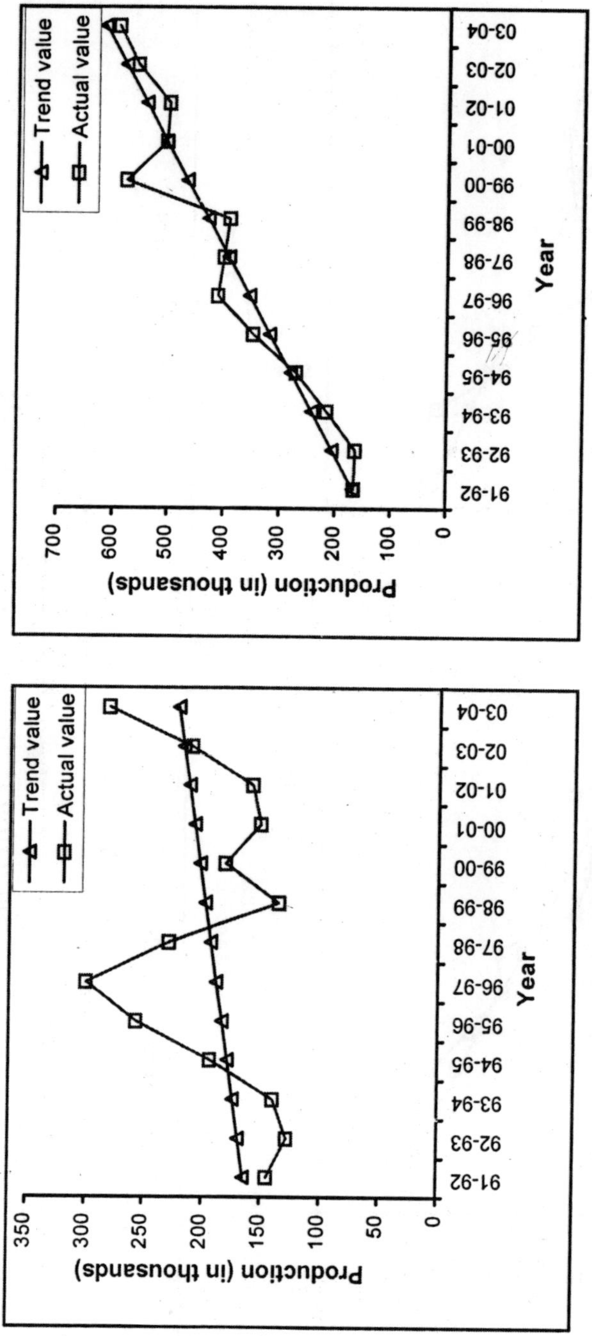

Commercial Vehicles **Passenger Cars**

Figure 1
Production trendes of Indian Automobile

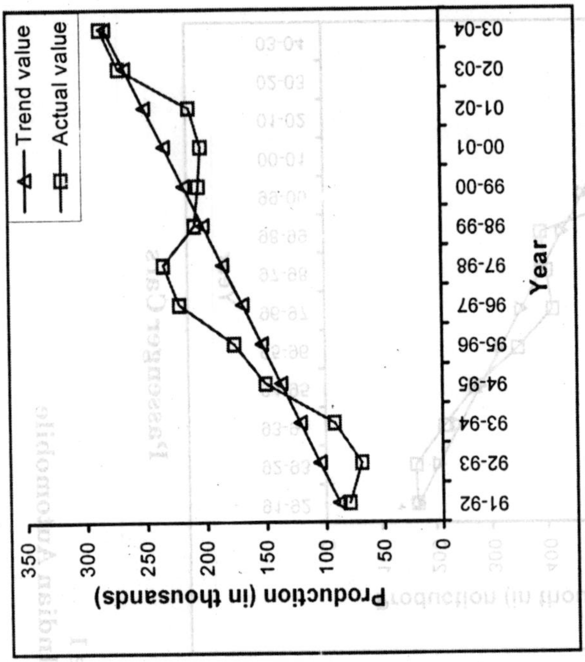

Three-Wheelers

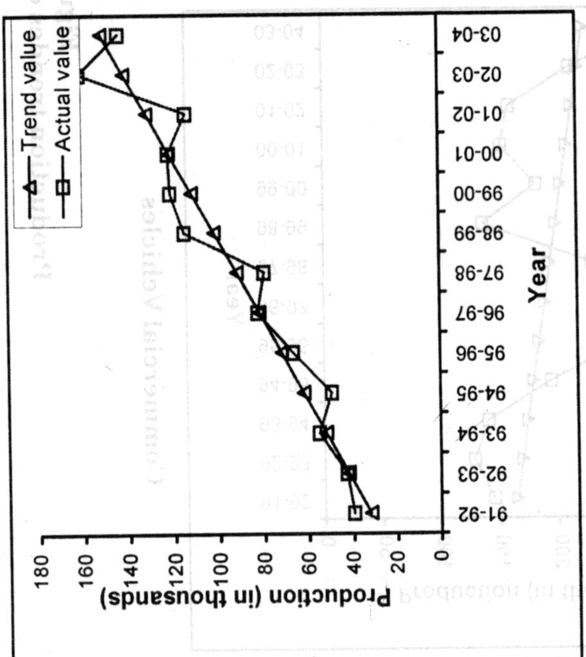

Multiutility Vehicles

Figure 1 (Contd.)
Production trendes of Indian Automobile

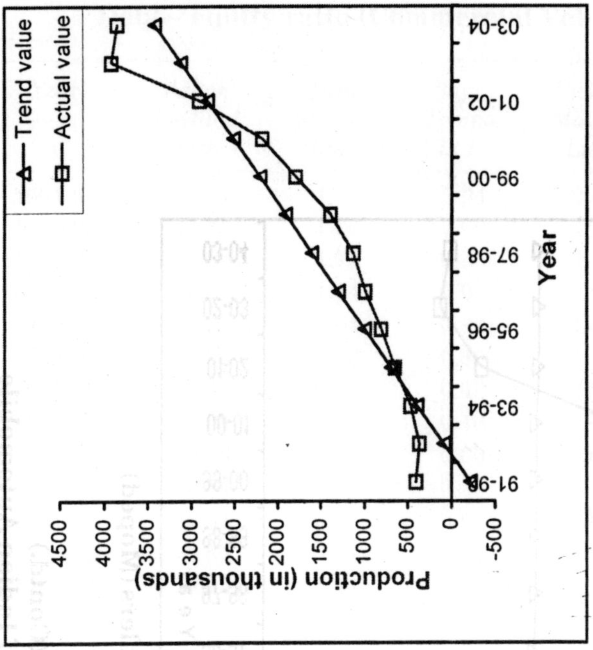

Two-Wheelers (Motor Cycle)

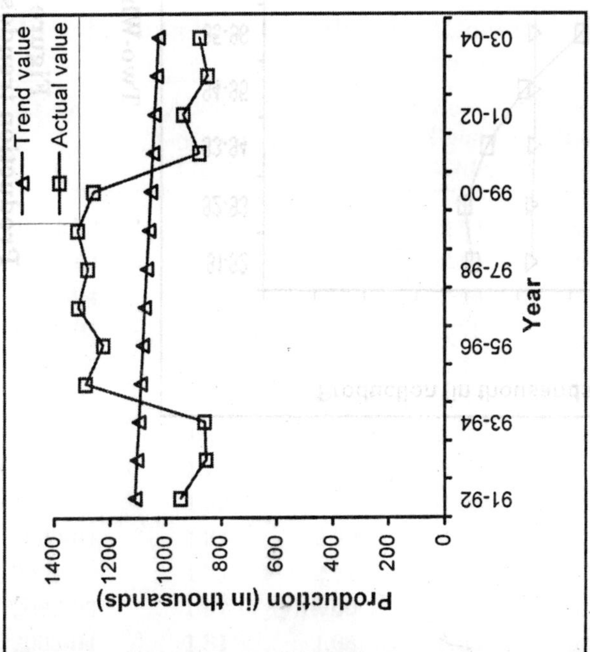

Three-Wheelers (Scooters)

Figure 1 (Contd.)
Production trendes of Indian Automobile

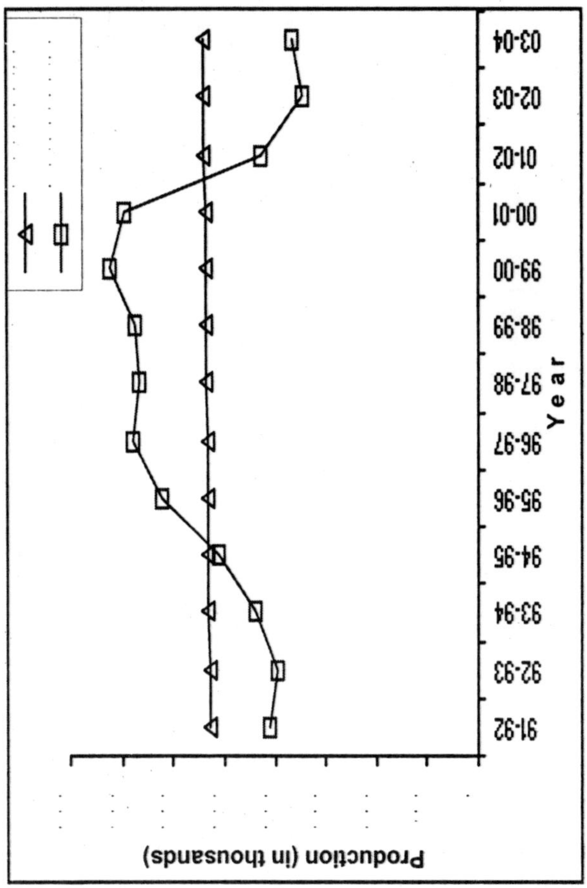

Two-Wheelers (Moped)

Figure 1 (Contd.)
Production trendes of Indian Automobile

0.92 for passenger cars and 0.93 multiutility vehicles. Such great variation in the value of R^2 implies that time explain production variation of Indian automobiles in different degree over the time. Further the production of scooters in India experienced tendency of decline in production over the study period. The negative value of β the time trend co-efficient confirms this however β being statistically is not significant.

Dispersions in Production of Indian Automobile Industry

This section of the chapter intends to examine company wise dispersion in production of Indian automobile industry over the study period of 13 years. This is achieved through estimation of mean, co-efficient of variation and compound annual growth rate. Further estimates of trend co-efficient for production of selected automobile industry has been computed. The estimates are presented in Table 4.4 and Table 4.5. The annual production of selected automobile industry during the study period has been shown in Appendix I.

It is observed from Table 4.4 that under commercial vehicles sector, Tata Motors Limited had highest mean production of commercial vehicles followed by Ashok Leyland Ltd and Bajaj Tempo Ltd.,. Another important observation which follows from Table 4.4 is that the mean production of commercial vehicles varies greatly in case of all the industries under commercial vehicles sector. From the CV value majority of the industries, three out of five industries (60 per cent) experienced moderately fluctuating variation in production during the study period. Swaraj Mazda Ltd alone experienced high fluctuating variation in production whereas Eicher Motors Ltd reveals the most erratically fluctuating series of production. The compound annual growth rate of production of commercial vehicles by all the selected industries was positive during the study period and it was highest in case of Eicher Motors Ltd and Swaraj Mazda Ltd.

It is clear from the Table 4.5 that the difference between actual production and trend values of production was significant only in case of Tata Motors Ltd as calculated value of chi-square 98.73 was higher than the table value of chi-square at 5 per cent level of significance and the null-hypothesis was rejected while the

Table 4.4
Annual production of selected automobile industry in India

Industry	*Range (in thousands)*	*Mean (in thousands)*	*CV*	*CAGR*
Commercial Vehicles				
Ashok Leyland Ltd.	18.43 - 49.15	32.67	0.25	4.41
Tata Motors Ltd.	85.57 - 320.07	168.84	0.40	8.65
Bajaj Tempo Ltd.	14.00 - 43.80	25.80	0.29	6.27
Eicher Motors Ltd.	2.85 - 44.76	9.31	1.18	15.20
Swaraj Mazda Ltd.	2.25 - 10.23	4.56	0.53	10.50
Passenger Cars and Multiutility Vehicles				
Hindustan Motors Ltd.	15.86 - 37.86	25.64	0.23	-0.70
Mahindra and Mahindra Ltd.	32.76 - 117.67	67.67	0.33	7.54
Maruthi Udyog Ltd.	121.89 - 472.91	298.12	0.37	10.30
Daewoo Motors India Ltd.	1.90 - 35.54	10.04	1.21	2.85

(Contd.)

(Contd. Table 4.4)

Industry	*Range (in thousands)*	*Mean (in thousands)*	*CV*	*CAGR*
Two and Three Wheelers				
Bajaj Auto Ltd.	773.31 - 1516.87	1229.56	0.20	4.40
LML Ltd.	110.65 - 494.34	203.50	0.66	7.77
Maharastra Scooters Ltd.	17.9[illegible] - 154.36	102.22	0.43	-3.49
TVS Motors India Ltd.	159.22 - 1143.34	616.22	0.56	17.20
Kinetic Motors Company Ltd.	69.50 - 124.71	103.35	0.17	1.15
Hero Honda Motors Ltd.	128.65 - 2064.70	692.26	0.96	25.60
Majestic Auto Ltd.	72.26 - 139.34	92.57	0.50	-27.00
Kinetic Engineering Ltd.	87.06 - 159.96	133.89	0.19	-0.90
Scooters India Ltd.	4.26 - 16.02	11.62	0.40	10.60

Source: Computed from the annual reports of the selected Industry

alternative hypothesis was accepted. However in remaining industry the differences in the actual production and trend values of production were not significant as per chi-square value. Hence the null hypothesis was accepted the results were as per the expectation, while the alternative hypothesis was rejected. Further, the linear model of time trend of production has proved to be good fit in case of three out of five industries, i.e., 60 per cent of industry examining here. This is revealed from the va!ue of R^2 the co-efficient of determination. The great variation in the value of R^2 implies that time explain production variation of different industries under commercial vehicles sector was in different degree over the time.

In passenger cars and multiutility vehicles sector, Maruthi Udyog Ltd had high mean value of production of passenger cars and multiutility vehicles followed by Mahindra and Mahindra Ltd, Hindustan Motors Ltd and Daewoo Motors India Ltd during the study period. It is observed from the Table 4.4 that three out of four industries (75 per cent) namely Maruthi Udyog Ltd, Mahindra and Mahindra Ltd, and Hindustan Motors Ltd, experienced moderately fluctuating variation in production during the study period. The analysis of compound annual growth rate of production indicates it was negative only in case of Hindustan Motors Ltd. Among the positive compound annual growth rates of production it is highest in case of Maruthi Udyog Ltd followed by Mahindra and Mahindra Ltd and Daewoo Motors India Ltd.

It is clear from the Table 4.5 that the null hypothesis was accepted and the results were as per expectations while the alternative hypothesis was rejected in case of Hindustan Motors Ltd as the calculated value of chi-square (18.02) was lower than the table value at 5 per cent level of significance. In the remaining three industries, the null hypothesis was rejected while the alternative hypothesis was accepted as the calculated value of chi-square was more than the table value of chi-square. Further, the linear model of time trend of production has proved to be good fit in Maruthi Udyog Ltd and Mahindra and Mahindra Ltd as per the value of R^2 indicates that time explain production variation of these two industries to the tune of 85 per cent and 69 per cent respectively. Further the negative values of β in case of Hindustan Motors Ltd implies that production declined over the study period.

Table 4.5
Estimates of trend co-efficients for production of selected automobile industry in India (1991-92 to 2003-04)

Industry	$P = \alpha + \beta t + e$				
	α	β	R^2	*F Value*	*Calculated value of Chi-square*
Commercial Vehicles					
Ashok Leyland Ltd.	23.29 (5.66)	1.34 (2.59)	0.38	6.69	16.51
Tata Motors Ltd.	71.05 (2.99)	13.97 (4.66)*	0.66	21.74	98.73
Bajaj Tempo Ltd.	14.88 (5.53)	1.56 (4.61)*	0.66	21.21	8.33
Eicher Motors Ltd.	- 3.37 (-0.65)	1.81 (2.78)	0.41	7.71	-2.61
Swaraj Mazda Ltd.	0.95 (1.17)	0.52 (5.05)*	0.70	25.55	4.14

(Contd.)

(Contd. Table 4.5)

Industry	$P = \alpha + \beta t + e$				
	α	β	R^2	*F Value*	*Calculated value of Chi-square*
Passenger Cars and Multiutility Vehicles					
Hindustan Motors Ltd.	26.60 (7.37)	- 0.14 (-0.30)	0.01	0.09	18.02
Mahindra and Mahindra Ltd.	34.31 (4.47)	4.77 (4.93)*	0.69	24.32	24.62
Maruthi Udyog Ltd.	115.91 (4.35)	26.03 (7.75)*	0.85	60.08	76.26
Daewoo Motors India Ltd.	5.03 (0.69)	0.72 (0.78)	0.05	0.61	115.82

(Contd.)

(Contd. Table 4.5)

Industry	α	β	R^2	F Value	Calculated value of Chi-square
	$P = \alpha + \beta t + e$				
Two and Three Wheelers					
Bajaj Auto Ltd.	893.77 (9.28)	47.97 (3.95)*	0.59	15.64	259.50
LML Ltd.	125.97 (1.61)	11.08 (1.12)	0.10	1.26	510.52
Maharastra Scooters Ltd.	141.11 (5.98)	- 5.56 (-1.87)	0.24	3.49	190.59
TVS Motors India Ltd.	1.27 (0.04)	87.85 (21.46)*	0.98	460.53	119.69
Kinetic Motors Company Ltd.	94.56 (9.23)	1.26 (0.97)	0.08	0.95	31.80
Hero Honda Motors Ltd.	- 396.91 (-2.51)	155.60 (7.82)*	0.85	61.15	-373.28
Majestic Auto Ltd.	131.58 (5.28)	- 5.57 (-1.78)	0.22	3.15	122.18
Kinetic Engineering Ltd.	139.78 (8.93)	- 0.84 (-0.43)	0.02	0.18	58.62
Scooters India Ltd.	5.09 (2.95)	0.93 (4.30)*	0.63	18.44	8.96

* Significant at 5 per cent level; Table value of Chi-square (0.05)=21.0 with df = 12

Source: Computed

Under two and three wheeler sectors, the mean value of production was the highest in case of Bajaj Auto Ltd followed by TVS Motors India Ltd, Hero Honda Motors Ltd, LML Ltd and so on. Table 4.4 reveals that Kinetic Motor India Ltd, Kinetic Engineering Ltd and Bajaj Auto Ltd experienced the lowest variation in its production series, while Hero Honda Motors Ltd, LML Ltd, TVS Motors India Ltd had the largest variation in its production during the study period as per the CV value. Further Maharashtra Scooters Ltd, Majestic Auto Ltd and Scooters India Ltd experienced moderately fluctuating variations in production series. It is observed from the Table 4.4 that three out of nine industries (33.33 per cent) namely Maharashtra Scooters Ltd, Majestic Auto Ltd and Kinetic Engineering Ltd had negative compound annual growth rate of production during the study period. Among the Industries having positive compound annual growth rate it was highest in Hero Honda Motors Ltd followed by TVS Motors India Ltd, Scooters India Ltd and LML Ltd.

From the Table 4.5, it is observed that the difference between the actual production and trend values of production was significant in all the selected industries under two and three wheelers sector except Scooters India Ltd as the calculated value chi-square was higher than table value chi-square at 5 per cent level. Hence, the null hypothesis was rejected while alternative hypothesis was accepted. The linear model of time trend of production has proved to be a good fit in case of TVS Motors India Ltd, Hero Honda Motors Ltd and Scooters India Ltd, as per R^2 value. The value of R^2 varies between 0.98 (TVS Motors India Ltd), 0.85 (Hero Honda Motors Ltd), and 0.63 (Scooters India Ltd) indicating that time explain production variations of these industries to the tune of 98 per cent, 85 per cent, and 63 per cent respectively. Further three industries, Viz., Maharashtra Scooters Ltd, Majestic Auto Ltd and Kinetic Engineering Ltd experienced tendency in production to decline over the study period, the negative values of β, the time trend co-efficient confirms this however β being statistically not significant.

Capacity Utilisation of Automobile Industry

In a developing economy, the need for optimum utilisation of industrial capacity can hardly be over-emphasised. Production below the capacity in industrial plants is the source of a significant loss in the growth of Gross National Product of a country. The production performance of a business enterprise can be appraised on the basis of capacity utilisation. Full utilisation of the installed capacity is the dominant desideratum in judging the operational efficiency of the business enterprise. "Through better utilisation of installed capacity, the economy should improve the capital output and capital labour ratios and should, consequently, result in more employment, more income and more competitiveness in export market without additional capital investment"[3].

Capacity utilization means that proportion of the total capacity which has been gainfully utilised for the production of required goods and services[4]. Capacity utilization ratio refers the relationship between production and installed capacity. Production means total output of a company during a particular year, while installed capacity is that capacity for which the concern has made arrangements to produce. The relationship has been calculated by dividing the figure of production by the figure of installed capacity in terms of percentages[5].

The over all performance of manufacturing business enterprise, to a great extent, depends upon its production performance. The production performance ultimately depends on the utilisation of production capacity. This is why maximum capacity utilisation is needed in an industry. It makes the production economical by reducing the cost of production and improving productivity. The capacity utilisation also helps indirectly in exploring the foreign market and finally contributing to the Gross National Product[6].

The automobile industry in India produces a large variety of products. The installed capacity and capacity utilisation ratio of different products of automobile industry during the study period are presented in Table 4.6.

The capacity utilisation ratio of commercial vehicles marked a fluctuating trend throughout the study period. It varied in range of 63.33 per cent from 29.29 per cent in 1998-99 to 92.62 per cent in 2003-04. The CV value came to 0.32, whereas average capacity utilization ratio remained 53.25 per cent during the period. The capacity utilisation ratio of passenger cars and multiutility vehicles

Table 4.6

Capacity Utilisation in Automobile Industry in India

(1991-92 to 2003-04)

Year	*Commercial Vehicles*		*Passenger Car and Multiutility Vehicles*		*Two and Three Wheelers*	
	Installed capacity (000')	*Capacity utilisation (%)*	*Installed capacity (000')*	*Capacity utilisation (%)*	*Installed capacity (000')*	*Capacity utilisation (%)*
1991-92	186.31	49.33	299.00	63.51	2508.50	49.46
1992-93	186.31	41.10	227.00	73.37	2808.50	45.89
1993-94	197.47	53.96	239.00	67.96	2964.60	47.71
1994-95	248.55	62.51	317.00	57.97	3328.10	52.81
1995-96	332.66	69.56	475.60	51.06	3779.08	55.06
1996-97	391.16	47.64	514.84	52.07	4416.18	55.34
1997-98	409.16	33.81	526.84	44.54	4724.68	58.41
1998-99	452.00	29.29	824.84	34.75	5339.68	59.43
1999-00	467.00	48.30	779.00	60.48	5789.18	49.37
2000-01	471.00	41.07	749.00	57.12	6372.88	46.84
2001-02	468.00	54.20	783.80	50.80	10487.70	43.84
2002-03	453.00	68.82	693.80	65.61	10143.50	49.25
2003-04	460.50	92.62	556.00	76.74	7483.50	58.01
Mean		**53.25**		**58.15**		**51.69**
CV		**0.32**		**0.20**		**1.01**
CAGR		**2.14**		**-0.38**		**0.25**

Source: CMIE Database.

also showed fluctuating trend during the study period. It varied from 34.75 per cent in 1998-99 to 76.74 per cent in 2003-04 indicating the range of 41.99 per cent with a low co-efficient being 0.20 although the installed capacity of the company has increased during the period of study, yet on an average 58.15 per cent capacity only has been utilised. The two and three wheelers sector revealed a fluctuating trend in capacity utilisation throughout the period of the study. It varied in range of 15.59 per cent from 43.84 per cent in 2001-02 to 59.43 per cent in 1998-99. The co-efficient variation being 1.01 also reflected erratic fluctuation in capacity utilisation ratios of two and three wheelers sector.

It is therefore, obvious that the Indian automobile industry has not utilised its plan capacity an average of more than 40 per cent which remains idle during the period. It is therefore suggested that the management should concentrate on overcoming the problem of power cuts, implementing research and development programs, adopting the latest technological know how and skills and making industrial relation cordial and congenial to increase the capacity utilisation ratio.

Dispersion on Capacity Utilisation Ratio of Indian Automobile Industry

This section of the chapter indents to examine industries wise capacity utilisation ratio of Indian automobile industry over the study period. This is achieved through estimation of mean, co-efficient of variation and compound annual growth rate. The estimates are presented in Table 4.7. The individual capacity utilisation ratio of selected automobile industry during the study period has been shown in Appendix II.

It is observed from Table 4.7 that under commercial vehicles sector on an average Swaraj Mazda Ltd had highest capacity utilization ratio (84.87 per cent) followed by Ashok Leyland Ltd (74.64 per cent) and Eicher Motors Ltd (67.04 per cent) during the study period. Ashok Leyland Ltd with co-efficient variation being 0.17 experienced lowest variation in capacity utilisation ratio over the study period while Bajaj Tempo Ltd suffered from largest variation (co-efficient of variation = 0.94) during the study period. However, the compound annual growth rate of capacity utilisation ratio of Ashok Leyland Ltd, Tata Motors Ltd and Bajaj Tempo Ltd were

Table 4.7

Capacity utilisation of selected automobile industry (Production as percentage of installed capacity)
(1991-92 to 2003-04)

Industry	Range (%)	Mean (%)	CV	CAGR (%)
Commercial Vehicles				
Ashok Leyland Ltd.	52.50 - 96.54	74.64	0.17	-1.19
Tata Motors Ltd.	16.57 - 46.57	30.08	0.33	-1.12
Bajaj Tempo Ltd.	3.76 - 93.43	37.01	0.94	-17.70
Eicher Motors Ltd.	43.25 - 106.57	67.04	0.30	1.85
Swaraj Mazda Ltd.	45.00 - 170.50	84.87	0.43	8.98
Passengers Cars and Multiutility Vehicles				
Hindustan Motors Ltd.	24.78 - 61.09	40.80	0.29	-2.54
Mahindra and Mahindra Ltd.	47.09 - 102.41	69.84	0.23	-4.01
Maruthi Udyog Ltd.	89.77 - 138.66	109.73	0.15	1.03
Daewoo Motors India Ltd.	2.83 - 40.85	14.52	0.90	-9.59

(Contd.)

(Contd. Table 4.7)

Industry	*Range (%)*	*Mean (%)*	*CV*	*CAGR (%)*
Two and Three Wheelers				
Bajaj Auto Ltd.	11.04 - 64.82	32.43	0.56	1.06
LML Ltd.	22.01 - 123.58	58.90	0.66	-2.09
Maharastra Scooters Ltd.	11.93 - 102.91	78.41	0.42	-13.80
TVS Motors India Ltd.	31.84 - 76.37	57.86	0.29	7.38
Kinetic Motors Company Ltd.	43.27 - 84.81	68.35	0.16	-3.10
Hero Honda Motors Ltd.	59.88 - 101.94	87.38	0.12	-0.23
Majestic Auto Ltd.	30.36 - 73.34	41.54	0.53	-22.20
Kinetic Engineering Ltd.	27.81 - 55.62	44.33	0.19	-2.26
Scooters India Ltd.	6.82 - 96.67	60.13	0.60	22.20

Source: Computed.

negative while remaining two industries it was positive over the study period. It is also observed from the Appendix II that the capacity utilisation ratio of Swaraj Mazda Ltd exceeds 100 per cent from 2000-01 to 2003-04.

Among the selected passenger cars and multiutility vehicles, Maruthi Udyog Ltd, the mean capacity utilisation ratio was more than hundred per cent during the study period followed by Mahindra and Mahindra Ltd. (69.84 per cent), Hindustan Motors Ltd (40.80 per cent) and Daewoo Motors Ltd (14.52 per cent). The analysis of co-efficient of variation reveals that Maruthi Udyog Ltd capacity utilization ratio was relatively stable (CV=0.15), while Daewoo Motors India Ltd suffered from largest variation (CV=0.90) during the study period. The remaining two industries experienced moderate variation in its capacity utilisation ratios. From the analysis of compound annual growth rate of capacity utilisation ratio, it is observed that only Maruthi Udyog Ltd had positive growth rate while the remaining three industries had negative growth rate during the study period.

The mean capacity utilization ratio was the highest in Hero Honda Motors Ltd (87.38 per cent) followed by Maharastra Scooters Ltd (78.41 per cent), Kinetic Motors India Ltd (68.35 per cent), Scooters India Ltd (60.13 per cent) LML Ltd (58.90 per cent) and TVS Motors India Ltd (57.86 per cent) in two and three wheelers sector during the study period. Among the selected industry Hero Honda Motors Ltd, Kinetic Motors Ltd and Kinetic Engineering Ltd had lowest variation in capacity utilisation ratios while LML Ltd, Scooters India Ltd and Bajaj Auto Ltd suffered from largest variation in capacity utilisation ratio during the study period. It is also observed from the Table 4.7 that the compound annual growth rate of capacity utilisation ratios were only positive in the case of TVS Motors India Ltd, Scooters India Ltd and Bajaj Auto Ltd and in remaining industries it was negative during the study period.

To conclude, the mean rates of capacity utilisation ratio vary greatly in case of all the industries under examination irrespective of the sector of which they belong.

Analysis of Sales Trend

'Sales' is the value of the output offered to the customers. It is the life blood of a business enterprise without which the business cannot survive. Further, 'sales' is the indicator of the operational efficiency of management in how efficiently the management has used the assets of the business. The higher the volume of sales, the more efficient the management. Sales is also related to profitability of an enterprise. If other things remain constant, the higher the amount of sales, the more profitable the business is and vice versa. The trend of sales indicates the direction in which forecast for further can be made. The trend analysis of sales helps to understand the growth of a business enterprise. For proper trend analysis, the trend should be studied atleast over a period of five or more years[7].

The sales performance of an enterprise can be measured in a number of ways. The sales performance of the industry as a whole can be compared with different years; also the comparison can be done in between the competitive industries. The analysis of market share can also significantly prove the sales performance of a company or of the industry as a whole. All these techniques have been adopted to appraise the sales performance of the Indian Automobile Industry in the present section.

An attempt has also been made to estimate trend co-efficient for sales of automobiles in India during the study period by fitting a linear regression model. The linear model fitted is as follows:

$$P=\alpha+\beta t+e$$

where P is rate of sales, t's is the time, and α and β are the parameters (intercept and co-efficient respectively) and e is the error term. To test whether the difference between actual sales and estimated sales was significant or not, the following hypothesis is framed and tested.

H_o - **There is no significant difference between actual sales and the trend values of sales among different years.**

(or)

H_a - **There is significant difference between actual sales and the trend values of sales among different years.**

The annual sales quantity of automobiles products such as commercial vehicles, passenger cars and multiutility vehicles and two and three wheelers from the year 1991-92 to 2003-04 are presented in Table 4.8. To study the trend of sales in automobile industry under study, in the year 1991-92 has been chosen on as a base year and figure of sales in the base year have been taken equal to 100. Index numbers have been calculated for the remaining year based on the amount of sales for the base year. Further, the product wise dispersion in sales of Indian automobile industry over the study period is achieved through estimation of mean, co-efficient of variation and compound annual growth rate. The estimates are also presented in Table 4.8.

Commercial Vehicles

The annual sales of commercial vehicles for the period of study has been shown in Table 4.8. The sales of commercial vehicles marked fluctuating trend throughout the study period. In the year 1991-92 the sales was 132.41 thousands which decreased to 114.83 thousands in 1992-93 showing decrease of 13 per cent in the indices. This was partly due to the increasing prices and partly due to the decrease in the quantity of the sales of commercial vehicles. The sales has increased considerably in the next three years and reached 248.23 thousands in the year 1995-96 at the indices of 187. But again in 2000-01 and 2001-02 and there was a decrease in sales of commercial vehicles. In the last three years the sales of commercial vehicles increased continuously and it registered 271.43 thousands in the year 2003-04 at the indices of 205. The mean value of sales of commercial vehicles was 172.36 thousands. The compound annual growth rate of sales of commercial vehicles was positive which worked out 3.92 per cent. The analysis of CV value indicates that the sales of commercial vehicles moderately fluctuated during the study period.

The results of estimates of trend co-efficient for sales of commercial vehicles are presented in Table 4.9. The yearly increase in sales of commercial vehicles comes to 4.05 thousands. The calculated value of chi-square comes to 151.23 which is high as compared to table value of chi-square at 5 per cent level of significance for V=12 is 21. Therefore the null hypothesis was rejected while the alternative hypothesis was accepted. This proves that difference between actual sales and trend value of sales of commercial vehicles among different years was significant.

Table 4.8
Annual Sales Units of Automobile in India

(in thousands)

Year	*Commercial Vehicles*	*Passenger Cars and Multiutility Vehicles*	*Two and Three Wheelers*
1991-92	132.41 (100)	176.21 (100)	1561.12 (100)
1992-93	114.83 (87)	189.30 (107)	1495.76 (96)
1993-94	143.96 (109)	246.77 (140)	1704.08 (109)
1994-95	190.27 (144)	288.99 (164)	2101.69 (135)
1995-96	248.23 (187)	398.03 (226)	2724.54 (175)
1996-97	228.71 (173)	511.88 (290)	3053.34 (195)
1997-98	150.44 (114)	503.12 (286)	3265.39 (209)
1998-99	134.60 (102)	496.10 (282)	3729.51 (239)
1999-00	165.05 (125)	661.33 (375)	3828.99 (245)
2000-01	144.29 (109)	641.31 (364)	3829.33 (245)
2001-02	130.62 (99)	633.15 (359)	4250.50 (272)
2002-03	185.84 (140)	689.52 (391)	4543.27 (291)
2003-04	271.43 (205)	730.91 (415)	5635.90 (361)
Mean	**172.36**	**474.36**	**3209.49**
CV	**0.29**	**0.41**	**0.39**
CAGR	**3.92**	**12.20**	**10.80**

Figures in brackets are indices.
Source: CMIE Database

Passenger Cars and Multiutility Vehicles

It is evident from the Table 4.8 that the sales trend of passenger cars and multiutility vehicles registered a rising trend throughout the period of study except in the year 1997-98 and 1998-99. In 1991-92 sales were 176.21 thousands which increased to 730.91 thousands in the year 2003-04 depicting an increase of 315 per cent in the indices. However in the year 1997-98 and 1998-99, there was also slight decrease in the sales of passenger cars and multiutility vehicles. This was due to cut throat competition in the market. The mean value of sales of passenger cars and mutliutility vehicles were 474.36 thousands during the study period. The analysis of CV value indicates that sales of passenger cars and multiutility vehicles moderately fluctuated during the study period. The compound annual growth rate of sales of passenger cars and multiutility vehicles was 12.20 per cent which is highest among all other products.

Table 4.9 shows the linear least square trend of sales of passenger cars and multiutility vehicles. The yearly increasing sales comes to 49.14 thousands. The calculated value of chi-square comes to 56.51 which is high as compared to table value of chi-square at 5 per cent level of significance. This proves that the difference between actual sales and trend value of sales of passenger cars and multiutility vehicles among different years was significant.

Two and Three Wheelers

The total sales figures in quantity of two and three wheelers have been presented in Table 4.8. The table reflected a rising trend in sales of two and three wheelers over the study period. Only in the year 1992-93 the sales declined by 4 per cent over the base year 1992-93. In 1991-92 the sales were 1561.12 thousands which increased to 5635.90 thousands in the year 2003-04 depicting an increase of 261 per cent in the indices. The mean value of sales of two and three wheelers was 3209.49 thousands during the study period and reflected moderate fluctuation in the sales of two and three wheelers as per CV value. Further on an average the sales of two and three wheelers registered a growth rate of 10.80 per cent per year during the study period.

Table 4.9 indicates that the yearly increase in sales of two and three wheelers comes to 318.35 thousands. The calculated value

Table 4.9
Estimates of Trend Co-efficients for Sales Units of Automobile in India
(1991-92 to 2003-04)

S. No.	*Type*	$P = \alpha + \beta t + e$				*Calculated value of Chi-square*
		α	β	R^2	*F Value*	
1.	Commercial Vehicles	143.99 (4.99)	4.05 (1.11)	0.10	1.24	151.23
2.	Passenger Cars and Multiutility Vehicles	130.41 (4.59)	49.14 (13.74)*	0.95	188.76	56.51
3.	Two and Three Wheelers	981.04 (6.37)	318.35 (16.41)*	0.96	269.29	235.66

* - Significant at 5 per cent level; Table value of Chi-square (0.05)=21.0 with df=12
Source: Computed.

of chi-square comes to 235.66 which is very high as compared to the table value of chi-square of 5 per cent level of significance. This proves that the difference between actual sales and trend values of sales of two and three wheelers among different years were significant.

Sales of Automobiles in India-Projections

The projections obtained for sales of commercial vehicles, passenger cars and multiutility vehicles and two and three wheelers by linear growth model has been presented in Table 4.10. It is evident from the Table 4.10 that commercial vehicles, passenger cars and multiutility vehicles were growing marginally where as two and three wheelers have fast emerging growing market in the years to come in our country.

Table 4.10

Projections for Sales Units of Automobile in India

(in thousands)

Year	*Commercial Vehicles*	*Passenger Cars and Multiutility Vehicles*	*Two and Three Wheelers*
2007-08	212.85	965.79	6392.99
2008-09	216.90	1014.93	6711.34
2009-10	220.95	1064.07	7029.69
2010-11	225.00	1113.21	7348.04
2011-12	229.05	1162.35	7666.39

Source: Computed.

It can be concluded that the linear model of time trend of sales has proved to be "good fit" in case of passenger cars and multiutility vehicles and two and three wheelers. This is revealed from the values of R^2 which varied from 0.10 for commercial vehicles, 0.95 for passenger cars and multiutility vehicles and 0.96 for two and three wheelers. Such a great variation in the value of R^2 implies that the time explain sales variation in different degree over the time. It is concluded that at present sales level of automobiles product is at a satisfactory level yet there is further scope to increase the level of growth rate per year regularly.

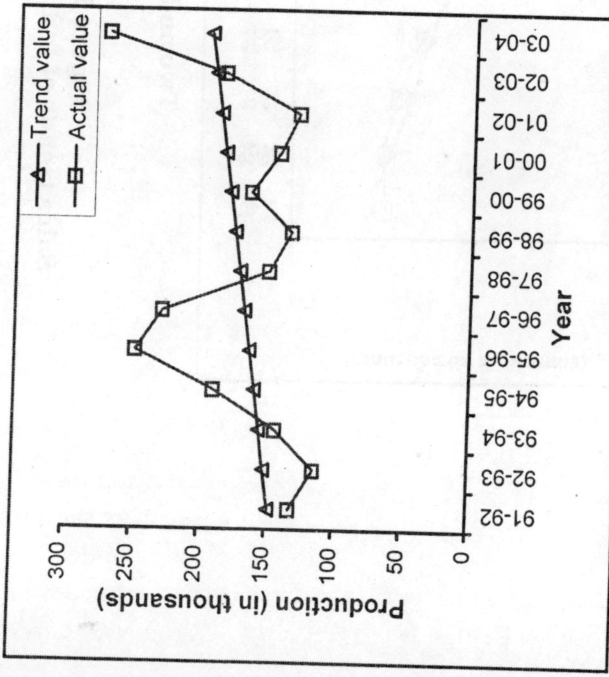

Commercial Vehicles

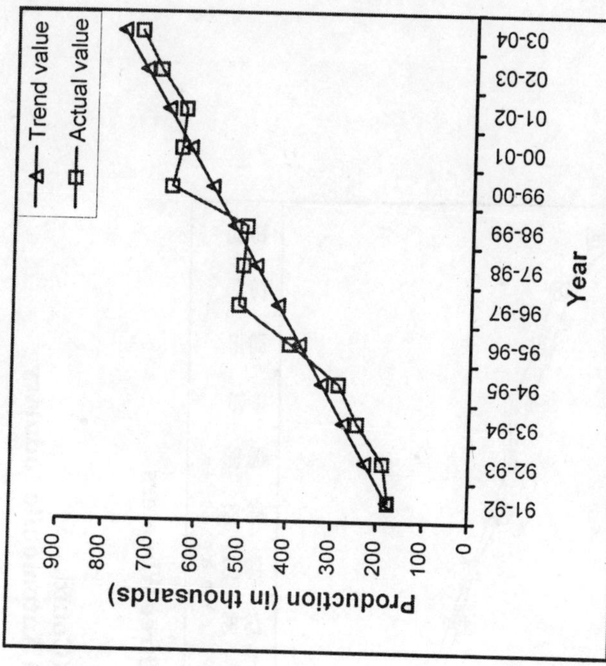

Passenger cars and Multiutility vehicles

Figure II
Sales trends of Indian Automobile Industry

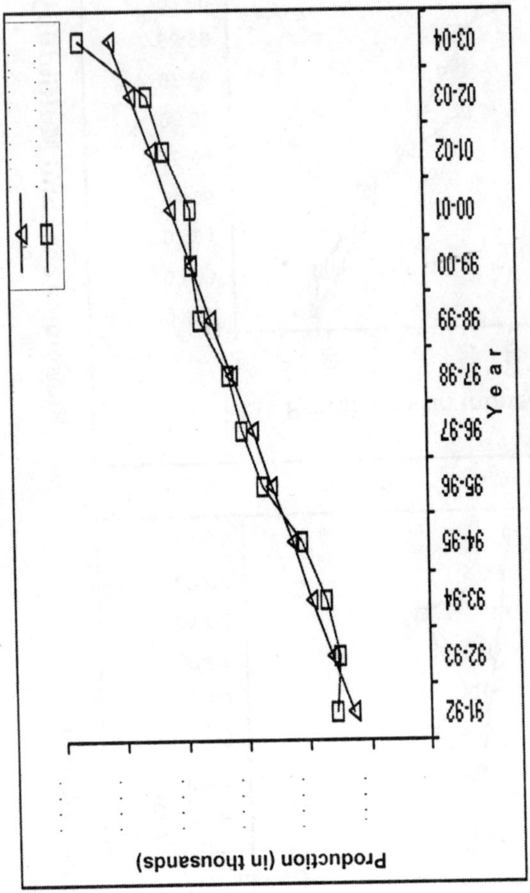

Two and Three Wheelers

Figure II (Contd.....)
Sales trends of Indian Automobile Industry

Dispersions in Sales of Indian Automobile Industry

This section of the chapter intends to examine company wise dispersion in sales of Indian automobiles over the study period. This is achieved through estimation of mean, co-efficient of variation and compound annual growth rate which were presented in Table 4.11 and 4.12. The annual sales of selected automobile industry during the study period is shown in Appendix III.

It is observed from Table 4.11 that under commercial vehicles sector. Tata Motors Ltd had the highest mean sales of commercial vehicles followed by Ashok Leyland and Bajaj Tempo Ltd. Another important observation which follows from Table 4.11 is that the mean sales of commercial vehicles vary greatly in case of all the industries under commercial vehicles sector. From the CV value, majority of the industries, three out of five industries (60 per cent) experienced moderately fluctuating variation in sales during the study period. Swaraj Mazda Ltd alone experiences high fluctuating variation in sales whereas Eicher Motors Ltd reveals the most eratically fluctuating series of sales. The compound annual growth rate of sales of commercial vehicles by all the selected industries was positive during the study period and it was the highest in case of Eicher Motors Ltd and Swaraj Mazda Ltd.

It is clear from the Table 4.12 that the difference between actual sales and trend values of sales was significant in the case of Tata Motors Ltd and Eicher Motors Ltd, as the calculated value of chi-square was higher than the table value of chi-square at 5 per cent level of significance and the null hypothesis was rejected while the alternative hypothesis was accepted. However in remaining industries the difference in the actual sales and trend value of sales was not significant as per chi-square value. Further the linear model at time trend of sales has proved to be good fit in all the industries examined here. This is revealed from the value of R^2 the co-efficient of determination. The great variation in the value of R^2 implies that time explain sales variation of different industries under commercial vehicles sector is in different degrees over the time.

In passenger cars and multiutility vehicles sectors, Maruthi Udyog Ltd had high mean value of sales of passenger cars and multiutility vehicles followed by Mahindra and Mahindra Ltd, Hindustan Motors Ltd and Daewoo Motors Ltd during the study period. It is observed from the Table 4.11 that three out of four industries (75 per cent) namely Maruthi Udyog Ltd, Mahindra and Mahindra Ltd and Hindustan Motors Ltd experienced moderately fluctuating variation in sales during the study period. The table also indicates that Daewoo Motors India Ltd experienced most erratically fluctuating series of sales over the study period. The analysis of compound annual growth rate of sales was negative only in case of Hindustan Motors Ltd. Among the positive compound annual growth rate of sales it was the highest in case of Maruthi Udyog Ltd followed by Mahindra and Mahindra Ltd and Daewoo Motors India Ltd.

It is clear from the Table 4.12 that the null hypothesis was accepted and the results were as per expectations while the alternative hypothesis was rejected in case of Hindustan Motors Ltd as the calculated value of chi-square (16.02) was lower than the table value at 5 per cent level of significance. In remaining three industries, the null hypothesis was rejected, while the alternative hypothesis was accepted as the calculated value of chi-square were more than the table value of chi-square. Further, the linear model at time trend of sales has proved to be good fit in Maruthi Udyog Ltd and Mahindra and Mahindra Ltd as per the value of R^2, co-efficient of determination. The value of R^2 indicates that time explain sales variation of these two industries are to the tune of 86 per cent and 76 per cent respectively. Further the negative value of β in case of Hindustan Motors Ltd implies sales decline over the study period.

Under two and three wheelers sectors, the mean value of sales were the highest in case of Bajaj Auto Ltd followed by TVS Motors India Ltd, Hero Honda Motors Ltd, LML Ltd and so on. Table 4.11 reveals that Kinetic Motors India Ltd, Kinetic Engineering Ltd and Bajaj Auto Ltd experienced the lowest variation in its sales series, while Hero Honda Motors Ltd, LML Ltd, TVS Motors India Ltd has the largest variations in its sales during the study period as per the CV value. Further Maharastra Scooters India Ltd, Majestic Auto Ltd and Scooters India Ltd experienced moderately fluctuating variation in sales series over the study period.

It is observed from the Table 4.11 that three out of nine industries (33.33 per cent) namely Maharastra Scooters Ltd, Majestic

Table 4.11
Annual Sales Units of Selected Automobile Industry in India

Industry	*Range (in thousands)*	*Mean (in thousands)*	*CV*	*CAGR (%)*
Commercial Vehicles				
Ashok Leyland Ltd.	20.57 - 48.65	32.74	0.24	4.38
Tata Motors Ltd.	75.71 - 295.46	164.58	0.38	8.49
Bajaj Tempo Ltd.	14.30 - 43.41	25.68	0.28	6.12
Eicher Motors Ltd.	3.00 - 44.24	9.26	1.17	15.10
Swaraj Mazda Ltd.	2.28 - 10.28	4.53	0.53	10.50
Passenger Cars and Multiutility Vehicles				
Hindustan Motors Ltd.	16.50 - 38.03	25.88	0.23	-1.01
Mahindra and Mahindra Ltd.	33.42 - 117.40	68.21	0.32	7.72
Maruthi Udyog Ltd.	124.6 - 5472.12	293.46	0.36	11.40
Daewoo Motors India Ltd.	2.03 - 35.79	9.97	1.20	2.93

(Contd.)

(Contd. Table 4.11)

Industry	*Range (in thousands)*	*Mean (in thousands)*	*CV*	*CAGR (%)*
Two and Three Wheelers				
Bajaj Auto Ltd.	665.54 - 1518.13	1210.34	0.24	5.70
LML Ltd.	110.80 - 485.34	202.77	0.65	7.81
Maharastra Scooters Ltd.	16.93 - 150.04	102.48	0.42	-10.00
TVS Motors India Ltd.	159.84 - 1146.86	605.77	0.54	17.80
Kinetic Motor Company Ltd.	70.98 - 124.06	103.58	0.16	1.07
Hero Honda Motors Ltd.	127.97 - 2070.15	692.01	0.95	25.60
Majestic Auto Ltd.	74.37 - 138.81	92.40	0.50	-27.30
Kinetic Engineering Ltd.	85.16 - 160.66	132.82	0.19	-1.20
Scooters India Ltd.	3.84 - 16.15	11.81	0.39	10.80

Source: Computed

Table 4.12

Estimates of Trend Co-efficients for Sales Units of Selected Automobile Industry in India (1991-92 To 2003-04)

Industry	$P = \alpha + \beta t + e$				
	α	β	R^2	*F Value*	*Calculated value of Chi-square*
Commercial Vehicles					
Ashok Leyland Ltd.	23.19 (6.32)	1.37 (2.95)*	0.44	8.72	12.87
Tata Motors Ltd.	73.18 (3.41)	13.06 (4.82)*	0.68	23.26	85.54
Bajaj Tempo Ltd.	14.94 (5.78)	1.53 (4.71)*	0.67	22.21	7.74
Eicher Motors Ltd.	-3.28 (-0.64)	1.79 (2.79)*	0.41	7.76	48.23
Swaraj Mazda Ltd.	0.92 (1.17)	0.52 (5.24)*	0.71	27.44	3.80

(Contd.)

(Contd. Table 4.12)

Industry	$P = \alpha + \beta t + e$			*F Value*	*Calculated value of Chi-square*
	α	β	R^2		
Passenger Cars and Multiutility Vehicles					
Hindustan Motors Ltd.	27.32 (7.52)	-0.21 (-0.45)	0.02	0.20	16.02
Mahindra and Mahindra Ltd.	33.70 (5.09)	4.93 (5.91)*	0.76	34.87	28.34
Maruthi Udyog Ltd.	116.91 (4.81)	25.22 (8.23)*	0.86	67.71	67.02
Daewoo Motors India Ltd.	4.88 (0.69)	0.73 (0.81)	0.06	0.66	109.68

(Contd.)

(Contd. Table 4.12)

Industry	$P = \alpha + \beta t + e$				
	α	β	R^2	*F Value*	*Calculated value of Chi-square*
Two and Three Wheelers					
Bajaj Auto Ltd.	782.94 (8.11)	61.06 (5.02)	0.70	25.19	265.85
LML Ltd.	124.995 (1.62)	11.11 (1.15)	0.11	1.31	484.21
Maharastra Scooters Ltd.	139.86 (5.997)	-5.34 (-1.82)	0.23	3.30	188.22
TVS Motors India Ltd.	-12.93 (-0.405)	88.39 (21.98)*	0.98	482.99	159.00
Kinetic Motor Company Ltd.	96.15 (9.78)	1.06 (0.86)	0.06	0.74	29.11
Hero Honda Motors Ltd.	-397.59 (-2.51)	155.66 (7.79)*	0.85	60.69	361.95
Majestic Auto Ltd.	131.81 (5.30)	-5.63 (-1.80)	0.23	3.22	123.15
Kinetic Engineering Ltd.	140.16 (9.10)	-1.05 (-0.54)	0.03	0.29	57.32
Scooters India Ltd.	4.92 (2.94)	0.94 (4.43)*	0.64	19.67	8.48

* - Significant at 5 percent level; Table value of Chi-square (0.05)=21.0 with df=12

Source: Computed.

Auto Ltd and Kinetic Engineering Ltd had negative compound annual growth rate of sales during the study period. Among the industries having positive compound annual growth rate, it was highest in Hero Honda Motors Ltd followed by TVS Motors India Ltd, Scooters India Ltd and LML Ltd.

From the Table 4.12 it is observed that the difference between the actual sales and trend value of sales was significant in all the selected industries of two and three wheelers sector except Scooters India Ltd as the calculated value chi-square were higher than the table value chi-square at 5 per cent level. Hence the null hypothesis was rejected, while alternative hypothesis was accepted. The linear model of time trend of sales has proved to be a "good fit" in case of TVS Motors India Ltd, Hero Honda Motors Ltd and Scooters India Ltd as per R^2 value. The value of R^2 varies between 0.98 (TVS Motors India Ltd) 0.85 (Hero Honda Motors Ltd), 0.70 (Bajaj Auto Ltd) and 0.64 (Scooters India Ltd) indicating that time explain sales variations of these industries are to the tune of 98 per cent, 85 per cent, 70 per cent and 64 per cent respectively. Further three industries viz., Maharastra Scooters Ltd, Majestic Auto Ltd and Kinetic Engineering Ltd experienced tendency in sales to decline over the study period. The negative value of β, the time trend co-efficient, confirms this. However β being statistically is not significant.

Dispersions in market share of Indian automobile industry

This section of this chapter intends to examine company wise dispersion in market share of Indian automobile industry over the study period. This is achieved through estimation of mean, co-efficient of variation and compound annual growth rate which are presented in Table 4.13. The annual market share of selected automobiles industry during the study period has been shown in Appendix IV.

It is observed from Table 4.13 that under commercial vehicles sector on an average Ashok Leyland Ltd had the highest market share ratio (35.62 per cent) followed by Tata Motors Ltd (34.22 per cent), Bajaj Tempo Ltd (11.50 per cent), Eicher Motors Ltd (10.65 per cent) and Swaraj Mazda Ltd (6.75 per cent) during the study period. Ashok Leyland Ltd with co-efficient variation being 0.19

Industry	*Range (%)*	*Mean (%)*	*CV*	*CAGR (%)*
Commercial Vehicles				
Ashok Leyland Ltd.	28.61 - 54.67	35.62	0.19	-0.39
Tata Motors Ltd.	26.18 - 57.67	34.22	0.26	0.37
Bajaj Tempo Ltd.	3.46 - 18.68	11.50	0.50	-11.50
Eicher Motors Ltd.	4.55 - 18.68	10.65	0.43	9.13
Swaraj Mazda Ltd.	3.33 - 12.12	6.75	0.40	7.73
Passenger Cars and Multiutility Vehicles				
Hindustan Motors Ltd.	2.67 - 15.72	8.31	0.47	-11.90
Mahindra and Mahindra Ltd.	36.45 - 57.23	42.17	0.33	11.60
Maruthi Udyog Ltd.	23.82 - 68.77	36.60	0.33	-7.11
Daewoo Motors India Ltd.	1.35 - 8.00	2.68	1.07	4.03

(Contd. Table 4.13)

Industry	*Range (%)*	*Mean (%)*	*CV*	*CAGR (%)*
Two and Three Wheelers				
Bajaj Auto Ltd.	13.26 - 24.65	18.80	0.19	4.68
LML Ltd.	7.05 - 14.36	11.58	0.19	-3.06
Maharastra Scooters Ltd.	1.31 - 12.59	7.80	0.47	-4.15
TVS Motors India Ltd.	10.31 - 16.78	12.93	0.12	0.56
Kinetic Motor Company Ltd.	8.76 - 14.25	11.75	0.16	-1.43
Hero Honda Motors Ltd.	8.27 - 13.22	10.54	0.15	-0.04
Majestic Auto Ltd.	7.50 - 10.34	9.04	0.13	-2.12
Kinetic Engineering Ltd.	8.50 - 13.75	9.72	0.20	0.60
Scooters India Ltd.	5.70 - 9.45	7.65	0.18	0.40

Source: Computed.

experienced lowest variation in market share ratio over the study period while Bajaj Tempo Ltd suffered from largest variation (co-efficient variation= 0.50) during the study period. However the compound annual growth rate of market share ratio of Ashok Leyland Ltd and Bajaj Tempo Ltd was negative while in the remaining three industries it was positive over the study period.

Among the selected passenger cars and multiutility vehicles on an average Mahindra and Mahindra Ltd has highest market share ratio (42.17 per cent) followed by Maruthi Udyog Ltd (36.60 per cent), Hindustan Motors Ltd (8.31 per cent) and Daewoo Motors Ltd (2.68 per cent) during the study period. The analysis of co-efficient of variation reveals that Mahindra and Mahindra Ltd and Maruthi Udyog Ltd (CV=0.33) and Hindustan Motors Ltd (CV=0.47) had experienced moderate fluctuation in its market share during the study period while Daewoo Motors India Ltd suffered from erratic variation (CV=1.07) during the study period. The analysis of compound annual growth rate of market share, it is observed that Mahindra and Mahindra Ltd and Daewoo Motors Ltd were positive growth rate of market share during the study period.

The mean market share was the highest in Bajaj Auto Ltd (18.80 per cent) followed by TVS Motors India Ltd (12.93 per cent), Kinetic Motors India Ltd (11.75 per cent), LML Ltd (11.58 per cent), Kinetic Engineering Ltd (9.72 per cent), Majestic Auto Ltd (9.04 per cent), Maharastra Scooters Ltd (7.80 per cent) and Scooters India Ltd (7.65 per cent) in Two and Three wheelers sector during the study period. Among the selected industries TVS Motors India Ltd, Majestic Auto Ltd, Hero Honda Motors Ltd, Scooters India Ltd, LML Ltd and Kinetic Engineering Ltd had lowest variation in market share, while Maharastra Scooters Ltd suffered from largest variation in market share over the study period. It is also observed from the Table 4.13 that the compound annual growth rate of market share was only positive in the case of Bajaj Auto Ltd, TVS Motors Ltd, Kinetic Engineering Ltd and Scooters India Ltd and in the remaining industries it was negative during the study period.

To conclude, the mean rates of market share vary greatly in case of all the industries under examination irrespective of the sector of which they belong.

References

1. S.A Sherlekar, Industrial Organisation and Management (Bombay: Himalya Publishing House, 1998), p. 375.
2. A. Aziz, Performance Appraisal-Accounting and Quantitative Approaches (Jaipur: Pointer Publishers, 2003), p. 22.
3. N. C. Joshi, Management- Concept and Analysis (New Delhi: Vivek Publishing Co., 1977), p.50.
4. Ibid., p.51.
5. A. N. Agarwal, Corporate Performance Evaluation (Jaipur: Pointer Publisher, 1991), p.66.
6. A. Aziz, opp. cite., p.36.
7. Sanjay J. Bhayani, A study on sales trend and cost structure of Indian Cement Industry, The Management Accountant, Jan 2006, Vol.41, No.1, pp. 66 - 72.

5

Profitability Analysis

The business firms are generally established with a view of earning profit from their business operations. But under different situation the object of the business firms may be changed to survival, growth and stability etc. Business firms are to survive in dynamic and expanding environment. It has to go on expanding the scale of its operation on a regular and continuing basis by generating sufficient profit. Profits are the soul of the business without which it is lifeless. Infact, profits are useful intermediate beacon towards which a firm's capital should be directed[1]. It is difficult for a business to breathe well without profit. It may be regarded as a mirror of the operating performance of the business activities. But in the real business environment of today, profit is thus, not the sole objective but one among the most important objectives, which normally guide and direct business operations.

The importance of profit in judging and directing business affairs has been recognized both by economic thinkers and accounting practitioners. According to economic thinkers, profits are the report card of the past, the incentive gold star for the future and also the stake for the new venture. Accountants ascertain profits, because profit index as they perceive, is not only a reliable measure of efficient performance in using productive resources. The ultimate test of any business enterprise is profit. Perhaps the most important reason for keeping accounts is that the information contained in them provides the means of measuring the progress of the business or "Testing its pulse"; and of indicating when and where remedial action, if necessary shall be taken[2].

These days managements are giving top priority to increase the profits and maximise their shareholders' wealth. The efficiency of a management is measured in terms of profit generated by the business. It is sometimes said that higher profitability implies greater efficiency[3]. Apart from the owners, the management of the company, and the creditors, both long-term and short-term, would be interested in the financial soundness of the firm. The management of a firm is generally eager to measure its operating efficiency of a firm and its ability to ensure adequate return to its shareholders depends ultimately on the profits earned. Moreover, profits provide money for repaying the debt used to finance the project and the resources for expansion.

Concept of Profitability

In the era of economic development, the profit and the profitability are two different concepts. Although both of them are controversial, even then both are inter-related and mutually inter-dependent. Profit is the absolute term and profitability is a relative concept. Notably, while profit is the residue of income, profitability is the profit-making ability of the enterprise. It may be remarked that the profit-making ability might denote a constant or improved or deteriorated state of affairs during a given period. Thus, profit is an absolute connotation, whereas profitability is a relative concept, despite being closely related to and mutually interdependent, as they are, profit and profitability are two different concepts. In other words, in spite of their generic nature, each one of them has a distinct role in business concerns might be the same and yet more often than note their profitability could differ when measured in terms of the size of investment[4]. An analysis of the profitability reveals as to how the position of profits stands as a result of total transactions made during the year.

Profitability implies profit-making ability of a business enterprise. Profitability may be defined as the ability of a given investment to earn a return from its use[5]. Profitability is a relationship of the earnings to total resources of the corporation[6]. Stanev remarked, profitability is an overall reflection of the strength and weakness of an enterprise[7]. Therefore, profitability is the main indicator of the efficiency and effectiveness of a business enterprise in achieving its goal of earning profit. Profitability as a relative measure enables the management to make prompt change in the financial and production policies in the light of the past performance. Many important management decisions pertaining to such issues as further expansion of plant, adoption of modern technology, raising of additional funds, payment of bonus and higher dividend are linked with this relative measure.

Measurement of Profitability

Profitability of a firm can be measured by its profitability ratios. In the process of performance appraisal of a business, profitability ratios can be calculated to measure the operating efficiency. The profitability ratios can be determined on the basis of either investment or sales and for this purpose a quantitative relationship between the profit and the investment or the sales is established. In the words of James C. Van Horne, "Profitability ratios are of two types: those showing profitability in relation to sales, and those showing profitability in relation to investment[8]. He further added, with all of the profitability ratios, comparisons of a company with similar companies are extremely valuable. Only by comparison are we able to judge whether the profitability of a particular company is good or bad, and why. Absolute figures give some insight, but it is a relative performance which is most important"[9]. The profitability of the company should also be evaluated in terms of its investment in assets and in terms of capital contributed by creditors and owners, as such if a company is unable to earn a satisfactory return on investments, its survival is threatened.

In this section it is attempted to study the various ratios suggested for measuring the performance in relation to profitability. The following profitability ratios have been computed and analysed for the selected sectors of Indian automobile industry during the study period.

I. Analysis of profit margin

(1) Operating profit margin ratio

(2) Net profit margin ratio

II. Analysis of return on investment

(1) Return on assets

(2) Return on networth

(3) Return on capital employed

III. Analysis of other profitability ratios

(1) Earnings per share

(2) Dividend per share

(3) Dividend payout ratio

In order to test the significance of variations in the mean percentage of profitability ratios between the sectors and the years, the following hypothesis is framed and tested.

Ho - There is no significant difference in the mean percentage of profitability ratios between the sectors and years.

Analysis of Profit Margin

The profit margin ratio is a profitability ratio measure the relationship between profit and sales. It indicates the efficiency or effectiveness with which the operations of the business are carried on. Poor operation performance may result in low profit margin ratio. Profit margin varies with the disproportionate variations in sales revenue in comparison to costs or the vice-versa. The profit margin can be increased either by making up prices or by reduction in costs or by both. Profitability can be analyzed either on the basis of operating profits or in regard to net profit. Operating profit reflects profit from the main business for which the corporation or enterprise was launched and offers the most reliable measure for the long-term perspective. On the other hand, the net profit reflects the net profit of operating and non-operating income. It equips the analyst with the most reliable measure of profitability from the short-term point of view.

To judge the profitability performance of selected automobile industry, the following ratios relating to profit margin have been computed and analysed.

Operating Profit Margin Ratio

The first profitability ratio in relation to sales is the gross operating profit margin[10]. The operating profit margin reflects the efficiency with which the management produces each unit of product. This ratio indicates the average spread between the cost of goods sold and sales[11]. It is one of the most carefully watched measures of profitability. A high operating profit ratio is the sign of managerial effectiveness. Conversely, a low ratio should be carefully investigated and compared with the ratios of similar corporations to diagnoses as also to remedy problem[12]. There is no standard norm for operating profit ratio and it may vary from business to business but the operating profit should be adequate to provide for fixed charges, interest and dividend.

Table 5.1 and Appendix V show a fluctuating trend in the operating profit margin ratio of the selected sectors of the automobiles industry during the study period. The average operating profit margin ratio varied from sector to sector, the highest average was 9.06 per cent in passenger cars and multiutility vehicles followed by two and three wheelers (8.79 per cent) and commercial vehicles (7.85 per cent). The average ratio of operating margin was higher than the industry average in passenger cars and multiutility vehicles and two and three wheelers. However this was not statistically significant. All the selected sectors witnessed the positive compound annual growth rate of this ratio during the study period. The growth rate of this margin was highest in commercial vehicles followed by passenger cars and multiutility vehicles and two and three wheelers. The CV value of this ratio shows the high fluctuations in the operating profit margin ratio of the selected sectors during the study period. The overall fluctuating trend of this ratio can be attributed to the factors like high operating expenses, market conditions, planned product mix and high rate of wages and salary.

In order to test the hypothesis, analysis of variance has been applied among all the sectors and between the years. Since the calculated value of F (2.06 and 0.58) is less than table value of F

(3.40) is at 5 per cent level between the years and sectors, it is concluded that null hypothesis is accepted. The acceptance of null hypothesis would indicate that there are no significant differences in this ratio between the years and sectors.

The company wise operating profit margin ratio of different sectors of Indian automobile industry is presented in Table 5.2. The performance of Ashok Leyland Ltd, Tata Motors Ltd and Bajaj Tempo Ltd under commercial vehicles sector were satisfactory because its average operating profit margin ratio was higher than the industry average. In passenger cars and multiutility vehicles, the performance of Mahindra and Mahindra Ltd and Maruthi Udyog Ltd were satisfactory because its average profit margin ratio was higher than the industry average. Bajaj Auto Ltd, Hero Honda Motors Ltd, Kinetic Engineering Ltd, TVS Motors Company Ltd and Maharastra Scooters Ltd under two and three wheelers sectors showed better performance regarding operating profit margin ratio. The table also reveals that a fluctuating trend of this ratio among the companies selected under different sectors of Indian automobiles industry.

Table 5.3 refers that the difference in the operating profit margin ratio was significant in between the companies of all the three sectors as calculated value of F was greater than table value of F at 5 per cent level of significance. However, these were insignificant in between the years in passenger cars and multiutility vehicles and two and three wheelers sectors as the calculated value of F was lower than the table value of F at 5 per cent level of significance.

Hence, the profitability of the selected sector measured through operating profit margin ratio is satisfactory and should be adequate to cover the fixed charges during the study period. Thus it can be concluded that the overall profitability of the selected automobile industry was satisfactory, due to satisfactory operating profit margin.

Net Profit Margin

Net profit margin enables one to measure the relationship between sales and net profits and it is an indicator of the efficiency of the management in manufacturing, selling and financing. A high net profit margin would ensure adequate return to the owners as well as enable a firm to withstand adverse economic conditions when the selling price is declining, cost of production is rising and demand for the product is falling [13]. In case the net profit margin is inadequate, the company will not be in a position to pay off its debts and give a satisfactory return to its share holders[14].

Table 5.1 and Appendix VI clear the position regarding the net profit ratio in the selected sectors of automobile industry. The net profit ratio of all the sectors witnessed a fluctuating trend during the study period. The average net profit margin varied from sector to sector. The highest average was 3.48 per cent in two and three wheelers followed by passenger cars and multiutility vehicles (2.74 per cent) and commercial vehicles (0.41 per cent). The average net profit margin ratio of passenger cars and multiutility vehicles and two and three wheeler sectors, was more than industry average ratio. However, these were significant only in two and three wheelers sector. The compound annual growth rate of these ratio was positive in case of commercial vehicles and passenger cars and multiutility vehicles. However, it was negative in case of two and three wheelers. The CV value of these ratio shows a very high fluctuation in the net profit margin of the selected sectors during the study period.

The analysis of variance result shows that there were significant differences in net profit margin ratio among the sectors as calculated value of F (3.95) is more than the table value of F (3.40) at 5 per cent level of significance. However there were no significant differences in net profit margin ratio between the years during the study period as calculated value of F (1.99) is less than table value of F (2.18) at 5 per cent level.

The net profit margin ratio of different companies selected under different sectors of Indian automobile industry is presented in Table 5.2.The analysis of table reveals that Ashok Leyland Ltd and Eicher Motors Ltd in commercial vehicles, Mahindra and Mahindra Ltd and Maruthi Udyog Ltd in passenger cars and multiutility vehicles and Bajaj Auto Ltd, Hero Honda Motors Ltd, Maharastra Scooters Ltd and TVS Motors Company Ltd in two and three wheelers have shown better performance in this ratio concerned. However, Hindustan Motors Ltd and Daewoo Motors India Ltd in passenger cars and multiutility vehicles and LML Ltd and Majestic Auto Ltd in two and three wheelers had negative net profit margin ratio which indicated the poor performance. This was due to increase of non-operating expenses in these companies during the study period. Therefore, these companies should take necessary action to improve their position. The table also reveals the high fluctuating trend of this ratio in all the companies selected under study.

Table 5.1
Analysis of profit margin ratio of Indian automobile industry (1991-92 to 2003-04)

Particulars	*Commercial Vehicles*	*Passengers Cars and Multiutility Vehicles*	*Two and Three Wheelers*	*Industry Average*
Operating profit margin				
Mean	7.85	9.06	8.79	8.49
CV	0.35	0.33	0.46	0.28
CAGR	5.78	1.67	0.49	-0.06
"t" Value	1.54	1.21	0.09	
Net profit margin				
Mean	0.41	2.74	3.48	2.21
CV	11.90	0.91	0.55	1.07
CAGR	8.79	2.14	-2.50	3.71
"t" Value	2.17*	0.26	2.15*	

***- Significant at 5 per cent level.**
Source: Computed

Analysis of variance-Results

Sources of variation	*Operating profit margin "F" Value*	*Net profit margin "F" Value*
Between the years	2.06	1.99
Between the sectors	0.58	3.95*

*- Significant at 5 per cent level; Critical value of $F_{0.05}$ (12,24) = 2.18 and $F_{0.05}$ (2,24) = 3.40
Source: Computed

Table 5.3 shows that difference in the net profit margin ratio was insignificant in between the years in all the sectors as the

Table 5.2

Analysis of profit margin ratio of selected Indian automobile industry (1991-92 to 2003-04)

Particulars	Operating profit margin			Net profit margin ratio		
	Mean	*CV*	*CAGR*	*Mean*	*CV*	*CAGR*
Commercial Vehicles						
Ashok Leyland Ltd.	13.00	0.08	-0.04	3.16	0.52	6.47
Tata Motors Ltd.	11.18	0.28	-3.57	2.19	1.57	-1.29
Bajaj Tempo Ltd.	9.31	0.37	-4.91	1.17	2.52	-6.84
Eicher Motors Ltd.	7.34	0.34	0.07	3.33	0.68	-4.59
Swaraj Mazda Ltd.	4.27	0.73	15.30	0.81	4.35	10.70
Passenger Cars and Multiutility Vehicles						
Hindustan Motors Ltd.	6.39	0.56	-12.20	-1.82	2.42	-4.98
Mahindra and Mahindra Ltd.	11.45	0.21	1.19	4.51	0.39	3.24
Maruthi Udyog Ltd.	10.04	0.43	4.31	3.63	0.86	-1.05
Daewoo Motors India Ltd.	2.24	5.83	4.06	-18.18	1.63	-1.79

(Contd.)

(Contd. Table 5.2)

Particulars	Operating profit margin			Net profit margin ratio		
	Mean	*CV*	*CAGR*	*Mean*	*CV*	*CAGR*
Two and Three Wheelers						
Bajaj Auto Ltd.	21.36	0.18	0.02	11.14	0.34	6.45
LML Ltd.	7.38	0.63	-16.10	-0.96	-7.07	-9.03
Maharastra Scooters Ltd.	9.28	0.49	36.40	5.34	0.46	-12.60
TVS Motors Company Ltd.	10.94	0.19	-2.40	5.01	0.42	0.96
Kinetic Motors Co. Ltd.	4.52	0.86	-1.77	0.99	3.47	15.90
Hero Honda Motors Ltd.	12.80	0.25	11.30	7.04	0.36	8.57
Kinetic Engineering Ltd.	11.66	0.62	-11.20	2.06	3.56	-10.60
Majestic Auto Ltd.	5.84	0.69	-11.60	-1.67	-2.77	4.02
Scooters India Ltd.	-6.81	5.80	16.00	2.33	1.24	11.50

Source: Computed

Table 5.3
Analysis of profit margin ratio of Indian automobile industry (1991-92 to 2003-04) - ANOVA Results

Sources of variation	*Operating profit margin*		*Net profit margin ratio*	
	F Value	*F Critic Value at 5% level*	*F Value*	*F Critic Value at 5% level*
Commercial Vehicles				
Between the years	2.44*	1.96	1.80	1.96
Between the companies	21.68*	2.56	2.40	2.57
Passenger Cars and Multiutility Vehicles				
Between the years	1.63	2.03	1.34	2.03
Between the companies	4.93*	2.87	6.83*	2.86
Two and Three Wheelers				
Between the years	0.80	1.85	1.84	1.85
Between the companies	3.81*	2.03	12.30*	2.03

calculated value of F was lower than the table value of F at 5 per cent level of significance. Hence the null hypothesis is accepted. However the differences between the company were significant in passenger cars and multiutility vehicles and two and three wheelers. Because calculated value F was more than the table value of F at 5 per cent level of significance and the null hypothesis was rejected. The difference was significant in between the companies because the amount of non-operating expenses was different between the companies under study.

The overall analysis of net profit margin ratio shows the ability of the company to withstand competition and adverse conditions during the study period. Thus, it can be concluded that the operating efficiency of automobile industry was satisfactory from the point of view of shareholders.

Analysis of Return on Investment

The profitability of a business enterprise is measured in relation to investment. It is the prime measure of the overall profitability of an enterprise. Return on Investment (ROI) measures the overall effectiveness of management in generating profits with its available assets[15]. This ratio reveals how profitability the firm's assets have been utilized. The rate of return on investment is the end product of the two-fold sequence of the profit margin path and can be ascertained by the multiplication of the investment-turnover with the percentage of profit margin on sales[16].

This overall measure can be looked in three different ways, depending on whether one investment is being total assets, capital employed and shareholders net worth. In order to analyse the profitability of the automobile industry in India, the following ratios have been computed and analysed.

Return on Assets

The return on assets of a company determines its ability to utilize the assets employed in the enterprises efficiently and effectively to earn good return. This ratio measure the percentage of profits earned per rupee of assets and thus is a measure of efficiency of the company in generating profits on its asset. The ratio can be very well used for inter-firm and inter-industry comparisons. Notably, neither the operating profit margin nor the turnover ratio by itself provides an adequate measure of operating efficiency. Further, while the net profit margin ignores the utilization of assets, the turnover ratio ignores profitability on sales, the return on assets ratio or earning power reveals these short comings[17]. An improvement in the earning power of the firm will result if there is an increase in turnover on existing assets and an increase in the net profit margin.

Table 5.4 and Appendix VII explain the fluctuating trend in the return on assets of the selected sectors of the automobile industry. The average return on assets ratio varied from sector to sector, the highest average was 9.70 per cent in two and three wheelers followed by commercial vehicles (5.86 per cent) and passenger cars and multiutility vehicles (2.91 per cent). The average return on assets ratio of two and three wheelers was more than industry average ratio and statistically significant at 5 per cent level. The compound annual growth rate of these ratio was positive in case of commercial vehicles and two and three wheelers, however it was negative in case of passenger cars and multiutility vehicles. The CV value of these ratio shows the very high fluctuation in commercial vehicles and passenger cars and multiutility vehicles. The overall fluctuating trend of this ratio can be influenced by the ability of the company to utilize the assets in the profitable way.

In order to test the hypothesis, analysis of variance has been applied between the sectors and between the years. Since, the calculated value of 'F' (5.04 and 8.37) more than the table value of 'F' (2.18 and 3.40) at 5 per cent level between the years and the between the sectors, it is concluded that there were significant differences between the return on assets ratio among the selected years and between the sectors during the study period.

The return on assets ratio of different companies selected under different sectors of Indian automobile industry are presented in Table 5.5. The analysis of the table reveals that Tata Motors Ltd and Eicher Motors Ltd in commercial vehicles sector, Mahindra and Mahindra Ltd and Maruthi Udyog Ltd in passenger cars and multiutility vehicles sector and Hero Honda Motors Ltd, TVS Motors Company Ltd and Bajaj Auto Ltd in two and three wheelers sectors had shown better performance in this ratio concerned. However

Hindustan Motors Ltd and Daewoo Motors India Ltd in passenger cars and multiutility vehicles and LML Ltd and Majestic Auto Ltd in two and three wheelers had negative return on assets ratio. It indicated the poor performance. This was due to net loss incurred by these companies during the study period. Therefore, these companies should take necessary action to improve its net profit position. The table also reveals the high fluctuating trend of this ratio in all the companies selected under study.

Table 5.6 shows that difference in the return on assets ratio between the years was significant in commercial vehicles and passenger cars and multiutility vehicles because the calculated value F was more than the table value of F at 5 per cent level of significance and the null hypothesis was rejected. However, the return on assets ratio between the companies were significant in passenger cars and multiutility vehicles and two and three wheelers sectors because the calculated value of F is greater than the table value of F.

The overall analysis of this ratio shows that the profitability of the selected sectors measured through this ratio was satisfactory except Hindustan Motors Ltd, Daewoo Motors India Ltd, LML Ltd and Majestic Auto Ltd and should be adequate to meet the future financial plans. On the whole, the overall trend of this ratio kept fluctuating during the period under study. It can be drawn from the foregoing discussion that the operating assets were effectively utilized in a profitable manner.

Return on Networth

There is no doubt that the preference shareholders are also the owners of a company. The real owners are the ordinary shareholders who bear all the risk, participate in management and are entitled to all the profits, remaining after outside claims, including preference dividends. The profitability of a company from the owners' point of view should, therefore be assessed in terms of the return on the owners equity. The ratio measures the ability of the management of enterprise to generate adequate returns for the capital invested by the owners of the company. The ratio is meaningful in the sense that it measures the residue of income, which really belongs to the owners.

This residue is measured in relation to the capital base, which takes into account not only the share capital paid by the owners, but also accumulated surplus or deficit. The earning of a satisfactory return is the most desirable objective of business. Thus, this ratio is of great interest to present as well as prospective shareholders and also of great concern to management[18]. As is the case for return on assets, the estimate of market value will have a large impact on this ratio. The return on owners' equity of the company should be compared with the ratios for other similar companies. This will reveal the relative performance and also the relative strength of the enterprise in attracting future investments.

Table 5.4 and Appendix VIII show a fluctuating trend in the return on networth ratio of the selected sectors of the automobile industry. The average return on networth varied from sector to sector. The highest average was 18.70 per cent in two and three wheelers followed by commercial vehicles (16.76 per cent) and passenger cars and multiutility vehicles (9.75 per cent). The average return on networth ratio of two and three wheelers and commercial vehicles sectors were more than industry average ratio. However these were not statistically significant. The compound annual growth rate of these ratio was positive in case of commercial vehicles only. However it was negative in case of passenger cars and multiutility vehicles and two and three wheelers. The CV value of these ratio shows the very high fluctuation in commercial vehicles and passenger cars and multiutility vehicles and moderate fluctuations in the two and three wheelers sectors. The overall fluctuating trend of this ratio can be attributed to the factors like demand and supply and planned product mix and efficient use of machinery.

In order to test the hypothesis, analysis of variance has been applied among all the selected sectors and between the years. Since, the calculated value of 'F' (2.37 and 3.67) is more than the table value of 'F' (2.18 and 3.40) at 5 per cent level between the years and sectors, it is concluded that there were significant differences between the return on networth ratio among the selected sectors and between the years during the study period.

The return on networth ratio of different companies selected under different sectors of Indian automobile industry is presented in Table 5.5. The analysis of table reveals that Swaraj Mazda Ltd and Eicher Motors Ltd in commercial vehicles, Maruthi Udyog Ltd in passenger cars and multiutility vehicles and TVS Motors Company Ltd, Hero Honda Motors Ltd, Bajaj Auto Ltd and Majestic Auto Ltd in two and three wheelers had shown better performance regarding return on networth ratios. However, Hindustan Motors Ltd and Daewoo Motors India Ltd in passenger cars and multiutility vehicles had negative return on networth showed better performance regarding return on networth ratio.

Table 5.6 shows that difference in the return on networth ratio was significant in between the companies of all the three sectors as calculated value of F was greater than table value of F at 5 per cent level of significance. However, these were insignificant in between the years in two and three wheelers sectors as the calculated value of F was lower than the table value of F at 5 per cent level of significance.

Hence, the profitability of the selected sector measured through return on networth ratio was satisfactory and should be adequate to cover the fixed charges during the study period. It can be generalized that on the whole the owners' equity was utilized profitably in all the sectors of Indian automobile industry except Hindustan Motors Ltd, Daewoo Motor India Ltd, LML Ltd and Majestic Auto Ltd during the study period.

Return on Capital Employed

The primary objective of making investment in any business is to obtain satisfactory return on the capital invested. Hence, the return on capital employed is used as a measure of success of a business in realizing this objective. It is the chief profitability ratio and the most important measure of performance as it indicates the comparative efficiency with which the whole company runs properly. Therefore, return on capital employed is a valuable yardstick to measure the overall performance of an undertaking. The return on capital employed shows the earning power of the capital invested. It indicates how the management has used the funds supplied by creditors and owners. The higher the ratio, the more efficient can be considered the enterprises in using funds entrusted to it. The comparison of this ratio with the ratios of similar business organizations will reveal the relative operating efficiency of a business enterprise. Further, an investor can judge the future prospects of business enterprises by taking into consideration the earning capacity of capital employed.

Table 5.4 and Appendix IX explain a fluctuating trend in the return on capital employed of the selected sectors of automobile industry. The average return on capital employed varied from sector to sector. The highest average was 22.10 per cent in two and three wheelers, followed by commercial vehicles (19.32 per cent) and passenger cars and multiutility vehicles (13.81 per cent). The average ratio of return on capital employed was higher than the industry average in two and three wheelers and commercial vehicles. However, these were statistically significant only in two and three wheelers. The compound annual growth rate of this ratio was positive only in commercial vehicles. The CV value shows that this ratio was highly fluctuating in commercial vehicles and passenger cars and multitutlity vehicles during the study period. The overall analysis of this ratio reveals that the ratio of return on capital employed improved significantly which was on account of considerable increases in profit margin as well as assets turnover. This was mainly because of optimization of output, material efficiency and rigid control on costs.

In order to test the hypothesis, analysis of variance has been applied among all the selected years and between the sectors. Since, the calculated value of 'F' (2.36 and 4.51) was more than the table value of 'F' (2.18 and 3.40) at 5 per cent level between the sectors and between the years, it is concluded that there were significant differences between the return on capital employed ratio among the selected years and between the sectors during the study period.

The company wise return on capital employed ratio of different sectors of Indian automobile industry is presented in Table 5.5. The performance of Swaraj Mazda Ltd and Eicher Motors Ltd under commercial vehicles sector was satisfactory because its average return on capital employed was higher than industry average. In passenger cars and multiutility vehicles, the performance of Maruthi Udyog Ltd were satisfactory because its average return on capital employed was higher than the industry average. Hero Honda Motors Ltd, TVS Motors Company Ltd and Bajaj Auto Ltd under two and three wheelers sector showed better performance regarding return

Table 5.4
Analysis of Return on Investment of Indian Automobile Industry (1991-92 to 2003-04)

Particulars	*Commercial Vehicles*	*Passengers Cars and Multiutility Vehicles*	*Two and Three Wheelers*	*Industry Average*
Return on assets				
Mean	5.86	2.91	9.70	6.16
CV	1.20	2.61	0.45	0.89
CAGR	7.78	-7.02	5.49	6.40
"t" Value	-0.28	-3.58	3.36*	
Return on networth				
Mean	16.76	9.75	18.70	15.07
CV	0.72	1.29	0.33	0.52
CAGR	3.36	-4.37	-6.42	-4.27
"t" Value	0.66	-2.71	1.27	
Return on capital employed				
Mean	19.32	13.81	22.10	18.40
CV	0.51	0.73	0.24	0.35
CAGR	4.65	-6.60	-2.36	0.33
"t" Value	0.43	-3.17	1.96*	

* - Significant at 5 per cent level
Source: Computed.

Analysis of Variance-Results

Sources of variation	*Return on Assets* "F" Value	*Return on networth* "F" Value	*Return on capital employed* "F" Value
Between the years	5.04*	2.37*	2.36*
Between the sectors	8.37*	3.67*	4.51*

*- Significant at 5 per cent level; Critical value of $F_{0.05}$ (12,24)=2.18 and $F_{0.05}$ (2,24) = 3.40
Source: Computed.

Table 5.5
Analysis of Return on Investment of Selected Indian Automobile Industry (1991-92 to 2003-04)

Particulars	*Return on assets*			*Return on networth*			*Return on capital employed*		
	Mean	*CV*	*CAGR*	*Mean*	*CV*	*CAGR*	*Mean*	*CV*	*CAGR*
Commercial Vehicles									
Ashok Leyland Ltd.	4.44	0.72	11.20	8.73	0.65	8.07	12.50	0.29	2.05
Tata Motors Ltd.	6.46	1.25	-0.70	9.96	1.32	-11.20	16.66	0.66	-7.43
Bajaj Tempo Ltd.	5.50	1.85	-10.20	8.17	1.86	-11.60	16.59	0.88	-12.40
Eicher Motors Ltd.	10.00	1.13	19.00	23.85	0.69	17.60	22.89	0.61	20.10
Swaraj Mazda Ltd.	5.56	4.83	28.80	36.71	0.85	28.80	25.36	0.93	33.40
Passenger Cars and Multiutility Vehicles									
Hindustan Motors Ltd.	-3.61	2.54	-8.60	-4.20	5.97	-15.30	7.73	1.09	-16.90
Mahindra and Mahindra Ltd.	7.81	0.46	2.33	13.75	0.63	5.26	16.67	0.38	-2.56
Maruthi Udyog Ltd.	12.28	1.03	-1.10	20.41	0.88	-12.40	28.61	0.78	-12.00
Daewoo Motors India Ltd.	-4.82	2.02	-2.08	-2.74	3.53	-5.53	1.82	3.22	-3.84

(Contd.)

(Contd. Table 5.5)

Particulars	*Return on assets*			*Return on networth*			*Return on capital employed*		
	Mean	*CV*	*CAGR*	*Mean*	*CV*	*CAGR*	*Mean*	*CV*	*CAGR*
Two and Three Wheelers									
Bajaj Auto Ltd.	16.03	0.35	-0.34	22.38	0.40	-2.74	28.27	0.41	-5.73
LML Ltd.	-2.32	-8.19	-7.82	-4.80	2.54	-21.80	11.50	1.28	-14.90
Maharastra Scooters Ltd.	9.97	0.64	-28.60	11.30	0.66	-29.70	17.72	0.73	-31.70
TVS Motors Company Ltd.	20.48	0.49	1.69	41.17	0.54	-2.35	40.99	0.41	-1.47
Kinetic Motors Company Ltd.	6.14	1.57	-5.62	10.31	1.58	-8.35	15.49	0.86	-18.20
Hero Honda Motors Ltd.	29.91	0.52	13.40	46.95	0.33	0.07	52.50	0.51	13.10
Kinetic Engineering Ltd.	4.86	1.66	-16.10	7.96	2.45	-18.5	13.37	0.72	-16.00
Majestic Auto Ltd.	-2.75	3.27	7.70	-16.92	1.76	27.80	10.42	0.91	-22.90
Scooters India Ltd.	5.00	1.60	14.90	6.48	1.55	17.80	7.97	1.43	14.20

Source: Computed.

Table 5.6
Analysis of Return on Investment of Indian Automobile Industry
(1991-92 to 2003-04)
ANOVA Results

Sources of variation	*Return on assets*		*Return on networth*		*Return on capital employed*	
	F Value	*F Critic Value at 5% level*	*F Value*	*F Critic Value at 5% level*	*F Value*	*F Critic Value at 5% level*
Commercial Vehicles						
Between the years	2.32*	1.96	3.61*	1.96	3.44*	1.96
Between the companies	0.37	2.56	8.98*	2.57	2.39	2.57
Passenger Cars and Multiutility Vehicles						
Between the years	5.72*	2.03	4.67*	2.03	4.64*	2.03
Between the companies	22.95*	2.87	10.80*	2.87	20.83*	2.87
Two and Three Wheelers						
Between the years	1.52	1.85	1.23	1.85	1.13	1.85
Between the companies	13.15*	2.04	10.80*	2.04	13.98*	2.04

* - Significant at 5 per cent level
Source: Computed.

on capital employed ratio during the study period. The table also reveals that fluctuating trend of this ratio among companies selected under different sectors of Indian automobile industry.

Table 5.6 shows that difference in the return on capital employed ratio was significant in between the years in commercial vehicles and passenger cars and multiutility vehicles sectors as the calculated value of F was more than the table value of F at 5 per cent level of significance. Hence, the null hypothesis was rejected. However, the difference in the return on capital employed ratio between the companies was significant in passenger cars and multiutility vehicles and two and three wheelers because calculated value of F was more than the table value of F at 5 per cent level of significance and the null hypothesis was rejected.

In fine, it can be inferred that the operating efficiency of the automobile industry was satisfactory and the management generally succeeded in investing the capital funds profitably.

Analysis of other Profitability Ratios

Earnings Per Share

Apart from the rates of return, the profitability of a company from the point of view of the equity shareholders is the earnings per share. It measures the profit available to the equity shareholders on a per share basis. Many enterprises fix their growth targets in terms of growth in earnings per share[19]. Shareholders and financial analyst place considerable emphasis on reported earnings per share and anticipated growth in earnings per share. The earnings per share calculations made over years indicate whether or not the firm's earning power on per share basis has changed over that period.

The earnings per share simply show the profitability of the firm on a per share basis, it does not reflect how much is paid as dividend and how much is retained in the business. But as a profitability index, it is a valuable and widely used ratio[20]. Further, earning per share is a good measure of profitability and when compared with earnings per share of similar other companies, it gives a view of the comparative earnings or earning power of the firm.

Table 5.7 and Appendix X show a fluctuating trend in the earnings per share of the selected sectors of the automobile industry.

The average earnings per share varied from sector to sector. The highest average was Rs. 48.64 in passenger cars and multiutility vehicles followed by two and three wheelers (Rs. 14.42) and commercial vehicles (Rs. 9.23). The average earnings per share ratio of passenger cars and multiutility vehicles sectors was more than industry average ratio. However, these were statistically significant in all the selected sectors. The compound annual growth rate of these ratio were positive in case of two and three wheelers, however it was negative in case of commercial vehicles and passenger cars and multiutility vehicles. The CV value of these ratio shows the high fluctuation in all the sectors during the study period. The overall fluctuating trend of this ratio can be attributed to the factors like profitability position and fluctuations in the market prices of the shares of the company.

The analysis of variance result shows that there were significant differences in earnings per share ratio among the sectors as calculated value of F (9.15) is more than the table value of F (3.40) at 5 per cent level of significance. However there were insignificant differences between the earnings per share ratio between the years during the study period as calculated value of F (1.10) is less than table value of F (2.18) at 5 per cent level.

The earning per share ratio of different companies selected under different sectors of Indian automobile industry is presented in Table5.8. The analysis of Maruthi Udyog Ltd under passenger cars and multiutility vehicles sector was satisfactory because its average earning per share ratio was higher than industry average, In two and three wheelers sectors, performance of Bajaj Auto Ltd and Kinetic Engineering Ltd was satisfactory because its average earning per share were higher than the industry average. Table also reveals the fluctuating trend of this ratio among industry selected under different sectors of Indian automobile industry.

Table 5.9 refers that the difference in the earnings per share was significant in between the companies of all the three sectors because calculated value of F was greater than table value of F at 5 per cent level of significance. However this ratio was insignificant in between the years in passenger cars and multiutility vehicles sector as the calculated value of F was lower than the table value F at 5 per cent level of significance.

It can be concluded that the position regarding earnings per share was good in all the selected sectors of the automobile industry during period under review highlighting their better performance and prospectus from the point of view of owners.

Dividend Per Share

The net profits after taxes belong to shareholders. But the income, which they really receive is the amount of earnings distributed as cash dividends. Therefore, a large number of present and potential investors may be interested in dividend per share rather than earnings per share. The market price of a share is a reflection of the collective judgement of a company to pay dividends, issue of bonus shares and right shares in the long run. In fact, earnings per share or dividend per share should be related to the market price of the share.

Table 5.7 and Appendix XI show a fluctuating trend in the dividend per share of the selected sectors of the automobile industry. The average dividend per share varied from sector to sector, the highest average was Rs.52.98 in two and three wheelers followed by commercial vehicles (Rs.26.94) and passenger cars and multiutility vehicles (Rs.18.16). The average dividend per share of two and three wheelers was more than industry average and this was statistically significant at 5 per cent level. The compound annual growth rate of this ratio was the highest in two and three wheelers followed by passenger cars and multiutility vehicles and commercial vehicles. The CV value of this ratio shows the highly fluctuating trend in the dividend per share of all the sectors except passenger cars and multiutility vehicles during the study period. The overall fluctuating trend of this ratio can be attributed to the factors like profitability position and board dividend policy.

In order to test the hypothesis, analysis of variance has been applied among all the selected years and between the sectors. Since, the calculated values of F (1.95) is less than the table value of F (2.18) at 5 per cent level between the years, it is concluded that there were no significant differences between the dividend per share between the years among the selected sectors. However, there were significant differences between the dividend per share of the different sectors, because the calculated value of 'F' (5.06) is more than the table value of 'F' (3.40) at 5 per cent level.

The company wise dividend per share of different sectors of Indian automobile industry is presented in Table 5.8. The performance of Ashok Leyland Ltd and Tata Motors Ltd in commercial vehicles. Mahindra and Mahindra Ltd in passenger cars and multiutility vehicles and Bajaj Auto Ltd, Kinetic Motors Co. Ltd and Hero Honda Motors Ltd in two and three wheelers was satisfactory because its average dividend per share was higher than the industry average. The table also reveals the fluctuating trend of this ratio among industry selected under different sectors of Indian automobile industry.

Table 5.9 refers that the difference in the dividend per share ratio was significant in between the industry of all the three sectors as calculated value of F was greater than table value of F at 5 per cent level of significance. However these were insignificant in between the years in passenger cars and multiutility vehicles and two and three wheelers sector as the calculated value of F was lower than the table value of F at 5 per cent level of significance. Therefore, null hypothesis is accepted.

Hence, the profitability of the selected sector measured through this ratio is satisfactory and the industry must frame the new dividend policy for the satisfaction of the shareholders.

Dividend Payout Ratio

Dividend payout ratio is a major aspect of the dividend policy of a company. It measures the relationship between the earnings belonging to the equity shareholders and the dividend paid to them. A ratio lower than 100 Per cent denotes the retention of distributable earnings whereas a ratio higher than 100 per cent indicates the distribution of a part of reserves by way of dividends. The investors have a marked preference for higher dividend payout ratio. The ratio is a test of managerial ability and reputation of company.

Table 5.7 and Appendix XII exhibit a fluctuating trend in the dividend pay out ratio of the selected sectors of the automobile industry. The average dividend payout ratio varied from sector to sector, the highest average was 335.97 in commercial vehicles followed by two and three wheelers (232.83) and passenger cars and multiutility vehicles (113.27). The average dividend payout ratio of two and three wheelers sector were more than industry average

Table 5.7
Analysis of Appropriation of Profit of Indian Automobile Industry
(1991-92 to 2003-04)

Particulars	*Commercial Vehicles*	*Passengers Cars and Multiutility Vehicles*	*Two and Three Wheelers*	*Industry Average*
Earnings per share				
Mean	9.23	48.64	14.42	24.10
CV	0.62	0.91	0.33	0.64
CAGR	-0.11	-7.25	5.57	0.47
"t" Value	-3.10*	3.04*	-2.78*	
Dividend per share				
Mean	26.94	18.16	52.98	32.69
CV	0.57	0.33	0.93	0.66
CAGR	4.27	7.41	19.70	12.70
"t" Value	-1.74	-1.70	2.62*	
Dividend payout ratio				
Mean	335.97	113.27	232.83	227.36
CV	0.39	0.49	0.68	0.33
CAGR	0.79	5.32	13.90	6.24
"t" Value	3.18*	-9.05*	0.22	

* - Significant at 5 per cent level
Source: Computed

Analysis of variance-Results

Sources of variation	*Earnings per share "F" Value*	*Dividend per share "F" Value*	*Dividend payout ratio "F" Value*
Between the years	1.10	1.95	1.15
Between the sectors	9.15*	5.06*	11.11*

*- Significant at 5 per cent level; Critical value of $F_{0.05}$ (12,24) = 2.18 and $F_{0.05}$ (2,24)=3.40

Source: Computed

Table 5.8
Analysis of Appropriation of Profit of Selected Indian Automobile Industry
(1991-92 to 2003-04)

Particulars	Earnings per share			Dividend per share			Dividend payout ratio		
	Mean	*CV*	*CAGR*	*Mean*	*CV*	*CAGR*	*Mean*	*CV*	*CAGR*
Commercial Vehicles									
Ashok Leyland Ltd.	6.73	0.60	9.60	35.08	0.53	7.59	638.01	0.57	7.96
Tata Motors Ltd.	11.05	0.89	-7.73	41.54	0.61	-13.30	477.46	0.81	-23.30
Bajaj Tempo Ltd.	11.82	0.97	-10.50	32.31	0.81	-16.40	245.55	1.19	-32.10
Eicher Motors Ltd.	6.71	0.87	21.90	13.08	1.01	37.00	172.36	1.01	59.50
Swaraj Mazda Ltd.	5.09	1.11	23.2	12.69	1.73	38.50	146.41	1.32	65.10
Passenger Cars and Multiutility Vehicles									
Hindustan Motors Ltd.	1.26	1.41	-5.25	1.54	2.44	-3.79	37.74	2.47	-2.94
Mahindra and Mahindra Ltd.	16.52	0.42	3.81	52.12	0.31	6.47	344.76	0.33	11.20
Maruthi Udyog Ltd.	172.41	1.01	-14.40	19.38	0.56	8.14	70.59	2.39	15.00
Daewoo Motors India Ltd.	0.42	3.57	-3.09	0.00	0.00	0.00	0.00	0.00	0.00

(Contd.)

(Contd. Table 5.8)

Particulars	*Earnings per share*			*Dividend per share*			*Dividend payout ratio*		
	Mean	*CV*	*CAGR*	*Mean*	*CV*	*CAGR*	*Mean*	*CV*	*CAGR*
Two and Three Wheelers									
Bajaj Auto Ltd.	41.49	0.40	9.17	102.31	0.51	9.25	260.39	0.31	0.07
LML Ltd.	2.39	1.23	-2.86	2.31	2.44	-1.49	42.75	2.47	-0.15
Maharastra Scooters Ltd.	14.96	0.63	-24.30	23.15	0.47	-10.30	211.51	0.74	8.38
TVS Motors Company Ltd.	21.66	0.76	19.00	55.54	0.78	37.00	183.08	0.58	35.9
Kinetic Motors Co. Ltd.	3.78	0.92	4.04	9.23	1.12	13.60	245.77	1.17	21.3
Hero Honda Motors Ltd.	22.08	0.57	7.70	252.77	1.51	33.70	1025.39	1.33	23.4
Kinetic Engineering Ltd.	22.20	0.60	-14.70	31.54	0.51	-19.80	126.70	0.49	-32.5
Majestic Auto Ltd.	0.49	2.61	5.20	0	0	0	0	0	0
Scooters India Ltd.	0.77	1.23	-1.11	0	0	0	0	0	0

Source: Computed.

Table 5.9
Analysis of Appropriation of Profit of Indian Automobile Industry (1991-92 to 2003-04)

ANOVA Results

Source of variation	*Earnings per share*		*Dividend per share*		*Dividend payout ratio*	
	F Value	*F Critic Value at 5% level*	*F Value*	*F Critic Value at 5% level*	*F Value*	*F Critic Value at 5% level*
Commercial Vehicles						
Between the years	4.20*	1.96	3.99*	1.96	1.02	1.96
Between the companies	3.02*	2.57	7.82*	2.57	6.82*	2.57
Passenger Cars and Multiutility Vehicles						
Between the years	1.09	2.03	1.70	2.03	0.95	2.03
Between the companies	12.13*	2.87	89.76*	2.87	25.33*	2.87
Two and Three Wheelers						
Between the years	2.15*	1.85	1.36	1.85	1.02	1.85
Between the companies	25.76*	2.04	5.43*	2.04	5.77*	2.04

* - Significant at 5 per cent level
Source: Computed.

ratio. However these were significant in commercial vehicles and passenger cars and multiutility vehicles sectors. The selected sector witnessed the positive compound annual growth rate of dividend payout ratio during the study period. The compound annual growth rate of this ratio was the highest in two and three wheelers, followed by passenger cars and multiutility vehicles and commercial vehicles. The CV value of this ratio shows a moderate fluctuation in the dividend payout ratio of the selected sectors during the study period.

To test the hypothesis, analysis of variance has been applied among all the selected sectors and between the years. Since, the calculated value of 'F' (1.15) is less than the table value of 'F' (2.18) at 5 per cent level between the years, it is concluded that there were no significant differences between the dividend payout ratio between the selected years. However, there were significant differences in the dividend payout ratio between the sectors. Because, the calculated value of 'F' (11.11) is more than the table value of 'F' (3.40) at 5 per cent level.

The dividend payout ratio of different companies selected under different sectors of Indian automobile industry is presented in Table 5.8. The performance of Ashok Leyland Ltd, Tata Motors India Ltd and Bajaj Tempo Ltd in commercial vehicles, Mahindra and Mahindra Ltd in passenger cars and mulitiutility vehicles and Bajaj Auto Ltd, Hero Honda Motors Ltd and Kinetic Motors Ltd in two and three wheelers were satisfactory because its average dividend payout ratio was higher than the industry average. The table also reveals the fluctuating trend of this ratio among industry selected under different sectors of Indian automobile industry during the study period.

Table 5.9 refers that the difference in the dividend payout ratio was significant in between the companies of all the three sectors as calculated value of F was greater than table value of F at 5 per cent level of significance. However, these were insignificant in between the years in all three sectors as the calculated value of F was lower than the table value of F at 5 per cent level. Hence, the fluctuation in the payout ratio in different years of different companies was the reflection of the companies efforts to maintain stable dividend policies irrespective of their actual earnings.

Table 5.10
ANOVA Results-Ratios Relating to Profitability-Comparison

Profitability ratios	*Between the years*		*Between the sectors*	
	F ratio	*H_o-Accepted / Rejected*	*F Ratio*	*H_o-Accepted / Rejected*
I. Profit margin				
1.Operating profit margin ratio	2.06	H_o - Accepted	0.58	H_o – Accepted
2. Net profit margin ratio	1.99	H_o – Accepted	3.95	H_o – Rejected
II. Return on investment				
1. Return on assets	5.04	H_o – Rejected	8.37	H_o – Rejected
2. Return on networth	2.37	H_o – Rejected	3.67	H_o – Rejected
3. Return on capital employed	2.36	H_o – Rejected	4.51	H_o – Rejected
III.Other profitability ratios				
1. Earnings per share	1.10	H_o – Accepted	9.15	H_o – Rejected
2. Dividend per share	1.95	H_o – Accepted	5.06	H_o – Rejected
3. Dividend payout ratio	1.15	H_o – Accepted	11.11	H_o – Rejected

Critical value of F at 5 per cent level: 2.18 & 3.40
Source: Computed

Profitability Analysis-ANOVA Results-Comparison

The results of ANOVA for testing the hypothesis of different years and different sectors of the selected Indian automobile industry are presented in Table 5.10. It is evident from the table that there were significant differences in all the profitability ratios between the years except operating profit margin, net profit margin ratio, earnings per share, dividend per share and dividend payout ratio during the study period. Similarly, there were significant differences in all the profitability ratios between the sectors except operating profit margin ratio during the study period.

Profitability Trends

Profitability of various industries would hardly diverge in a world of perfection, because, future can easily be predicated. However, real world is far from perfection. A number of dynamic forces (e.g., changes in income, technology, population, etc.) operate simultaneously in a real imperfect and uncertain world. Consequently, profitability of different concerns and industries gets greatly affected.

Rate of profit which is one of the most used and popular financial measure of performance of a concern and an industry, plays a pivotal role in the growth process of the concern, the industry and the whole economy. It reflects the financial stability and also enhances the earning capacity of the concern. It plays dual role in the investment process of the economy by attracting fresh investment on one hand, and generating internal source of finance on the other hand. However, low rate of profit or loss repels any fresh inflow of investment and induces existing capital to quit towards the fields of higher rates of profit. It thus reflects investors' and lenders' need of knowing financial indicator of performance and is a key factor in determining the commercial viability of the concern and the industry.

The current rate of profit is an indicator and source of and a need for the expansions of business through re-investment and through attracting and observing new capital in the industry. Hence, investors and lenders are interested in knowing the profitability of a concern and industry over time or at a point of time. The celebrated tendency of rates of profit to fall over long period of time had been theoretically developed by classical economists like Adam Smith, David Ricardo, etc., their critic Karl Marx and also by neoclassical writers like Alfred Marshall. The study therefore intends to empirically examine whether the rate of profit in Indian automobile industry has a tendency to rise or fall over a period of 1991-92 to 2003-04. The objective is not to test the validity of classical hypothesis, as the economic conditions as assumed by classical writers do not prevail in the country. However, knowledge about whether profitability is raising or falling over the period 1991-92 to 2003-04 would throw interesting results for formulation of future policies.

An attempt has been made in this study to examine the trends in rates of profit of selected Indian automobile Industries over the period 1991-92 to 2003-04. Further an attempt has also been made to capture the industry vise variations in the series of profit rates, which reveals the dispersion of the series for each industry over the study period. In this study a ratio of profits to capital employed and expresses in percentage terms has been used for this purpose. The rate of profit on capital employed indicates the earning power of capital of long term nature and thus examine long-term profitability better. The linear regression model fitted is as follows:

$$P = \alpha + \beta t + e$$

where P is rate of profit, t is the time and α and β are the parameters (intercept and co-efficient respectively) and e is the error term. The results of the application of above stated model to the profitability of Indian automobile industries are presented in Table 5.11.

Table 5.11 reveals that the linear model of time trend of profitability has proved to be a "good fit" in case of ten out of eighteen industries, i.e., 55.55 per cent of the industries examined. This is revealed from value of R^2, the co-efficient of determination. All these ten industries, viz., Tata Motors Ltd, Eicher Motors Ltd, Swaraj Mazda Ltd (commercial vehicles), Hindustan Motors Ltd, Maruthi Udyog Ltd (passenger cars and multiutility vehicles), Maharastra Scooters Ltd, TVS Motors Company Ltd, Hero Honda Motors Ltd, Kinetic Engineering Ltd and Majestic Auto Ltd (two and three wheelers), experienced a strong tendency in profitability to decline over the study period. The negative values of β, the time

Table 5.11
Results of Regression of Rates of Profit on Time for Indian Automobile Industries (1991-92 to 2003-04)

Sl. No.	Industry	$P = \alpha + \beta t + e$ α	β	R^2	F value
1.	Ashok Leyland Ltd.	10.124 (4.813)	0.340 (1.283)	0.13	1.65
2.	Tata Motors Ltd.	20.174 (3.017)	-0.591 (2.595)*	0.47	35.41
3.	Bajaj Tempo Ltd.	24.326 (2.815)	-1.113 (1.022)	0.09	1.05
4	Eicher Motors Ltd.	5.300 (0.867)	-2.514 (3.265)*	0.49	10.66
5.	Swaraj Mazda Ltd.	-10.312 (-1.313)	-5.096 (5.147)*	0.71	26.50
	Commercial Vehicles Sector	**14.182 (2.700)**	**-0.862 (3.303)***	**0.51**	**31.45**
6.	Hindustan Motors Ltd.	14.682 (3.208)	-0.993 (2.723)*	0.46	29.69
7.	Mahindra and Mahindra Ltd.	19.261 (5.016)	-0.370 (0.765)	0.05	0.59
8.	Maruthi Udyog Ltd.	42.541 (3.293)	-1.990 (3.223)*	0.40	34.15
9.	Daewoo Motors India Ltd.	3.541 (0.996)	-0.246 (0.550)	0.03	0.30
	Passenger Cars and Multiutility Vehicles Sector	**17.112 (2.802)**	**-0.477 (0.621)**	**0.03**	**0.39**
10.	Bajaj Auto Ltd.	39.047 (6.420)	-1.540 (2.010)	0.27	4.04
11.	LML Ltd.	22.676 (2.768)	-1.596 (1.546)	0.18	2.39
12.	Maharashtra Scooters Ltd.	40.083 (17.393)	-3.194 (11.001)*	0.92	121.03
13.	TVS Motors Company Ltd.	44.803 (4.378)	-0.553 (2.429)*	0.39	24.16
14.	Kinetic Motors Co. Ltd.	20.817 (2.601)	-0.761 (0.754)	0.05	0.57
15.	Hero Honda Motors Ltd.	6.892 (1.253)	-6.526 (9.419)*	0.89	88.72
16.	Kinetic Engineering Ltd.	26.508 (6.914)	-1.877 (3.885)*	0.58	15.09

(Contd.)

(Contd. Table 5.11)

Sl. No.	*Industry*	*P = α + βt + e*	*Sl. No.*	*Industry*	*P = α + βt + e*
17.	Scooters India Ltd.	5.344 (0.771)	0.375 (0.429)	0.02	0.18
	Two and Three wheelers Sector	**25.512 (8.442)**	**-0.487 (3.280)***	**0.43**	**36.38**
	Whole Automobile Industry	**18.935 (5.030)**	**-0.234 (3.072)***	**0.48**	**51.26**

Notes: Figures in brackets are t values; * significant at 5 per cent level.
Source: Computed.

trend co-efficient, confirms this as these are observed to be statistically significant. Statistically significant negative values of b indicate strong negative relationship between profitability and time over the study period. Table further reveals that b assumes different values (negative) for different industries and ranges in value from -0.50 for Tata Motors Ltd to -6.50 for Hero Honda Motors Ltd during the study period this implies that profitability of different industries declined at different rates over this period.

Only in case of two industries viz., Ashok Leyland Ltd and Scooters India Ltd, the sign for b, the time trend co-efficient is positive, implying a tendency of profit rate to rise over time. However b being statistically non significant, the results are not discussed. In case of eight industries, no definite trend could be observed as the results are statistically non significant. The value of co-efficient of determination, R^2, varied in case of industries having strong declining tendency of profit rate over time, from 0.39 for TVS Motors Company Ltd to 0.92 for Maharastra Scooters Ltd. Such great variation in the value of R^2 implies that time explain profitability variation of different industries in different degree over the time. This means that time explain variations in profitability of the above two industries to the extent of 39 per cent and 92 per cent respectively over the study period.

Sector wise time trend regression results are also presented in Table 5.11. It may be noted from the table that out of three sectors shown, commercial vehicles and two and three wheelers sectors, as well as whole automobile industry, all had a strong

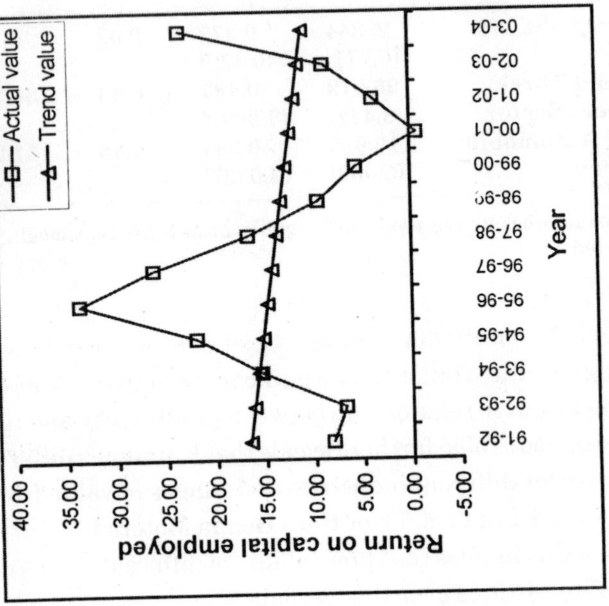

Passenger Cars and Multiutility Vehicles

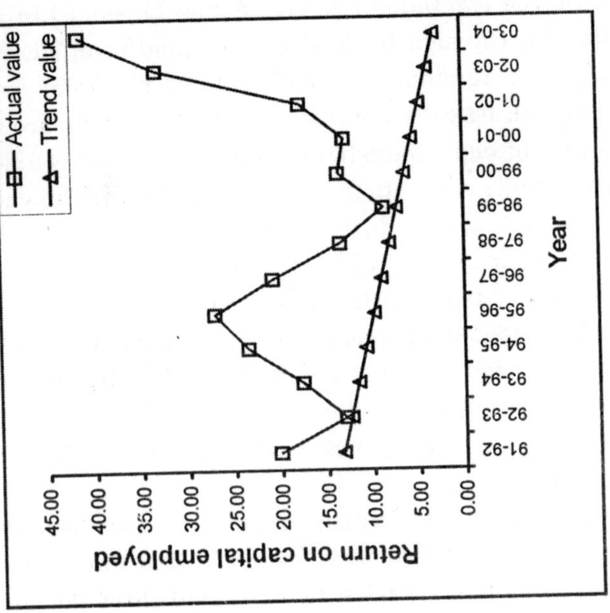

Commercial Vehicles

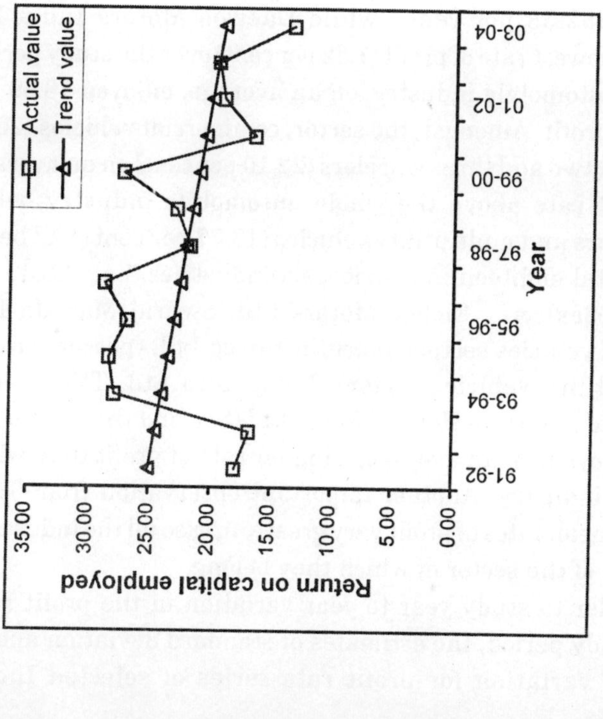

Two and Three Wheelers

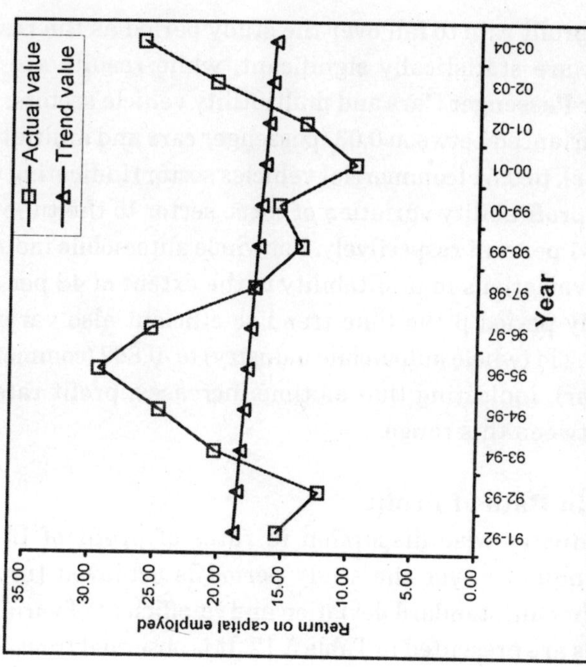

Industry Average

Profitability Trends in Indian Automobile Industry

Figure-III

tendency for profit rate to fall over the study period as the results for R^2 and β, are statistically significant, while results are non significant for Passenger Cars and multiutility vehicle sectors. The value of R^2 varianced between 0.03 (passenger cars and multiutility vehicles sector), to 0.51 (commercial vehicles sector) indicating that time explain profitability variation of these sector to the tune of 3 per cent and 51 per cent respectively. For whole automobile industry time explain variations in profitability to the extent of 48 per cent over the study period β the time trend co-efficient also varies in value from - 0.234 (whole automobile industry) to -0.862 (commercial vehicles sector), indicating that as time increases, profit rates of sector fall between this range.

Dispersion in Rate of Profit

The industry-wise dispersion in rates of profit of Indian automobile industry over the study period is achieved through estimation of mean, standard deviation and co-efficient of variation. The estimates are presented in Table 5.12. It is observed from Table 5.12 that on an average, Hero Honda Motors Ltd experienced highest profit rate (52.58 per cent), while Daewoo Motors India Ltd experienced lowest rate of profit (1.82 per cent) over the study period. The whole automobile industry, on an average, enjoyed 18.69 per cent rate of profit. Amongst, the sector, commercial vehicles (20.21 per cent) and two and three wheelers (22.10 per cent) on an average, had a profit rate above the whole automobile industry, while passenger cars and multiutility vehicles (13.77 per cent) had below it. Out of total eighteen industries, six industries, i.e., (33.33 per cent industries) viz., Eicher Motors Ltd, Swaraj Mazada Ltd. (commercial vehicles sector), Maruthi Udyog Ltd. (passenger cars and multiutility vehicles sector), Bajaj Auto Ltd, TVS Motors Company Ltd and Hero Honda Motors Ltd (two and three wheelers sectors), enjoyed, on an average, a higher rate of profit than whole automobile industry. Another important observation from Table 5.12 is that mean rates of profit vary greatly in case all the industries, irrespective of the sector of which they belong.

In order to study year to year variation in the profit rates over the study period, the estimates of standard deviation and co-efficient of variation for profit rate series of selected Indian

Table 5.12
Industry wise Variations in Profitability of Indian automobile Sector
(1991-92 - 2003-04)

S. No	*Industry*	*Mean*	*S.D*	*CV*
1.	Ashok Leyland Ltd.	12.50	3.70	0.30
2.	Tata Motors Ltd.	16.66	11.06	0.66
3.	Bajaj Tempo Ltd.	16.54	14.71	0.89
4.	Eicher Motors Ltd.	22.89	13.95	0.61
5.	Swaraj Mazda Ltd.	25.36	23.61	0.93
	Commercial Vehicles Sector	**20.21**	**9.18**	**0.45**
6.	Hindustan Motors Ltd.	7.73	8.39	1.09
7.	Mahindra and Mahindra Ltd.	16.67	6.41	0.38
8.	Maruthi Udyog Ltd.	28.61	22.41	0.78
9.	Daewoo Motors India Ltd.	1.82	5.86	3.22

(Contd.)

(Contd. Table 5.12)

S. No	Industry	Mean	S.D	CV
	Passenger Cars and Multiulity Vehicles Sector	**13.77**	**10.11**	**0.73**
10.	Bajaj Auto Ltd.	28.27	11.57	0.41
11.	LML Ltd.	11.50	7.00	0.61
12.	Maharastra Scooters Ltd.	17.72	12.99	0.73
13.	TVS Motors Company Ltd.	40.99	16.86	0.41
14.	Kinetic Motors Co. Ltd.	15.49	13.36	0.86
15.	Hero Honda Motors Ltd.	52.58	26.95	0.51
16.	Kinetic Engineering Ltd.	13.37	9.61	0.72
17.	Majestic Auto Ltd.	10.42	9.45	0.91
18.	Scooters India Ltd.	7.97	11.38	1.43
	Two and Three Wheelers Sector	**22.10**	**5.27**	**0.24**
	Whole Automobile Industry	**18.69**	**6.12**	**0.33**

Source: Computed from annual reports of the respective industries.

automobile industries are worked out and presented in Table 5.12. These measures reveal the extent of variation of actual values of profit rate of each industry from its mean value of the series. The higher values of co-efficient of variation indicate larger dispersion among the profit rate series of respective industries and vice-versa. Ashok Leyland Ltd, with co-efficient of variation being 0.30 experienced the lowest variation in profit rates over the study period while Daewoo Motors Ltd, with the lowest mean profit rate suffered from the largest dispersions, co-efficient variation assuming value equal to 3.22. Among the sector, two and three wheelers sector had the lowest variations in profit rates (CV = 0.24) while passenger cars and multiutility vehicles sectors suffered from the largest variation (CV = 0.73) during the study period.

The selected automobile industries are dividend arbitrarily into relatively stable (CV with value up to 0.25), moderately fluctuating (CV laying between 0.251 and 0.500), highly fluctuating (CV lying between 0.501 and 0.750) and erratically fluctuating (CV above 0.750), then it is observed from Table 5.12 that majority of the industries, eight out of eighteen industries (44.44 per cent) experienced erratically fluctuating variations in profit rate series. These industries are Bajaj Tempo Ltd and Swaraj Mazda Ltd (commercial vehicles), Hindustan Motors Ltd, Maruthi Udyog Ltd, Daewoo Motors India Ltd (passenger cars and multiutility vehicles) and Kinetic Engineering Ltd, Majestic Auto Ltd and Scooters India Ltd (two and three wheelers). Six out of eighteen industries (33.33 per cent) experienced highly fluctuating variations in profit rate series. These industries are Tata Motors Ltd and Eicher Motors Ltd (commercial vehicles) LML Ltd, Maharastra Scooters Ltd, Hero Honda Motors Ltd and Kinetic Engineering Ltd (two and three wheelers). Four out of eighteen industries (22.23 per cent) experienced moderately fluctuating variations in profit rate series. These industries are Ashok Leyland Ltd (commercial vehicles) Mahindra and Mahindra Ltd (passenger cars and multiutility vehicles) and Bajaj Auto Ltd and TVS Motors Company Ltd (two and three wheelers). As far as the whole automobile industry variations are concerned, it experienced moderately fluctuating series of profit rates over the study period.

Determinants of Profitability

The question of determination of profit is of great importance. The profit of a business may be measured by studying the profitability of investment in it. Profitability is a relative term and its measurement can be achieved by profit and its relation with the other objects by which the profit is effected. It is the test of efficiency, powerful motivational factor and the measure of control in any business. Actually profitability is highly sensitive economic variable which is affected by a host of factors operating through a variety of ways. Some of them affect product prices and quantities, some affect the cost of production while others make changes in capital stock, size, market share and growth of the firm. Further, corporate policy relating to various functions will affect profitability. Some of them are relevant in short run while others have impact in the long run. It is doubtful to build a theory of profitability, which accounts for all such factors. Because of these difficulties, it is quite natural to analyse the variation in profitability by taking the partial approach i.e., to find the effect of certain major variables, ignoring the implications of other left out independent variables at a time. In this part an attempt is made to identify the major determinants of profitability in Indian automobile industry with the help of empirical data for the year 1991-92 to 2003-04.

There are a number of cross sectional studies which provide direct evidence about the determinants of profitability. These studies include Shepherd (1972), Berry (1975), Agarwal V.K. (1978), Ramachandran (1980), Chaudhury (1982), Clarkson & Miller (1982), Ravenscraft (1983), Hay & Morris (1979), Narayana (1984), Amato Swilder (1985), Agarwal, R.N. (1987), Chandrasekaran (1993), Sidhu & Bhatia (1998). Vijayakumar (2002) and Vijayakumar and Kathirvel (2003). The review of above empirical works facilitates to understand various structural and non-structural variables that determine profitability. It gives an idea of extensive and diversed works on determinants of profitability.

The objective of this part is to examine determinants of profitability of Indian automobile industry during the period 1991-92 to 2003-04. Determinants of profitability are analysed using the technique of ordinary least squares. Based on existing theories and relevant econometric empirical works, variables are selected. The variables occurring in the models and their measurement are described in methodology. While using the regression technique, efforts are made to reduce the problem of multi-collinearity and auto correlation.

Specification of Profitability Model

In order to explain the profitability of selected sectors of Indian automobile industry, the model specified for estimating profitability function is as follows:

$$P = b_0 + b_1 S + b_2 L + b_3 CR + b_4 ITR + b_5 FATR + b_6 OESR + b_7 VI + b_8 PP + b_9 GRA$$

Where,

S	- Size
L	- Leverage
CR	- Current Ratio
ITR	- Inventory Turnover Ratio
FATR	- Fixed Assets Turnover Ratio
OESR	- Operating Expenses to Sales Ratio
VI	- Vertical Integration
PP	- Past Profitability
GRA	- Growth Rate of Assets

The model was estimated using ordinary least square method, while estimating, checks were made for model violation such as multicollinarity.

Analysis of Results

The model described above has been estimated for all the selected sectors of automobile industry and whole industry and the results are presented in Table 5.13 to 5.14. It presents beta coefficient and t values of the variables.

Whole Industry

For the whole automobile industry, model explains 99 percentage of variation in profitability of firms included in the industry (Table 5.13.) The analysis shows that all the variables except past profitability are found to be statistically significant in explaining

Table 5.13
Determinants of Profitability in Indian Automobile Industry- Multiple Regression Model
[Dependent Variable: Ratio of Profit Margin on Sales (P)]
[P = 32.59 + 16.48 S-0.49 L + 10.79 CR – 0.71 ITR – 3.57 FATR – 9.76 OESR + 13.05 VI – 0.07 PP + 0.20 GRA]

Variables	*Beta Co-efficient*	*t value*	*Significant /Not Significant*
Constant	32.59	2.878	
Size (S)	16.48	3.625*	Significant
Leverage (L)	-0.49	1.648**	Significant
Current Ratio (CR)	10.79	3.472*	Significant
Inventory Turnover Ratio (ITR)	-0.71	3.215*	Significant
Fixed Assets Turnover Ratio (FATR)	- 3.57	4.416*	Significant
Operating Expenses to Sales Ratio (OESR)	-9.76	4.316*	Significant
Vertical Integration (VI)	13.05	5.759*	Significant
Past Profitability (PP)	-0.07	0.705	Not Significant
Growth Rate of Assets (GRA)	0.20	6.054*	Significant
R^2 = 0.99			
Adj R^2 = 0.95			
F = 27.30			
D.W = 2.03			

D.W - Durbin - Watson statistics; * - significant at 0.05 level; ** - significant at 0.10 level
Source: Computed.

profitability of Indian automobile industry. It is evident from the results that size is stronger determinant of profitability followed by vertical integration, current ratio, growth rate of assets, past profitability, leverage, inventory turnover ratio, fixed assets turnover ratio and operating expenses to sales ratio. As expected size, leverage, operation expenses to sales ratio, vertical integration and growth rate of assets did support our hypothesis with the expected sign. However the co-efficient of current ratio, inventory turnover ratio, fixed assets turnover ratio and post profitability did not support our hypothesis rather these appear with opposite sign.

It is evident from the result that co-efficient of size shows the increase of 16.48 per cent in profitability as a result of one per cent increase in size, which is statistically significant at 5 per cent level. The co-efficient of leverage indicates that a decrease of 0.49 per cent in profitability as a result of one per cent increase in leverage which is significant at 10 per cent level. It is appeared from the result that value of one per cent increase in current ratio resulted in 10.79 per cent increase in profitability, which is significant at 5 per cent level. Further, one per cent increase in inventory turnover ratio, fixed assets turnover ratio and operating expenses to sales ratio shows 0.71 per cent, 3.57 per cent and 9.76 per cent decrease in profitability respectively during the study period. All these co-efficients are statistically significant. It is also apparent from the table that co-efficient of vertical integration and growth rate of assets show 13.05 per cent and 0.20 per cent increases in profitability as the result of one per cent increase, which is significant at 5 per cent level. However, the co-efficient of past profitability shows that 0.07 per cent decrease in profitability as a result of one per cent increase in past profitability. This is not statistically significant.

The overall explanatory power of regression appears to be good. This may be inferred from the co-efficient of determination (R^2) which is the measure of extent of movement in the dependent variable that is explained by the independent variables. It is 99 per cent and the adjusted explanation is around 95 per cent.

Commercial Vehicles

For the commercial vehicles, model explains 94 percentage of variation in profitability of firms included in the industry (Table 5.14). The analysis shows that all the variables except current ratio and growth rate of assets are found to be statistically significant in explaining profitability of commercial vehicles sector. It is evident from the results that size is stronger determinant of profitability followed by vertical integration, fixed assets turnover ratio, past profitability, growth rate of assets, inventory turnover ratio, leverage, current ratio and operating expenses to sales ratio. As expected size, leverage, current ratio, fixed assets turnover ratio, operating expenses to sales ratio, vertical integration and past profitability did support our hypothesis with the expected sign.

Table 5.14
Determinants of Profitability in Commercial Vehicles Sector- Multiple Regression Model

[Dependent Variable: Ratio of profit margin on sales (P)]
[P = - 26.09 + 16.11 S – 0.98 L - 14.38 CR – 0.18 ITR + 5.27 FATR - 30.63 OESR + 13.32 VI + 0.38 PP - 0.02 GRA]

Variables	*Beta Co-efficient*	*t value*	*Significant / Not significant*
Constant	-26.09	2.275	
Size (S)	16.11	2.922*	Significant
Leverage (L)	-0.98	2.611*	Significant
Current Ratio (CR)	-14.38	1.398	Not significant
Inventory Turnover Ratio (ITR)	-0.18	2.062*	Significant
Fixed Assets Turnover Ratio (FATR)	5.27	3.154*	Significant
Operating Expenses to Sales Ratio (OESR)	-30.63	3.276*	Significant
Vertical Integration (VI)	13.32	1.967**	Significant
Past Profitability (PP)	0.38	2.331**	Significant
Growth Rate of Assets (GRA)	-0.02	1.226	Not significant

R^2 = 0.94
Adj R^2 = 0.77
F = 15.38
D.W = 2.16

D.W - Durbin - Watson statistics; * - significant at 0.05 level; ** - significant at 0.10 level
Source: Computed

However the co-efficient of inventory turnover ratio and growth rate of assets did not support our hypothesis rather these appear with opposite sign.

It is evident from the results that co-efficient of size shows the increase of 16.11 per cent in profitability as a result of one Percent increase in size, which is statistically significant at 5 per cent level. Further, one per cent increase in leverage, current ratio and inventory turnover ratio shows 0.98 per cent, 14.38 per cent and 0.18 per cent decrease in profitability respectively during the study period. All these co-efficient are statistically significant except current ratio. The co-efficient of fixed assets turnover ratio shows the increase of 5.27 per cent in profitability as a result of one per cent increase in fixed assets turnover ratio, which statistically significant at 5 per cent level. The co-efficient of operating expenses to sales ratio decrease in 30.63 per cent in profitability as a result of one per cent increase in operating expenses to sales ratio which is significant at 5 per cent level. Further one per cent increase in vertical integration and past profitability shows 13.32 per cent and 0.38 per cent increase in profitability respectively during the study period. All these co-efficient are statistically significant at 10 per cent level. However, the co-efficient of growth rate of assets shows that 0.02 per cent decrease in profitability as a result of one per cent increase in growth rate of assets. This is not statistically significant.

The overall explanatory power of regression appears to be good. This may be inferred from the co-efficient of determination (R^2) which is the measure of extent of movement in the dependent variable that is explained by the independent variables. It is 94 per cent and adjusted explanation is around 77 per cent.

Passenger Cars and Multiutility Vehicles

For the passenger cars and multiutility vehicles, model explains 95 percentage of variation in profitability of firms included in the industry (Table 5.15). The analysis shows that all the variables except past profitability are found to be statistically significant in explaining profitability of passenger cars and multiutility vehicles sectors. It is evident from the results that size is the strongest determinant of profitability followed by current ratio, fixed assets turnover ratio, past profitability, growth rate of assets, leverage, inventory turnover ratio, vertical integration and operating expenses to sales ratio. As expected size, leverage, fixed assets turnover ratio, operating expenses to sales ratio and past profitability did support our hypothesis with the expected sign. However the co-efficient of current ratio, inventory turnover ratio, vertical integration and

Table 5.15
Determinants of Profitability in Passenger Cars and Multiutility Vehicles sector - Multiple Regression Model

[Dependent Variable: Ratio of profit margin on sales (P)]
[P = 256.59 + 84.36 S - 2.63 L + 20.89 CR - 3.35 ITR + 9.01 FATR - 497.41 OESR - 482.28 VI + 0.13 PP - 0.98 GRA]

Variables	*Beta Co-efficient*	*t value*	*Significant / Not Significant*
Constant	256.59	2.488	
Size (S)	84.36	2.682*	Significant
Leverage (L)	-2.63	1.683**	Significant
Current Ratio (CR)	20.89	1.787**	Significant
Inventory Turnover Ratio (ITR)	-3.35	2.843*	Significant
Fixed Assets Turnover Ratio (FATR)	9.01	2.369*	Significant
Operating Expenses to Sales Ratio (OESR)	-497.41	3.062*	Significant
Vertical Integration (VI)	-482.28	2.992*	Significant
Past profitability (PP)	0.13	0.274	Not Significant
Growth Rate of Assets (GRA)	-0.98	3.046*	Significant

R^2 = 0.95
Adj R^2 = 0.79
F = 11.02
D.W = 1.93

D.W - Durbin - Watson statistics ; * - significant at 0.05 level; ** - significant at 0.10 level
Source: Computed

growth rate of assets did not support our hypothesis rather these appear with opposite sign.

It is evident from the results that co-efficient of size shows the increase of 84.36 per cent in profitability as a result of one per cent increase in size, which is statistically significant at 5 per cent level. The co-efficient of leverage indicates that a decrease at 2.63 per cent in profitability as a result of one per cent increase in leverage which is significant at 10 per cent level. It is appeared from the result that value of one per cent increase in current ratio resulted in 20.89 per cent increase in profitability, which is statistically significant at 10 per cent level. Further, one per cent increase in inventory turnover ratio, operating expenses to sales ratio, vertical integration and growth rate of assets shows 3.35 per cent, 497.41 per cent, 482.28 per cent and 0.98 per cent decrease in profitability respectively during the study period. All these co-efficient are statistically significant. It is evident from the result that value of one per cent increase in fixed assets turnover ratio resulted in 9.01 per cent increase in profitability, which is significant at 5 per cent level. However, the co-efficient of past profitability shows that 0.13 per cent increase in profitability as a result of one per cent increase in past profitability. This is not statistically significant.

The overall explanatory power of regression appears to be good. This may be inferred from the co-efficient of determination (R^2) which is the measure of extent of movement in the dependent variable that is explained by the independent variables. It is 95 per cent and adjusted explanation is around 79 per cent.

Two and Three Wheelers

For the two and three wheelers, model explains 94 percentage of variation in profitability of firms included in the industry (Table 5.16). The analysis shows that all the variable except leverage and growth rate of assets are found to be statically significant in explaining profitability of two and three wheelers sector. It is evident from the results that size is stronger determinant of profitability followed by inventory turnover ratio, past profitability, growth rate of assets, leverage, vertical integration, fixed assets turnover ratio, operating expenses to sales ratio and current ratio. As expected size, leverage, current ratio, inventory turnover ratio, operating expenses to sales ratio and past profitability did support our hypothesis with the expected sign. However the co-efficient of fixed assets turnover ratio, vertical integration and growth rate of assets did not support our hypothesis rather these appear with opposite sign.

It is evident from the results that co-efficient of size shows the increase of 23.53 per cent in profitability as a result of one per cent increase in size, which is statistically significant at 5 per cent

Table 5.16
Determinants of Profitability in Two and Three Wheelers Sector- Multiple Regression Model

[Dependent Variable: Ratio of Profit Margin on Sales (P)]

[P = 70.63 + 23.53 S – 1.41 L – 37.66 CR + 3.72 ITR – 5.53 FATR - 29.34 OESR – 3.71 VI + 1.33 PP - 0.03 GRA]

Variables	*Beta Co-efficient*	*t value*	*Significant / Not Significant*
Constant	70.63	2.112	
Size (S)	23.53	1.998**	Significant
Leverage (L)	-1.41	0.634	Not significant
Current Ratio (CR)	- 37.66	2.364*	Significant
Inventory Turnover Ratio (ITR)	3.72	2.268**	Significant
Fixed Assets Turnover Ratio (FATR)	-5.53	1.667**	Significant
Operating Expenses to Sales Ratio (OESR)	- 29.34	1.639**	Significant
Vertical Integration (VI)	-3.71	1.652**	Significant
Past Profitability (PP)	1.33	3.682*	Significant
Growth Rate of Assets (GRA)	-0.03	0.647	Not Significant

R^2 = 0.94
Adj R^2 = 0.75
F = 11.65
D.W = 2.12

D.W-Durbin -Watson statistics; * - significant at 0.05 level; **- significant at 0.10 level
Source: Computed.

level. The co-efficient of leverage indicates that a decrease of 1.41 per cent in profitability as a result of one per cent increase in leverage. This is not statistically significant. It is appeared from the result that a decrease of 37.66 per cent in profitability as a result at one per cent increase in current ratio, which is statistically significant at 5 per cent level. It is also apparent from the table that co-efficient of inventory turnover ratio and past profitability shows

3.72 per cent and 1.33 per cent increase in profitability as the result of one per cent increase, which is statistically significant. Further, one per cent increase in fixed assets turnover ratio, operating expenses to sales ratio and vertical integration shows 5.53 per cent, 29.34 per cent and 3.71 per cent decreases in profitability respectively during the study period. All these co-efficients are statistically significant at 10 per cent level. However, the co-efficient of growth rate of assets shows that 0.03 per cent decrease in profitability as a result of one per cent increase in growth rate of assets. This is not statistically significant.

The overall explanatory power of regression appears to be good. This may be inferred from the co-efficient of determination (R^2) which is the measure of extent of movement in the dependent variable that is explained by the independent variables. It is 94 per cent and the adjusted explanation is around 75 per cent.

References

1. J.P. Bradley (1968). Administrative Financial Management (New York: Holt Rinechart and Winston, Inc.), p. 173.
2. Duck R.E.V. and Jervis, F.R.J. (1964). Management Accounting, George G. Harrap & Company, p. 98.
3. N.P. Agarwal (1981). Analysis of Financial statements: A case study of Aluminium Industry in India, National Publishing House, New Delhi.
4. R.S. Kulshreshtha, Profitability in India's Steel Industry-During the decade 1960-70 (A thesis submitted for the degree of Ph.D., Dept. of E.A.F.M. University of Rajashthan, 1973), p. 83.
5. Howard and Upton (1961). Introduction to Business finance. (New York: Mcgraw Hill), p.150.
6. Slavin.A, et al. (1968). Basic Accounting for Management and Financial control (New York : Holt, Rinshart and Winsron, Inc.,), p. 173.
7. Stanev quoted in the Charted Accountant, May 1975.
8. James C.Van Horne (1978). Fundamentals of Financial Management, (New Delhi: Prentice Hall), p. 40.
9. Ibid., p.43.
10. Waston J.F and. Brigham E.F (1978). Managerial Finance (6th Edn. The Dryden Press, Hinsdale. Illinois), p.148.

11. Anthony R.N and Reece J.S. (1975). Management Accounting Principles (Home wood, Illinois, Richard D.Irwin, Inc.,), p.245.
12. Ralph, D.Kennedy, and Stewart, M. (1968). Financial Statement (Home Wood III; Richard D.Irwin, Inc.), p.404.
13. Khan M.Y and Jain P.K (1996). Financial Management, (New Delhi: Tata McGraw-Hill Publishing Co., Ltd.), p.139.
14. Pandey I.M (1980). Concept of Earning Power, Accounting Journal, Vol.W, (Rajastan Accounting Association), p.46.
15. Lawrence J. Gitman (1982). Principles of Management Finance (New York, Herper & Row Publishers), p. 204.
16. Ibid., p. 204.
17. James C. Van Horne (1981). Fundamentals of Financial Management (New Delhi, Prentice Hall), p. 155.
18. Pandey. I.M. (1996). Financial Management (New Delhi, Vikas Publishing House Private Ltd.,), p. 449.
19. John Sizer (1979). An insight in to the Management Accounting (London; Pitman), p.170.
20. Pandey I.M., op. cit., p. 552.

6

Analysis of Financial Structure and Financial Strength

Analysis of Financial Structure

Accounting regarding the "Financial structure of a business consists of three elements: assets, liabilities and capital. The financial structure provides an insight in to the various types of sources tapped to finance, the total assets employed in a business enterprise. That part of financial structure which represents long-term sources is known as capital structure. Since the balance sheet is a detailed form of the fundamental, or structure equation, it is set for the financial structure of an enterprise. It states the nature and amount of each of the various assets, liabilities and property interest of the owner or owners. Stating the nature of the assets, liabilities and capital is not so difficult as stating their amounts. The financial structure can be made initially from the point of view of the time for which funds are needed. It includes both the sources of finance, i.e., long term and short term. Thus financial structure refers to the makeup of permanent capital of firm.

Over the past, many researchers have tried to establish the factors which influence a firm's financial structure. The association between a firm's financial structure and its size, profitability similar other operating characteristics have gained considerable importance. Some of them have presented affirmative evidences in respect of a particular factor or a group of factors as determinant of corporate financial structure, others have presented dissenting evidences in respect of the same factor or factors to be a clear determinant of financial structure. Scott[1] and Scott et al[2] presented empirical evidences claiming that industrial class has got influence on the firm's financial structure. Remmers, et al[3] in their study, however, presented dissenting evidence arguing that neither size nor industry class is a clear determinant of the firm's financial structure. Therefore in this part an attempt has been made to study the corporate financial structure relationship with reference to size, profitability, operating leverage, external financing and income gearing. Attempts are also made here to offer an econometric interpretation to the factors which determine the financial structure of selected Indian automobile industry. Testing of the hypothesis, formulated in chapter I thus falls within the scope of discussion of this chapter.

Financial Leverage and Industry Class

The first hypothesis relates to the possible association between industry class and financial structure. Firms in the same industry should experience similar amount of business risk because they produce similar products, incur similar set of rules, regulations, guidelines and environment. Since business risk has got relationship with the types of product, and the product with types of industries, there is reason to believe that a firm's financial structure is influenced by its industrial classification. The same logic should also hold good for inter-industry comparison. Since industries deal with different products, operate under different environment, rely on different technology, have different cost structure, their business risks should essentially be different. As such, their financial structures should also be different.

To test whether the financial leverage of selected sectors of Indian automobile industry significantly differs, Analysis of Variance (ANOVA) has been applied and result of which is displayed in Table 6.1. It is evident from Table 6.1 that F ratio (82.62) is much higher than the table value of F (3.40) at 5 per cent level of significance.

This indicates that the means of the financial leverages of the selected sectors of Indian automobile industry differ significantly. Thus the null hypothesis that financial leverage is independent of industrial class is rejected leading to the conclusion that financial leverage depends upon industrial class.

Financial Leverage and Size

Large firms are generally more diversified, enjoy easier access to capital markets, receive higher credit ratings, and pay lower rates of interest on borrowed capital. Moreover as the level of activity increases with size, more debt is expected in the financial structure of large corporations. Hence, size of the firm should be positively related to its financial structure. The same logic should also hold good for inter-industry variations. In order to test the validity of the second null hypothesis that financial leverage and industry size are independent, correlation co-efficient between financial leverage and industry size have been calculated for all the three sectors namely commercial vehicles, passenger cars and multiutility

Table 6.1

Analysis of Variance (ANOVA) for Financial Leverages of Indian Automobile Industry

Sectors	*Mean*	*No. of items*
Commercial Vehicles	0.468	13
Passenger Cars and Multiutility Vehicles	0.542	13
Two and Three Wheelers	0.268	13
Mean	0.425	13

Source of variations	*Sum of squares*	*Df*	*Mean square*	*F ratio*	*F Value (at 5%)*
Between the years	0.238	12	0.019	6.27	2.18
Between the sectors	0.522	2	0.261	82.62	3.40
Error	0.076	24	0.003		
Total	0.836	38			

Source : Computed.

vehicles, two and three wheelers and whole industry during the study period. To test the significance of correlation co-efficient, t values have also been computed.

Table 6.2 exhibits details of empirical results found in respect of the hypothesis concerning financial leverage and industry size. It is apparent from Table 6.2 that not only there exists positive correlations between financial leverages and industry size but also the relations are statistically significant at 5 per cent level in case of all the sectors and whole industry during the study period. Therefore, the null hypothesis that leverage is independent of industry size is rejected and hence concluded that size has got bearing on financial structure.

Financial Leverage and Profitability

The third hypothesis is pertaining to the relationship between a firm's profitability and its financial structure. A firm's ability to generate internal surpluses for business expansion depends upon its earning capacity. A more profitable firm may be considered to be in a better position to generate internal funds by way of reserves and surpluses. As reserves and surpluses will grow, the firm's dependence on external financing will decline, and consequently its dependence on dept capital too. This is because, a firm going for external funds will certainly prefer low-cost source and debt will be the first choice. Hence, a negative relationship should exist between a firm's financial leverage and its profitability. This phenomenon should also be true for industry level comparison, for profitability differs from industry to industry. In order to test the validity for the null hypothesis that financial leverage and profitability are independent of each other, correlation co-efficient between financial leverage and profitability have been calculated along with t value for all the three sectors and whole industry and empirical results are presented in Table 6.2.

It is evident from the Table 6.2 that the existence of negative correlation between financial leverage and profitability in commercial vehicles, two and three wheelers and whole industry and also the relation are statistically significant at 5 per cent level. Although empirical evidences indicate the existence of negative correlation between financial leverage and profitability in passenger cars and multiutility vehicles sector the relations could not be found statistically significant. Thus the null hypothesis that financial leverage is independent of profitability is rejected and concluded that there exists negative correlation between them.

Financial Leverage and Operating Leverage

The fourth hypothesis relates to the suspected influence of operating leverage on financial structure. Ferri and Jones[4] define operating leverage as "the use of fixed costs in the firm's production scheme but is generally associated with the employment of fixed assets". According to them, the use of fixed assets can magnify the variability of the firm's future income and hence, "operating leverage should be negatively related to the firm's financial structure". Determining the validity of this hypothesis in case of Indian automobile industry was thus the purpose of the fourth test. In order to test the validity of the null hypothesis that financial leverage and operating leverage have got no association between them, correlation co-efficient between financial leverages and operating leverages have been calculated along with t value for all the three sectors of automobile industry and whole industry and empirical results are presented in Table 6.2.

In case of Indian automobile industry, however a definite conclusion could not be reached as far as the relationship between operating leverage and financial leverage is concerned. Empirical evidences from Table 6.2 show that there exists negative correlation between operating leverage and financial leverage in case of commercial vehicles, passenger cars and multiutility vehicles and whole industry but also the relationships are statistically significant at 5 per cent level. Interestingly in case of two and three wheelers positive correlation between financial leverage and operating leverage, could not be found statistically significant. Thus, the null hypothesis that operating leverage and financial leverage are independent of each other could not be fully rejected in the sense there exists both negative as well as positive correlation between them in different sectors in the same period.

Financial Leverage and External Financing

The fifth hypothesis relates to the association between the external financing and financial structure. Generally firms prepare internal to external financing and they will prefer the safest security first, i.e., they will choose debt before equity financing, in case they seek external financing to finance real investments with a positive net present value. This implies that when external financing will increase, the proportion of debt in the total financing will also increase. Hence there should exist, a positive relationship between external financing and firm's financial leverage. This logic should also be valid for inter- industry comparison.

Empirical evidence from Table 6.2 shows that there exists a strong and statistically significant positive relationship between financial leverage and external financing in case of commercial vehicles, two and three wheelers and whole industry. The Table 6.2 further shows that the existence of negative significant correlation between financial leverage and external financing in case of passenger cars and multiutility vehicles sector. Thus the null hypothesis that financial leverage and external financing are independent of each other could not be fully rejected in the sense there exists both positive as well as negative correlation between them in different industry in the same period.

Financial Leverage and Income Gearing

The sixth and the last hypothesis relates to the possible association between income gearing and a firm's financial leverage. Income gearing is considered to be a measure of corporate vulnerability to fluctuations in general economic conditions[5]. Since firms operate under different economic conditions,and economic conditions have bearing on capital as well as debt markets, there should exist relationship between income gearing and a firm's financial leverage.

Empirical evidence from Table 6.2 shows that there exists a statistically significant positive relationship between income gearing and corporate financial structure in case of passenger cars and multiutility vehicles, two and three wheelers and whole industry. In case of commercial vehicles, the relations though positive is found to be statistically insignificant. Thus, while rejecting the null hypothesis that there is no association between income gearing and financial leverage, it may conclude that income gearing and financial leverage are positively correlated.

Table 6.2
Statement showing correlation coefficients, t-values and levels of significance of financial leverage and different factors

Industry class	*Correlation between*	*r-value*	*t value*	*Significant / Not significant*
Commercial Vehicles	FL and size	0.475	9.36*	Significant
	FL and profit	-0.641	2.73*	Significant
	FL and ol	-0.440	2.42*	Significant
	FL and ef	0.694	11.28*	Significant
	FL and ig	0.280	1.38	Not Significant
Passenger Cars and Multiutility Vehicles	FL and size	0.028	6.51*	Significant
	FL and profit	-0.795	1.11	Not Significant
	FL and ol	-0.429	1.87*	Significant
	FL and ef	-0.192	8.71*	Significant
	FL and ig	0.570	2.14	Significant
Two and Three Wheelers	FL and size	0.566	5.96*	Significant
	FL and profit	-0.705	7.65*	Significant
	FL and ol	0.064	0.58	Not significant
	FL and ef	0.933	7.43*	Significant
	FL and ig	0.479	6.17*	Significant
Whole Industry	FL and size	0.540	7.61*	Significant
	FL and profit	-0.733	3.72*	Significant
	FL and ol	-0.402	2.23*	Significant
	FL and ef	0.565	9.58*	Significant
	FL and ig	0.591	2.59*	Significant

FL - Financial Leverage profit - profitability
ol - operating leverage ef - external financing
ig - income gearing
* - Significant of at 0.05 level
Source: Computed.

Determinants of Financial Structure-econometric Analysis

In this part an attempt is made to measure the degree of relationship that exists between a firm's financial structure and the different factors which have bearing on the financial structure. The objective of this discussion is to examine the determinants of financial structure in the selected sectors of Indian automobile industry during the study period. Based on earlier empirical studies, the specific factors are chosen for analyzing determinants of financial structure in Indian automobile industry. The specific factors, which have been taken in to consideration are Payout Ratio (PR), Operating Leverage (OL), Size (S), Profitability (PROFIT), External Financing (EF) and Income Gearing (IG). These factors have been taken as the independent variables and Financial Leverage (FL) as the dependent variable. Multiple regression analysis has been applied to measure the effects of the independent variables on the dependent variable. The model to be estimated using from specific cross section data proposed is as follows :

$$\mathbf{FL = bo + b_1\,PR + b_2\,OL + b_3\,S + b_4\,PROFIT + b_5\,EF + b_6\,IG.}$$

The results of the regression analysis in respect of whole industry, commercial vehicles, passenger cars and multitulity vehicles and two and three wheelers have been presented through Table 6.3 to Table 6.6.

Whole Industry

Analysis of the regression results of Indian automobile industry (Table 6.3) reveals that the adjusted R^2 is 0.88 and the F ratio is significant, which implies that the independent variables collectively explain 88 percentage of the total variations in the dependent variable. The analysis shows that variables like operating leverage, size, profitability, external financing and income gearing which are found to be statistically significant in explaining financial structure of Indian automobile industry. However the other variable namely payout ratio is found to be statistically insignificant in explaining financial structure of Indian automobile industry. As far as the importance of individual variables are concerned, size followed by external financing, operating leverage, profitability and income gearing are found to be the most important factors explaining the variations in the financial structure of Indian automobile industry during the study period. The results thus indicate that the independent variables explaining the dependent variable well during the study period.

Commercial Vehicles

Analysis of regression results of the factors determining financial structure of commercial vehicles sector are presented in Table 6.4. It is evident from the table that the independent variables explain about 90 per cent variation in the dependent variable in this sector. The analysis shows that factors like payout ratio, size, profitability, external financing and income gearing are found to be

Table 6.3

Factors Determining the Financial Structure of Indian Automobile Industry - Regression Analysis

[Dependent variable-Financial Leverage (FL)]

$(FL = b_0 + b_1\ PR + b_2\ OL + b_3\ S + b_4\ PROFIT + b_5\ EF + b_6\ IG)$

Independent variables	*Regression co-efficients*	*t value*	*Significant / Not significant*
Payout Ratio (PR)	-0.0033	0.082	Not significant
Operating Leverage (OL)	-0.0023	1.442**	Significant
Size (S)	0.0001	1.412**	Significant
Profitability (PROFIT)	-0.0159	6.039*	Significant
External Financing (EF)	0.0001	2.352*	Significant
Income Gearing (IG)	-0.1460	1.973*	Significant

Constant = 0.77
Std. error of the estimate = 0.02
R^2 = 0.94
Adj R^2 = 0.88
* - Significant at 0.05 level
** - Significant at 0.10 level
Source: Computed.

ANOVA

Source of variance	*Sum of squares*	*Df*	*Mean square*	*F ratio*	*Significance*
Regression	0.0779	6	0.0129	15.66	0.002
Residual	0.0049	6	0.0008		
Total	0.0828	12			

Table 6.4
Factors Determining the Financial Structure of Commercial Vehicles - Regression Analysis

[Dependent variable - Financial Leverage (FL)]
$(FL = b_0 + b_1\ PR + b_2\ OL + b_3\ S + b_4\ PROFIT + b_5\ EF + b_6\ IG)$

Independent variables	*Regression co-efficients*	*t value*	*Significant / Not significant*
Payout Ratio (PR)	0.0336	1.682**	Significant
Operating Leverage (OL)	0.0012	0.295	Not significant
Size (S)	0.0001	2.020*	Significant
Profitability (PROFIT)	-0.0090	2.311*	Significant
External Financing (EF)	-0.0001	3.103*	Significant
Income Gearing (IG)	-0.0279	1.472**	Significant

Constant = 0.71
Std. error of the estimate = 0.04
R^2 = 0.90
Adj R^2 = 0.80
* - Significant at 0.05 level
** - Significant at 0.10 level
Source: Computed

ANOVA

Source of variance	*Sum of squares*	*Df*	*Mean square*	*F ratio*	*Significance*
Regression	0.1060	6	0.0177	8.969	0.009
Residual	0.0119	6	0.0019		
Total	0.1179	12			

statistically significant in explaining the financial structure of commercial vehicles sector. However, operating leverage is found to be statistically insignificant. It is evident from the results that payout ratio is the stronger determinant of financial structure followed by size, external financing, profitability and income gearing. The overall explanatory power of regression appears to be good. This may be inferred from the co-efficients of determinants (R^2). It is 90 per cent and the adjusted explanation is around 80 per cent.

Passenger Cars and Multiutility Vehicles

The results of analysis of the regression of passenger cars and multiutility vehicles are presented in Table 6.5. Analysis of the regression results shows that the adjusted R^2 is 0.61 and the F ratio is significant, which implies that the independent variables collectively explain 61 percentage of the total variations in the dependent variable. The analysis shows that operating leverage, size, profitability and external financing are found to be statistically significant in explaining financial structure of passenger cars and multiutility vehicles. The other factors payout ratio and income gearing are found to be statistically insignificant. It is also found that operating leverage has been the most important factor influencing the financial leverage of passenger cars and multiutility vehicles followed by size, profitability and external financing. The results thus indicate that the independent variables explain dependent variable well during the study period.

Two and Three Wheelers

The results of regression analysis of the factor determining the financial structure of two and three wheelers sector are presented

Table 6.5

Factors determining the financial structure of Passenger Cars and Multiutility Vehicles - Regression Analysis

[Dependent variable – Financial Leverage (FL)]

$(FL = b_0 + b_1\ PR + b_2\ OL + b_3\ S + b_4\ PROFIT + b_5\ EF + b_6\ IG)$

Independent variables	*Regression co-efficients*	*t value*	*Significant / Not significant*
Payout Ratio (PR)	-0.0072	0.238	Not significant
Operating Leverage (OL)	0.0018	1.529**	Significant
Size (S)	0.0002	1.823**	Significant
Profitability (PROFIT)	-0.0027	2.471*	Significant
External Financing (EF)	-0.0001	1.978*	Significant
Income Gearing (IG)	0.0969	0.841	Not significant

Constant = 0.68
Std. error of the estimate = 0.06
R^2 = 0.80
Adj R^2 = 0.61
* - Significant at 0.05 level
** - Significant at 0.10 level
Source: Computed.

ANOVA

Source of variance	*Sum of squares*	*df*	*Mean square*	*F ratio*	*Significance*
Regression	0.0915	6	0.0153	4.076	0.056
Residual	0.0224	6	0.0037		
Total	0.1139	12			

Table 6.6
Factors determining the financial structure of Two and Three Wheelers - Regression Analysis

[Dependent variable-Financial Leverage (FL)]

$$(FL = b_0 + b_1\ PR + b_2\ OL + b_3\ S + b_4\ PROFIT + b_5\ EF + b_6\ IG)$$

Independent variables	*Regression co-efficients*	*t value*	*Significant / Not Significant*
Payout Ratio (PR)	0.1290	1.463**	Significant
Operating Leverage (OL)	0.0049	1.489**	Significant
Size (S)	-0.0004	1.356**	Significant
Profitability (PROFIT)	-0.0032	0.823	Not Significant
External Financing (EF)	0.0001	1.469**	Significant
Income Gearing (IG)	0.2770	2.276*	Significant

Constant = 0.23
Std. error of the estimate = 0.02
R^2 = 0.95
Adj R^2 = 0.89
* - Significant at 0.05 level
** - Significant at 0.10 level
Source: Computed.

ANOVA

Source of variance	*Sum of squares*	*Df*	*Mean square*	*F ratio*	*Significance*
Regression	0.0821	6	0.0137	17.79	0.001
Residual	0.0046	6	0.0008		
Total	0.0867	12			

in Table 6.6. It is found from the Table 6.6 that the independent variables collectively explain about 89 per cent of the total variations in the dependent variable in two and three wheelers sector during the study period. The analysis shows that factors like payout ratio, operating leverage, size, external financing and income gearing are found to be statistically significant in explaining financial structure of two and three wheelers sector. However, profitability is found to be statistically insignificant in explaining financial structure. As far as individual variables are concerned, it is found that income gearing, followed by payout ratio, operating leverage, external financing and size are the most significant variables influencing the financial structure of two and three wheelers sector during the study period. The results also indicate that the independent variables explain the dependent variable well in two and three wheelers sector during the study period.

Analysis of Financial Strength

Financial strength may be described as one's ability to overcome or meet a financial obligation. The term financial strength has a reference to the ability of a business to meet the claims of creditors not only under current economic and business conditions but also under the unfavorable situations that may occur in future; to take advantage of business dealings or expansion which require presently owned resources, additional funds obtained through the sale of long term debt obligations and capital stock, or a favorable credit rating, and to continue interest and dividend payments without interruption[6]. There are two aspects of the financial strength of a business - the short term and the long term. The short-term financial strength may be described as the liquidity (or) technical solvency of the business. The long-term financial strength depends on the structure that has been imposed on the business in financing more permanent asset requirements. Bankers and current creditors are interested in the current debt paying ability of a business, that is, the short-term financial strength of the business. Debenture holders and long-term lenders are mostly concerned with the long-term financial strength of the business.

To Judge the financial strength of Indian automobile industry, the ratios relating to short-term and long-term financial strength has been computed and analyzed in the following paragraph.

Short-term Financial Strength

Short-term financial strength is the ability of a firm to meet its current obligations as and when they become due for payment. The importance of short-term financial strength can hardly be overstressed. Liquidity ratios measure the ability to meet short-term obligations and reflect the short-term financial strength of the firm. The ratios, which indicate the liquidity of a firm, are mainly the current ratio and the quick ratio.

Current Ratio

The Current ratio is a test of the ability of the firm to meet its short-term commitments well in time. The greater extent to which current assets exceed current liabilities, the easier a company can meet its short-term obligations. It expresses the "Working Capital" relationship of current assets available to meet the company's current obligations. The significance of current ratio is that it is not only a measure of solvency but is an index of the working capital available in an enterprise[7]. A good current ratio may mean a good umbrella for creditors against the rainy day, but to the management, it reflects bad financial planning or presence of idle assets or over capitalization[8].

The rule of thumb about the current ratio has been set at 2:1, i.e., the current assets of a business should be twice the amount of current liabilities in order to call the business as technically solvent. The purpose in fixing this standard of 2:1 is that current liabilities should be met on time as and when they occur and there should be no difficulty in carrying on the usual operations. The above-mentioned rule of 2:1, however, cannot by any means be taken as a general guide to the desirability or otherwise of the current ratio of all types of business. The above "2 to 1" rule suggests a liquidation theory of solvency[9]. In nutshell, higher the current ratio, the greater the margin of safety, the more the firm's ability is to meet its current obligations. However, too high ratio may be favourable to creditors, but is not beneficial for the firms, because its shows poor utilisation of its current assets.

After calculating the current ratio of a firm, it is compared with other firms in the same industry and industry average. A ratio lower than that of the industry average suggests that the company may have liquidity problems. A satisfactory current ratio for a company will be within the close range of the industry average.

Table 6.7 and Appendix XXXVII show the fluctuating trend in the current ratio of the selected automobile industry. The average current ratio varied from sector to sector, the highest average was 1.22 in commercial vehicles followed by two and three wheelers (1.18) and passenger cars and multiutility vehicles (1.10). The average current ratio of commercial vehicles was more than industry average ratio, however, this was not statistically significant. The compound annual growth rate of this ratio was positive only in case of Two and Three wheelers, however, it was negative in other two sectors. The CV value of this ratio shows that moderate fluctuation in the selected sectors of automobile industry during the study period. The overall fluctuating trend of this ratio can be caused by the changes in the working capital of the industry. Individual sector average of current ratio is some what similar to industry average (1.17).

In order to test the hypothesis, analysis of variance has been applied between the sectors and between the years. Since the calculated value of F is less than the table value of F at 5 per cent level, it is concluded that there were no significant differences between the current ratio among the selected years and between the sectors during the study period.

The current ratio for the industry- wise automobile companies for the study period is presented in Table 6.8. The table reveals that Ashok Leyland Ltd, Bajaj Tempo Ltd and Eicher Motors Ltd in commercial vehicles sector, Mahindra and Mahindra Ltd in passenger cars and multiutility vehicle sectors and Scooters India Ltd, Kinetic Motors Company Ltd, Kinetic Engineering Ltd and TVS Motors Company Ltd in two and three wheelers sector had shown better performance in this ratio concerned. The table also reveals that moderate fluctuating trend of the current ratio in all the companies selected under the study.

Table 6.9 shows that difference in the current ratio between the year and between the company were significant in commercial vehicles sector because the calculated value of F was more than the table value of F at 5 per cent level of significance and the null hypothesis was rejected. However, current ratio between the companies was significant only in passenger cars and multiutility vehicles and two and three wheeler sectors because calculated value of F is greater than the table value of F.

The inferences drawn from the above analysis shows that all the industries group invariably showed low average current ratio except Ashok Leyland Ltd in commercial vehicles sector, none has ever achieved the required norm of 2:1 ratio. But, the ratio during the study period for all the industry group was quite satisfactory.

Liquidity Ratio

The current ratio in not a sufficient indicator of the weakness or soundness of the liquidity of a company. The important question is whether the current assets are held in liquid form or not. If working capital is tied up in inventories and prepaid expenses, which cannot be converted promptly into cash, the company may be unable to honour its obligations for want of cash funds. Therefore, the solvency of a company can be better judged by quick ratio. The quick ratio is an important device for judging the liquidity position of a business. The ratio is designed to show the amount of near cash or cash items available for meeting immediate payments. This ratio is a true test of a going concern solvency of a business. As a general rule, when the quick assets are more than or equal to current liabilities, the financial position may be considered to be satisfactory. The quick ratio indicates the ability of the business to meet its commitments as they fall due for payment. The standard norm of this ratio is 1:1 since in that case yield will be sufficient to meet current liabilities. Like current ratio, liquid ratio within close range to the industry average is desirable.

Table 6.7 and Appendix XXXVIII show fluctuating tend in the liquidity ratio of the selected sectors of the automobile industry. The average liquidity ratio varied from sector to sector, the highest average was 1.16 in two and three wheelers followed by commercial vehicles (1:11) and passenger cars and multiutility vehicles 0.91. The average liquidity ratio of two and three wheelers and commercial vehicles sector was more than industry average ratio. However, this was statistically significant only in case of two and three wheelers. The compound annual growth rate of this ratio was positive in case of passenger cars and multiutility vehicles and two and three wheelers sector. The CV value of this ratio shows a moderate fluctuation in all the three sectors during the study period. Since, the calculated value of F was less than the table value of F at 5 per cent level between the years and sector, it is concluded that there were no significant differences between the liquid ratio among the selected sectors and between the years during the study period.

Table 6.8 shows the liquidity ratio of different companies selected under different sectors of Indian automobile industry during the study period. The analysis of table reveals that all the selected companies except Majestic Auto Ltd in two and three wheelers sector had shown better performance regarding liquidity ratio. It is also noticed from the Table 6.9 that the difference in the liquidity ratio was significant in between the companies of commercial vehicles and two and three wheelers sector as the calculated value of F was greater than the table value of F at 5 per cent level of significance. However, these were insignificant in between the years during the study period. To interprete the above analysis it may thus be stated that all the selected companies of automobile industry did maintain satisfactory level of liquidity ratio.

Interest Coverage Ratio

It is one of the most conventional coverage ratio used to test the firms servicing debt capacity. Interest cover is nothing but profit cover of interest i.e., number of times interest on loans and debenture is covered by available profit. Greater the cover better is the position of the debenture holder and loan creditors regarding possibility of timely payment of interest.

Table 6.7 and Appendix XXXIX explain a fluctuating trend in the interest coverage ratio of the selected sectors of Indian automobile industry. The average interest coverage ratio varied from sector to sector. The highest average was 55.96 times in two and three wheelers, followed by passenger cars and multiutility vehicles (3.58) and commercial vehicles (1.30). The interest coverage was very high in two and three wheelers sector. This was due to better coverage of Bajaj Auto Ltd, Maharastra Scooters India Ltd and Hero Honda Motors Ltd during the study period. The analysis of t value reveals that the average interest coverage ratio was significanly different from the industry average at 5 per cent level

Table 6.7
Analysis of Short-term Financial Strength of Indian Automobile Industry
(1991-92 to 2003-04)

Particulars	*Commercial Vehicles*	*Passenger Cars and Multiutility Vehicles*	*Two and Three Wheelers*	*Industry Average*
Current ratio				
Mean	1.22	1.10	1.18	1.17
CV	0.16	0.23	0.11	0.09
CAGR	-4.38	-2.75	2.13	-1.47
"t" Value	1.093	-1.726	0.649	
Liquidity ratio				
Mean	1.11	0.91	1.16	1.06
CV	0.29	0.25	0.19	0.13
CAGR	-4.74	3.13	3.04	0.56
"t" Value	0.533	-2.705	3.009	
Interest coverage ratio				
Mean	1.30	3.58	55.96	20.28
CV	0.93	1.02	1.00	0.94
CAGR	-14.20	12.20	26.00	22.40
"t" Value	-3.347	-3.267	3.320	

* - Significant at 5 per cent level
Source: Computed

Analysis of variance – Results

Sources of variation	*Current ratio* "F" *Value*	*Liquidity ratio* "F" *Value*	*Interest coverage ratio* "F" *Value*
Between the years	0.905	0.743	1.057
Between the sectors	1.190	2.945	12.040

*- Significant at 5 per cent level; Critical value of $F_{0.05}$ (12,24)=2.18 and $F_{0.05}$ (2.24) =3.40
Source: Computed

of significance. The compound annual growth rate of this ratio was positive in passenger cars and multiutility vehicles and two and three wheelers sector. The CV value indicates the very high

Table 6.8
Analysis Of Short-term Financial Strength Of Selected Indian Automobile Industry (1991-92 to 2003-04)

Particulars	*Current ratio*			*Liquidity ratio*			*Interest coverage ratio*		
	Mean	*CV*	*CAGR*	*Mean*	*CV*	*CAGR*	*Mean*	*CV*	*CAGR*
Commercial Vehicles									
Ashok Leyland Ltd.	2.17	0.18	-1.12	1.99	0.28	-5.24	2.06	0.61	4.42
Tata Motors Ltd.	1.10	0.16	-3.47	1.09	0.39	-5.72	2.51	0.86	-6.78
Bajaj Tempo Ltd.	1.30	0.08	-0.93	0.67	0.40	0.32	4.25	1.16	-2.45
Eicher Motors Ltd.	1.31	0.20	-3.40	0.98	0.30	-3.89	3.86	1.03	26.30
Swaraj Mazda Ltd.	1.02	0.06	1.39	0.68	0.31	7.82	3.38	1.70	25.20
Passenger Cars and Multiutility Vehicles									
Hindustan Motors Ltd.	1.20	0.12	-0.85	0.88	0.32	-4.34	0.74	1.18	-5.98
Mahindra and Mahindra Ltd.	1.53	0.16	-1.79	2.31	1.74	-11.50	3.48	0.55	5.57
Maruthi Udyog Ltd.	1.18	0.22	1.94	0.89	0.37	4.05	7.32	0.12	11.60
Daewoo Motors India Ltd.	0.87	0.82	-10.80	1.57	0.92	-1.93	-0.95	-3.60	4.28

(Contd.)

(Contd. Table 6.8)

Particulars	*Current ratio*			*Liquidity ratio*			*Interest coverage ratio*		
	Mean	*CV*	*CAGR*	*Mean*	*CV*	*CAGR*	*Mean*	*CV*	*CAGR*
Two and Three Wheelers									
Bajaj Auto Ltd.	1.30	0.15	-2.02	1.12	0.16	-0.21	202.19	1.52	39.40
LML Ltd.	0.88	0.47	1.13	0.63	0.49	-0.69	1.10	1.25	-3.94
Maharastra Scooters Ltd.	1.01	0.11	-0.45	2.25	0.28	-4.96	140.52	1.41	-6.54
TVS Motors Company Ltd.	1.41	0.27	2.28	0.81	0.47	-5.57	8.73	0.77	15.30
Kinetic Motors Company Ltd.	1.44	0.15	-1.14	1.08	0.29	3.78	3.26	0.93	-1.85
Hero Honda Motors Ltd.	0.91	0.30	-7.78	0.58	0.26	-2.57	139.91	1.54	50.40
Kinetic Engineering Ltd.	1.43	0.11	-1.28	2.63	0.27	2.86	2.71	0.77	-9.98
Majestic Auto Ltd.	0.89	0.16	-2.71	0.39	1.18	-2.29	1.21	1.14	-4.54
Scooters India Ltd.	1.62	0.97	17.60	0.94	1.00	7.54	4.06	0.95	19.60

Source: Computed.

Table 6.9
Analysis of Short-term Financial Strength of Indian Automobile Industry - Anova Results (1991-92 to 2003-04)

Particulars	*Current ratio*		*Liquidity ratio*		*Interest coverage ratio*	
	F Value	*F Critic Value at 5% level*	*F Value*	*F Critic Value at 5% level*	*F Value*	*F Critic Value at 5% level*
Commercial Vehicles						
Between the years	2.556	1.960	1.810	1.960	3.989	1.960
Between the companies	68.175	2.565	32.021	2.565	1.122	2.565
Passenger Cars and Multiutility Vehicles						
Between the years	0.550	2.033	0.967	2.033	0.855	2.033
Between the companies	5.202	2.866	1.280	2.866	9.110	2.866
Two and Three Wheelers						
Between the years	0.412	1.854	1.730	1.854	1.481	1.854
Between the companies	2.832	2.036	31.160	2.036	4.439	2.036

* - Significant at 5 per cent Level
Source: Computed.

fluctuation in the interest coverage ratio in all the three sectors during the study period. Since, the calculated value of F is more that the table value of F at 5 per cent level of significance between the sector, it is concluded that there were significant differences between interest coverage ratio among the selected sectors during the study period.

The interest coverage ratio of different companies selected under different sectors of automobile industry is presented in Table 6.8. The analysis of table reveals that all the selected companies in all the three sectors except Daewoo Motors India Ltd in passenger cars and multiutility vehicles had shown better performance regarding interest coverage ratio. Table 6.9 shows that the difference in the interest coverage ratio between the companies was significant in passenger cars and multiutility vehicles and two and three wheelers sector as calculated value of F was higher than the table value of F at 5 per cent level of significance. The inference drawn from the above analysis is that all the selected companies of automobile industry showed comparatively better performance in maintaining their interest coverage ratio during the study period.

Long-term Financial Strength

The long term creditors, debenture holders and financial institutions would judge the soundness of a firm on the basis of the long-term financial strength in terms of its ability to pay the interest regularly as well as to repay the principal amount as and when it falls due. To examine the long-term solvency of a firm, capital structure ratios are calculated. These ratios indicate the proportion between funds provided by owners and outsiders. As a general rule, there should be an 'appropriate' mix of debt and owners equity in financing the firm's assets. To judge the long-term financial strength of selected Indian automobile industry the following ratios have been computed and analysed in the following paragraph.

Debt-equity Ratio

The relationship between borrowed funds and owners equity is a popular measure of the long-term financial strength of a concern. This relationship is reflected by the debt-equity ratio. This ratio is employed as a principal tool for analyzing the composition of financial structure. From the creditor's point of view, the debt-equity ratio measures the extent to which their interests are covered by owned funds. The higher the coverage of owned funds, the lower will be the ratio and the greater will be the protection to the creditors against possible losses in the event of liquidation. This ratio is also important for judging the financial policy followed by the concern. An ideal norm of the ratio is 1:1 that is the long-term debt should not exceed the owned funds in the business.

The proportion of debt and equity of company depends upon the nature of the business. This ratio differs from industry to industry. According to the guidelines issued by the Financial Ministry to the Financial Institutions, "The debt equity ratio in case of project engaging an investment of less than Rs. 5 crores will be in range of 1:1 and 1.5:1 and in the case of projects those investments range between Rs. 5 crores and Rs.10 crores, the debt-equity ratio will be in the range of 1.5:1 to 2:1. Similarly, where the investment on the project exceeds Rs. 10 crores which is considered capital intensive, the debt equity ratio will be 2:1 or more"[10]

Table 6.10 and Appendix LX reveal a fluctuating trend in the debt equity ratio of the selected sectors of Indian automobile industry. It is evident from the table that none of the selected sectors if automobile industry had debt equity ratio of 2:1 during the study period. However, the mean debt equity ratio varied from sector to sector, the highest average was 1.92 in passenger cars and multiutility vehicles followed by commercial vehicles (1.66) and two and three wheelers (1.06). The mean of this ratio was near to standard norms (2:1) in case of passenger cars and multiutility vehicles and commercial vehicles. It shows that the sector adopted a sound financial policy during the study period and the long term solvency position of the company can be called good when compared to two and three wheelers sector. The average debt equity ratio of commercial vehicles and passenger cars and multiutility vehicles were more than the industry average, however, this was not statistically significant. The compound annual growth rate of this ratio was negative in all the three sectors during the study period. The high CV value of this ratio of selected sectors proves that there was a very high fluctuation in this ratio during the study period.

In order to test whether there are significant differences of this ratio between the years and between the sector, analysis of variance has been applied. It is evident from Table 6.10 that there was a significance difference in this ratio between the years only since the calculated value of F was greater that table value of F at 5 per cent level of significance.

The debt equity ratio for the company - wise automobile industry is presented in Table 6.11. The table reveals that Eicher Motors Ltd and Swaraj Mazda Ltd in commercial vehicles, Mahindra and Mahindra Ltd, Hindustan Motor Ltd and Daewoo Motor India Ltd in passenger cars and multiutility vehicles and LML Ltd and Majestic Auto Ltd in two and three wheelers showed better performance in this ratio is concerned. The analysis of CV of this ratio shows that high fluctuating trend in the debt equity ratio of all the company selected under the study. Majority of the companies showed negative compound annual growth rate of this ratio during the study period.

It is evident from the Table 6.12 that debt equity ratio between the companies in passenger cars and multiutility vehicles and two and three wheelers only was significant because the calculated value of F was more than the critical value of F at 5 percent level of significance.

It is concluded that the long-term financial position of commercial vehicles and passenger cars and multiutility vehicles may be considered more satisfactory than the two and three wheelers sectors of Indian automobile industry during the study period.

Fixed Assets to Networth Ratio

The long term investors, creditors and shareholders are we concerned with the investment policy of management in fixed assets. The investment in fixed assets involves commitments of funds for longer period into the future and usually are difficult and costly to reserve, often they are in large increments. Therefore, the management should be very cautious in deciding about the investment in fixed assets. The management has also to decide about the funds to be used as working capital in the business. This ratio is an important tool for judging the margin of safety for long-term creditors. The lesser the ratio, the greater is the margin of safety for long-term creditors[11]. If net worth is less that the fixed assets, it implies that the loan funds are used to finance a part from fixed assets, when the amount of ownership funds exceeds the value of fixed assets apart from the net working capital is provided by the share holders.

The fixed assets to networth ratio of the selected sectors of Indian automobile industry for the study period is presented in Table 6.10 and Appendix LXI. The table reveals that the fixed assets to networth ratio of the selected sectors show the fluctuating trend during the study period. The fixed assets to networth ratio varied between 1.94 times in case of passenger cars and multiutility vehicles, 1.59 times in commercial vehicles and -0.98 times in two and three wheelers sector. The mean fixed assets to networth ratio of commercial vehicles and two and three wheelers sectors were more than the industry average. However, this was not statistically significant. The compound annual growth rate of this ratio was positive only in commercial vehicles sector for the study period. The analysis of CV value reveals that the fixed assets to networth ratio witnessed very high fluctuations in two and three wheelers sector whereas moderate fluctuations in commercial vehicles and passenger cars and multiutility vehicles sector during the study period.

In order to examine the significant effect of different years and category of sectors on the fixed assets to net worth ratio, F test has been made which is exhibited in the Table 6.10. The table reveals that the calculated value of F is smaller than table value for given degrees of freedom at 5 per cent level. Thus it is interpreted that nature of sector and years does not hold any effect on said fixed assets to net worth ratio.

Table 6.11 shows the fixed assets to networth ratio of different companies selected under different sectors of automobile industry during the study period. The analysis reveals that different companies have different value of fixed assets to net worth ratio during the study period. However, companies under commercial vehicles and passenger cars and multiutility vehicles showed better performance compared to companies under two and three wheelers sector. The analysis of CV ratio also shows that all these companies experienced very high fluctuation in this ratio during the study

Table 6.10
Analysis of Long-term Financial Strength of Indian Automobile Industry (1991-92 to 2003-04)

Particulars	*Commercial Vehicles*	*Passenger Cars and Multiutility Vehicles*	*Two and Three Wheelers*	*Industry Average*
Debt – equity ratio				
Mean	1.66	1.92	1.06	1.55
CV	0.73	0.89	0.60	0.61
CAGR	-11.30	-17.30	-5.06	-11.80
"t" Value	0.306	1.229	-2.712	
Fixed assets to networth ratio				
Mean	1.59	1.94	-0.98	0.85
CV	0.28	0.29	-7.61	2.91
CAGR	4.91	-1.05	0.00	4.16
"t" Value	0.985	1.451	-1.212	

*- Significant at 5 per cent level;
Source: Computed.

Analysis of variance-Results

Sources of variation	*Debt-equity ratio* "F" Value	*Fixed assets to networth ratio* "F" Value
Between the years	2.620	0.971
Between the sectors	2.450	1.742

*-Significant at 5 per cent level; Critical value of $F_{0.05}(12,24)$=2.183 and $F_{0.05}(2,24)$ = 3.40
Source: Computed.

period. It is alsoevident that majority of the companies in two and three wheelers sector had negative compound annual growth rate of this ratio during the study period.

The F test exhibited in Table 6.12 reveals that except passenger cars and multiutility vehicles in all other sectors the calculated value of F is smaller than the table value of F at 5 per

Table 6.11
Analysis of Long-term Financial Strength of Selected Indian Automobile Industry (1991-92 to 2003-04)

Particulars	*Debt – equity ratio*			*Fixed assets to networth ratio*		
	Mean	*CV*	*CAGR*	*Mean*	*CV*	*CAGR*
Commercial Vehicles						
Ashok Leyland Ltd.	1.08	0.43	-7.06	1.40	0.26	2.96
Tata Motors Ltd.	0.96	0.41	-8.31	1.69	0.27	3.05
Bajaj Tempo Ltd.	0.50	0.52	4.40	3.11	0.34	6.59
Eicher Motors Ltd.	1.53	0.87	-18.60	1.96	0.51	-1.33
Swaraj Mazda Ltd.	3.20	1.72	-11.30	-2.50	-4.34	2.57
Passenger Cars and Multiutility Vehicles						
Hindustan Motors Ltd.	2.51	0.37	-0.98	3.72	0.64	8.18
Mahindra and Mahindra Ltd.	10.66	0.37	-2.65	1.27	0.40	-0.91
Maruthi Udyog Ltd.	0.53	1.08	-21.30	1.47	0.28	-2.70
Daewoo Motors India Ltd.	6.79	0.70	-1.40	10.52	1.55	4.50

(Contd.)

(Contd. Table 6.11)

Particulars	*Debt – equity ratio*			*Fixed assets to networth ratio*		
	Mean	*CV*	*CAGR*	*Mean*	*CV*	*CAGR*
Two and Three Wheelers						
Bajaj Auto Ltd.	0.26	0.65	-7.45	1.04	0.48	-0.45
LML Ltd.	3.67	1.42	-10.80	-6.56	-3.74	0.62
Maharastra Scooters Ltd.	0.05	0.20	3.49	0.17	0.12	-0.44
TVS Motors Company Ltd.	1.00	0.91	-15.30	1.56	0.24	1.08
Kinetic Motors Company Ltd.	0.78	0.53	1.26	1.48	0.26	-0.70
Hero Honda Motors Ltd.	0.57	0.81	22.30	1.46	0.33	-0.36
Kinetic Engineering Ltd.	1.01	0.48	8.36	2.15	0.27	-0.12
Majestic Auto Ltd.	1.76	0.78	4.51	5.20	2.62	0.47
Scooters India Ltd.	0.35	1.29	-11.70	0.44	1.09	-0.34

Source: Computed

Table 6.12
Analysis of Long-term Financial Strength of Indian Automobile Industry - ANOVA Results (1991-92 to 2003-04)

Particulars	*Debt – equity ratio*		*Fixed assets to net worth ratio*	
	F Value	*F Critic Value at 5% level*	*F Value*	*F Critic Value at 5% level*
Commercial Vehicles				
Between the years	1.010	1.960	1.182	1.960
Between the companies	2.191	2.565	2.551	2.565
Passenger Cars and Multiutility Vehicles				
Between the years	0.579	2.033	1.084	2.033
Between the companies	23.889	2.866	3.652	2.866
Two and Three Wheelers				
Between the years	1.105	1.854	0.207	1.854
Between the companies	4.695	2.036	1.307	2.036

Source: Computed

cent level. Thus it may be assumed that nature of sector and years do not affect significantly fixed assets to networth ratio during the study period.

The conclusion drawn from the above analysis is that commercial vehicles and passenger cars and multiutility vehicles showed comparatively better performance in all respects in maintaining above said ratio doing the study period.

Assessment of Financial Health of Indian Automobile Industry

In this part, an attempt has been made to have an insight into the financial stability and operational health of the selected Indian automobile industry. Altman's 'Z' score analysis has been applied by financial analysts to evaluate the general trend in the financial health of an enterprise over a period. Many of the individual accounting ratios used frequently to predict the financial performance of an enterprise may only provide warnings when it is too late to take a corrective action. Further, single ratio does not convey much of the sense. There is no internationally accepted standard for financial ratio against which the results can be compared. Therefore, Edwin I. Altman (1968)[12] combined a number of accounting ratios (liquidity, leverage, activity and profitability) to form an index of the profitability, which are effective indicators of corporate performance in predicting bankruptcy well over a year or two in advance. In this direction a variety of studies have been conducted, over the period, by applying Multiple Discriminant Analysis (MDA) to predict the corporate failure, as for instance, Bevar (1996)[13], Argenti John (1976)[14], Gupta (1974)[15], Ohlson (1980)[16], Etebari (1987)[17], Makridakis (1991)[18] and Sastry (1994)[19].

The objective of this part is to predict the financial health and viability of the selected Indian automobile industry with an objective to improve its operational efficiency and effectiveness, productivity and profitability. The data collected are first analysed with the help of the accounting ratios. These different ratios are combined into a single measure 'Z' score analysis with the help of Multiple Discriminant Analysis (MDA). The formula used to evaluate the 'Z' score analysis as established by Altman is:

$$Z = 0.012X_1 + 0.014X_2 + 0.033X_3 + 0.004X_4 + 0.999X_5$$

Where 'Z' is the overall index

x_1 - ratio of working capital to total assets (WC/TA X 100)

x_2 - ratio of net operating profit to net sales (NOP/S X 100)

x_3 - ratio of earning before interest and taxes to total assets (EBIT/TA X 100)

x_4 - ratio of market value of equity to book value of debt (MVE/BV X 100)

x_5 - ratio of sales to total assets (S / TA)

Variables used in Z- score analysis

The following accounting ratios are used as variables to combine them into a single measure, which is efficient in predicting bankruptcy

x_1 - The ratio of working capital to total assets. It is the measure of the net liquid assets of a concern to the total capitalization.

x_2 - The ratio of net operating profit to net sales. It indicates the efficiency of the management in manufacturing, sales, administration and other activities.

x_3 - The ratio of earning before interest and taxes to total assets. It is a measure of productivity of assets employed in an enterprise. The ultimate existence of an enterprise is based on the earning power.

x_4 - The ratio of market value of equity to book value of debt. It is reciprocal of the familiar debt-equity ratio. This measure shows how much assets of an enterprise can decline in value before the liabilities exceed the assets and the concern becomes insolvent.

x_5 - The ratio of sales to total assets. The capital turnover ratio is a standard financial measure for illustrating the sales generating capacity of the assets.

Measurement of financial health

According to Altman (1968), the following three situations are considered for studying financial health of selected sectors of the Indian automobiles industry (Table 6.13)

I. Bellow 'Z' score of 1.8, the unit is considered to be in bankruptcy zone. Its failure is certain and extremely likely and would occur probably with in a period of 2 years.

II. If a unit has a 'Z' score between 1.8 and 3, its financial viability is considered to be healthy. The failure in this situation is uncertain to predict

Table 6.13
Altman Guidelines for Healthy Zone

	Situation	*'Z' Scores*	*Zones*
I	Below 1.8	Bankruptcy zone	Certain to all
II	1.8-3	Healthy zone	Uncertain to predict
III	3 and above	Too Healthy zone	Not to all

Source: Altman (1968).

III. **Above 'Z' score of 3, the unit is in too healthy zone. Its financial health is very viable.**

Automobile industry

The Z score with respect to Indian automobile industry for the period has been computed and presented in Table 6.14. Further using the data point, the scores obtained over the period have been represented graphically in Figure IV. It is imperative from the analysis that the Z score for the automobile industry is not less than 1.8 during the study period. It shows that financial health of automobile industry during the study period is never in bankruptcy zone. This shows that the better financial performance of automobile industry during the study period. It is also revealed that its financial health lies both between healthy zone and too healthy zone during the study period.

Table 6.14

Altman Z score of Indian Automobile Industry (1991-92 to 2003-04)

Year	X_1	X_2	X_3	X_4	X_5	*Z Score*
1991 - 92	18.34	3.26	7.28	19.60	2.51	3.13
1992 - 93	19.76	3.19	7.14	37.16	1.82	2.56
1993 - 94	12.53	5.12	14.18	47.35	2.24	3.21
1994 - 95	6.10	5.92	15.71	33.03	2.30	3.17
1995 - 96	-1.40	6.03	18.00	28.49	2.76	3.59
1996 - 97	12.53	5.79	12.03	17.11	1.88	2.61
1997 - 98	13.42	6.16	10.69	29.80	1.49	2.27
1998 - 99	15.96	5.40	9.28	28.80	1.59	2.33
1999 - 00	17.06	4.13	8.58	32.77	1.74	2.48
2000 – 01	15.48	1.94	5.42	33.11	1.79	2.38
2001 – 02	15.50	2.55	6.94	26.61	1.81	2.42
2002 – 03	15.74	3.14	9.03	49.19	2.51	3.33
2003 – 04	9.31	3.50	12.02	52.59	2.70	3.57

X_1 - working capital to total assets;
X_2 - net operating profit to net sales
X_3 - earnings before interest and taxes to total assets
X_4 - market value of equity to book value of debt;
X_5 - sales to total assets
Source: Computed.

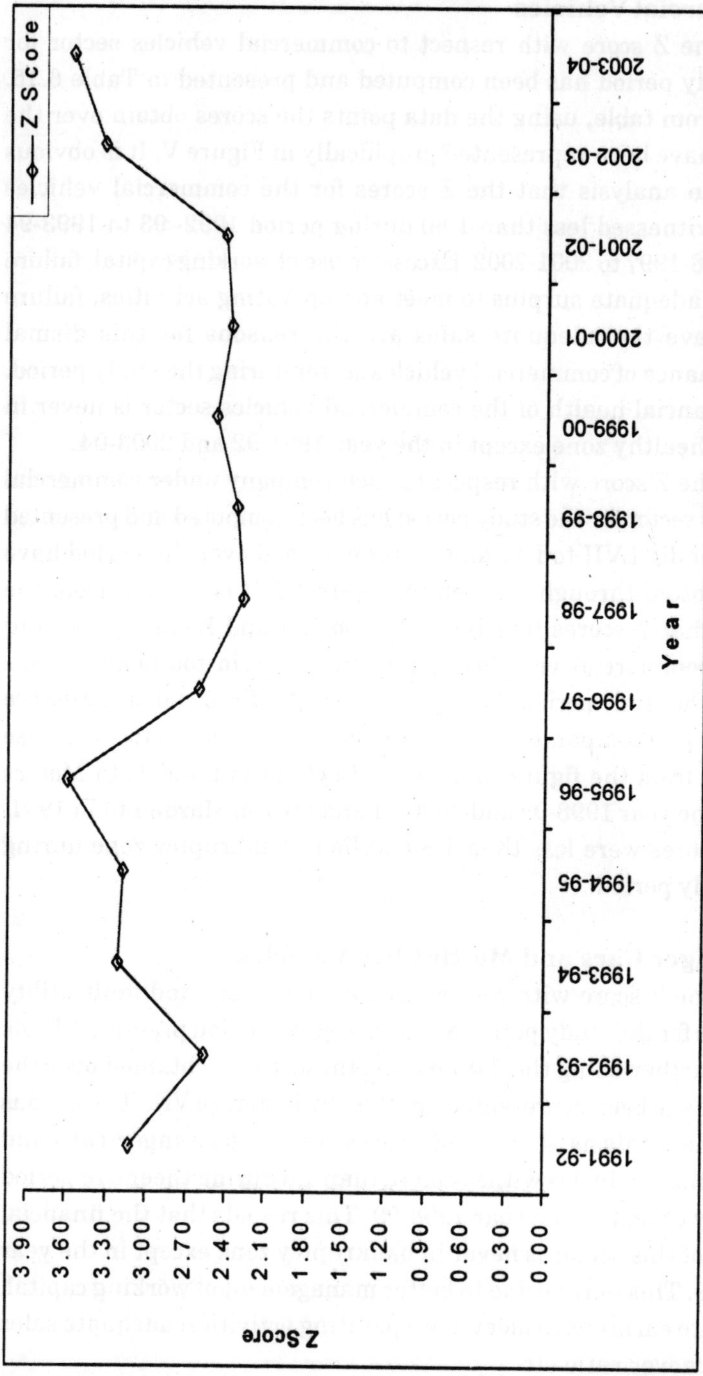

Figure IV Altman Z score of Indian Automobile Industry (1991-92 to 2003-04)

Commercial Vehicles

The Z score with respect to commercial vehicles sector for the study period has been computed and presented in Table 6.15. Apart from table, using the data points the scores obtain over the period have been represented graphically in Figure V. It is obvious from the analysis that the Z scores for the commercial vehicles sector witnessed less than 1.80 during period 1992- 93 to 1993-94 and 1996-1997 to 2001-2002. Excessive use of working capital, failure to earn adequate surplus to meet non-operating activities, failure to achieve the adequate sales are the reasons for this dismal performance of commercial vehicles sector during the study period. The financial health of the commercial vehicles sector is never in the too healthy zone except in the year 1991-92 and 2003-04.

The Z score with respect to each company under commercial vehicles sector for the study period has been computed and presented in Appendix LVII to LXI and scores obtained over the period have been plotted through a graph in Figure VI. It is evident from the figure that Z scores fore Bajaj Tempo Ltd and Eicher Motor Ltd under commercial vehicles sector always lie in too healthy zone during the study period. This shows the better financial performance of these two companies under commercial vehicles sector. It is also evident from the figure that Ashok Leyland Ltd and Tata Motors Ltd in the year 1998-99 and 2000-01 and Swaraj Mazda Ltd in 1994-95, Z scores were less than 1.8 and lie in bankruptcy zone during the study period.

Passenger Cars and Multiutility Vehicles

The Z score with respect to passenger cars and multiutility vehicles for the study period has been computed and presented Table 6.16. Further using the data points, these scores obtained over the period have been represented graphically in Figure VII. It is obvious from the analysis that the Z scores for the passenger cars and multiutility vehicles witness more than 1.8 during theentire period of study except in the year 1998-99. This reveals that the financial health of this sector is never in bankruptcy zone except in the year 1998-99. This may be due to better management of working capital, adequate earnings to meet non-operating activities, adequate sales and turnover ratio etc.

Table 6.15
Altman Z score of Commercial Vehicles (1991-92 to 2003-04)

Year	X_1	X_2	X_3	X_4	X_5	Z Score
1991 - 92	0.55	0.06	0.15	0.25	3.28	3.29
1992 - 93	0.53	0.08	0.10	0.25	1.36	1.40
1993 - 94	0.44	0.08	0.14	0.54	1.66	1.67
1994 - 95	0.42	0.10	0.20	0.85	1.89	2.02
1995 - 96	0.38	0.12	0.21	0.26	1.88	1.90
1996 - 97	0.47	0.12	0.19	0.21	1.61	1.63
1997 - 98	0.41	0.09	0.11	0.25	1.11	1.12
1998 - 99	0.29	008	0.08	0.26	1.07	1.08
1999 - 00	0.23	0.06	0.10	0.26	1.50	1.51
2000 - 01	0.17	0.02	0.03	0.25	1.52	1.52
2001 - 02	0.14	0.05	0.09	0.92	1.55	1.56
2002 - 03	0.01	0.08	0.20	0.35	2.58	2.59
2003 - 04	-0.12	0.09	0.29	0.19	3.19	3.20

X_1 - working capital to total assets; X_2 - net operating profit to net sales
X_3 - earnings before interest and taxes to total assets
X_4 - market value of equity to book value of debt ; X_5 - sales to total assets
Source: Computed.

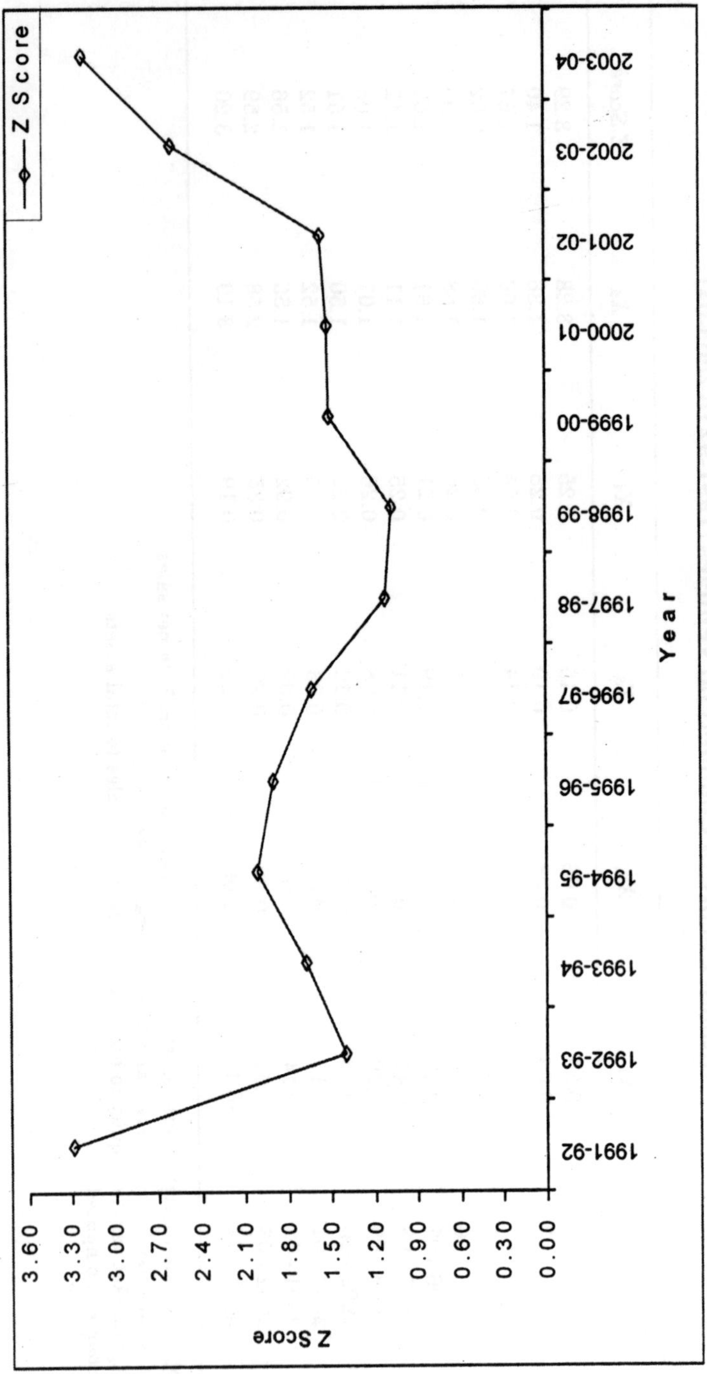

Figure V Altman Z score of Commercial Vehicles (1991-92 to 2003-04)

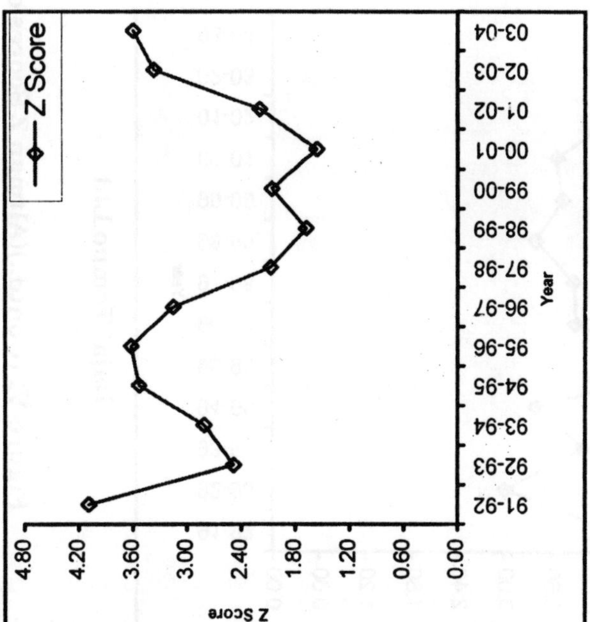

Ashok Leyland Ltd

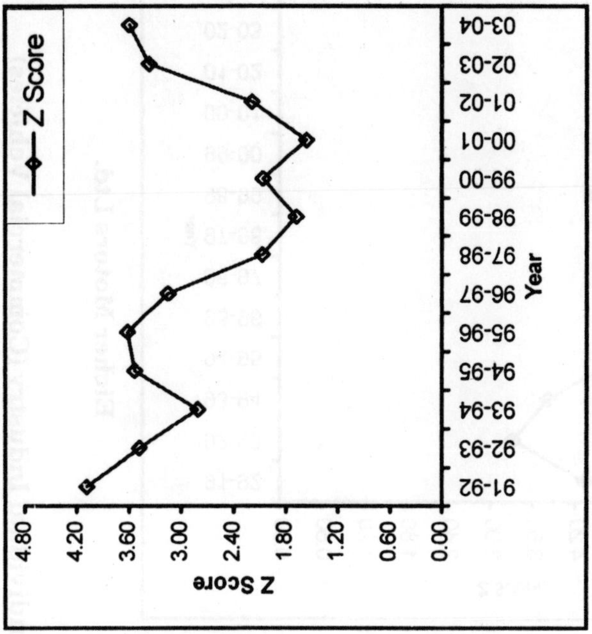

Tata Motors Ltd

Figure-VI (Altman Z Scores of Individual Industry (Commercial Vehicles)

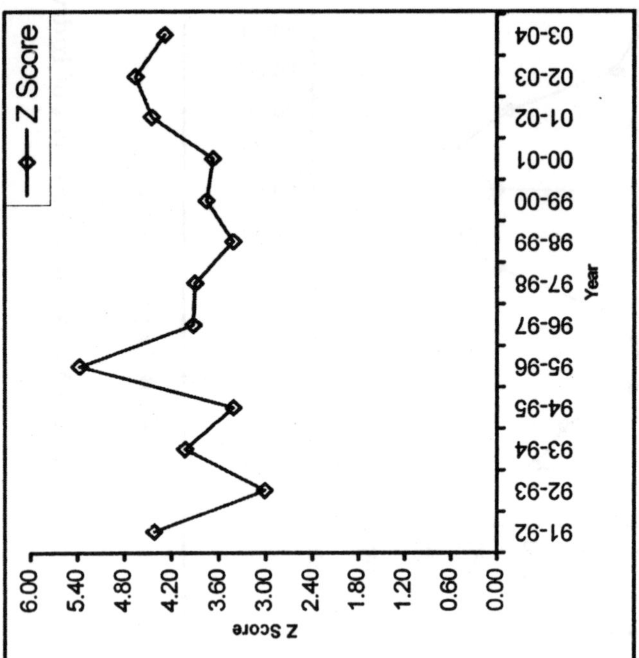

Bajaj Tempo Ltd

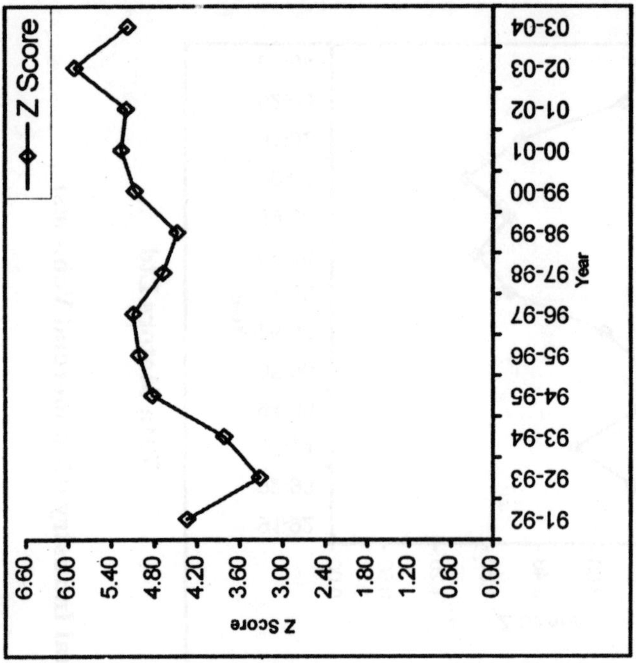

Eicher Motors Ltd.

Figure-VI (Contd..)(Altman Z Scores of Individual Industry (Commercial Vehicles)

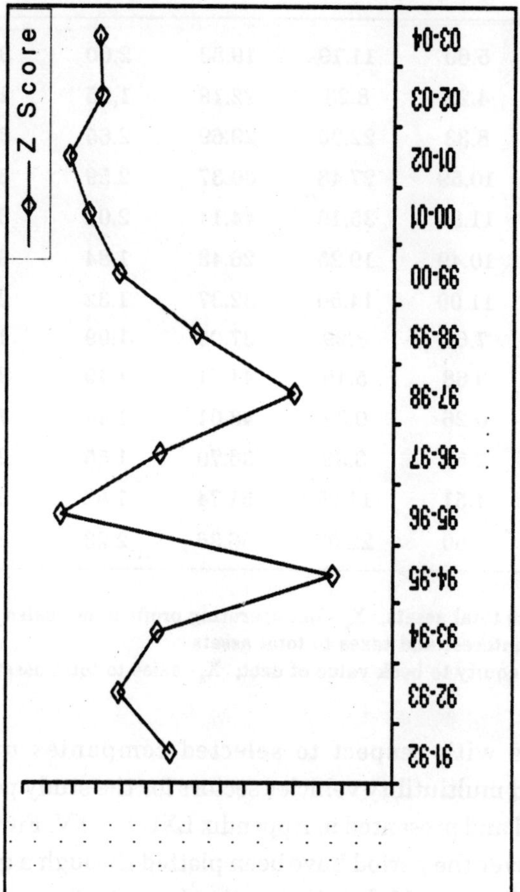

Swaraj Mazda Ltd

Figure-VI (Contd..) (Altman Z Scores of Individual Industry (Commercial Vehicles)

Table 6.16
Altman Z score of Passenger Cars and Multiutility Vehicles (1991-92 to 2003-04)

Year	X_1	X_2	X_3	X_4	X_5	*Z Score*
1991 - 92	38.51	5.60	11.19	19.83	2.00	3.03
1992 - 93	35.51	4.22	8.23	22.19	1.95	2.84
1993 - 94	16.21	8.33	22.20	29.69	2.65	3.87
1994 - 95	-3.79	10.59	27.48	30.37	2.59	3.78
1995 - 96	-25.65	11.34	35.16	44.14	2.02	3.19
1996 - 97	18.20	10.49	19.25	26.43	1.84	3.00
1997 - 98	11.22	11.00	14.50	32.37	1.32	2.28
1998 - 99	18.64	7.60	8.29	37.05	1.09	1.67
1999 - 00	24.11	3.68	5.15	44.71	1.40	3.58
2000 - 01	20.29	0.26	0.38	43.01	1.44	1.96
2001 - 02	24.44	2.57	3.98	36.70	1.55	2.23
2002 - 03	39.14	4.51	11.25	51.74	1.82	3.09
2003 - 04	14.82	7.60	22.07	56.36	2.23	3.58

X_1 - working capital to total assets; X_2 - net operating profit to net sales
X_3 - earnings before interest and taxes to total assets
X_4 - market value of equity to book value of debt; X_5 - sales to total assets
Source: Computed.

The Z score with respect to selected companies under passenger cars and multiutility vehicles sectors for the study period has been computed and presented in Appendix LXII to LXV. Further, the scores obtain over the period have been plotted through a graph and presented in Figure VIII. It is imperative from the figures that all the selected companies under this sector except Daewoo Motors Ltd showed fluctuating trend for the study period, have never reached the bankruptcy zone. However, Daewoo Motors Limited showed dismal performance in this regard during the study period 1996-97 to 2003-04. This was attributed to under trading owing to excess working capital, failed to achieve adequate sales, under utilisation of capacity etc.

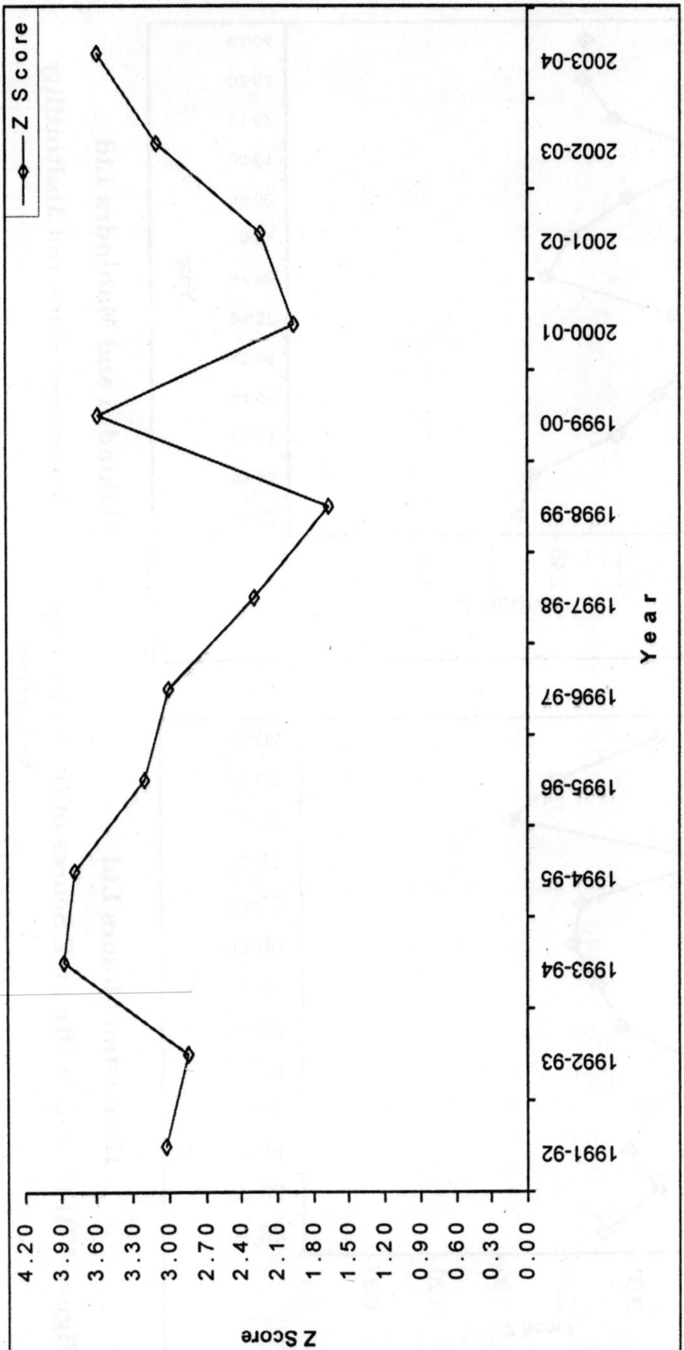

Figure VII Altman Z score of Passenger Cars and Multiutility Vehicles (1991-92 to 2003-04)

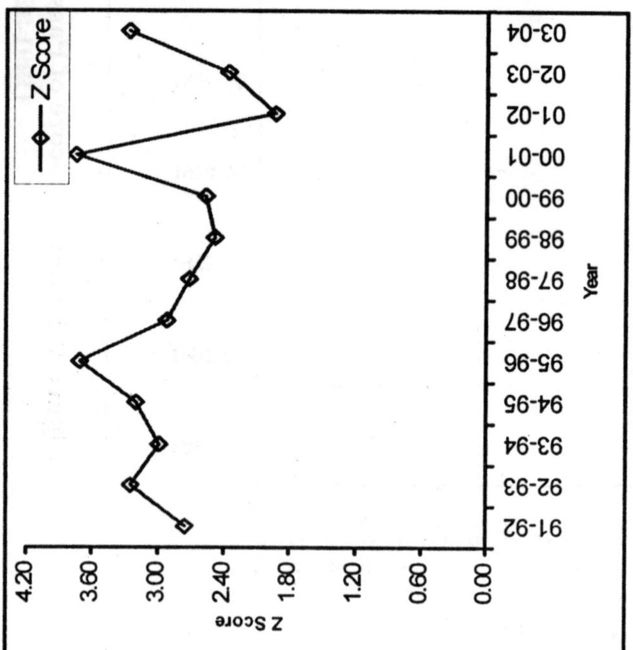

Hindustan Motors Ltd

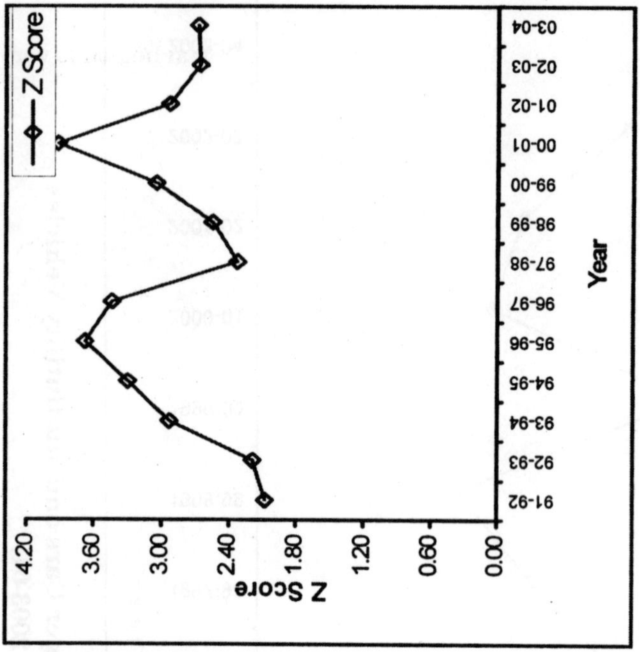

Mahindra and Mahindra Ltd

Figure-VIII (Contd..)(Altman Z Scores of Individual Industry (Passenger Cars and Multiutility Vehicles)

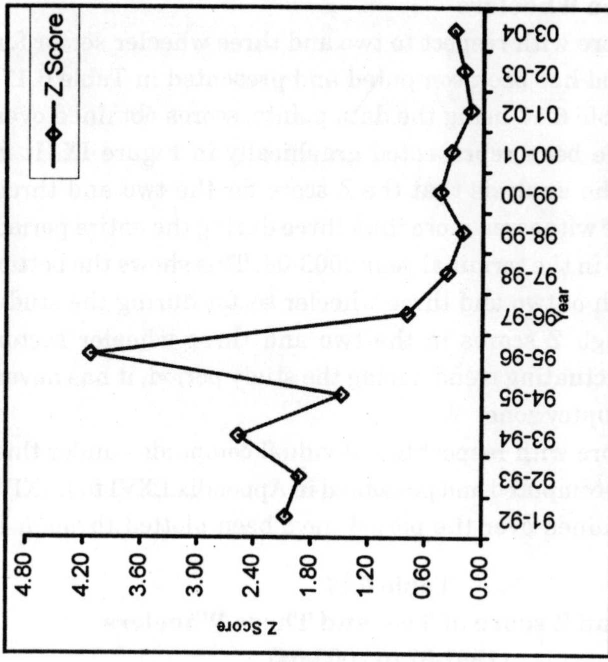

Daewoo Motors India Ltd

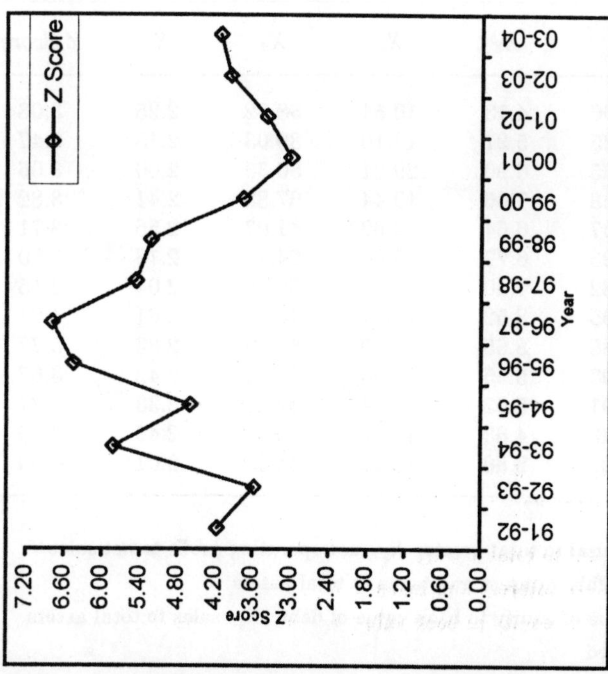

Maruti Udyog Ltd

Figure-VIII (Contd..)(Altman Z Scores of Individual Industry (Passenger Cars and Multiutility Vehicles)

Two and Three Wheelers

The Z score with respect to two and three wheeler sector for the study period has been computed and presented in Table 6.17. Apart from Table 6.17 using the data points, scores obtained over the period have been represented graphically in Figure IX. It is evident from the analysis that the Z score for the two and three wheeler sectors witnessed more than three during the entire period of study except in the terminal year 2003-04. This shows the better financial health of two and three wheeler sector during the study period. Although Z scores in the two and three wheeler sector witnessed a fluctuating trend during the study period, it has never reached bankruptcy zone.

The Z score with respect to individual companies under this sector has been computed and presented in Appendix LXVI to LXXIV and scores obtained over the period have been plotted through a

Table 6.17
Altman Z score of Two and Three Wheelers
(1991-92 to 2003-04)

Year	X_1	X_2	X_3	X_4	X_5	*Z Score*
1991 - 92	15.96	4.13	10.51	38.72	2.25	3.08
1992 - 93	23.25	5.27	13.10	89.03	2.15	3.47
1993 - 94	20.95	6.90	20.21	50.33	2.00	3.06
1994 - 95	21.68	7.06	19.44	67.88	2.41	3.82
1995 - 96	21.07	6.64	18.62	41.07	2.56	3.71
1996 - 97	18.93	6.77	16.66	24.70	2.18	3.20
1997 - 98	28.62	7.40	17.46	56.78	2.04	3.15
1998 - 99	28.95	8.52	19.47	49.09	2.61	4.01
1999 - 00	26.85	8.65	20.49	53.34	2.33	3.77
2000 - 01	25.97	5.55	15.86	56.07	2.42	3.67
2001 - 02	21.91	5.03	16.74	42.20	2.33	3.47
2002 – 03	8.06	4.83	15.65	44.47	2.45	3.40
2003 – 04	13.22	2.80	13.71	44.87	2.01	2.93

X_1 - working capital to total assets; X_2 - net operating profit to net sales

X_3 - earnings before interest and taxes to total assets

X_4 - market value of equity to book value of debt; X_5 - sales to total assets

Source: Computed.

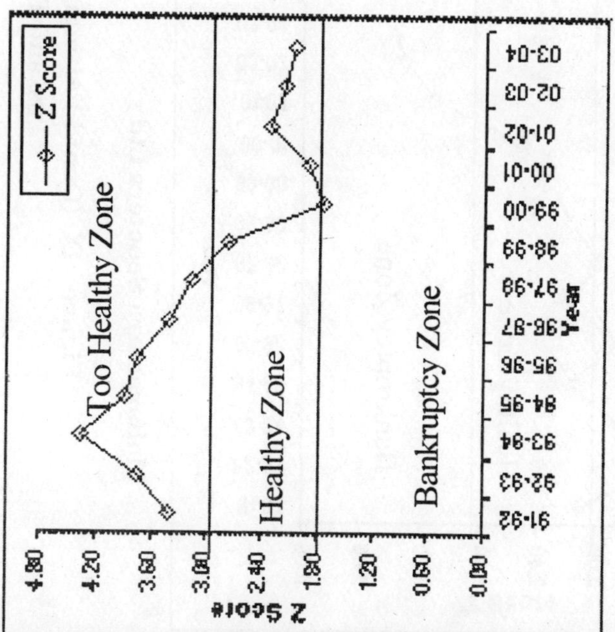

Bajaj Auto Ltd

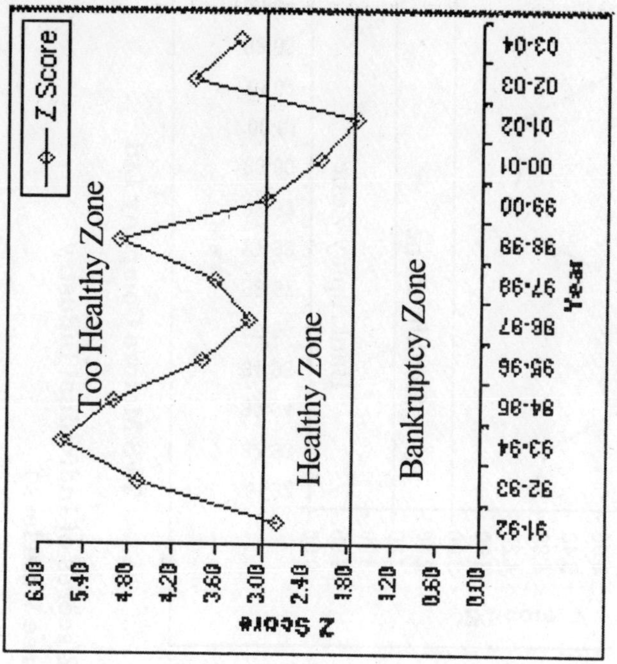

LML Ltd

Figure - IX Altman Z scores of Individual Industry (Two and Three Wheelers)

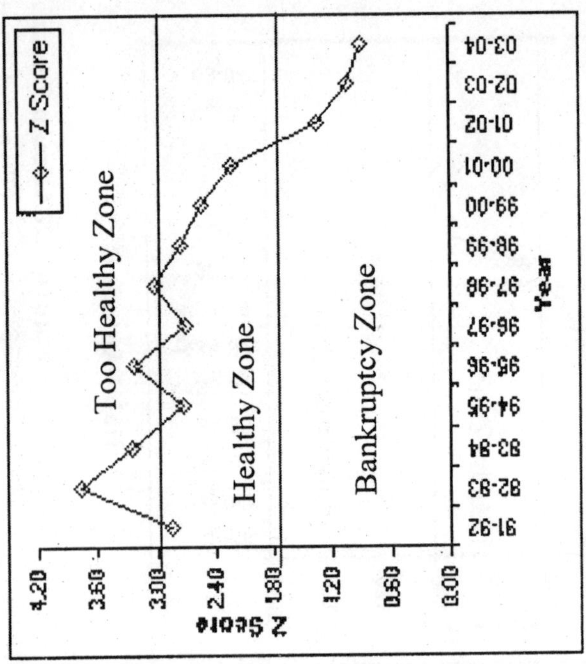

Maharashtra Scooters Ltd

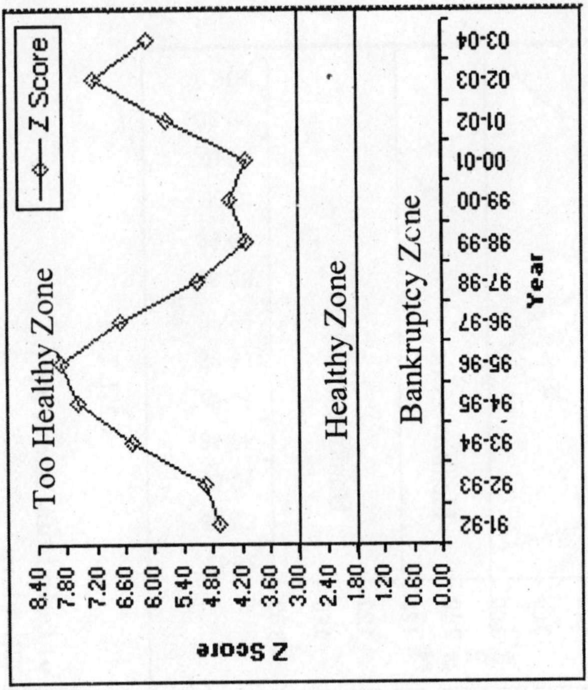

TVS Motors Company Ltd

Figure - IX (Contd.) Altman Z scores of Individual Industry (Two and Three Wheelers)

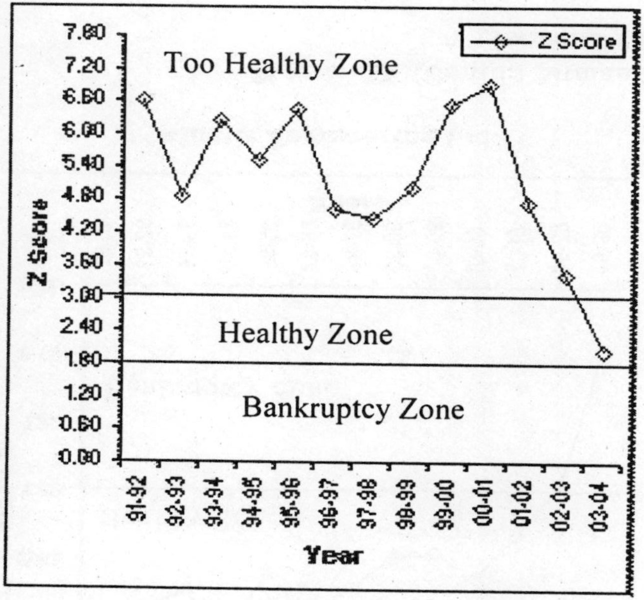

Kinetic Motors Company Ltd

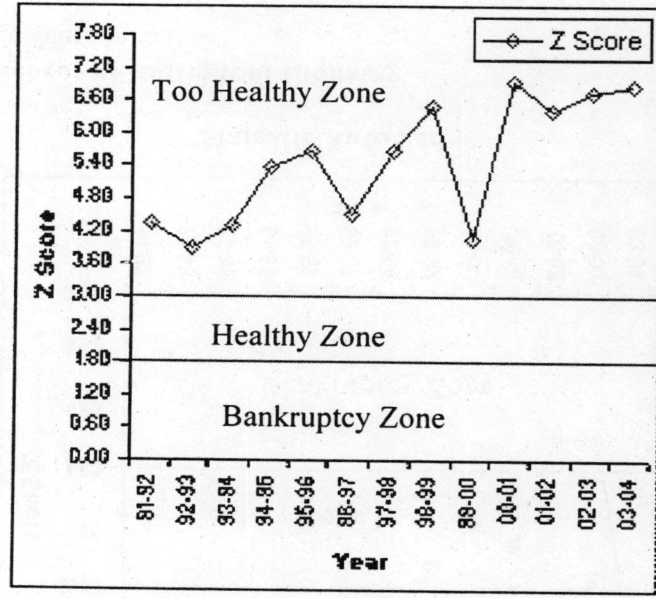

Hero Honda Motors Ltd

Figure - IX (Contd.) Altman Z scores of Individual Industry (Two and Three Wheelers)

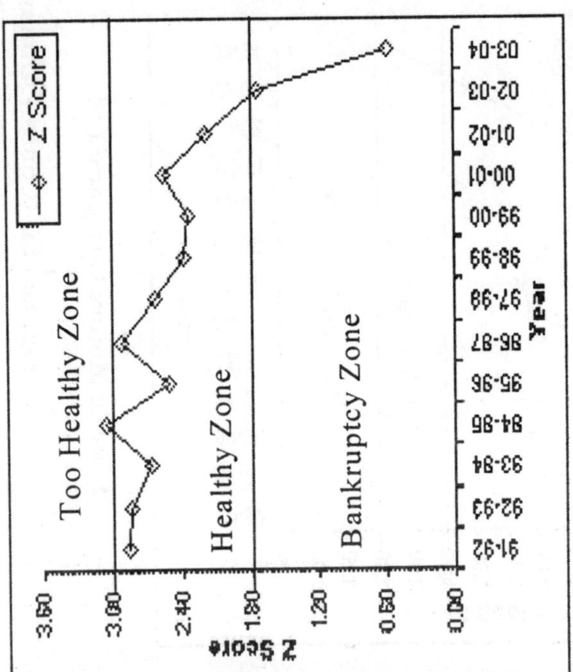

Kinetic Engineering Ltd.

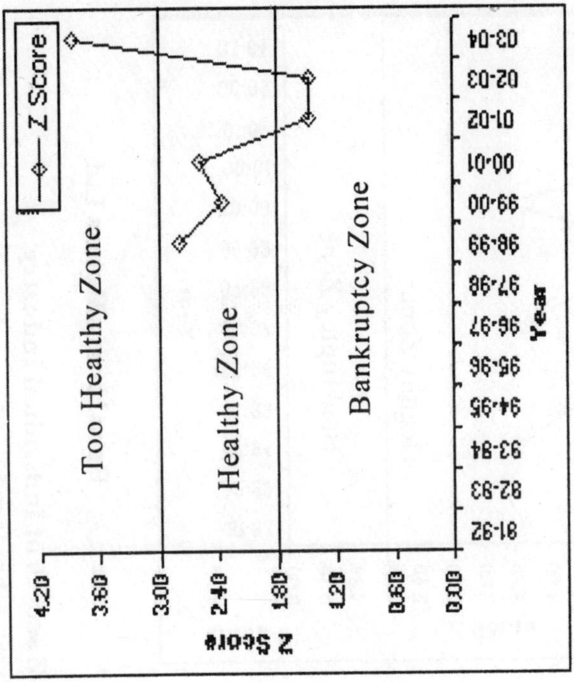

Majestic Auto Ltd

Figure - IX (Contd.) Altman Z scores of Individual Industry (Two and Three Wheelers)

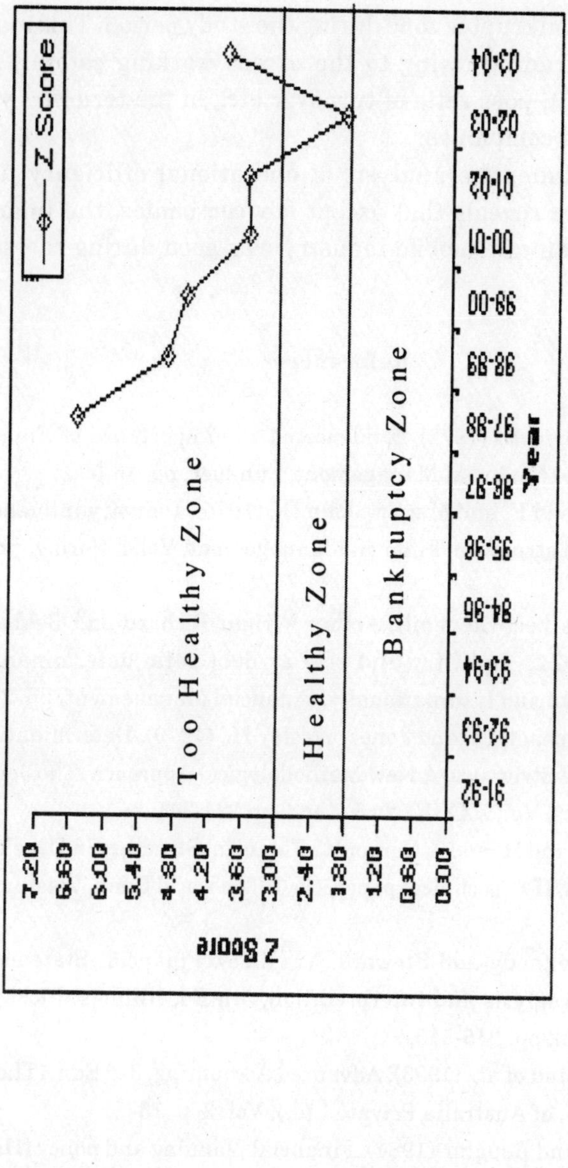

Scooters India Ltd.

Figure - IX (Contd.) Altman Z scores of Individual Industry (Two and Three Wheelers)

graph in Figure X. It is obvious from the figure that Maharastra Scooters Ltd and all other companiesfinancial health was sound and lies in healthy and too health zone during the study period. However, in the terminal years 2001-02 to 2003-04 the Z scores as Maharastra Scooters Ltd, Kinetic Engineering Ltd and Majestic Auto Ltd lie in the bankruptcy zone during the study period. This may be due to undertrading owing to the excess working capital, poor operating profit, poor ratio of turnover etc., in the terminal years by the selected companies.

To conclude, the analysis of operational efficiency using Altman Z score reveals that except few companies, the financial health of Indian automobile industry was good during the study period.

References

1. Scott, David F. (1972). Evidence on the importance of Financial Structure, Financial Management, Summer, pp. 45-50.
2. Scott, David F. and Martin, John D., (1975). Industry influence on Financial structure, Financial Management, Vol.4, Spring, pp. 67-75.
3. Remmers Lee, Stonenill, Arthur Wright Richard and Bekhuisen Theo (1974). Industry and size as debt ratio determinants in Manufacturing Internationally, Financial Management, pp. 24-32.
4. Ferri, Michael, G., and Jones, Wesley H., (1979). Determination of Financial Structure: A New Methodological Approach, The Journal of Finance, Vol, XXXIV, No.3. June, pp.331-344.
5. Singh, A and Hamid J, Corporate Financial Structure in Developing countries, IFC Technical paper, No.1, The world Bank, Washington, D.C.
6. Ralph Kennedy and Steward. Y. (1968). Financial Statements - Forms, Analysis and Interpretation, 5th Ed, (Illinois; Richard D. Irwin Inc), pp. 215-216.
7. R.K.Yorston et al., (1993). Advanced Accounting, 3rd Edn. (The Law Book Co., of Australia Private Ltd.), Vol. 3, p. 134.
8. Walker and Boughn (1984). Financial planning and policy (Harper International Student Edition Reprint), p. 151.

9. Guthman H.G., and Dougall H.E., (1982). Corporate Financial Policy, (New Delhi : Prentice Hall), p. 61.
10. The Economic Times (New Delhi), May 17, 1983, p.1.
11. Hunt, Willian and Donaldson, (1965). Basic Business Finance (Illinois : Richard D.Jrwinm)
12. Edwin I. Altman (1968). Financial Ratios - Discriminate analysis and prediction of corporate bankruptcy, Journal of Finance, Vol.9, pp. 589-609.
13. Bevar. W.R. (1966). Financial ratios as prediction of failure, Journal of Accounting Research, pp.71-110.
14. Argenti John (1976). Corporate collapse - the causes and symptoms,(New york: Mc.Graw Hill), p.91
15. Gupta, L.O (1979). Financial ratios as forwarding predicators of sickness, ICICI, Bombay, pp. 65-69.
16. Ohlson, S. (1980). Financial ratios and the prediction of bankruptcy, Journal of Accounting Research, pp. 109-131.
17. Etebari, A. (1987). Financial ratio criteria: A hypothesis and empirical test, Working paper, University of New Harcshrie, pp. 27-32.
18. Makridakis, S. (1991). Wear car we learn from corporate failure, Lang Range Planning. Vol.1 (244), pp. 115-225.
19. Sastry, K.S. (1994). Uses of 'Z' score of selective privatization marrtioused note, Indian Journal of Finance and Research, New Delhi. pp. 85-88.

7

Analysis of Economic Value Added (EVA) and Market Value Added (MVA)

Maximizing shareholders value is becoming the new corporate standard in India. The corporates, which gave the lowest preference to the shareholders' inquisitiveness, are now bestowing the utmost inclination to it. Shareholder's wealth is measured in terms of the returns they receive on their investment. The returns can either be in the form of dividends or in the form of capital appreciation or both. Capital appreciation in turn depends on the subsequent changes in the market value of the shares. This market value of shares is influenced by a number of factors, which can be company specific, industry specific and macro-economic in nature[1].

An important goal of financial management is to maximise the wealth of the organisation highest capital employees wealth and consequently enhance the value of the firm. Shareholder wealth is traditionally reflected by either standard accounting parameters (such as profits, earnings and cash flow from operations) or financial ratios (including earnings per share, return on capital employed, return on networth, net profit margin, operating profit margin etc. All these indicators failed to measure the true economic worth due to manipulative accounting techniques to state higher or lower earnings, depending on non meaningful decision on how to record revenues or expenses. Standard accounting principles fail to reflect the varying cost of capital among the business with in a company or the difference in risk in the case of alternative business strategies in the earnings.

This financial information is used by managers, shareholders and other interested parties to assess their firm's current performance, and also by stakeholders to predict its future performance. The question that then arises is, whether these measures of corporate performance are linked to the expectation of the shareholders or not. The problem with these performance measure is the lack of a proper benchmark for comparison. To help corporates to generate value for shareholders, value-based management system has been developed. Indeed, value-based management, which seeks to integrate finance hypothesis with strategic economic philosophy, is considered as one of the most significant contributions to corporate financial planning[2].

Over the past several years, an alternative performance measure called Economic Value Added (EVA) has been gaining acceptance around the globe and has also been acknowledged by institutional firms as a credible performance measure. In order to overcome the limitations of accounting based measures of financial performance, Joel M Stern and G. Bennett Stewart & Co., introduced a modified concept of economic profit in 1990, in the name of Economic Value Added (EVA) as a measure of business performance. Stern Stewart has claimed that EVA, as a tool of financial management, was neither 'just a phenomenon' nor was it limited to 'for profit' organizations. Economic Value Added has been put to use for management performance evaluation, and more than just a measure of performance, it is the framework for a complete financial management (for improving scarce capital allocation; and valuation of a target company at the time of acquisition).

EVA as a Tool of Financial Performance Measurement

Shareholder value creation is the new buzzword today and Economic Value Added (EVA) is its most popular measure. In simple terms EVA is nothing but returns generated above cost of capital. It is the Net Operating Profit After Tax (NOPAT) minus an appropriate change for the opportunity cost of all capital invested (WACC) in an organisation. EVA is an estimate of "economic profit" or the amount by which earnings exceed or fall short of the required minimum rate of return that shareholders and lenders could get by investing capital in other securities of analogous risk[3].

EVA as a tool of financial measurement enlightens whether the operating profit is enough to cover the cost of capital. Shareholders must earn sufficient returns for the risk they have taken in investing their funds in companies' capital. According to Business Standard - KPMG, if a company's EVA is negative, the firm is destroying shareholders' wealth even though it may be reporting a positive and growing earning per share and return on capital employed[4]. The EVA framework, which is becoming more and more admired tool for measuring the financial performance of corporates, offers a consistent approach to set goals and measure performance, communicate with investors, evaluate strategies, allocate capital valuing acquisitions and determine incentive bonuses. It is one of the several ongoing initiatives for a new corporate.

The evaluation and growth of the concept EVA, which may be realistically in young age in the west, has been going through its childhood in country like India. It may be quite emerging concept in the mind of Indian corporate policy makers and managers. Hence, this chapter examines in detail the EVA of selected automobile industry. It consists of sub-parts like EVA- based ranking of selected companies, industry - wise and sector - wise trends in EVA - based ranking, results and discussion on statistically established trends. The chapter also examines the linear regression analysis in the midst of Market Value Added (MVA) and other traditional financial variables like EVA, EPS, ROCE, NOPAT and RONW of sample companies. It also discusses multiple regression analysis amid MVA and other financial variables of sample companies on sector-wise.

EVA of Selected Companies

EVA-based performance framework not only provides a far more accurate report card on corporate financial performance than conventional measures, but also has considerable implications for companies on how to make strategic decisions and manage the healthier financial performance in their pursuit of shareholder value. EVA created by the selected Automobile industry during the study

Table 7.1
EVA of sample companies

(Rs. in crores)

Sl. No	*Industry*	*91-92*	*92-93*	*93-94*	*94-95*	*95-96*	*96-97*	*97-98*
1.	Ashok Leyland Ltd.	193.33	-200.47	178.07	121.34	226.19	244.25	249.12
		(5)	(17)	(5)	(5)	(4)	(3)	(6)
2.	Tata Motors Ltd.	272.29	-343.86	467.12	477.77	777.68	433.04	961.36
		(1)	(18)	(1)	(1)	(1)	(1)	(1)
3.	Bajaj Tempo Ltd.	30.84	-14.37	20.79	13.21	28.86	-4.88	11.12
		(9)	(9)	(11)	(11)	(11)	(15)	(13)
4.	Eicher Motors Ltd.	5.63	-1.62	4.06	15.63	18.21	14.28	8.58
		(15)	(5)	(15)	(10)	(12)	(10)	(16)
5.	Swaraj Mazda Ltd.	-2.47	-0.25	-0.08	4.52	11.60	10.71	10.46
		(18)	(3)	(17)	(14)	(15)	(11)	(14)
6.	Hindustan Motors Ltd.	98.51	-82.42	120.30	78.29	116.58	47.50	134.10
		(7)	(14)	(7)	(7)	(7)	(7)	(7)
7.	Mahindra and Mahindra Ltd.	122.47	-77.17	195.48	125.50	216.76	113.71	423.90
		(6)	(13)	(4)	(4)	(5)	(6)	(4)
8.	Maruthi Udyog Ltd.	266.56	-158.32	256.63	414.49	584.49	311.83	834.13
		(2)	(15)	(2)	(2)	(2)	(2)	(2)
9.	Daewoo Motors India Ltd.	-0.86	-1.21	2.45	-6.80	62.03	-48.81	-87.12
		(17)	(4)	(16)	(17)	(8)	(18)	(18)

(Contd.)

(Contd. Table 7.1)

Sl. No	Industry	98-99	99-00	00-01	01-02	02-03	03-04
1.	Ashok Leyland Ltd.	134.05	250.08	283.39	222.16	129.23	234.91
		(2)	(8)	(4)	(6)	(4)	(4)
2.	Tata Motors Ltd.	-900.70	1888.03	199.99	25.98	-1937.03	360.56
		(18)	(1)	(6)	(10)	(17)	(3)
3.	Bajaj Tempo Ltd.	-53.81	-14.84	-4.04	1.59	30.78	24.88
		(12)	(17)	(16)	(16)	(6)	(11)
4.	Eicher Motors Ltd.	3.33	22.81	23.00	22.82	5.21	38.26
		(5)	(13)	(9)	(13)	(8)	(8)
5.	Swaraj Mazda Ltd.	4.54	7.08	8.85	12.48	7.43	18.62
		(4)	(16)	(11)	(14)	(7)	(12)
6.	Hindustan Motors Ltd.	-66.55	138.27	6.58	68.64	-167.24	-44.35
		(13)	(9)	(14)	(8)	(14)	(17)
7.	Mahindra and Mahindra Ltd.	-178.50	961.95	307.59	395.52	-104.02	139.67
		(15)	(4)	(3)	(5)	(16)	(5)
8.	Maruthi Udyog Ltd.	-452.34	1419.86	-39.45	621.12	-2852.98	30.86
		(17)	(3)	(17)	(2)	(18)	(9)
9.	Daewoo Motors India Ltd.	-161.33	-15.29	-91.12	-185.09	-101.02	-58.01
		(14)	(18)	(18)	(18)	(13)	(18)

(Contd.)

(Contd. Table 7.1)

Sl. No	Industry	91-92	92-93	93-94	94-95	95-96	96-97	97-98
10	Bajaj Auto Ltd.	242.82 (4)	-175.98 (16)	231.55 (3)	278.45 (3)	414.44 (3)	237.60 (4)	535.21 (3)
11	LML Ltd.	256.28 (3)	130.25 (1)	123.90 (6)	110.86 (6)	118.75 (6)	166.24 (5)	255.71 (5)
12	Maharastra Scooters Ltd.	36.69 (8)	-29.20 (10)	21.97 (10)	9.65 (12)	15.66 (13)	-2.29 (14)	19.08 (10)
13	TVS Motors India Ltd.	22.44 (11)	0.15 (2)	31.50 (8)	39.35 (8)	43.23 (9)	38.87 (8)	103.30 (8)
14	Kinetic Motors Company Ltd.	9.14 (14)	-7.98 (8)	6.57 (13)	4.14 (15)	7.01 (16)	-0.15 (13)	9.10 (15)
15	Hero Honda Motors Ltd.	2.31 (16)	-5.59 (7)	28.46 (9)	22.32 (9)	29.46 (10)	37.81 (9)	85.38 (9)
16	Kinetic Engineering Ltd.	12.78 (13)	-4.96 (6)	9.09 (12)	6.83 (13)	12.15 (14)	5.98 (12)	15.03 (11)
17	Majestic Auto Ltd.	28.41 (10)	-49.00 (12)	5.45 (14)	-5.97 (16)	-4.18 (17)	-15.16 (17)	-1.07 (17)
18	Scooters India Ltd.	15.46 (12)	-37.27 (11)	-0.38 (18)	-7.88 (18)	-7.27 (18)	-14.68 (16)	12.05 (12)

(Contd.)

(Contd. Table 7.1)

Sl. No	*Industry*	*98-99*	*99-00*	*00-01*	*01-02*	*02-03*	*03-04*
10	Bajaj Auto Ltd.	-425.16 (16)	1452.88 (2)	422.51 (1)	811.70 (1)	2223.75 (1)	87.48 (7)
11	LML Ltd.	276.42 (1)	462.71 (5)	401.60 (2)	410.00 (4)	290.32 (2)	362.97 (2)
12	Maharastra Scooters Ltd.	-28.90 (11)	69.39 (10)	7.58 (12)	23.43 (11)	135.48 (3)	25.14 (10)
13	TVS Motors India Ltd.	3.07 (6)	252.27 (7)	112.90 (7)	129.29 (7)	-304.01 (15)	117.14 (6)
14	Kinetic Motors Company Ltd.	-1.65 (9)	27.00 (12)	19.09 (10)	28.47 (9)	-33.18 (10)	-21.16 (15)
15	Hero Honda Motors Ltd.	39.97 (3)	278.14 (6)	254.86 (5)	496.11 (3)	-34.30 (11)	494.32 (1)
16	Kinetic Engineering Ltd.	-1.09 (8)	36.60 (11)	23.11 (8)	22.93 (12)	-38.55 (12)	-40.10 16)
17	Majestic Auto Ltd.	-1.97 (10)	14.78 (14)	6.99 (13)	-5.47 (17)	-27.78 (9)	6.31 (13)
18	Scooters India Ltd.	1.05 (7)	10.24 (15)	3.72 (15)	3.55 (15)	94.98 (5)	-1.90 (14)

Figures in parenthesis denotes EVA based ranking of selected companies.
Source: Computed

period is depicted in Table 7.1. The table shows that out of eighteen industry, sixteen industry has generated positive EVA during the study period except in the year 1992-93, 1994-95, 1996-97, 1998-99, 2002-03 and 2003-04 and two companies have destroyed their shareholder wealth during the same period. In the year 1992-93 the number of companies generating negative EVA went up to sixteen, eleven in the year 1998-99 and ten in the year 2002-03. It would be worthwhile to mention here that during this period the economy of the nation faced showery time. Political instability at Union Government level and Kargil War may be the qualified grounds to such downhill state of affairs in the economy. In the year 2001-02 in which Indian economy revealed the optimistic wind, witnessed that sixteen companies are created wealth for the shareholders and only two have destroyed the same. However the number of companies generate negative EVA increased to ten in the year 2002-03. It may be extrapolated that the year 2003-04 may be able to see the economy in a slightly good health yet again.

It may be observed from Table 7.1 that LML Ltd was the only company out of eighteen companies who have been constantly generating the positive EVA all the way throughout the period of study. On the other hand, Daewoo Motors Indian Ltd was the only company who has been annihilating the wealth of shareholders right through the period under reference except in the year 1993-94 and 1995-96. Ashok Leyland Ltd, Eicher Motors Ltd, TVS Motors India Ltd, Bajaj Auto Ltd and Hero Honda Motors Ltd created positive EVA during the major part of thirteen years period. Rest of the companies displayed high instability on this front.

On the whole the Table 7.1 concludes that about one-third (6 out 18), of the sample companies have been able to govern affirmative EVA during period under study whereas remaining companies make is feasible to append a very little to the value of shareholders.

EVA Based Ranking of Selected Companies

Table 7.1 also presents EVA - based ranking of sample companies. It is evident from the table that companies like LML Ltd. Bajaj Auto Ltd. Maruthi Udyog Ltd and Tata Motors Ltd. are toping in the list during the study period. On the other the companies

Table 7.2

EVA - Based Frequencies Distribution of Sample Companies

EVA	*91-92*	*92-93*	*93-94*	*94-95*	*95-96*	*96-97*	*97-98*
Negative	2	16	2	3	2	6	2
Up to Rs.10 crores	3	1	5	4	1	1	2
Rs.10-25 crores	3		2	3	4	2	5
Rs.25-50 crores	3		2	1	3	3	
Rs.50-100 crores	1			1	1		1
Rs.100-500 crores	6	1	7	6	5	6	5
Above Rs. 500 crores					2		3
Total	**18**	**18**	**18**	**18**	**18**	**18**	**18**

(Contd.)

(Contd. Table 7.2)

EVA	98-99	99-00	00-01	01-02	02-03	03-04
Negative	11	2	3	2	10	5
Up to Rs.10 crores	4	1	5	2	2	1
Rs. 10-25 crores		3	3	4		2
Rs. 25-50 crores	1	2		2	1	3
Rs. 50-100 crores		1		1	1	1
Rs. 100-500 crores	2	5	7	5	3	6
Above Rs. 500 crores		4		2	1	
Total	**18**	**18**	**18**	**18**	**18**	**18**

like Swaraj Mazda Ltd, Daewoo Motors India Ltd, Kinetic Engineering Ltd, Majestic Auto Ltd and Scooters India Ltd has been loosing the grounds. Rest of the companies has indexed unsteady position during the study period.

EVA based frequencies distribution of sample companies are shown in Table 7.2. It is clear from the table that 16 companies in 1992-93, 11 in 1998-99 and 10 in 2002-03 are reporting negative EVA and the remaining companies generating positive EVA during the study period. It is also observed that 33 $^{1}/_{3}$ per cent of the company have added to the economic value between Rs.100 crores to Rs.500 crores during the study period and only two companies in 1995-96, 3 in 1997-98, 4 in 1999-00, 2 in 2001-02 and 1 in 2002-03 reported an EVA of over Rs.500 crores.

Sector-wise Trends in EVA

Table 7.3 presents sector - wise EVA of sample companies. It is evident from Table 7.3 that the mean EVA generated for the Automobile industry was Rs.79.53 crores during the study period. The mean EVA generated was the highest in two and three wheelers sector followed by commercial vehicles and passenger cars and multiutility vehicles sector. Two and three wheelers sector and commercial vehicles sector should perform well in this regard because their average was more than the industry average. It is also evident from the table that all the selected sectors and whole industry witnessed very high fluctuation in their EVA during the study period. Table 7.3 further reported that the commercial vehicles, passenger cars and multiutility vehicles sector and whole industry registered negative compound annual growth rate of EVA during the study period.

The economic value added of selected industry under commercial vehicles sector during the study period is also presented in Table 7.3. The mean EVA was the highest in Tata Motors Ltd, followed by Ashok Leyland Ltd, Eicher Motors Ltd, Swaraj Mazda Ltd and Bajaj Tempo Ltd. All the industry under the sector had registered very high fluctuation in their EVA during the study period. It is also evident from the table that two companies namely Tata Motors Ltd and Bajaj Tempo Ltd registered negative compound annual growth rate of EVA during the study period.

Table 7.3 depicts the EVA generated by the selected companies under passenger cars and multiutility vehicles sector during the study period. Table 7.3 portrays that Daewoo Motors India Ltd showed negative EVA throughout the study period except in the year 1993-94 and 1995-96. The mean EVA generated was the highest in Mahindra and Mahindra Ltd followed by Maruthi Udyog Ltd and Hindustan Motors Ltd. All the companies registered very high

Table 7.3

EVA – Sector – wise Trends (1991-92 - 2003-04)

S. No.	*Industry*	*Mean (Rs. in crores)*	*CV*	*CAGR*
1.	Ashok Leyland Ltd.	174.28	0.71	15.70
2.	Tata Motors Ltd.	206.33	4.45	-9.22
3.	Bajaj Tempo Ltd.	5.39	4.50	-4.89
4.	Eicher Motors Ltd.	13.86	0.80	14.70
5.	Swaraj Mazda Ltd.	7.19	0.82	20.80
	Commercial Vehicles Sector	**81.41**	**2.42**	**-3.16**
6.	Hindustan Motors Ltd.	34.48	2.82	-22.40
7.	Mahindra and Mahindra Ltd.	131.30	3.41	2.50
8.	Maruthi Udyog Ltd.	95.14	10.55	-17.30
9.	Daewoo Motors India Ltd.	-53.24	-1.32	-8.77
	Passenger Cars and Multiutility Vehicles Sector	**51.92**	**7.42**	**-9.01**
10.	Bajaj Auto Ltd.	487.47	1.42	19.60
11.	LML Ltd.	258.92	0.48	9.88
12.	Maharastra Scooters Ltd.	23.36	1.81	13.60
13.	TVS Motors Company Ltd.	45.35	2.77	16.00
14.	Kinetic Motors Company Ltd.	3.57	4.87	-0.73
15.	Hero Honda Motors Ltd.	133.02	1.40	30.50
16.	Kinetic Engineering Ltd.	4.60	4.84	-4.13
17.	Majestic Auto Ltd.	-3.74	-5.15	-2.53
18.	Scooters India Ltd.	5.51	5.46	11.00
	Two and Three Wheelers Sector	**105.27**	**0.92**	**20.80**
	Whole Automobile Industry	**79.53**	**2.45**	**-1.24**

Table 7.4
Paired Test of Sector-wise EVA of Sample Companies

Paired sample test	Paired differences: Mean	Std Deviation	Std error of Mean	95 % Confidence Level: Lower	95 % Confidence Level: Upper	t	df	Sig (2 –tailed)
EVA 91-92 – EVA 92-93	148.49	187.69	44.24	55.10	241.78	3.36	17	.004
EVA 92-93 – EVA 93-94	-153.46	222.50	52.44	-264.10	-42.81	-2.93	17	.009
EVA 93-94 – EVA 94-95	-6.33	47.30	11.15	-23.45	23.59	.016	17	.995
EVA 94-95 – EVA 95-96	-53.89	80.84	19.05	-94.09	-13.68	-2.83	17	.012
EVA 95-96 – EVA 96-97	60.88	105.66	24.90	8.34	113.42	2.45	17	.026
EVA 96-97 – EVA 97-98	-111.31	178.05	41.97	-199.85	-22.77	-2.65	17	.017
EVA 97-98 – EVA 98-99	299.39	535.38	126.19	33.15	565.63	2.37	17	.030
EVA 98-99 – EVA 99-00	-503.97	832.52	196.23	-917.85	-89.97	-2.57	17	.020
EVA 99-00 – EVA 00-01	295.27	539.71	127.21	26.88	563.66	2.32	17	.033
EVA 00-01 – EVA 01-02	-64.34	192.02	45.26	-159.83	31.15	-1.42	17	.173
EVA 01-02 – EVA 02-03	373.56	1030.43	242.88	-138.86	885.99	1.54	17	.142
EVA 02-03 – EVA 03-04	-299.70	1041.73	245.54	-817.74	218.34	-1.22	17	.239
EVA 91-92 – EVA 03-04	-9.05	149.57	35.25	-83.43	65.33	-0.26	17	.800

Sources: Computed.

fluctuation in their EVA during the study period. Only Mahindra and Mahindra Ltd witnessed positive compound annual growth rate of EVA and the rest of the company showed negative compound annual growth rate of EVA.

The EVA generated by the companies under two and three wheeler sectors during the study period is presented in Table 7.3. It is evident from the Table 7.3 that Majestic Auto Ltd generated negative EVA in majority of the years, followed by Scooters India Ltd. The rest of the companies had registered a mixed trend of EVA during the study period. Among the selected companies, Bajaj Auto Ltd, LML Ltd, Hero Honda Motors Ltd and TVS Motors India Ltd had shown improved performance with record to EVA generation during the study period. All the selected companies under this sector had registered very high fluctuation in their EVA during the study period. Kinetic Motors Company Ltd, Kinetic Engineering Ltd and Majestic Auto Ltd had registered negative compound annual growth rate of EVA and the rest of the companies showed positive compound annual growth rate of EVA during the study period.

The sector wise paired test provided the value of t test in Table 7.4. The table exhibits that there has been significant deviation (at 5% level) in the EVA of respective years except for the year 1994-95 and 2001-02 to 2003-04.

Comparison of EVA and Conventional Method of Financial Performance

Analysing the corporate performance of Indian automobile industry based on Return on Capital Employed (ROCE) - the conventional benchmarks and on the new "trendier" one i.e., EVA, the results can be well exhibited in Table 7.5. From the table, it can be inferred that Indian automobile industry depicts a rosy picture in terms of return on capital employed. The mean value of return on capital employed of automobile industry during the study period 18.40 per cent i.e., for every Rs.100 investment, the return is Rs. 18.40 whereas EVA as a percentage of capital employed is only 14.07 i.e., for every Rs. 100 investment, the company has added value of Rs. 14.07. The same picture is reflected as in the case of commercial vehicles sector and passenger cars and multiutility vehicles sector during the study period. But in case of two and three wheelers

Table 7.5

Comparison of EVA Vs Conventional Method of Financial Performance

(in percentage)

Year	*Commercial Vehicles*		*Passengers Cars and Multiutility Vehicles*		*Two and Three Wheelers*		*Industry average*	
	ROCE	*EVA/CE*	*ROCE*	*EVA/CE*	*ROCE*	*EVA/CE*	*ROCE*	*EVA/CE*
1991-92	16.09	13.12	8.13	20.18	17.94	36.67	14.05	23.32
1992-93	7.78	-4.10	6.82	-11.82	16.82	8.67	10.47	-2.42
1993-94	17.63	13.40	15.33	19.07	27.88	33.78	20.28	22.08
1994-95	23.47	16.98	21.96	15.96	28.36	26.62	24.60	19.85
1995-96	27.15	21.55	33.75	20.40	26.90	25.89	29.27	22.61
1996-97	20.18	10.49	26.30	7.72	28.74	16.72	25.28	11.64
1997-98	13.43	13.64	16.61	17.21	21.77	28.18	17.27	19.68
1998-99	8.72	1.56	9.48	-8.52	22.94	7.98	13.71	0.34
1999-00	11.23	10.86	5.53	22.56	27.29	42.45	14.68	25.29
2000-01	12.90	10.48	-0.67	2.31	16.55	24.98	9.59	12.59
2001-02	17.63	10.98	3.72	9.98	19.09	30.18	13.48	17.05
2002-03	33.07	19.65	8.72	-38.25	19.57	15.73	20.45	-0.96
2003-04	41.31	16.26	23.33	1.60	13.47	17.69	26.04	11.85
Mean	**19.32**	**11.91**	**13.81**	**6.03**	**22.10**	**24.22**	**18.40**	**14.07**
CV	**0.51**	**0.58**	**0.73**	**2.88**	**0.24**	**0.43**	**0.35**	**0.69**
CAGR	**4.65**	**5.09**	**-6.60**	**- 14.00**	**-2.36**	**-0.96**	**0.33**	**-5.37**

Source: Computed.

sector, EVA as a percentage of capital employed showed better performance than the return on capital employed. Thus, the comparison shows that divergence exists between the performance results given by traditional measure and EVA. The traditional measures do not reflect the real value addition to shareholders' wealth and thus EVA has to be measured to have an idea about the shareholders value addition.

Market Value Added (MVA) of Selected Companies

The MVA explains the value added to a particular equity share over its book value. It informs how much value has been added in the economic value of the shareholders. In view of that, a company with an objective of pleasing to the eyes of the shareholders' wealth should endeavor to take advantage of its MVA. MVA can be estimated by subtracting the book value of shares from the market value of shares. It is silent that EVA helps in pushing up the MVA of an organization. Thus, EVA can be considered as an internal measure and MVA as the external measure of a company's financial performance.

Table 7.6 presents MVA calculation of selected companies of Indian automobile industry. On the base of the table, it may be observed that out of 18 companies, 15 companies have registered positive MVA throughout the study period. It indicates that the market value of these companies is dominating over the book value. On the otherhand, Hindustan Motors Ltd (1997-98, 1999-00, 2000-01 and 2001-02), Daewoo Motors Ltd (1997-98 and 1999-2004) and Scooters India Ltd (except 1998-99, 1999-00, 2001-02 and 2003-04) have registered negative MVA during the study period. It shows that the book value of these companies is dominated over the market value.

MVA based Ranking of Selected Companies

Table 7.6 also provides MVA based ranking. Glancing all the way through the table, it is noticed that companies like Maruthi Udyog Ltd, Bajaj Auto Ltd, Tata Motors Ltd, Ashok Leyland Ltd, Mahindra and Mahindra Ltd and TVS Motors India Ltd are topping the list and on the other side companies like Scooters India Ltd, Daewoo Motors India Ltd, Hindustan Motors Ltd, Majestic Auto

Ltd and Kinetic Engineering Ltd are struggling in terms of MVA over the period.

Sector Wise Trends in MVA

Table 7.7 portrays whole automobile industry and sector wise information pertaining to MVA. It is evident from Table 7.7 that among the three sectors, passenger cars and mutiutility vehicles sector have been generating highest market value added throughout the study period. This was due to the better market value added of Maruthi Udyog Ltd and Mahindra and Mahindra Ltd. It was followed by commercial vehicles sector and two and three wheelers. Table 7.7 also shows that all the selected sectors of automobile industry has been generating positive aggregate MVA throughout the period.The growth of MVA is more consistence in case of passenger cars and multiutility vehicles whereas less consistent in case of commercial vehicles and two and three wheelers sector. Table also brings out that only the commercial vehicles sector had registered negative compound annual growth rate of MVA during the study period.

The market value added of selected companies under commercial vehicles sector during the study period is also presented in Table 7.7 Table 7.7 reveals that the mean MVA of Tata Motors Ltd were the highest followed by Ashok Leyland Ltd, Bajaj Tempo Ltd, Eicher Motors Ltd and Swaraj Mazda Ltd. Table 7.7 brings out that all the selected companies under the commercial vehicles sector had registered very high fluctuations in their MVA except Bajaj Tempo Ltd which registered moderate fluctuations during the study period. Further, Table 7.7 provided that the two companies namely Tata Motors Ltd and Bajaj Tempo Ltd had registered negative compound annual growth rate of MVA and rest of the companies had positive compound annual growth rate of MVA during the study period.

Table 7.7 presents MVA of selected companies under passengers cars and multiutility vehicles sector. The table shows that the companies like Maruthi Udyog Ltd and Mahindra and Mahindra Ltd are top in the list and it was followed by Hindustan Motors Ltd and Daewoo Motors Ltd. All the selected companies except Maruthi Udyog Ltd had registered very high fluctuation in

Table 7.6

MVA of sample companies

(Rs. in crores)

Sl. No	Industry	91-92	92-93	93-94	94-95	95-96	96-97	97-98
1.	Ashok Leyland Ltd.	424.31 (4)	464.71 (4)	917.28 (4)	1190.49 (4)	1233.30 (5)	611.30 (6)	328.25 (7)
2.	Tata Motors Ltd.	6283.94 (2)	3503.05 (2)	6069.37 (2)	6444.12 (2)	10112.67 (1)	10700.65 (1)	4334.61 (3)
3.	Bajaj Tempo Ltd.	305.25 (7)	159.37 (7)	350.98 (6)	344.69 (6)	356.93 (6)	282.64 (7)	184.20 (9)
4.	Eicher Motors Ltd.	39.60 (16)	16.40 (16)	67.50 (13)	55.50 (14)	57.96 (14)	12.44 (17)	29.20 (14)
5.	Swaraj Mazda Ltd.	41.27 (15)	17.06 (15)	35.15 (17)	28.90 (17)	30.18 (17)	25.53 (15)	29.55 (13)
6.	Hindustan Motors Ltd.	110.63 (10)	47.31 (11)	181.07 (10)	142.11 (11)	150.23 (11)	43.35 (14)	-8.39 (16)
7.	Mahindra and Mahindra Ltd.	384.56 (5)	367.86 (5)	880.37 (5)	841.78 (5)	1575.30 (4)	1685.95 (4)	928.68 (5)
8.	Maruthi Udyog Ltd.	12099.24 (1)	6377.44 (1)	10654.64 (1)	9175.90 (1)	9478.58 (2)	9461.12 (2)	10979.28 (1)
9.	Daewoo Motors India Ltd.	24.92 (17)	12.48 (17)	60.57 (16)	94.04 (13)	100.11 (12)	188.56 (10)	-21.98 (18)

(Contd.)

(Contd.Table 7.6)

Sl. No	*Industry*	*98-99*	*99-00*	*00-01*	*01-02*	*02-03*	*03-04*
10.	Ashok Leyland Ltd.	1027.56 (5)	511.40 (6)	676.71 (5)	1047.77 (5)	213.17 (4)	2468.99 (5)
11.	Tata Motors Ltd.	295.41 (7)	2345.58 (4)	2054.88 (4)	4359.15 (4)	727.81 (4)	1206.66 (7)
12.	Bajaj Tempo Ltd.	228.25 (8)	340.08 (8)	219.67 (8)	122.03 (9)	371.03 (9)	340.97 (9)
13.	Eicher Motors Ltd.	55.56 (11)	39.90 (11)	31.74 (11)	128.56 (8)	317.52 (11)	293.49 (10)
14.	Swaraj Mazda Ltd.	42.64 (13)	27.89 (13)	21.88 (13)	62.12 (12)	172.52 (11)	293.49 (10)
15.	Hindustan Motors Ltd.	9.49 (18)	-28.47 (17)	-84.34 (17)	-23.38 (17)	664.39 (8)	101.49 (13)
16.	Mahindra and Mahindra Ltd.	1785.92 (4)	926.04 (5)	417.72 (5)	462.88 (7)	1465.79 (6)	2643.29 (4)
17.	Maruthi Udyog Ltd.	10544.05 (1)	14144.72 (1)	10156.94 (1)	9771.41 (1)	9361.00 (1)	12219.21 (1)
18.	Daewoo Motors India Ltd.	140.00 (10)	-56.74 (18)	-301.09 (18)	-348.11 (18)	-249.46 (18)	-120.64 (18)

(Contd.)

(Contd. Table 7.3)

Sl. No	Industry	91-92	92-93	93-94	94-95	95-96	96-97	97-98
19.	Bajaj Auto Ltd.	2951.28 (3)	1586.69 (3)	2598.31 (3)	4731.38 (3)	4887.86 (3)	4552.39 (3)	6777.89 (2)
20.	LML Ltd.	105.47 (11)	78.10 (10)	234.04 (8)	167.32 (9)	187.27 (9)	274.17 (8)	343.08 (6)
21.	Maharastra Scooters Ltd.	71.83 (14)	35.56 (13)	62.67 (15)	53.29 (16)	55.22 (16)	46.47 (13)	64.08 (10)
22.	TVS Motors India Ltd.	349.27 (6)	175.10 (6)	305.15 (7)	260.11 (7)	269.35 (7)	268.88 (9)	315.08 (8)
23.	Kinetic Motors Company Ltd.	130.04 (9)	93.36 (9)	171.23 (11)	145.69 (10)	150.93 (10)	146.01 (11)	64.07 (11)
24.	Hero Honda Motors Ltd.	264.47 (8)	133.27 (8)	231.39 (9)	246.58 (8)	255.52 (8)	655.81 (5)	1117.02 (4)
25.	Kinetic Engineering Ltd.	88.51 (12)	45.78 (12)	94.75 (12)	94.72 (12)	98.17 (13)	57.37 (12)	34.87 (12)
26.	Majestic Auto Ltd.	74.99 (13)	34.84 (14)	64.86 (14)	54.48 (15)	56.61 (15)	21.68 (16)	17.16 (15)
27.	Scooters India Ltd.	-36.17 (18)	-26.60 (18)	-18.84 (18)	-21.53 (18)	-21.00 (18)	-17.27 (18)	-11.28 (17)

(Contd.)

(Contd. Table 7.3)

Sl. No	Industry	98-99	99-00	00-01	01-02	02-03	03-04
28.	Bajaj Auto Ltd	5365.98 (2)	3180.98 (3)	3180.98 (3)	4697.99 (3)	7714.77 (2)	9212.27 (3)
29.	LML Ltd.	190.83 (9)	84.12 (9)	40.16 (9)	114.74 (10)	150.58 (12)	124.08 (12)
30.	Maharastra Scooters Ltd.	54.10 (12)	27.96 (12)	17.10 (14)	70.24 (11)	120.15 (13)	156.58 (11)
31.	TVS Motors India Ltd.	301.92 (6)	411.64 (7)	331.72 (7)	1021.94 (6)	1778.70 (5)	1800.73 (6)
32.	Kinetic Motors Company Ltd.	41.25 (14)	51.53 (10)	36.80 (10)	43.85 (13)	33.80 (14)	38.19 (15)
33.	Hero Honda Motors Ltd.	4352.66 (3)	3533.09 (2)	4312.72 (2)	5531.69 (2)	6633.43 (3)	9662.88 (2)
34.	Kinetic Engineering Ltd.	32.47 (15)	25.33 (14)	24.42 (12)	29.30 (14)	31.11 (15)	24.24 (16)
35.	Majestic Auto Ltd.	14.86 (17)	6.42 (15)	8.78 (15)	17.20 (15)	24.62 (16)	39.32 (14)
36.	Scooters India Ltd.	14.97 (16)	3.38 (16)	-7.64 (16)	3.20 (16)	-0.30 (17)	12.68 (17)

Figures in parenthesis denotes MVA based ranking of selected companies.
Source: Computed.

Table 7.7
MVA – Sector – wise Trends (1991-92 to 2003-04)

S. No.	*Industry*	*Mean (Rs.crores)*	*CV*	*CAGR*
1.	Ashok Leyland Ltd.	1003.02	0.65	8.64
2.	Tata Motors Ltd.	4495.22	0.74	-16.70
3.	Bajaj Tempo Ltd.	277.39	0.31	-0.54
4.	Eicher Motors Ltd.	99.63	1.31	17.00
5.	Swaraj Mazda Ltd.	63.71	1.25	13.80
	Commercial Vehicles Sector	**1187.83**	**0.53**	**-6.34**
6.	Hindustan Motors Ltd.	100.43	1.87	-19.00
7.	Mahindra & Mahindra Ltd.	1105.09	0.62	7.03
8.	Maruthi Udyog Ltd.	10340.26	0.18	1.58
9.	Daewoo Motors India Ltd.	-36.72	-4.67	-39.30
	Passenger Cars and Multiutility Vehicles Sector	**2877.27**	**0.18**	**1.85**
10.	Bajaj Auto Ltd.	4726.06	0.46	8.36
11.	LML Ltd.	161.07	0.53	-2.70
12.	Maharastra Scooters Ltd.	64.25	0.58	3.59
13.	TVS Motors Company Ltd.	583.81	0.98	15.30
14.	Kinetic Motors Company Ltd.	88.21	0.60	-14.00
15.	Hero Honda Motors Ltd.	2840.81	1.09	38.20
16.	Kinetic Engineering Ltd.	52.39	0.58	-11.90
17.	Majestic Auto Ltd.	33.52	0.68	-11.60
18.	Scooters India Ltd.	-9.72	-1.61	13.80
	Two and Three Wheelers Sector	**948.68**	**0.62**	**14.60**
	Whole Automobile Industry	**1671.26**	**0.20**	**2.41**

their MVA during the study period. Table 7.7 also brings out values relating to compound annual growth rate of MVA of selected companies. It is evident from the table that 2 out of 4 companies had registered negative growth rate and rest of the companies had registered positive growth rate of MVA during the study period.

Table 7.7 brings out the values relating to MVA of selected companies under two and three wheelers. Table 7.7 showed that Bajaj Auto Ltd, Hero Honda Motors Ltd, TVS Motors India Ltd and LML Ltd comparatively top in the list. On the otherhand, Scooters India Ltd and Majestic Auto Ltd are struggling on their front with

Table 7.8
Paired Test of Sector-wise MVA of Sample Companies

Paired sample test	*Paired differences*					*t*	*df*	*Sig (2 –tailed)*
	Mean	*Std Deviation*	*Std error of Mean*	*95 % Confidence Level*				
				Lower	*Upper*			
MVA 91-92 – MVA 92-93	588.42	1458.95	343.88	-137.09	1313.94	1.71	17	0.105
MVA 92-93 – MVA 93-94	-546.60	114.46	262.68	-1110.80	7.61	-2.08	17	0.053
MVA 93-94 – MVA 94-95	-60.50	636.99	150.14	-377.27	256.26	-0.40	17	0.692
MVA 94-95 – MVA 95-96	-276.98	865.49	204.00	-707.38	153.42	-1.36	17	0.192
MVA 95-96 – MVA 96-97	1.01	249.15	58.73	-122.89	124.91	.02	17	0.987
MVA 96-97 – MVA 97-98	195.09	1680.98	396.21	-640.84	1031.02	.49	17	0.629
MVA 97-98 – MVA 98-99	55.97	1332.60	314.10	-606.72	718.66	.18	17	0.861
MVA 98-99 – MVA 99-00	-59.83	1179.06	277.91	-646.16	526.50	-0.22	17	0.832
MVA 99-00 – MVA 00-01	246.43	966.30	227.76	-234.10	726.96	1.08	17	0.294
MVA 00-01 – MVA 01-02	-331.86	682.31	166.82	-671.16	7.74	-2.06	17	0.055
MVA 01-02 – MVA 02-03	-241.21	1236.32	291.40	-856.02	373.60	-0.83	17	0.419
MVA 02-03 – MVA 03-04	-5.11.87	999.03	235.47	-1008.67	-15.06	-2.17	17	0.044
MVA 91-92 – MVA 03-04	-941.92	2960.68	697.84	-2414.24	530.39	-1.35	17	0.195

Source: Computed.

regard to MVA during the study period. It is also noticed that all the selected companies have registered very high fluctuations in their MVA during the study period. The analysis of compound annual growth rate of MVA showed mixed trend among the selected companies under the sector during the study period.

The sector-wise paired test provided the value of the t-test in Table 7.8. The table exhibits that there has been no significant deviation in MVA in respect of years except for the year 1993-94, 2001-02 and 2003-04.

MVA vis-a-vis other financial variables-Linear Regression and Multiple Regression Analysis

In this section an attempt to find the relevance of Stern and Stewart's claim that MVA of the firm is largely positive association with or driven by its EVA generating capacity and other financial variables like EPS, ROCE, NOPAT and RONW. Based on the sample of 18 companies of Indian automobile industry for a period of 13 years, the analysis of this section is divided into two parts: in the first part, the linear regression analysis between dependent and particular selected independent variables (s) has been examined and in the second part multiple regression analysis between MVA and other financial variables has been looked at for the selected sectors of automobile industry during the study period.

Linear Regression analysis of MVA and selected financial variables

In this section, results of correlation co-efficients, linear regression, Durbin-Watson model, F-statistics and t-statistics have been determined between dependent variable (MVA) and independent variables. The values hence obtained have their particular statistical sense. The regression co-efficients for independent variables like EVA, EPS, ROCE, NOTPAT and RONW so worked out portray the temperament of association between the dependent and particular independent variable. The t-statistics and F-statistics so calculated determine the level of significant or insignificant association between the variables. Durbin-Watson model allows the researcher to establish the auto-correlation, if any between dependent and independent variable (the desirable value is two and any value more than two signifies negative auto-correlation and vice versa); values of adjusted R^2 indicate the extent of variation in the dependent variable which may be explicated by independent variable (s) and the standard error speaks about the limits within which the estimated value as the dependent variable is expected to lie.

MVA-EVA Analysis

Table 7.9 offers the explanation about the regression analysis between MVA and EVA during the study period for the whole automobile industry and its three sectors. Table 7.9 provides the values of R, R-square and adjusted R-square for the whole industry 0.165, 0.03 and -0.06 respectively. It sounds that there exists poor relationship between MVA and EVA in automobile industry, as the value of adjusted R-square in negative. Interestingly, the t and F statistics give the identical results but both of them lead to insignificant association between the variables under reference. It is evident from the table that the overall results in passenger cars and multiutility vehicles does not differ from whole industry and statistical association between MVA and EVA is again insignificant. Table 7.9 suggests that EVA are serially correlated in commercial vehicles and two and three wheelers sector and adjusted R-square value is also positive. The t and F statistics are resulting identical values and secure that in commercial vehicles and two and three wheelers sector relationship between MVA and EVA is fairly significant. However, the MVA-EVA analysis supports the hypothesis of Stern and Stewart's that MVA of firm is largely positive associated with EVA in all the selected sectors of Indian Automobile industry.

MVA-EPS Analysis

The linear regression analysis between MVA and EPS is presented by Table 7.10 for the study period. It is evident from the Table 7.10 that the correlation co-efficients between MVA and EPS for the whole industry is 0.306 and value of R-square and adjusted R-square is very low and may not be adequate for the fitness of the model. The t and F statistics suggest that the association between MVA and EPS of automobile industry is not significant and EPS does not suitably explain the MVA. It is evident from the table that the correlation co-efficients between MVA and EPS in passenger cars and multiutility vehicles and two and three wheelers 0.223 and

Table 7.9
MVA - EVA: Linear Regression Analysis
Dependent variable - Market Value Added (MVA)
Independent variable - Economic Value Added (EVA)

Independent variable	*Co-efficient*	*t*	*Multiple R*	*R Square*	*Adjusted R Square*	*Std. Error of the Estimate*	*Durbin-Watson*	*F Value*
Commercial Vehicles								
EVA	1.041	1.138	0.325	0.11	0.03	623.52	0.83	1.30
Passenger Cars and Multiutility Vehicles								
EVA	0.321	0.796	0.233	0.06	-0.03	537.98	1.78	0.63
Two and Three Wheelers								
EVA	2.602	1.562	0.426	0.18	0.11	558.29	0.86	2.44
Whole Industry:								
EVA	0.280	0.556	0.165	0.03	-0.06	339.76	1.23	0.31

Source: Computed.

Table 7.10
MVA - EPS: Linear Regression Analysis
Dependent variable - Market Value Added (MVA)
Independent variable - Earning Per Value (EPS)

Independent variable	*Co-efficient*	*t*	*Multiple R*	*R-Square*	*Adjusted R -Square*	*Std. Error of the Estimate*	*Durbin-Watson*	*F Value*
Commercial Vehicles								
EPS	46.84	1.566	0.427	0.18	0.11	596.11	0.84	2.45
Passenger Cars and Multiutility Vehicles								
EPS	2.67	0.760	0.223	0.05	-0.04	539.28	1.99	0.58
Two and Three Wheelers								
EPS	30.09	0.840	0.246	0.06	-0.03	598.19	0.34	0.71
Whole Industry								
EPS	6.53	1.068	0.306	0.09	0.12	327.93	1.37	1.14

Source: Computed.

0.246 respectively and value of adjusted R-square is negative. This shows the poor fitness of the model. Both t statistics and F statistics certify that the association between these two variables is insignificant as presented in the table. It is again noticed from the table that the variables are clearly correlated in commercial vehicles sector and adjusted R-square value is also positive. The t and F statistics are resulting identical values and secured that EPS of commercial vehicles sector has been able to describe MVA in better term than the other sectors. The overall results showed that EPS is positively associated with MVA in all the three sectors and the whole industry during the study period.

MVA-ROCE Analysis

Table 7.11 offers the explanation about the regression analysis between MVA and ROCE during the study period for the whole automobile industry and its three sectors. Table 7.11 provides the values of R, R-square and adjusted R-square are 0.756, 0.57 and 0.53 respectively. It sounds that the good fitness of the model. Interestingly, t and F statistics give the identical result but both of them lead to significant association between the variable under reference. In two and three wheelers sector the results are just about similar to whole industry. Table 7.11 suggests that the variables are clearly correlated in two and three wheelers sector and adjusted R-square value is also positive. The t and F statistics are resulting identical values and secure that in two and three wheelers sector the association between MVA and ROCE is fairly significant. However, in case of passenger cars and mutitutility vehicles and commercial vehicles sector the values of R, R-square and adjusted R-square showed that there exists poor relationship between MVA and ROCE in these sectors. Interestingly, t and F statistics give the identical results but both of them lead to insignificant association between the variables under reference. The overall results showed that ROCE is positively associated with MVA in all the three sectors and the whole industry during the study period.

MVA-NOPAT Analysis

Liner regression analysis between MVA and NOPAT is presented in Table 7.12. In Table 7.12 the statistical association

Table 7.11
MVA – ROCE: Linear Regression Analysis
Dependent variable - Market Value Added (MVA)
Independent variable – Return On Capital Employed (ROCE)

Independent variable	*Co-efficient*	*t*	*Multiple R*	*R-Square*	*Adjusted R -Square*	*Std. Error of the Estimate*	*Durbin-Watson*	*F Value*
Commercial Vehicles								
ROCE	19.587	1.061	0.305	0.09	0.01	627.87	0.78	1.13
Passenger Cars and Multiutility Vehicles								
ROCE	9.765	0.629	0.186	0.04	-0.05	543.56	1.90	0.40
Two and Three Wheelers								
ROCE	53.56**	1.804	0.478	0.23	0.16	542.08	0.53	3.26
Whole Industry								
ROCE	38.99*	3.830	0.756	0.57	0.53	225.51	1.34	14.67

* * - Significant at 0.10 level
* - Significant at 0.05 level
Source: Computed.

Table 7.12
MVA – NOPAT: Linear Regression Analysis
Dependent variable - Market Value Added (MVA)
Independent variable – Net Operating Profit After Tax (NOPAT)

Independent variable	*Co-efficient*	*t*	*Multiple R*	*R-Square*	*Adjusted R Square*	*Std. Error of the Estimate*	*Durbin-Watson*	*F Value*
Commercial Vehicles								
NOPAT	3.044	1.231	0.348	0.12	0.04	618.02	0.74	1.52
Passenger Cars and Multiutility Vehicles								
NOPAT	3.295*	2.568	0.612	0.38	0.32	437.47	1.33	6.59
Two and Three Wheelers								
NOPAT	10.870*	7.896	0.922	0.85	0.84	238.99	1.21	62.34
Whole Industry								
NOPAT	4.034*	4.698	0.817	0.67	0.64	198.68	1.52	22.08

* - Significant at 0.05 level.
Source: Computed.

between MVA and NOPAT of all the three sectors and the whole industry are provided. The table reveals that the value of R, R-square and adjusted R-square are high and it may be adequate for the fitness of the model in case of whole industry, passenger cars and multiutility vehicles sector and two and three wheelers sector. The t and F statistics also suggest that the association between MVA and NOPAT is significant and NOPAT is suitable to explain in the MVA of these sectors and whole industry during the study period. The results regarding the association of MVA and NOPAT in commercial vehicles sector slightly differ. The table reveals that value of adjusted R-square is very low and it may not be adequate for the fitness of the model, the t and F statistics also suggest that the association between the MVA and NOPAT is not significant and NOPAT do not suitably explain the MVA of commercial vehicles sector during the study period. The overall analysis showed that NOPAT is positively associated with MVA in all the three sectors and whole industry.

MVA-RONW Analysis

Table 7.13 tenders the elucidation concerning the regression analysis between MVA and RONW during the study period. The Table 7.13 provides the values of R, R-square and adjusted R-square. Table 7.13 suggests that variables are clearly correlated in whole industry, commercial vehicles and two and three wheelers sector and adjusted R-square value is also positive. The t and F statistics are resulting identical values and secured that in these sectors and whole industry the relationship between MVA and RONW is fairly significant. However, in case of passenger cars and multiutility vehicles,

Table 7.13 provides the value of R, R-square and adjusted R-square are 0.08, 0.01 and -0.08 respectively. It sounds that there exists poor relationship between and MVA and RONW in passenger cars and multiutility vehicles sector. The t and F statistics also give identical results but both of them lead to insignificant association between the variables under reference. The overall analysis showed that RONW is negatively association with MVA only in case of two and three wheelers sector during the study period.

Table 7.13

MVA – RONW: Linear Regression Analysis

Dependent variable - Market Value Added (MVA)

Independent variable – Return On Net Worth (RONW)

Independent variable	*Co-efficient*	*t*	*Multiple R*	*R-Square*	*Adjusted R - Square*	*Std. Error of the Estimate*	*Durbin-Watson*	*F Value*
Commercial Vehicles								
RONW	29.044*	2.209	0.554	0.31	0.24	548.61	1.39	4.88
Passenger Cars and Multiutility Vehicles								
RONW	3.364	0.266	0.080	0.01	-0.08	551.48	1.97	0.07
Two and Three Wheelers								
RONW	-62.75*	2.943	00.664	0.44	0.39	461.56	1.19	8.66
Whole Industry:								
RONW	20.59**	1.874	0.492	0.24	0.17	299.95	1.48	3.51

* - Significant at 0.05 level

* * - Significant at 0.10 level

Source: Computed.

MVA vis-a-vis other financial variables-Multiple Regression Analysis

The evidence of the majority of empirical study regarding EVA suggests that there is a positive relationship between EVA and MVA. However, when the explaining power of EVA versus traditional performance measures regarding returns is considered, the results are mixed. This is in continuation with the analysis made in the previous part, an attempt has been made in this part to find out sector-wise trends as far as the factors affecting MVA are concerned. The purpose of this analysis whether a particular independent variable or a set of variables emerges as the most explanatory variable of the MVA during the study period. In order to meet this objective, multiple regression analysis has been considered on sector-wise and whole industry during the study period. The results of multiple regression analysis are presented in this section.

Whole industry

Table 7.14 brings out the determinants of market value added for whole automobile industry during the study period. It is observed

Table 7.14

Determinants of MVA - Multiple Regression Analysis (Whole Industry)

Dependent variable: Market Value Added (MVA)

Independent variables	*Co-efficients*	*t value*	*Significant / Not significant*
Constant	730.11	5.058	
EVA	0.41	1.923	Significant **
EPS	1.28	2.362	Significant **
ROCE	63.02	3.331	Significant *
NOPAT	2.15	2.297	Significant **
RONW	-33.78	2.39	Significant *
R^2 = 0.90			
Adj R^2 = 0.84			
F = 23.12			
DW = 1.53			

EVA - Economic Value Added; ROCE - Return on Capital Employed ; EPS - Earnings Per Share; NOPAT - Net Operating Profit After Tax ; RONW- Return On Net Worth.

* - Significant at 0.05 level; * * - Significant at 0.10 level

Source: Computed.

Table 7.15

Determinants of MVA - Multiple Regression Analysis (Commercial Vehicles)

Dependent variable: Market Value Added (MVA)

Independent variables	*Co-efficients*	*t value*	*Significant / Not significant*
Constant	770.31	1.954	
EVA	0.33	2.364	Significant *
EPS	109.77	1.952	Significant **
ROCE	78.99	1.914	Significant **
NOPAT	1.71	2.551	Significant *
RONW	38.51	1.949	Significant **
R^2 = 0.75			
Adj R^2 = 0.56			
F = 17.97			
DW = 1.63			

EVA - Economic Value Added; ROCE - Return on Capital Employed ;
EPS - Earnings Per Share; NOPAT - Net Operating Profit After Tax ;
RONW- Return On Net Worth.
* - Significant at 0.05 level; * * - Significant at 0.10 level
Source: Computed.

from the Table 7.14 that all the selected independent variables exists significant influence on MVA of automobile industry during the study period. Co-efficient of determination, R^2 in the case is 0.90 implying that changes in MVA are predicated by these independent variables to the extent of 90 per cent. It is also evident from the table that ROCE is found in strong association with MVA followed by NOPAT, EPS and EVA. However, RONW is negatively related with MVA during the study period. The value of Adjusted R^2 and F value shows the good fitness of the model. From these regression results it can be concluded that all the selected independent variables are well explain the MVA of automobile industry during the study period.

Commercial Vehicles

Table 7.15 portrays the results of multiple regression analysis for commercial vehicles sector. It is revealed from the Table 7.21 that all the selected independent variables that are found statistically significant with MVA of commercial vehicles sector during the study period. Co-efficients of determination, R^2 in this case is 0.75 implying that change in MVA is predicted by these independent variables to the extent of 75 per cent only. It is also found that EPS is strongly associated with MVA followed by ROCE, RONW, NOPAT and EVA during the study period. The value of F statistic and adjusted R^2 showed the good fitness of the model.

Passenger cars and Multiutility vehicles

Table 7.16 gives an account of multiple regression analysis between MVA and other financial variables in respect of passenger cars and multiutility vehicles sector. The result provided by this table witnessed that the variables noticed significantly associated with MVA are EVA, EPS, ROCE and NOPAT. The co-efficient of determination, R^2 in this case is 0.83 implying that changes in MVA is predicted by these independent variables to the extent of 83 per cent. Once again the ROCE has emerged as the most important variable in determining MVA of passenger cars and multiutility vehicles sector followed by NOPAT, EVA and EPS. The value of R^2 and F shows the good fitness of the model.

Table 7.16
Determinants of MVA- Multiple Regression Analysis (Passenger Cars and Multiutility Vehicles)
Dependent variable: Market Value Added (MVA)

Independent variables	*Co-efficients*	*t value*	*Significant / Not significant*
Constant	2181.88	7.725	
EVA	0.35	2.058	Significant **
EPS	0.34	3.099	Significant *
ROCE	24.15	2.834	Significant *
NOPAT	5.42	3.422	Significant *
RONW	-44.20	1.774	Not significant

R^2 = 0.83
Adj R^2 = 0.68
F = 30.37
DW = 1.94

EVA - Economic Value Added; ROCE - Return on Capital Employed ;
EPS - Earnings Per Share; NOPAT - Net Operating Profit After Tax ;
RONW- Return On Net Worth.
* - Significant at 0.05 level; * * - Significant at 0.10 level
Source: Computed.

Table 7.17
Determinants of MVA- Multiple Regression Analysis (Two and Three Wheelers)
Dependent variable: Market Value Added (MVA)

Independent variables	*Co-efficients*	*t value*	*Significant / Not significant*
Constant	-460.41	1.694	
EVA	1.57	2.950	Significant *
EPS	49.36	2.832	Significant *
ROCE	1.04	1.053	Not significant
NOPAT	16.93	10.188	Significant *
RONW	20.99	2.374	Significant **
R^2 = 0.97			
Adj R^2 = 0.95			
F = 49.81			
DW = 1.98			

EVA - Economic Value Added; ROCE - Return on Capital Employed ;
EPS - Earnings Per Share; NOPAT - Net Operating Profit After Tax ;
RONW- Return On Net Worth.
* - Significant at 0.05 level; * * - Significant at 0.10 level

Source: Computed.

Two and Three wheelers

Table 7.17 describes the results of multiple regression for determinants of MVA for two and three wheelers sector during the study period. It is explicit from the table that all the independent variables except ROCE significantly associated with MVA of two and three wheelers sector during the study period. Co-efficient of determination, R^2 in this case is 0.97 implying that changes in MVA is predicted by selected independent variables to the extent of 97 per cent. Among the selected independent variables, EPS is strongly associated with MVA followed by RONW, NOPAT, and EVA However, the ROCE has not emerged as one of the most important variables explaining MVA in case of two and three wheelers sector. The value of t, F and adjusted R^2 sounds the good fitness of the model.

References

1. Mangala, Deepa and Joura Simpy, (2002). Linkage between Economic Value Added and Market Value: An Analysis in Indian context, Indian Management Studies Journal, pp.55-56.

2. Mc Taggart, James et al., (1994). The Value imperative, Free Press; New York, pp 4-6.
3. Jani Shweta, (2003). Godrej Retools for Value, Business Standard, p. 6.
4. Purikh, Parag, (2002). The Universe of Wealth Creation, PPFAS-Financial Advisory Services Ltd-Online, p.2.

8

Findings and Conclusion

The corporate sector is the backbone of the Indian economy so far, as it provides a vital, effective and organized system for the growth of industrial as well as non - industrial sectors of the economy. The rapid growth of corporate sector in India and the increasing scale of its operations and investments have turned it into the most dominant form of economic organization. The ever increasing importance of the corporate sector in the economic growth of the country has attracted several academicians, professional institutions, researchers and administrators. There is need to study industries' financial and operating performance which ultimately shall determine the overall industrial development in future. The present study is a small endeavor in that direction.

The study in general aims at making financial and operating performance of Indian automobile industry after liberalisation. The study specifically aimed at assessing the trends in the production, capacity utillisation, sales and market shares, analysing profitability position and its trend and determinants of profitability, analysing financial health, nature of factors which affect financial structure and economic value added analysis of Indian automobile industry.

This study covers three sectors of Indian automobile industry, viz., commercial vehicles, passenger cars and multiutility vehicles and two and three wheelers. The selected sectors include 26 companies. Out of 26 companies, 13 years data is available only for 18 companies. Therefore all the 18 companies are included in the sample which accounts for 69.23 per cent of the total companies available in the Indian automobile industry. Further, sample companies represent 98.74 percentage of market share in commercial vehicles, 89.76 percentage in passenger cars and multiutility vehicles and 99.81 percentage in two and three wheelers sector. The period covered under the study extends over 13 years from 1991-92 to 2003-04. The data for the study were taken from "PROWESS" database which is the most reliable on the empowered corporate database of Centre for Monitoring Indian Economy (CMIE). The important statistical techniques used in the study are correlation, multiple regression, analysis of variance, t-test, F-test, arithmetic mean, co-efficients of variation and compound annual growth rate besides simple percentages, ratios and graphs.

This chapter, being the concluding part of the study is made an endeavor to present a summarized version of the findings of the present study. The summary of the major findings are given below.

Production Trend

The production of all the three selected sectors of the Indian automobile industry marked fluctuating trend throughout the study period. The mean value of production was the highest in two and three wheelers sector followed by passenger cars and multiutility vehicles and commercial vehicles. With a view of making an inter-industry comparison of the overall production performance, production trends are taken under consideration. The time series analysis of production and application of chi-square test revealed that the production of the selected sectors of Indian automobile industry did not increase as per expectation. The projections of production of automobiles in India showed that passenger cars, two wheelers and motorcycle have growing good market potential in our country. Findings also reveal that by the year 2012 A.D., motorcycles may have more than 80 per cent market share replacing scooters and mopeds.

Dispersions in production of industries under three sectors revealed through the mean value of the series and values of co-efficient of variation for each industry. It is observed that Tata

Motors Ltd and Ashok Leyland Ltd in commercial vehicles, Maruthi Udyog Ltd and Mahindra and Mahindra Ltd in passenger cars and multiutility vehicles and Bajaj Auto Ltd, Hero Honda Motors Ltd and TVS Motors India Ltd in two and three wheelers showed better performance in this regard.

Capacity Utilisation

The capacity utilisation ratio of commercial vehicles sector varied in a range of 63.33 per cent from 29.29 per cent to 92.62 per cent, passenger cars and multiutility vehicles varied 41.99 per cent from 34.75 per cent to 76.74 per cent and two and three wheelers sector varied in a range of 15.59 per cent from 43.84 per cent to 59.43 per cent during the study period. It is therefore obvious that the Indian automobile industry has not utilised its plants capacity an average of more than 40 per cent which remains idle during the study period. The mean capacity utilisation was the highest (being more than 100 per cent) in Maruthi Udyog Ltd which indicates that company utilised its plants effectively and efficiently among the selected industries. Swaraj Mazda Ltd, Ashok Leyland Ltd and Eicher Motors Ltd in commercial vehicles, Maruthi Udyog Ltd and Mahindra and Mahindra Ltd in passenger cars and multiutility vehicles and Hero Honda Motors Ltd, Maharastra Scooters Ltd and Kinetic Motors Company Ltd in two and three wheelers sector showed better performance with regard to their capacity utilisation. The capacity utilization of the selected industries varies greatly irrespective of the sector of which they belong.

Sales Trend

The sales of passenger cars and multiutility vehicles and two and three wheelers sector marked rising trend throughout the study period. However, sales of commercial vehicles marked fluctuating trend. The time series analysis of sales and application of chi-square test revealed that sales in the selected sectors did not increase as per expectation. The projection of sales of automobiles in India revealed that commercial vehicles, passenger cars and multiutility vehicles were growing marginally whereas two and three wheelers have fast emerging growing market in the years to come in our country. The analysis of company-wise dispersion in sales of Indian automobiles industry over the study period reflected in the same picture with regard to production performance.

Trends in Market Share

The analysis of company-wise dispersion in market shares of Indian automobile industry revealed that the mean rates of market share vary greatly in case of all the industries under examination irrespective of the sector of which they belong. It is observed that Ashok Leyland Ltd and Tata Motors Ltd in commercial vehicles, Mahindra and Mahindra Ltd and Maruthi Udyog Ltd in passenger cars and multiutility vehicles and Bajaj Auto Ltd, TVS Motors India Ltd and Kinetic Motors Company Ltd in two and three wheelers sector had the highest market share during the study period.

Profitability Performance

The profitability performance of Indian automobile industry under review has been studied by computing various ratios relating to profitability. The profitability ratio can been determined on the basis of sales and investment. The profitability of the selected sector measured through operating profit margin ratio is satisfactory in all the three sectors of Indian automobile industry and showed adequate to cover the fixed charges and dividend reserve during the study period. The mean operating profit margin ratio was the highest in passenger cars and multiutility vehicles followed by two and three wheelers and commercial vehicles. The overall fluctuating trend of this ratio in all the sectors of Indian automobile industry can be attributed to the factors like high operating expenses, market condition, planned product mix and high rate of wages and salary. The overall analysis of net profit margin ratio shows the ability of the companies to withstand competition and adverse conditions during the study period. However, Hindustan Motors Ltd and Daewoo Motors India Ltd in passenger cars and multiutility vehicles and LML Ltd and Majestic Auto Ltd in two and three wheelers had negative mean net profit margin ratio which indicated the poor performance. This was due to increase of non-operating expenses in these companies during the study period. All the selected companies should be in a position to pay off debt and give a satisfactory return to its shareholders during the study period. The overall analysis of profit margin ratio shows that the operating efficiency of Indian automobile industry was satisfactory from the point view of shareholders.

When profitability is also measured in relation to assets, the results seem to be encouraging in the sense that the resources of the Indian automobile industry were being utilised in a profitable manner. The analysis of return on assets ratio depicts that operating assets were effectively utilised in profitable manner by the selected companies of Indian automobile industry during the study period, except Hindustan Motors Ltd and Daewoo Motors India Ltd in passenger cars and multiutility vehicles and LML Ltd and Majestic Auto Ltd in two and three wheelers sector. The overall fluctuating trend of return on assets ratio can be influenced by the ability of the industry to utilise its assets in the profitable manner.

The analysis of return on networth ratio also reveals that owners equity was utilised profitability by all the selected companies during the study period except Hindustan Motors Ltd, Daewoo Motors India Ltd, LML Ltd and Majestic Auto Ltd during the study period. The overall analysis of return on capital employed ratio showed that this ratio has been improved significantly during the study period which was on account of considerable increase in profit margin as well as assets turnover. In fine it can be inferred that the operating efficiency of the Indian automobile industry was satisfactory and the management generally succeeded in investing capital funds. It is significant to note that the position regarding earnings per share, dividend per share and dividend payout ratio in all the selected companies of the Indian automobile industry during the period under review highlighting the better performance and prospects from the view point of shareholders. However, the fluctuating trend of the ratio can be attributed to the factors like profitability position, fluctuation in the market prices and board dividend policy.

The observation made from F-test clearly shows that there were significant differences in all the profitability ratio between the year except operating profit margin, net profit margin, earnings per share, dividend per share and dividend payout during the study period. Similarly, there were significant differences in all the profitability ratio between the sectors except operating profit margin during the study period. Hence, the analyses of profitability of selected sectors of Indian automobile industry during the period under review highlighted their better performance and prospects from the point of view of owners.

Profitability Trend

The analysis of profitability trend reveals that the linear model of time trend of profitability has proved to be good fit in case of 10 out of 18 industries (55.55 per cent) examined. The results shows that Tata Motors Ltd, Eicher Motors Ltd, Swaraj Mazda Ltd (commercial vehicles), Hindustan Motors Ltd, Maruthi Udyog Ltd (passenger cars and multiutility vehicles) and Maharastra Scooters Ltd, TVS Motor Company Ltd, Hero Honda Motors Ltd, Kinetic Engineering Ltd and Majestic Auto Ltd (two and three wheelers) experienced a strong tendency in profitability to decline over the study period. The falling tendency of profit rate of these industry is the proof of adverse effect of various controls on prices, output, expansion, investment, distribution etc., exerted by government on these industries over time. Only in case of two industries viz., Ashok Leyland Ltd and Scooters India Ltd, the time trend co-efficient of profit rate is positive, implying a tendency of profit rate of rise over time. The sector-wise time trend regression results reveal that all the three sectors had a strong tendency for profit rate to fall over the study period. Further, variation in the value of R^2 implies that time explain profitability variations of different industry in different degree over the time.

The industry-wise dispersion in rate of profit of Indian automobile industry over the study period showed that Hero Honda Motors Ltd experienced highest profit rate, while Daewoo Motors India Ltd experienced lowest rate of profit over the study period. Another observation made is that mean rate of profit for Indian automobiles industry varied greatly irrespective of the sector to which they belong. The relative dispersion in the series of profit rate is captured by the value of co-efficients of variation. It is observed that majority of industries (8 out of 18) experienced erratically fluctuating variation in profit rate series. Further, 6 out of 18 industries experienced highly fluctuating variance and 4 out of 18 industries have moderately fluctuating variation in profit rate series.

Determinants of Profitability

The determinants of profitability in Indian automobile industry during the study period are analysed using the technique of ordinary least square. In Automobile industry model explains 99 percentage of variation in profitability of firm included in the industry. The analysis reveals that size is the strongest determinant of profitability of Indian automobile industry followed by vertical integration, current ratio, growth rate of assets, and past profitability. For the commercial vehicles sector, model explains 94 percentage of variation in profitability of firms included in this sector. It is evident from the result that size is the strongest determinant of profitability in commercial vehicles followed by vertical integration, fixed assets turnover ratio, past profitability and growth rate of assets. For the passenger cars and multiutility vehicles, model explains 95 percentage of variation in profitability of firms included in this sector. The analysis shows that size is the strongest determinant of profitability in passenger cars and multiutility vehicles followed by current ratio, fixed assets turnover ratio, past profitability and growth rate of assets. The selected variables explain 94 percentage of variation in profitability of firms in two and three wheelers sector. The results portray that size is the stronger determinant of profitability followed by inventory turnover ratio, past profitability, growth rate of assets and vertical integration in this sector.

The overall analysis of determinants of profitability reveals that size, vertical integration, growth rate of assets, fixed assets turnover ratio and past profitability significantly explain the profitability of Indian automobile industry during the study period. Further, among the selected variables, size is the strongest determinant of profitability in all the three sectors and the automobile industry. The overall explanatory power of regression appears to be good in all the selected sectors of Indian automobile industry. This may be inferred from the co-efficients of determinations (R^2) which is the measure of the extent of movement in the dependent variable that is explained by the independent variables.

Analysis of Financial Structure

The analysis of variance carried out for the financial leverages of Indian automobile industry reveals 82.62 as calculated value of F which is much higher than its table value (i.e., 3.40) at 5 per cent level of significance. This indicates that the means of financial leverage of the three sectors of automobile industry differed significantly. Hence, the null hypothesis that financial leverage is independent of industry size was rejected leading to the conclusions that financial structure depends upon industry class. The relationship between financial leverage and size was found to be positive and significant at 5 per cent level. Therefore, the null hypothesis that leverage is independent of industry size is rejected and hence concluded that size has got bearing on financial structure. The analysis of financial leverage and profitability reveals that the null hypothesis that financial leverage is independent of profitability is rejected and thus concluded that there exists negative correlation between them. As far as financial leverage and operating leverage concerned, both negative as well as positive correlation between them in different sectors were noticed. Thus the null hypothesis that operating leverage and financial leverage are independent of each other could not be fully rejected in the case of automobile industry. The same picture is reflected as in the case of relationship between financial leverage and external financing. Further, the null hypothesis that there is no association between income gearing and financial leverage was rejected consequently leading to the conclusion that, depending upon the time period and nature of industry, there exists a positive correlation between financial leverage and income gearing.

Determinants of Financial Structure

The analysis of determinants of financial structure of Indian automobile industry reveals that the selected variables collectively explain 88 percentage of total variation in Indian automobile industry, 90 per cent in commercial vehicles sector, 60 per cent in passenger cars and multiutility vehicles sector and 89 per cent in two and three wheelers sector during the study period. As far as the importance of individual variation of concern, size followed by external financing, operating leverage, profitability and income gearing are found to be most important factors explaining the variations in the financial structure of Indian automobile industry during the study period.

Analysis of Financial Strength

The overall analysis of assessing the financial strength shows that the Indian automobile industries are able to meet its current obligation as and when they become due for payment. Although the current ratio was less than the standard norms, even then the liquidity position of the selected industry may be considered satisfactory as its liquidity ratio close or above to the standard norm. Another interesting inference drawn from the analysis is that except Ashok Leyland Ltd in commercial vehicle sector none has ever achieved the required norm of 2:1 ratio during the study period. Further, analysis of interest coverage ratio also reveals that all the selected industries have the ability to meet fixed interest charges during the study period. The analysis of long-term financial strength as reviewed by debt equity ratio and fixed assts to net worth ratio concluded that the long-term financial position of commercial vehicles sector and passenger cars and multiutility vehicles sectors may be considered satisfactory than the two and three wheelers sector of Indian automobile industry.

Assessment of Financial Health

The assessment of financial health of Indian automobile industry has been made by using Altman Z score. The analysis shows that the financial health of Indian automobile industry during the study period is never in bankruptcy zone. This shows the better financial performance of Indian automobile industry. However, in case of commercial vehicles sector for the period 1991-92 to 1993-94 and 1996-97 to 2001-02, the financial health is in bankruptcy zone which was due to excessive use of working capital, failed to earn adequate surplus to meet non-operating activities and failure to achieve the adequate sales. It is also obvious from the analysis that the financial health of passenger cars and multiutility vehicles sector is never in bankruptcy zone except in the year 1998-99. It is also evident from the analysis that the Z score for the two and three wheelers sector witnessed more than three during the entire period of study shows the better financial health of two and three wheelers sector. The overall analysis concluded that, assessment of financial health using Altman Z score model portrayed that except a few industries, the financial health of Indian automobile industry was good during the study period.

Analysis of EVA and MVA

The analysis of EVA created by the sample company concludes that about 1/3 of the sample companies have been able to govern affirmative EVA during period under study whereas remaining companies make it feasible to append a very little to the value of share holders. Company's like LML Ltd, Bajaj Auto Ltd and Maruthi Udyog Ltd are all toping in the list during the study period. On the other hand companies like Swaraj Mazda Ltd, Daewoo Motors India Ltd, Kinetic Engineering Ltd and Majestic Auto Ltd have been losing the ground. Remaining companies have indexed unsteady position during the study period. Sector-wise trends in EVA reviews the significant deviation in then EVA during the study period. The comparison of EVA and traditional method of financial performance shows that the traditional method does not reflect the real value addition to the shareholders wealth.

The analysis of market value added indicates the 15 out of 18 companies have registered positive MVA throughout the study period. Further, it is noticed that companies like Maruthi Udyog Ltd, Bajaj Auto Ltd, Tata Motors Ltd, Ashok Leyland Ltd, Mahindra and Mahindra Ltd and TVS Motors India Ltd are topping the list and on the other hand company like Scooters India Ltd, Daewoo Motors India Ltd, Hindustan Motors Ltd, Majestic Auto Ltd and Kinetic Engineering Ltd are struggling in terms of MVA over the period. The analysis of sector-wise trends in MVA exhibits that there has been no significant deviation in MVA in respect of years except the terminal years.

The linear regression analysis between MVA and other financial variables reviews that EVA, EPS, ROCE and NOPAT, all highly significant in explaining MVA movement of sample companies. Further, the market value added is positively influenced by EVA, EPS, ROCE and NOPAT. The sector-wise multiple regression analysis showed that EVA is positively influenced by the market value added of all the sectors of Indian automobile industry by supporting Stern Stewart's Claim.

Suggestions

Keeping in view of the above observation relating to the study, the following measures are suggested which would go a long way to improve the performance of Indian automobile industry.

1. It is suggested that still there is a need for Indian automobile industry to adopt producing and selling wide range of products, to adopt better market strategy, by reducing cost and revising selling prices to enhance the value of turnover so as to go ahead in the era of competitions.
2. It is obvious from the study that Indian automobile industry has not utilised its plan capacity on an average of more than 40 per cent which remain idle during the study period. It is therefore suggested that the management of the selected unit should concentrate on overcoming the problem of power cuts, implementing R & D programs, application of latest technology and making industrial relation cordial and congenial to increase the capacity utilisation.
3. The profitability trend of selected Indian automobile industry experienced a strong tendency in profitability to decline over the study period. Therefore, it is suggested that all the selected industries should undertake cost control measures further so that increased profit margin of the companies may enhance the earning power ratio. In this regard further reduction of excise duty, tariff and surcharge of sales tax and steps to control of operating expenses are the measures suggested for the improvement of profitability trend.
4. Cost accounting and cost audit should be made mandatary in automobile industry and they should be called to prepare cost sheet along with their annual financial statement.
5. A systematic, prompt and regular flow of information and its analysis is important for improving productivity, efficiency and profitability. A suitable management information system needs to be evolved which will take care of the data requirement of administrative offices as well as other units like factory etc., for internal management and control. Appropriate organizational arrangements should be made for the successful implementation of management information system in Indian automobile industry.
6. At present, in India, the financial statements are presented on historical cost basis. As such these statements do not exhibit the correct realizable value of the assets on the date of the balance sheet. Thus, the true profitability can't be ascertained

on the basis of the figures given in the balance sheet on historical cost basis. It is, therefore, suggested that a supplementary statement should be included in the annual report showing the figures of assets and liabilities on the basis of current values.

7. At present, the profit and loss account of multi-product concerns is disclosed in a consolidated form which can't measure and judge the performance and profitability of each activity. Hence, the profit and loss accounts should be prepared on departmental activity basis by such multiproduct concerns.
8. The policy of borrowed of financing in automobile industry was not proper. So the company use wisely the borrowed funds and should try to reduce the fixed charge burden gradually by decreasing borrowed funds and by enhancing in owners fund.
9. It is also suggested that EVA has been used as a performance evaluation tool of the organisation. The cost drives of EVA like sales growth, operating profit margin, cost of capital etc., should be identified and the performance should be measured based on the improvement made in this value drivers. It appears to be useful in spotting changes in a company's on going performances that are hidden in EPS.
10. A vehicle retirement programme which will assist not only in fleet modernization and reduction of emission but will also provide quantum fillip to the demand should be put in place.
11. There is a need to brief the international communities on technological and quality related capabilities at Indian automobile industry. Substantive efforts are required for educating opinion leaders and build a strong 'made in India' brand in overseas markets. Existing incentives for promoting exports are considered inadequate. An institutional mechanism such as the Automobile Export Promotion Council, which can address industry- specific issues and facilitate exports is urgently required.
12. Tariff rationalization and taming of avoidable competition between rail and road transport sectors should be carried out. In this unhealthy competition, both the industries are unable to realize their full potential.

13. The automobile industry is impeded by power the state of road infrastructure in the country. Because of the road condition the penetration level of automobile in India is very low compared to other developing countries. Therefore it is suggested that take road building seriously and start massed for project on the road in the next fifteen years are imperative. The automobile market will stagnant show if this is not done.
14. To meet the emerging challenge of new emission norms the Indian automobile industry has started making investment in introducing new technology. A higher safety and emission standards regimes required adequate infrastructure for testing and certification of domestically produced and imported product. However, the existing testing infrastructure in the country is limited and grossly inadequate to meet the emerging requirements of the industry. Therefore, the Government in close co-operation and co-ordination with the industry has initiated steps for upgrading the existing testing facilities and setting up of new testing infrastructure in the country.
15. Method of production by the Indian automobile industry is based on the assembly of different components in a knock down condition. The MNC's have not been improving the quality of produce in India rather they have been in a sense "importing" high quality products into the country. This is actually providing in India cost of fuel is important and at the same this fuel quality needs to be improved in terms of gumming tendency, and dust contamination.
16. The inverted duty structure of customs duty on raw materials components and finished goods needs to be corrected. The Government should grant certain funds to leading Indian automobiles companies for R & D so that Indian vehicles can really become world class in five years time. Vehicles with 100 per cent local content should be given a concessional excise duty of 50 per cent of the normal rate. Further, all local constraints like the outdated industrial disputes act, Factories act and the like which make local manufacturing far more difficult, should be modified without further delay.
17. The Indian automobile market is still in its evolutionary or early growth stage. Therefore, no fixed or widely accepted

method of segmenting the market has evolved yet. Segmentation has mostly been done on product types or price ranges. Therefore, it is suggested that segmentation on psychographic or behavioral parameters have been adopted as seen in developed car market.

Scope for Further Research

Any research study can explore only a limited filed of knowledge. There are many aspects which need to be researched further. In the present case also there is a considerable scope for further research. In spite of every attempt to make this study more intensive there are quite many fields remained unveiled owing to constrains of time and resources. Financial study, specially, has numerous dimensions. Each component of the financial statement has got scope for an extensive study. An analysis of the social profitability of the automobile industry with the help of value added and the other techniques can provide an ample scope for research. A concetrable scope for further research also exists in the area of diversification, mergers, takeover etc.,. Another interesting theme would be to identify sick and healthy units separately in the automobile industry and find out discriminating characteristic of each group with respect to performance. A study can also be undertaken in the area of performance appraisal comparing private sector and public sector.

The findings of the study may not have universal applicability since the study is confined to a definite period and to a definite scheme of corporate sector in India. Hence, to arrive at any general conclusion, the hypothesis need further testing by way of addition research in the same filed in different periods and even in different fields in the same period. Last but not least one can make a comparative study of corporate performance in the pre liberalization and the post liberalisation period. Therefore research work in above mentioned area would be of great practical significance and would throw more light on the operation of automobile industry in our country.

Conclusion

Easier and faster mobility of people and goods across the regions, countries and continents is a cherished yearning of mankind.

The automobile industry's potential for facilitating the mobility is enormous. Wheels of development across the globe would have to be powered by this industry. However, a seamless development of this industry across countries and continents alone will help in realization of this objective. For such seamless and barrier free development of the sector, countries will have to come together and develop better understanding. Industry across countries will have to meet challenges of newer technologies, alternative fuels and affordability of automobiles by people at large through constructive cooperation. The earlier we are able to achieve this the better it would be for the world development.

Appendices

APPENDIX I

Annual production of selected automobile industry in India

(in thousands)

Industry	*91-92*	*92-93*	*93-94*	*94-95*	*95-96*	*96-97*	*97-98*
Commercial Vehicles							
Ashok Leyland Ltd.	24.58	18.43	23.79	30.38	37.90	45.26	33.20
Tata Motors Ltd.	94.59	86.29	85.57	133.97	181.40	218.39	154.79
Bajaj Tempo Ltd.	14.00	14.91	22.86	24.04	28.03	26.54	26.17
Eicher Motors Ltd.	4.24	2.85	3.42	4.81	5.89	6.63	5.35
Swaraj Mazda Ltd.	2.41	2.25	2.80	3.51	4.50	4.01	2.93
Passenger Cars and Multiutility Vehicles							
Hindustan Motors Ltd.	16.84	23.11	27.89	28.48	31.30	28.57	26.92
Mahindra and Mahindra Ltd.	32.76	38.82	53.29	46.63	65.38	80.48	79.00
Maruthi Udyog Ltd.	121.89	128.00	164.15	205.49	277.78	336.81	354.34
Daewoo Motors India Ltd.	2.46	1.90	2.38	2.75	11.19	18.42	5.40

(Contd.)

(Contd. Appendix-I)

Industry	*98-99*	*99-00*	*00-01*	*01-02*	*02-03*	*03-04*
Commercial Vehicles						
Ashok Leyland Ltd.	26.50	36.28	33.78	31.82	33.65	49.15
Tata Motors Ltd.	129.32	204.52	171.03	180.06	234.98	320.07
Bajaj Tempo Ltd.	22.13	27.75	25.74	26.13	33.31	43.80
Eicher Motors Ltd.	5.19	6.95	8.52	9.66	12.81	44.76
Swaraj Mazda Ltd.	2.88	4.01	5.21	6.36	8.20	10.23
Passenger Cars and Multiutility Vehicles						
Hindustan Motors Ltd.	23.51	37.86	28.24	23.22	21.58	15.86
Mahindra and Mahindra Ltd.	72.12	76.98	63.15	66.33	87.10	117.67
Maruthi Udyog Ltd.	338.10	407.60	350.38	358.11	359.96	472.91
Daewoo Motors India Ltd.	8.56	35.54	34.24	7.67	-	-

(Contd.)

(Contd. Appendix-I)

Industry	*91-92*	*92-93*	*93-94*	*94-95*	*95-96*	*96-97*	*97-98*
Two and Three Wheelers							
Bajaj Auto Ltd.	905.54	773.31	816.12	1261.70	1302.03	1439.18	1354.28
LML Ltd.	-	110.65	121.72	160.34	232.75	255.57	297.50
Maharastra Scooters Ltd.	96.27	101.05	104.64	105.62	126.62	154.36	145.02
TVS Motors India Ltd.	167.90	159.22	201.85	288.72	442.81	576.02	649.14
Kinetic Motors Company Ltd.	99.95	101.39	82.78	69.50	113.80	110.90	114.16
Hero Honda Motors Ltd.	135.26	128.65	147.57	183.49	230.08	269.48	407.30
Majestic Auto Ltd.	139.04	111.54	109.19	115.85	158.52	159.96	155.44
Kinetic Engineering Ltd.	92.86	83.49	104.80	118.96	119.04	139.34	137.74
Scooters India Ltd.	4.77	4.26	4.62	7.97	11.33	15.80	16.02

(Contd.)

(Contd. Appendix-I)

Industry	*98-99*	*99-00*	*00-01*	*01-02*	*02-03*	*03-04*
Two and Three Wheelers						
Bajaj Auto Ltd.	1381.76	1269.13	1212.76	1294.63	1457.03	1516.87
LML Ltd.	494.34	275.82	211.21	167.65	-	317.97
Maharastra Scooters Ltd.	153.66	140.53	91.74	60.13	31.36	17.90
TVS Motors India Ltd.	712.43	794.18	868.83	871.87	1134.54	1143.34
Kinetic Motors Company Ltd.	100.70	116.69	124.71	115.56	117.68	75.73
Hero Honda Motors Ltd.	532.74	761.21	1035.68	1423.00	1680.28	2064.70
Majestic Auto Ltd.	159.72	154.74	149.71	139.56	100.24	87.06
Kinetic Engineering Ltd.	127.76	111.81	107.86	79.74	-	-
Scooters India Ltd.	15.31	15.34	13.04	13.01	14.09	15.49

Source: CMIE Database.

APPENDIX II

Capacity utilisation of selected automobiles industry (production as percentage of installed capacity)

Industry	*91-92*	*92-93*	*93-94*	*94-95*	*95-96*	*96-97*	*97-98*
Commercial Vehicles							
Ashok Leyland Ltd.	89.38	67.02	86.51	79.64	81.75	86.00	63.84
Tata Motors Ltd.	24.67	24.69	32.17	46.57	40.19	43.95	23.30
Bajaj Tempo Ltd.	46.67	49.70	76.20	80.13	93.43	14.58	10.51
Eicher Motors Ltd.	70.67	47.50	57.00	80.17	98.17	55.25	44.58
Swaraj Mazda Ltd.	48.20	45.00	56.00	70.20	90.00	80.20	58.60
Passenger Cars and Multiutility Vehicles							
Hindustan Motors Ltd.	26.73	36.42	43.15	56.91	61.09	55.22	49.11
Mahindra and Mahindra Ltd.	74.03	89.86	102.41	75.04	82.62	73.40	62.30
Maruthi Udyog Ltd.	89.77	93.82	121.62	99.07	107.50	131.54	138.66
Daewoo Motors India Ltd.	2.83	12.67	15.87	18.33	12.86	21.17	6.21

(Contd.)

(Contd. Appendix-II)

Industry	*98-99*	*99-00*	*00-01*	*01-02*	*02-03*	*03-04*
Commercial Vehicles						
Ashok Leyland Ltd.	52.50	71.54	66.30	62.74	66.62	96.54
Tata Motors Ltd.	16.91	37.02	16.57	23.45	27.27	34.32
Bajaj Tempo Ltd.	5.04	8.71	6.00	3.76	6.80	79.64
Eicher Motors Ltd.	43.25	57.92	53.25	80.50	106.75	76.51
Swaraj Mazda Ltd.	57.60	80.20	104.20	106.00	136.67	170.50
Passenger Cars and Multiutility Vehicles						
Hindustan Motors Ltd.	31.64	41.67	40.25	32.23	32.06	24.78
Mahindra and Mahindra Ltd.	57.57	61.76	47.09	50.26	58.02	73.54
Maruthi Udyog Ltd.	94.40	113.91	98.43	100.85	101.85	135.12
Daewoo Motors India Ltd.	9.84	40.85	39.36	8.82	-	-

(Contd.)

(Contd. Appendix-II)

Industry	*91-92*	*92-93*	*93-94*	*94-95*	*95-96*	*96-97*	*97-98*
Two and Three Wheelers							
Bajaj Auto Ltd.	11.71	11.04	44.07	58.28	45.68	38.62	40.81
LML Ltd.	-	55.33	60.86	80.17	116.38	85.19	74.38
Maharastra Scooters Ltd.	91.69	96.24	99.66	100.59	101.30	102.91	96.68
TVS Motors Company Ltd.	33.58	31.84	40.37	38.50	52.10	67.77	76.37
Kinetic Motors Comapany Ltd.	74.90	84.81	82.78	69.50	75.87	63.37	65.23
Hero Honda Motors Ltd.	90.17	85.77	98.38	101.94	95.87	59.88	81.46
Majestic Auto Ltd.	55.62	44.62	34.88	37.01	50.65	51.11	49.66
Kinetic Engineering Ltd.	30.36	34.79	43.67	49.57	62.65	73.34	59.89
Scooters India Ltd.	7.63	6.82	13.20	21.25	47.21	65.83	96.97

(Contd.)

(Contd. Appendix-II)

Industry	*98-99*	*99-00*	*00-01*	*01-02*	*02-03*	*03-04*
Two and Three Wheelers						
Bajaj Auto Ltd.	31.13	28.44	19.26	15.99	11.51	64.82
LML Ltd.	123.58	61.29	30.69	22.01	-	55.78
Maharastra Scooters Ltd.	102.44	93.69	61.16	40.09	20.91	11.93
TVS Motors Company Ltd.	56.99	63.53	69.51	69.75	75.64	76.22
Kinetic Motors Comapany Ltd.	57.54	66.68	71.26	66.03	67.25	43.27
Hero Honda Motors Ltd.	81.96	80.13	86.31	88.94	93.35	91.76
Majestic Auto Ltd.	51.03	49.44	47.83	34.67	32.03	27.81
Kinetic Engineering Ltd.	55.55	48.61	46.90	44.59	-	-
Scooters India Ltd.	92.79	92.97	78.85	78.85	85.39	93.88

Source: CMIE Database.

APPENDIX III

Annual Sales Quantity of Selected Automobile Industry in India

(in thousands)

Industry	*91-92*	*92-93*	*93-94*	*94-95*	*95-96*	*96-97*	*97-98*
Commercial Vehicles							
Ashok Leyland Ltd.	23.42	20.57	24.23	29.88	37.40	43.35	31.55
Tata Motors Ltd.	89.73	75.71	95.21	137.70	181.22	209.26	152.93
Bajaj Tempo Ltd.	14.30	15.15	23.00	24.05	27.98	25.49	24.69
Eicher Motors Ltd.	4.11	3.00	3.37	4.86	5.88	6.58	5.28
Swaraj Mazda Ltd.	2.33	2.28	2.81	3.52	4.23	3.73	3.30
Passenger Cars and Multiutility Vehicles							
Hindustan Motors Ltd.	18.07	23.13	28.20	28.38	33.57	29.01	25.69
Mahindra and Mahindra Ltd.	33.42	38.89	52.10	48.19	69.97	75.57	76.95
Maruthi Udyog Ltd.	124.65	127.24	165.23	206.72	275.26	338.56	353.26
Daewoo Motors India Ltd.	2.43	2.03	2.33	2.80	10.98	16.62	6.50

(Contd.)

(Contd. Appendix-III)

Industry	*98-99*	*99-00*	*00-01*	*01-02*	*02-03*	*03-04*
Commercial Vehicles						
Ashok Leyland Ltd.	29.74	38.22	32.48	29.68	36.44	48.65
Tata Motors Ltd.	128.86	199.14	170.51	171.57	232.29	295.46
Bajaj Tempo Ltd.	22.67	28.50	24.71	27.14	32.69	43.41
Eicher Motors Ltd.	5.32	6.93	8.44	9.63	12.72	44.24
Swaraj Mazda Ltd.	2.98	3.98	5.07	6.22	8.10	10.28
Passenger Cars and Multiutility Vehicles						
Hindustan Motors Ltd.	23.55	38.03	28.20	23.10	21.05	16.50
Mahindra and Mahindra Ltd.	70.55	76.43	62.93	77.39	86.89	117.40
Maruthi Udyog Ltd.	333.77	353.16	350.62	352.20	362.25	472.12
Daewoo Motors India Ltd.	8.49	35.79	33.39	8.28	-	-

(Contd.)

(Contd. Appendix-III)

Industry	91-92	92-93	93-94	94-95	95-96	96-97	97-98
Two and Three Wheelers							
Bajaj Auto Ltd.	810.79	665.54	808.70	1029.86	1301.97	1415.82	1333.80
LML Ltd.	-	110.80	124.16	157.46	227.70	257.04	294.65
Maharastra Scooters Ltd.	97.16	101.03	104.40	105.78	126.27	150.04	138.34
TVS Motors India Ltd.	168.48	159.84	184.24	289.82	410.81	513.40	648.40
Kinetic Motors Company Ltd.	108.43	101.39	78.50	70.98	112.78	108.49	113.76
Hero Honda Motors Ltd.	134.99	127.97	148.15	183.65	230.16	268.93	407.55
Majestic Auto Ltd.	133.35	115.55	108.55	118.26	157.72	160.66	153.85
Kinetic Engineering Ltd.	74.37	81.93	104.35	119.08	120.03	138.81	138.62
Scooters India Ltd.	4.63	3.84	5.15	7.55	11.67	14.71	16.15

(Contd.)

(Contd. Appendix-III)

Industry	*98-99*	*99-00*	*00-01*	*01-02*	*02-03*	*03-04*
Two and Three Wheelers						
Bajaj Auto Ltd.	1423.50	1412.61	1209.09	1358.97	1445.67	1518.13
LML Ltd.	485.34	283.07	207.69	172.73	-	315.35
Maharastra Scooters Ltd.	152.60	146.67	96.76	65.34	30.93	16.93
TVS Motors India Ltd.	703.25	801.00	863.45	866.31	1119.1	1146.86
Kinetic Motors Company Ltd.	102.51	119.77	124.06	112.93	111.79	81.13
Hero Honda Motors Ltd.	530.55	761.62	1029.51	1425.30	1677.54	207.15
Majestic Auto Ltd.	161.32	148.02	153.38	130.52	100.28	85.16
Kinetic Engineering Ltd.	126.76	111.20	108.72	77.39	-	-
Scooters India Ltd.	15.16	15.49	12.10	13.07	14.37	15.37

Source: CMIE Database.

APPENDIX IV

Annual market share of selected automobile industry in India

(in thousands)

Industry	*91-92*	*92-93*	*93-94*	*94-95*	*95-96*	*96-97*	*97-98*
Commercial Vehicles							
Ashok Leyland Ltd.	28.61	54.57	34.40	31.65	31.41	31.05	35.47
Tata Motors Ltd.	35.59	26.18	30.56	42.99	35.46	39.94	34.00
Bajaj Tempo Ltd.	18.68	11.23	22.64	17.94	16.48	11.93	8.00
Eicher Motors Ltd.	10.84	4.55	6.75	7.20	6.47	5.75	9.80
Swaraj Mazda Ltd.	6.28	3.47	5.65	5.11	4.57	3.33	5.72
Passenger Cars and Multiutility Vehicles							
Hindustan Motors Ltd.	12.55	15.72	14.45	10.55	9.10	6.98	6.41
Mahindra and Mahindra Ltd.	0.00	43.14	45.60	47.67	43.97	48.40	48.97
Maruthi Udyog Ltd.	68.77	41.14	39.95	41.78	41.29	36.62	41.33
Daewoo Motors India Ltd.	-	-	-	-	5.64	8.00	3.29

(Contd.)

(Contd. Appendix-IV)

Industry	*98-99*	*99-00*	*00-01*	*01-02*	*02-03*	*03-04*
Commercial Vehicles						
Ashok Leyland Ltd.	39.28	38.46	39.39	35.15	31.68	31.88
Tata Motors Ltd.	34.00	27.04	24.93	25.85	30.64	57.67
Bajaj Tempo Ltd.	8.00	9.31	7.62	6.82	7.43	3.46
Eicher Motors Ltd.	9.80	11.69	13.84	18.68	17.93	15.15
Swaraj Mazda Ltd.	5.72	7.18	8.51	12.12	10.97	9.18
Passenger Cars and Multiutility Vehicles						
Hindustan Motors Ltd.	6.33	7.18	6.50	4.88	4.71	2.67
Mahindra and Mahindra Ltd.	54.21	57.23	42.44	36.45	39.03	41.13
Maruthi Udyog Ltd.	36.36	29.27	26.01	25.04	24.48	23.82
Daewoo Motors India Ltd.	3.20	6.32	5.71	1.38	1.35	0.00

(Contd.)

(Contd. Appendix-IV)

Industry	*91-92*	*92-93*	*93-94*	*94-95*	*95-96*	*96-97*	*97-98*
Two and Three Wheelers							
Bajaj Auto Ltd.	16.00	13.26	14.00	15.25	16.12	18.30	21.35
LML Ltd.	12.54	11.84	10.43	12.56	13.70	11.45	13.73
Maharastra Scooters Ltd.	1.31	9.37	12.59	9.27	9.06	10.13	10.47
TVS Motors Company Ltd.	13.19	12.33	13.06	13.67	12.70	13.26	12.42
Kinetic Motors Company Ltd.	15.04	10.23	12.79	11.83	12.17	11.24	13.10
Hero Honda Motors Ltd.	13.22	13.00	10.00	9.00	8.40	8.27	10.79
Kinetic Engineering Ltd.	10.00	10.34	10.00	9.00	10.00	8.50	11.21
Majestic Auto Ltd.	11.00	12.02	9.26	8.59	6.40	8.50	11.21
Scooters India Ltd.	5.70	6.61	5.87	8.83	9.45	8.35	9.42

(Contd.)

(Contd. Appendix-IV)

Industry	*98-99*	*99-00*	*00-01*	*01-02*	*02-03*	*03-04*
Two and Three Wheelers						
Bajaj Auto Ltd.	19.26	21.23	20.45	22.05	22.45	24.65
LML Ltd.	14.36	12.65	11.77	10.63	7.84	7.05
Maharastra Scooters Ltd.	9.21	10.50	9.18	5.71	2.98	1.59
TVS Motors Company Ltd.	11.74	10.31	12.21	11.50	14.94	16.78
Kinetic Motors Company Ltd.	8.82	10.14	11.44	12.99	14.25	8.76
Hero Honda Motors Ltd.	10.08	10.21	9.99	10.31	11.45	12.25
Kinetic Engineering Ltd.	8.00	7.50	7.50	8.75	8.40	8.32
Majestic Auto Ltd.	9.20	9.50	7.50	9.25	10.20	13.75
Scooters India Ltd.	8.53	7.97	8.90	7.43	6.49	5.85

APPENDIX V
Operating profit margin ratio

Year	*Commercial Vehicles*	*Passenger Cars and Multiutility Vehicles*	*Two and Three Wheelers*	*Industry average*
1991-92	8.49	5.59	9.68	7.92
1992-93	6.41	4.57	10.16	7.05
1993-94	7.26	9.44	-3.77	4.31
1994-95	9.58	10.56	10.19	10.11
1995-96	11.73	13.07	10.10	11.63
1996-97	11.48	10.82	11.47	11.26
1997-98	9.54	13.29	11.62	11.48
1998-99	10.50	10.53	11.17	10.73
1999-00	7.18	8.10	11.64	8.97
2000-01	7.21	4.48	8.17	6.62
2001-02	2.75	7.49	7.60	5.95
2002-03	5.55	8.40	8.18	7.38
2003-04	4.37	11.47	5.04	6.96

APPENDIX VI
Net profit margin ratio

Year	*Commercial Vehicles*	*Passenger Cars and Multiutility Vehicles*	*Two and Three Wheelers*	*Industry average*
1991-92	-13.96	1.38	0.57	-4.00
1992-93	0.39	-1.50	2.14	0.34
1993-94	2.57	0.66	4.59	2.61
1994-95	5.19	4.88	5.19	5.09
1995-96	0.33	5.96	4.89	3.73
1996-97	0.01	4.30	4.84	3.05
1997-98	3.18	6.28	5.34	4.93
1998-99	1.06	2.90	5.20	3.05
1999-00	1.22	-0.14	5.55	2.21
2000-01	-3.34	3.46	2.73	0.95
2001-02	0.51	0.38	1.82	0.90
2002-03	3.22	1.92	1.45	2.20
2003-04	4.93	5.10	0.88	3.64

APPENDIX VII
Return on assets

Year	*Commercial Vehicles*	*Passenger Cars and Multiutility Vehicles*	*Two and Three Wheelers*	*Industry average*
1991-92	0.46	-4.82	5.38	0.34
1992-93	0.54	-3.94	0.56	-0.95
1993-94	4.27	1.26	10.27	5.27
1994-95	12.37	9.18	15.27	12.27
1995-96	16.20	18.32	14.44	16.32
1996-97	15.69	11.71	12.02	13.14
1997-98	3.87	10.61	14.40	9.63
1998-99	1.08	5.47	12.05	6.20
1999-00	1.82	1.99	13.22	5.68
2000-01	-5.08	-7.16	8.09	-1.38
2001-02	0.93	-2.07	7.67	2.18
2002-03	8.32	-0.69	5.83	4.49
2003-04	15.71	-1.99	6.93	6.88

APPENDIX VIII
Return on net worth

Year	*Commercial Vehicles*	*Passenger Cars and Multiutility Vehicles*	*Two and Three Wheelers*	*Industry average*
1991-92	12.85	-9.31	19.27	7.60
1992-93	4.05	5.21	17.44	8.90
1993-94	6.78	14.56	31.83	17.72
1994-95	43.53	19.78	26.07	29.79
1995-96	28.73	32.69	20.58	27.33
1996-97	22.95	19.44	18.54	20.31
1997-98	16.00	19.93	17.36	17.76
1998-99	3.80	8.28	19.99	10.69
1999-00	7.67	0.94	23.45	10.69
2000-01	7.21	-11.25	11.15	2.37
2001-02	14.20	1.22	15.28	10.23
2002-03	18.66	6.94	14.58	13.39
2003-04	31.41	18.30	7.53	19.08

APPENDIX IX
Return on capital employed

Year	*Commercial Vehicles*	*Passenger Cars and Multiutility Vehicles*	*Two and Three Wheelers*	*Industry average*
1991-92	16.09	8.13	17.94	14.05
1992-93	7.78	6.82	16.82	10.47
1993-94	17.63	15.33	27.88	20.28
1994-95	23.47	21.96	28.36	24.60
1995-96	27.15	33.75	26.90	29.27
1996-97	20.81	26.30	28.74	25.28
1997-98	13.43	16.61	21.77	17.27
1998-99	8.72	9.48	22.94	13.71
1999-00	11.23	5.53	27.29	14.68
2000-01	12.90	-0.67	16.55	9.59
2001-02	17.63	3.72	19.09	13.48
2002-03	33.07	8.72	19.57	20.45
2003-04	41.31	23.33	13.47	26.04

APPENDIX X
Earnings per share

Year	*Commercial Vehicles*	*Passenger Cars and Multiutility Vehicles*	*Two and Three Wheelers*	*Industry average*
1991-92	6.88	14.89	6.48	9.42
1992-93	6.05	8.72	6.60	7.12
1993-94	15.41	20.06	10.68	15.38
1994-95	10.39	52.70	12.89	25.33
1995-96	14.62	87.49	17.20	39.77
1996-97	10.78	101.81	18.71	43.77
1997-98	4.69	129.28	17.88	50.62
1998-99	2.25	103.38	18.03	41.22
1999-00	3.73	66.81	23.57	31.37
2000-01	4.50	2.59	13.02	6.70
2001-02	4.93	28.60	14.30	15.94
2002-03	14.75	4.18	14.95	11.29
2003-04	21.04	11.86	13.20	15.37

APPENDIX XI
Dividend per share

Year	*Commercial Vehicles*	*Passenger Cars and Multiutility Vehicles*	*Two and Three Wheelers*	*Industry average*
1991-92	19.40	7.13	13.56	13.36
1992-93	14.40	9.00	14.44	12.61
1993-94	23.40	13.75	19.89	19.01
1994-95	29.00	20.00	23.33	24.11
1995-96	34.00	18.75	28.00	26.92
1996-97	38.00	20.00	30.56	29.52
1997-98	17.00	21.25	28.33	22.19
1998-99	13.00	21.25	33.33	22.53
1999-00	18.00	20.00	41.67	26.56
2000-01	15.00	13.75	43.89	24.21
2001-02	19.00	20.00	126.67	55.22
2002-03	44.00	21.25	129.56	64.94
2003-04	66.00	30.00	155.56	83.85

APPENDIX XII
Dividend payout ratio

Year	*Commercial Vehicles*	*Passenger Cars and Multiutility Vehicles*	*Two and Three Wheelers*	*Industry average*
1991-92	182.99	80.99	106.90	123.63
1992-93	653.80	109.45	104.90	289.38
1993-94	287.59	87.30	108.60	161.16
1994-95	227.95	80.20	115.43	141.19
1995-96	188.32	69.69	131.31	129.77
1996-97	414.11	116.25	195.32	241.89
1997-98	418.52	129.40	167.65	238.52
1998-99	377.41	65.84	201.22	214.82
1999-00	469.14	61.73	121.69	217.52
2000-01	226.38	132.85	305.30	221.51
2001-02	247.61	150.74	561.41	319.92
2002-03	343.57	269.82	458.38	357.26
2003-04	330.26	118.29	448.63	299.06

APPENDIX XIII

Operating profit margin ratio (Commercial Vehicles)

Year	*Ashok Leyland Ltd.*	*Tata Motors Ltd.*	*Bajaj Tempo Ltd.*	*Eicher Motors Ltd.*	*Swaraj Mazda Ltd.*
1991-92	10.97	13.71	13.77	5.78	-1.79
1992-93	11.98	10.69	09.33	1.45	-1.40
1993-94	11.17	10.27	09.13	4.74	0.97
1994-95	12.03	13.45	09.21	9.32	3.89
1995-96	14.03	14.28	15.54	9.43	5.37
1996-97	14.29	14.92	13.28	8.16	6.77
1997-98	12.12	13.90	10.89	5.96	7.72
1998-99	11.31	10.96	04.66	7.06	5.98
1999-00	11.64	07.24	05.75	7.82	4.26
2000-01	12.08	04.27	04.95	8.05	5.11
2001-02	12.71	08.14	06.65	8.42	5.35
2002-03	11.80	11.16	08.29	11.32	6.59
2003-04	11.11	12.38	09.57	7.91	6.65

APPENDIX XIV

Net profit margin ratio (Commercial Vehicles)

Year	*Ashok Leyland Ltd.*	*Tata Motors Ltd.*	*Bajaj Tempo Ltd.*	*Eicher Motors Ltd.*	*Swaraj Mazda Ltd.*
1991-92	2.33	4.45	3.17	-6.34	1.12
1992-93	0.47	1.02	[illegible]88	-5.78	5.75
1993-94	2.92	2.80	[illegible]2	-2.29	-2.22
1994-95	4.59	5.69	3.03	0.27	5.09
1995-96	5.53	6.85	4.08	4.16	4.75
1996-97	4.96	0.01	[illegible].93	2.66	3.62
1997-98	0.89	4.11	0.63	3.94	1.44
1998-99	0.96	1.52	-5.15	1.68	2.93
1999-00	2.93	0.82	-2.20	1.33	4.51
2000-01	3.43	-6.31	-2.82	1.48	5.29
2001-02	3.42	-0.62	0.25	2.02	3.48
2002-03	3.85	2.84	3.89	3.48	5.36
2003-04	4.86	5.34	3.98	3.87	2.15

APPENDIX XV

Return on assets (Commercial Vehicles)

Year	*Ashok Leyland Ltd.*	*Tata Motors Ltd.*	*Bajaj Tempo Ltd.*	*Eicher Motors Ltd.*	*Swaraj Mazda Ltd.*
1991-92	3.15	17.42	8.52	3.33	-34.73
1992-93	0.49	0.14	10.28	-14.42	-40.42
1993-94	3.53	4.59	13.34	-5.90	-29.61
1994-95	4.53	12.76	14.04	15.30	02.17
1995-96	5.89	14.82	14.69	15.24	24.35
1996-97	5.51	13.12	2.66	12.04	10.15
1997-98	0.79	4.51	1.57	4.69	18.49
1998-99	0.98	1.51	-13.15	8.92	05.71
1999-00	3.74	1.19	-6.79	15.97	06.68
2000-01	4.36	-9.33	-8.29	19.90	08.24
2001-02	4.81	-1.13	0.89	16.42	11.79
2002-03	7.17	7.46	16.12	29.49	45.74
2003-04	12.75	16.79	17.69	8.98	43.69

APPENDIX XVI

Return on networth (Commercial Vehicles)

Year	*Ashok Leyland Ltd.*	*Tata Motors Ltd.*	*Bajaj Tempo Ltd.*	*Eicher Motors Ltd.*	*Swaraj Mazda Ltd.*
1991-92	13.35	20.71	17.20	12.99	0.00
1992-93	0.41	3.12	16.70	0.00	0.00
1993-94	8.67	8.42	16.80	0.00	0.00
1994-95	10.24	28.27	16.32	55.82	107.02
1995-96	11.60	27.63	22.00	39.50	42.90
1996-97	12.04	25.15	04.14	27.69	45.75
1997-98	0.59	7.96	02.28	08.03	61.11
1998-99	0.62	-0.26	-17.75	15.64	20.76
1999-00	7.16	-4.98	-10.93	27.37	19.74
2000-01	8.10	-14.28	-14.40	32.14	24.48
2001-02	8.53	-0.29	1.42	23.99	32.34
2002-03	12.37	11.86	25.57	43.51	62.24
2003-04	19.75	26.20	26.84	23.37	60.90

APPENDIX XVII

Return on capital employed (Commercial Vehicles)

Year	*Ashok Leyland Ltd.*	*Tata Motors Ltd.*	*Bajaj Tempo Ltd.*	*Eicher Motors Ltd.*	*Swaraj Mazda Ltd.*
1991-92	14.33	24.95	24.42	16.73	0.00
1992-93	10.38	12.07	16.43	0.00	0.00
1993-94	11.03	12.63	29.22	0.00	0.00
1994-95	11.69	26.86	28.70	29.47	20.65
1995-96	13.62	30.95	40.71	28.57	21.91
1996-97	14.26	26.99	14.58	24.70	23.52
1997-98	07.90	11.94	07.71	13.39	26.19
1998-99	07.43	06.45	-0.14	17.54	19.33
1999-00	11.15	04.60	-0.19	24.35	17.56
2000-01	11.29	-0.16	-0.91	27.26	27.04
2001-02	12.47	06.95	07.21	30.54	30.97
2002-03	14.99	18.64	21.77	52.56	57.41
2003-04	22.00	33.77	33.19	32.52	85.05

APPENDIX XVIII

Earnings per share (Commercial Vehicles)

Year	*Ashok Leyland Ltd.*	*Tata Motors Ltd.*	*Bajaj Tempo Ltd.*	*Eicher Motors Ltd.*	*Swaraj Mazda Ltd.*
1991-92	7.76	11.63	13.45	1.54	0.00
1992-93	0.66	2.40	14.94	0.00	0.00
1993-94	4.53	7.91	14.87	0.00	0.00
1994-95	5.94	23.29	17.07	5.30	0.37
1995-96	9.51	21.92	28.31	6.18	7.20
1996-97	10.01	29.01	04.46	5.74	4.70
1997-98	1.45	10.97	02.89	1.80	6.36
1998-99	1.60	3.48	0.00	3.75	2.44
1999-00	6.21	2.23	0.00	7.71	2.49
2000-01	7.30	0.00	0.00	11.56	3.65
2001-02	7.76	0.00	1.21	9.24	6.45
2002-03	9.47	8.87	23.77	18.28	13.35
2003-04	15.32	21.93	32.65	16.17	19.12

APPENDIX XIX

Dividend per share (Commercial Vehicles)

Year	*Ashok Leyland Ltd.*	*Tata Motors Ltd.*	*Bajaj Tempo Ltd.*	*Eicher Motors Ltd.*	*Swaraj Mazda Ltd.*
1991-92	27.00	40.00	30.00	0.00	0.00
1992-93	12.00	30.00	30.00	0.00	0.00
1993-94	27.00	40.00	50.00	0.00	0.00
1994-95	35.00	60.00	50.00	0.00	0.00
1995-96	40.00	60.00	70.00	0.00	0.00
1996-97	50.00	80.00	50.00	10.00	0.00
1997-98	10.00	55.00	10.00	10.00	0.00
1998-99	10.00	30.00	10.00	15.00	0.00
1999-00	35.00	25.00	0.00	20.00	10.00
2000-01	40.00	0.00	0.00	20.00	15.00
2001-02	45.00	0.00	0.00	25.00	25.00
2002-03	50.00	40.00	50.00	35.00	4500
2003-04	75.00	80.00	70.00	35.00	70.00

APPENDIX XX

Dividend payout ratio (Commercial Vehicles)

Year	*Ashok Leyland Ltd.*	*Tata Motors Ltd.*	*Bajaj Tempo Ltd.*	*Eicher Motors Ltd.*	*Swaraj Mazda Ltd.*
1991-92	347.94	343.94	223.05	0.00	0.00
1992-93	1818.18	1250.00	200.80	0.00	0.00
1993-94	596.03	505.69	336.25	0.00	0.00
1994-95	589.23	257.62	292.91	0.00	0.00
1995-96	420.61	273.72	247.26	0.00	0.00
1996-97	499.50	275.77	1121.08	174.22	0.00
1997-98	689.66	501.37	346.02	555.55	0.00
1998-99	625.00	862.07	0.00	400.00	0.00
1999-00	563.61	1121.08	0.00	259.40	401.61
2000-01	547.95	0.00	0.00	173.01	410.96
2001-02	579.90	0.00	0.00	270.56	387.60
2002-03	527.98	450.96	210.35	191.47	337.08
2003-04	489.56	364.80	214.40	216.45	366.11

APPENDIX XXI

Operating profit margin ratio (Passenger Cars and Multiutility Vehicles)

Year	*Hindustan Motors Ltd.*	*Mahindra and Mahindra Ltd.*	*Maruthi Udyog Ltd.*	*Daewoo Motors India Ltd.*
1991-92	5.40	07.71	07.81	01.44
1992-93	5.84	07.77	06.89	02.37
1993-94	10.68	11.37	10.76	04.94
1994-95	10.03	12.80	14.39	05.03
1995-96	10.00	13.63	14.58	14.06
1996-97	09.93	13.53	13.90	05.92
1997-98	10.13	13.98	14.94	-05.63
1998-99	05.92	13.52	13.17	-0.40
1999-00	04.90	14.31	07.06	16.31
2000-01	01.56	08.92	01.44	11.65
2001-02	03.90	08.94	05.92	-36.61
2002-03	05.21	10.75	06.98	04.61
2003-04	-0.40	11.67	12.64	05.38

APPENDIX XXII

Net profit margin ratio (Passenger Cars and Multiutility Vehicles)

Year	*Hindustan Motors Ltd.*	*Mahindra and Mahindra Ltd.*	*Maruthi Udyog Ltd.*	*Daewoo Motors India Ltd.*
1991-92	-6.09	1.85	1.19	-12.87
1992-93	-4.47	1.83	1.61	-16.11
1993-94	1.85	4.12	3.08	-11.13
1994-95	2.43	5.81	5.96	-6.78
1995-96	4.07	6.11	6.55	8.30
1996-97	3.11	6.01	6.33	0.38
1997-98	3.03	6.37	7.78	-11.14
1998-99	-1.91	5.68	6.29	-11.07
1999-00	-3.39	6.13	3.48	-09.09
2000-01	-7.07	2.82	-3.22	-17.24
2001-02	-2.84	2.61	1.16	-113.79
2002-03	-2.78	3.27	1.44	-19.23
2003-04	-9.63	5.98	5.50	-16.56

APPENDIX XXIII

Return on assets (Passenger Cars and Multiutility Vehicles)

Year	*Hindustan Motors Ltd.*	*Mahindra and Mahindra Ltd.*	*Maruthi Udyog Ltd.*	*Daewoo Motors India Ltd.*
1991-92	-7.64	3.04	3.26	-17.92
1992-93	-6.35	3.93	3.97	-17.30
1993-94	3.17	7.19	10.14	-15.45
1994-95	4.81	10.53	23.29	-01.90
1995-96	9.32	12.86	31.15	19.95
1996-97	6.43	10.02	30.27	0.11
1997-98	5.29	09.60	28.67	-1.13
1998-99	-3.34	07.96	18.19	-0.95
1999-00	-7.97	9.36	9.52	-2.95
2000-01	-19.82	4.05	-7.78	-5.07
2001-02	-6.52	3.56	3.24	-8.56
2002-03	-5.68	5.45	3.74	-6.26
2003-04	-18.67	13.97	2.00	-5.26

APPENDIX XXIV

Return on networth (Passenger Cars and Multiutility Vehicles)

Year	*Hindustan Motors Ltd.*	*Mahindra and Mahindra Ltd.*	*Maruthi Udyog Ltd.*	*Daewoo Motors India Ltd.*
1991-92	-38.61	-7.69	9.05	0.00
1992-93	0.00	8.91	11.93	0.00
1993-94	14.33	21.69	22.20	0.00
1994-95	14.11	19.00	46.00	0.00
1995-96	25.36	20.35	50.14	34.92
1996-97	16.71	20.91	39.41	0.74
1997-98	14.97	20.95	35.45	0.00
1998-99	-10.79	16.28	21.95	0.00
1999-00	-29.53	15.13	11.93	0.00
2000-01	-61.22	05.95	-09.70	0.00
2001-02	0.00	6.64	03.91	0.00
2002-03	0.00	9.57	04.47	0.00
2003-04	0.00	21.03	18.59	0.00

APPENDIX XXV

Return on capital employed (Passenger Cars and Multiutility Vehicles)

Year	*Hindustan Motors Ltd.*	*Mahindra and Mahindra Ltd.*	*Maruthi Udyog Ltd.*	*Daewoo Motors India Ltd.*
1991-92	3.81	9.85	18.84	0.00
1992-93	0.00	12.99	14.27	0.00
1993-94	15.32	19.49	26.50	0.00
1994-95	15.86	22.29	49.69	0.00
1995-96	20.52	28.03	65.24	21.20
1996-97	18.42	24.38	59.96	02.42
1997-98	16.37	19.38	54.03	0.00
1998-99	07.17	15.05	34.03	0.00
1999-00	05.77	17.41	14.60	0.00
2000-01	-2.78	8.38	-05.44	0.00
2001-02	0.00	7.28	05.63	0.00
2002-03	0.00	11.34	09.10	0.00
2003-04	0.00	20.06	25.45	0.00

APPENDIX XXVI

Earnings per share (Passenger Cars and Multiutility Vehicles)

Year	*Hindustan Motors Ltd.*	*Mahindra and Mahindra Ltd.*	*Maruthi Udyog Ltd.*	*Daewoo Motors India Ltd.*
1991-92	0.00	8.30	26.37	0.00
1992-93	0.00	7.21	27.65	0.00
1993-94	1.65	13.48	65.10	0.00
1994-95	2.87	20.78	187.16	0.00
1995-96	4.75	16.51	323.27	5.41
1996-97	3.56	20.06	383.57	0.06
1997-98	3.56	23.77	489.99	0.00
1998-99	000	21.51	391.99	0.00
1999-00	0.00	23.24	243.99	0.00
2000-01	0.00	10.35	0.00	0.00
2001-02	0.00	08.85	78.99	0.00
2002-03	0.00	11.84	04.88	0.00
2003-04	0.00	28.89	18.56	0.00

APPENDIX XXVII

Dividend per share (Passenger Cars and Multiutility Vehicles)

Year	*Hindustan Motors Ltd.*	*Mahindra and Mahindra Ltd.*	*Maruthi Udyog Ltd.*	*Daewoo Motors India Ltd.*
1991-92	0.00	22.50	06.00	0.00
1992-93	0.00	30.00	06.00	0.00
1993-94	0.00	45.00	10.00	0.00
1994-95	0.00	65.00	15.00	0.00
1995-96	10.00	45.00	20.00	0.00
1996-97	10.00	50.00	20.00	0.00
1997-98	0.00	55.00	30.00	0.00
1998-99	0.00	55.00	30.00	0.00
1999-00	0.00	55.00	25.00	0.00
2000-01	0.00	55.00	0.00	0.00
2001-02	0.00	50.00	30.00	0.00
2002-03	0.00	55.00	30.00	0.00
2003-04	0.00	90.00	30.00	0.00

APPENDIX XXVIII

Dividend payout ratio (Passenger Cars and Multiutility Vehicles)

Year	*Hindustan Motors Ltd.*	*Mahindra and Mahindra Ltd.*	*Maruthi Udyog Ltd.*	*Daewoo Motors India Ltd.*
1991-92	0.00	301.20	22.75	0.00
1992-93	0.00	416.09	21.70	0.00
1993-94	0.00	333.82	15.36	0.00
1994-95	0.00	312.80	08.01	0.00
1995-96	0.00	272.56	06.19	0.00
1996-97	210.53	249.25	05.21	0.00
1997-98	280.09	231.38	06.13	0.00
1998-99	0.00	255.70	07.65	0.00
1999-00	0.00	236.66	10.25	0.00
2000-01	0.00	531.40	0.00	0.00
2001-02	0.00	564.97	37.98	0.00
2002-03	0.00	464.53	614.75	0.00
2003-04	0.00	311.53	161.64	0.00

APPENDIX XXIX

Operating profit margin ratio (Two and Three Wheelers)

Year	*Bajaj Auto Ltd.*	*LML Ltd.*	*Maharastra Scooters Ltd.*	*TVS Motors Ltd.*	*Kinetic Motors Ltd.*
1991-92	16.52	4.45	16.08	10.89	4.38
1992-93	16.56	11.25	14.47	9.77	3.61
1993-94	21.57	14.30	14.13	11.85	6.36
1994-95	24.20	11.09	11.92	11.92	5.13
1995-96	25.00	08.97	11.19	12.10	3.65
1996-97	25.41	11.81	09.15	12.75	3.53
1997-98	26.63	9.42	08.24	14.24	4.37
1998-99	25.39	10.46	08.03	11.88	5.19
1999-00	22.25	07.74	11.26	13.23	8.66
2000-01	14.37	02.82	01.67	8.15	8.25
2001-02	18.71	-0.34	04.60	6.76	8.82
2002-03	20.12	2.52	07.67	9.39	4.23
2003-04	20.95	1.45	02.27	9.35	-6.79

(Contd.)

(Contd. Appendix-XXIX)

Year	*Hero Honda Motors Ltd.*	*Kinetic Engineering Ltd.*	*Majestic Auto Ltd.*	*Scooters India Ltd.*
1991-92	10.49	16.16	8.16	-
1992-93	10.38	16.49	8.89	-
1993-94	9.14	15.64	10.55	-137.43
1994-95	9.52	14.04	8.98	-5.08
1995-96	9.26	13.57	6.60	0.56
1996-97	11.34	12.80	4.69	11.77
1997-98	11.90	13.34	5.43	10.99
1998-99	13.55	11.61	7.19	07.30
1999-00	14.41	14.82	5.91	06.46
2000-01	13.36	13.07	5.76	06.09
2001-02	16.73	10.42	-0.79	03.50
2002-03	18.61	11.21	-4.04	03.90
2003-04	17.72	-11.63	8.56	03.44

(Contd.)

APPENDIX XXX

Net profit margin ratio (Two and Three Wheelers)

Year	*Bajaj Auto Ltd.*	*LML Ltd.*	*Maharastra Scooters Ltd.*	*TVS Motors Ltd.*	*Kinetic Motors Ltd.*
1991-92	3.74	-17.46	8.60	1.94	0.02
1992-93	3.97	-2.34	6.47	2.04	0.28
1993-94	9.01	6.63	6.60	6.65	3.37
1994-95	13.91	6.03	6.47	8.26	2.79
1995-96	15.27	3.87	6.63	5.69	1.63
1996-97	13.69	5.12	5.58	6.57	0.70
1997-98	13.68	-	5.57	6.63	0.61
1998-99	14.43	3.14	5.56	6.25	1.15
1999-00	13.57	0.87	8.41	6.83	3.65
2000-01	8.39	-6.62	0.54	3.46	3.76
2001-02	10.58	-8.21	3.47	2.45	3.83
2002-03	11.66	-3.45	0.96	4.00	0.42
2003-04	12.88		4.57	4.23	-9.39

(Contd.)

(Contd. Appendix-XXX)

Year	*Hero Honda Motors Ltd.*	*Kinetic Engineering Ltd.*	*Majestic Auto Ltd.*	*Scooters India Ltd.*
1991-92	5.12	3.14	-	-
1992-93	4.74	4.09	-	-
1993-94	4.25	4.81	-	-
1994-95	4.08	5.14	-	-
1995-96	4.17	6.77	-	-
1996-97	6.58	5.33	-	-
1997-98	6.69	5.46	-	9.29
1998-99	8.12	2.68	0.37	5.09
1999-00	8.31	4.64	-1.21	4.86
2000-01	7.85	4.38	-1.70	4.51
2001-02	9.94	2.06	-9.97	2.20
2002-03	10.49	-0.15	-13.15	2.24
2003-04	11.16	-21.63	3.99	2.12

APPENDIX XXXI

Return on assets (Two and Three Wheelers)

Year	*Bajaj Auto Ltd.*	*LML Ltd.*	*Maharastra Scooters Ltd.*	*TVS Motors Ltd.*	*Kinetic Motors Ltd.*
1991-92	8.22	-14.56	18.38	6.56	8.46
1992-93	9.15	-46.73	14.67	7.41	0.95
1993-94	20.74	-7.91	14.57	29.37	14.68
1994-95	23.45	23.55	12.64	40.56	11.08
1995-96	25.72	19.82	14.08	30.42	7.93
1996-97	21.90	10.56	12.80	28.73	2.43
1997-98	18.17	13.86	11.22	21.34	2.03
1998-99	16.67	10.75	11.44	17.14	4.35
1999-00	13.60	1.83	15.34	20.01	16.50
2000-01	9.63	-12.59	00.67	10.66	18.18
2001-02	12.60	-15.05	2.42	10.89	11.56
2002-03	13.64	-13.63	0.35	22.87	0.95
2003-04	14.92	-	1.00	20.26	-19.24

(Contd.)

(Contd. Appendix-XXXI)

Year	*Hero Honda Motors Ltd.*	*Kinetic Engineering Ltd.*	*Majestic Auto Ltd.*	*Scooters India Ltd.*
1991-92	15.52	5.83	-	-
1992-93	12.58	6.97	-	-
1993-94	13.54	7.44	-	-
1994-95	16.16	9.99	-	-
1995-96	17.61	14.41	-	-
1996-97	21.31	10.41	-	-
1997-98	26.35	8.77	-	27.89
1998-99	31.70	3.98	0.74	11.69
1999-00	37.78	6.06	-2.27	10.15
2000-01	36.86	6.22	-3.35	6.50
2001-02	56.07	2.21	-15.16	3.53
2002-03	53.79	-0.13	-26.57	1.24
2003-04	49.56	-18.93	10.88	3.96

APPENDIX XXXII
Return on networth (Two and Three Wheelers)

Year	Bajaj Auto Ltd.	LML Ltd.	Maharastra Scooters Ltd.	TVS Motors Ltd.	Kinetic Motors Ltd.
1991-92	13.61	4.45	22.01	19.22	21.69
1992-93	14.57	11.25	16.72	16.36	2.03
1993-94	33.75	14.30	16.27	71.37	18.51
1994-95	39.11	11.09	14.23	81.45	17.79
1995-96	33.73	8.97	15.91	50.56	12.58
1996-97	27.81	11.81	14.91	51.11	5.40
1997-98	23.93	-	12.43	43.79	5.03
1998-99	22.43	24.23	12.96	37.86	8.39
1999-00	17.03	4.29	16.75	66.98	28.40
2000-01	10.33	-27.98	0.69	18.63	26.40
2001-02	15.94	0	2.55	15.89	20.77
2002-03	17.63	0	0.36	34.29	1.86
2003-04	21.10	0	1.05	27.76	-34.77

(Contd.)

(Contd. Appendix-XXXII)

Year	*Hero Honda Motors Ltd.*	*Kinetic Engineering Ltd.*	*Majestic Auto Ltd.*	*Scooters India Ltd.*
1991-92	46.62	11.54	34.30	0
1992-93	34.88	13.98	47.17	0
1993-94	27.48	14.65	90.15	0
1994-95	28.18	16.01	26.77	0
1995-96	30.55	24.17	8.78	0
1996-97	42.79	16.99	-0.35	-3.58
1997-98	44.26	16.94	-21.68	31.52
1998-99	47.82	8.57	1.22	16.43
1999-00	51.30	14.68	-5.35	16.95
2000-01	45.82	14.29	0	12.15
2001-02	7[illegible].41	5.81	0	6.13
2002-03	[illegible]9	-0.34	0	2.31
2003-04	6[illegible].1	-53.83	0	2.32

APPENDIX XXXIII

Return on capital employed (Two and Three Wheelers)

Year	Bajaj Auto Ltd.	LML Ltd.	Maharastra Scooters Ltd.	TVS Motors Ltd.	Kinetic Motors Ltd.
1991-92	21.5	0	36.01	25.60	17.41
1992-93	22.83	0	33.45	23.69	8.66
1993-94	45.15	38.25	32.30	43.65	21.21
1994-95	46.82	32.33	24.59	58.11	23.89
1995-96	41.96	23.30	24.71	66.03	16.25
1996-97	38.17	27.94	21.57	59.86	10.27
1997-98	32.07	-	16.16	47.41	10.17
1998-99	28.12	19.83	16.58	31.36	12.10
1999-00	20.12	9.47	20.63	62.08	33.31
2000-01	9.94	-1.58	0.84	18.75	34.07
2001-02	18.03	0	1.97	18.59	25.59
2002-03	20.88	0	1.90	41.04	5.42
2003-04	21.89	0	-0.31	36.68	-16.97

(Contd.)

(Contd. Appendix-XXXIII)

Year	*Hero Honda Motors Ltd.*	*Kinetic Engineering Ltd.*	*Majestic Auto Ltd.*	*Scooters India Ltd.*
1991-92	26.25	20.31	14.34	0
1992-93	23.21	19.40	20.15	0
1993-94	22.08	16.56	31.69	0
1994-95	30.85	16.88	21.80	0
1995-96	35.66	23.68	10.55	0
1996-97	38.37	18.43	6.03	38.01
1997-98	44.49	16.77	6.58	22.30
1998-99	53.29	13.22	9.12	13.87
1999-00	66.15	15.09	6.58	12.26
2000-01	64.86	14.00	0	8.04
2001-02	94.84	8.63	0	4.21
2002-03	99.22	5.14	0	2.55
2003-04	83.21	-14.27	8.64	2.36

APPENDIX XXXIV

Earnings per share (Two and Three Wheelers)

Year	*Baja Auto Ltd.*	*LML Ltd.*	*Maharastra Scooters Ltd.*	*TVS Motors Ltd.*	*Kinetic Motors Ltd.*
1991-92	11.89	0.59	20.07	1.38	2.94
1992-93	13.83	0	17.81	1.64	0.29
1993-94	38.72	0	19.86	7.81	3.97
1994-95	38.34	6.38	19.82	14.61	4.37
1995-96	52.53	7.44	28.69	15.22	3.38
1996-97	54.35	4.18	27.20	23.19	1.43
1997-98	38.08	4.75	12.69	29.26	1.34
1998-99	44.39	6.25	14.77	34.77	2.29
1999-00	50.13	1.49	21.71	44.81	9.09
2000-01	25.13	0	1.97	26.31	9.99
2001-02	51.50	0	4.66	22.42	9.15
2002-03	51.42	0	0.22	54.49	0.88
2003-04	69.09	0	5.04	5.65	0

(Contd.)

(Contd. Appendix-XXXIV)

Year	Hero Honda Motors Ltd.	Kinetic Engineering Ltd.	Majestic Auto Ltd.	Scooters India Ltd.
1991-92	9.53	11.94	-	-
1992-93	9.78	16.04	-	-
1993-94	9.66	16.06	-	-
1994-95	9.74	22.79	-	-
1995-96	13.19	34.37	-	-
1996-97	25.03	33.05	-	-
1997-98	37.96	33.70	-	3.10
1998-99	29.70	26.40	2.09	1.65
1999-00	46.99	36.23	0	1.70
2000-01	12.06	40.44	0	1.27
2001-02	22.67	17.59	0	0.71
2002-03	26.78	0	0	0.75
2003-04	33.91	0	4.29	0.78

APPENDIX XXXV

Divided per share (Two and Three Wheelers)

Year	*Baja Auto Ltd.*	*LML Ltd.*	*Maharastra Scooters Ltd.*	*TVS Motors Ltd.*	*Kinetic Motors Ltd.*
1991-92	50	0	25	0	0
1992-93	50	0	25	0	0
1993-94	80	0	30	12	0
1994-95	80	0	35	25	0
1995-96	100	0	40	30	10
1996-97	100	0	40	35	10
1997-98	80	15	20	50	10
1998-99	80	15	20	70	15
1999-00	100	0	20	80	25
2000-01	80	0	10	80	25
2001-02	140	0	10	90	25
2002-03	140	0	6	120	0
2003-04	250	0	20	130	0

(Contd.)

(Contd.Appendix-XXXV)

Year	*Hero Honda Motors Ltd.*	*Kinetic Engineering Ltd.*	*Majestic Auto Ltd.*	*Scooters India Ltd.*
1991-92	22	25	0	0
1992-93	25	30	0	0
1993-94	27	30	0	0
1994-95	30	40	0	0
1995-96	32	40	0	0
1996-97	35	40	0	0
1997-98	40	40	0	0
1998-99	75	40	0	0
1999-00	100	50	0	0
2000-01	150	50	0	0
2001-02	850	25	0	0
2002-03	900	0	0	0
2003-04	1000	0	0	0

APPENDIX XXXVI

Dividend payout ratio (Two and Three Wheelers)

Year	Baja Auto Ltd.	LML Ltd.	Maharastra Scooters Ltd.	TVS Motors Ltd.	Kinetic Motors Ltd.
1991-92	420.52	0	124.56	0	0
1992-93	361.53	0	140.37	0	0
1993-94	206.61	0	151.06	153.65	0
1994-95	208.66	0	176.59	171.12	0
1995-96	190.37	0	139.42	197.11	295.86
1996-97	184.00	315.79	147.05	150.93	699.30
1997-98	210.08	0	157.60	170.88	746.27
1998-99	180.22	240.00	130.41	201.32	655.02
1999-00	198.77	0	92.12	178.49	275.03
2000-01	318.34	0	507.61	304.07	250.25
2001-02	271.84	0	214.59	401.43	273.22
2002-03	272.27	0	272.27	220.22	0
2003-04	361.85	0	496.03	230.88	0

(Contd.)

(Contd. Appendix-XXXVI)

Year	*Hero Honda Motors Ltd.*	*Kinetic Engineering Ltd.*	*Majestic Auto Ltd.*	*Scooters India Ltd.*
1991-92	230.85	187.03	0	0
1992-93	255.62	186.80	0	0
1993-94	279.50	186.80	0	0
1994-95	308.01	175.52	0	0
1995-96	242.61	116.38	0	0
1996-97	139.83	121.03	0	0
1997-98	105.37	118.69	0	0
1998-99	252.53	151.52	0	0
1999-00	212.81	138.01	0	0
2000-01	1243.81	123.64	0	0
2001-02	3749.45	142.13	0	0
2002-03	3360.72	0	0	0
2003-04	2948.98	0	0	0

APPENDIX XXXVII
Current ratio

Year	*Commercial Vehicles*	*Passenger Cars and Multiutility Vehicles*	*Two and Three Wheelers*	*Industry average*
1991-92	1.38	1.24	0.94	1.19
1992-93	1.40	1.24	1.04	1.23
1993-94	1.39	1.20	1.21	1.27
1994-95	1.44	1.65	1.14	1.41
1995-96	1.41	1.18	1.09	1.23
1996-97	1.40	1.15	1.07	1.21
1997-98	1.16	0.86	1.14	105
1998-99	1.12	0.89	1.29	1.10
1999-00	1.14	0.89	1.29	1.11
2000-01	1.05	0.83	1.31	1.06
2001-02	0.97	0.79	1.22	0.99
2002-03	0.95	1.04	1.40	1.13
2003-04	1.00	1.33	1.19	1.17

APPENDIX XXXVIII
Liquidity ratio

Year	*Commercial Vehicle*	*Passenger Cars and Multiutility Vehicles*	*Two and Three Wheelers*	*Industry average*
1991-92	1.02	0.96	0.75	0.91
1992-93	1.22	0.92	1.10	1.08
1993-94	1.20	0.80	1.05	1.02
1994-95	1.21	0.69	1.01	0.97
1995-96	1.16	0.48	0.98	0.87
1996-97	1.56	0.82	1.07	1.15
1997-98	1.74	0.81	1.22	1.26
1998-99	1.29	1.11	1.38	1.26
1999-00	1.09	0.81	1.45	1.12
2000-01	0.84	1.13	1.28	1.08
2001-02	0.82	1.04	1.44	1.10
2002-03	0.67	1.41	1.39	1.16
2003-04	0.65	0.91	094	0.83

APPENDIX XXXIX
Interest coverage ratio

Year	*Commercial Vehicles*	*Passenger Cars and Multiutility Vehicles*	*Two and Three Wheelers*	*Industry average*
1991-92	1.50	0.58	33.67	11.92
1992-93	0.97	0.81	2.64	1.47
1993-94	1.98	1.68	6.04	3.23
1994-95	3.44	2.37	9.34	5.05
1995-96	3.44	4.41	13.30	7.05
1996-97	2.63	9.55	23.96	12.05
1997-98	0.43	3.89	88.69	31.00
1998-99	0.58	1.23	60.38	20.73
1999-00	0.37	-0.16	54.74	18.32
2000-01	0.31	1.23	25.04	8.86
2001-02	-0.02	5.18	78.22	27.79
2002-03	0.28	12.17	156.11	56.19
2003-04	0.98	3.66	175.41	60.02

APPENDIX XL
Debt equity ratio

Year	*Commercial Vehicles*	*Passenger Cars and Multiutility Vehicles*	*Two and Three Wheelers*	*Industry average*
1991-92	3.02	3.49	1.36	2.62
1992-93	2.06	6.23	2.90	3.73
1993-94	1.91	4.34	1.60	2.62
1994-95	1.06	1.75	0.71	1.17
1995-96	0.76	1.04	0.54	0.78
1996-97	4.57	1.24	0.69	2.17
1997-98	3.00	1.06	0.73	1.60
1998-99	1.07	1.08	0.87	1.01
1999-00	1.00	1.14	0.74	0.96
2000-01	0.96	1.25	0.66	1.04
2001-02	0.99	1.30	0.83	0.92
2002-03	0.68	0.76	1.33	0.51
2003-04	0.47	0.28	0.78	1.55

APPENDIX XLI

Fixed assets to networth ratio

Year	*Commercial Vehicles*	*Passenger Cars and Multiutility Vehicles*	*Two and Three Wheelers*	*Industry average*
1991-92	0.97	2.26	-1.05	0.73
1992-93	1.66	2.61	-0.91	1.12
1993-94	1.74	2.46	1.46	1.89
1994-95	1.27	1.81	1.12	1.40
1995-96	1.12	1.64	1.10	1.29
1996-97	1.07	0.96	1.28	1.10
1997-98	1.25	0.98	0.94	1.06
1998-99	1.45	1.90	1.61	1.65
1999-00	1.75	2.19	1.52	1.82
2000-01	0.09	2.42	1.63	2.05
2001-02	2.22	2.70	2.78	2.57
2002-03	2.24	1.97	-25.57	-7.22
2003-04	1.82	1.57	1.38	1.59

APPENDIX XLII

Current ratio (Commercial Vehicles)

Year	*Ashok Leyland Ltd.*	*Tata Motors Ltd.*	*Bajaj Tempo Ltd.*	*Eicher Motors Ltd.*	*Swaraj Mazda Ltd.*
1991-92	1.71	1.18	1.53	1.43	1.05
1992-93	2.10	1.17	1.49	1.31	0.94
1993-94	2.21	1.23	1.36	1.27	0.90
1994-95	2.41	1.23	1.29	1.33	0.92
1995-96	2.38	1.12	1.23	1.50	0.99
1996-97	2.13	1.20	1.20	1.42	1.04
1997-98	2.47	1.36	1.21	1.57	1.07
1998-99	2.93	1.27	1.20	1.62	1.08
1999-00	2.48	1.08	1.24	1.50	1.06
2000-01	2.20	0.91	1.29	1.40	1.04
2001-02	1.87	0.88	1.27	0.98	1.02
2002-03	1.71	0.88	1.31	0.78	1.04
2003-04	1.58	0.76	1.34	0.89	1.10

APPENDIX XLIII
Liquidity ratio (Commercial Vehicles)

Year	*Ashok Leyland Ltd.*	*Tata Motors Ltd.*	*Bajaj Tempo Ltd.*	*Eicher Motors Ltd.*	*Swaraj Motors Ltd.*
1991-92	2.11	1.12	0.79	0.73	0.37
1992-93	2.32	1.11	0.56	0.91	0.28
1993-94	1.68	1.21	0.66	1.51	0.47
1994-95	2.57	1.01	0.57	1.06	0.65
1995-96	2.32	0.98	0.55	1.01	0.56
1996-97	1.98	1.52	1.45	1.33	0.67
1997-98	2.60	1.68	0.41	1.19	0.68
1998-99	2.56	1.18	0.45	1.28	0.83
1999-00	2.33	1.91	0.48	0.91	0.98
2000-01	1.93	0.63	0.53	0.89	0.86
2001-02	1.26	0.73	0.66	0.61	0.94
2002-03	1.27	0.52	0.76	0.56	0.68
2003-04	0.95	0.51	0.89	0.70	0.83

APPENDIX XLIV
Interest coverage ratio (Commercial Vehicles)

Year	*Ashok Leyland Ltd.*	*Tata Motors Ltd.*	*Bajaj Tempo Ltd.*	*Eicher Motors Ltd.*	*Swaraj Mazda Ltd.*
1991-92	1.48	2.52	3.02	1.29	-0.83
1992-93	1.01	1.11	3.40	0.06	-0.73
1993-94	1.53	1.32	6.41	0.59	0.05
1994-95	1.94	3.48	7.97	2.45	1.35
1995-96	2.35	5.22	7.60	2.36	2.14
1996-97	2.15	4.74	2.18	2.32	1.76
1997-98	1.04	1.80	1.79	1.55	2.67
1998-99	1.05	0.98	-1.46	2.44	1.64
1999-00	1.69	0.60	-0.15	4.71	1.93
2000-01	1.77	-0.02	-0.13	7.54	2.12
2001-02	2.15	0.85	1.12	6.74	2.75
2002-03	2.78	2.65	6.56	14.78	8.14
2003-04	5.82	7.38	16.99	3.40	21.00

APPENDIX XLV
Debt – equity ratio (Commercial Vehicles)

Year	*Ashok Leyland Ltd.*	*Tata Motors Ltd.*	*Bajaj Tempo Ltd.*	*Eicher Motors Ltd.*	*Swaraj Motors Ltd.*
1991-92	2.17	1.16	0.94	2.47	8.36
1992-93	1.88	1.66	0.69	4.00	0.00
1993-94	1.28	1.78	0.25	4.28	0.00
1994-95	0.81	1.14	0.05	2.22	0.00
1995-96	0.76	0.64	0.22	1.42	0.00
1996-97	0.99	0.63	0.39	1.12	19.72
1997-98	1.13	0.79	0.42	0.89	4.48
1998-99	1.03	0.90	0.46	0.69	2.28
1999-00	0.88	0.86	0.60	0.62	2.04
2000-01	0.84	0.86	0.80	0.49	1.79
2001-02	0.84	0.93	0.77	0.50	1.92
2002-03	0.83	0.74	0.54	0.39	0.90
2003-04	0.62	0.44	0.36	0.77	0.16

APPENDIX XLVI
Fixed assets to networth ratio (Commercial Vehicles)

Year	*Ashok Leyland Ltd.*	*Tata Motors Ltd.*	*Bajaj Tempo Ltd.*	*Eicher Motors Ltd.*	*Swaraj Mazda Ltd.*
1991-92	1.99	1.52	2.57	1.93	-3.18
1992-93	1.16	1.72	2.53	4.48	-3.27
1993-94	1.22	1.96	2.04	2.56	-2.31
1994-95	0.87	1.48	1.78	1.62	-2.47
1995-96	0.96	1.11	2.19	1.31	-37.62
1996-97	1.09	0.99	2.37	1.15	5.01
1997-98	1.14	1.22	2.50	1.27	2.20
1998-99	1.29	1.44	3.22	1.27	1.84
1999-00	1.32	1.83	4.08	1.27	1.67
2000-01	1.37	2.39	4.71	1.13	1.67
2001-02	1.64	2.34	5.08	2.27	1.69
2002-03	1.91	2.29	4.10	2.04	1.30
2003-04	1.84	1.68	3.28	3.20	0.95

APPENDIX XLVII

Current ratio (Passenger Cars and Multiutility Vehicles)

Year	*Hindustan Motors Ltd.*	*Mahindra and Mahindra Ltd.*	*Maruthi Udyog Ltd.*	*Daewoo Motors India Ltd.*
1991-92	1.06	1.49	1.35	1.07
1992-93	0.99	1.49	1.54	0.95
1993-94	1.08	1.71	1.09	0.92
1994-95	1.19	1.72	0.80	2.90
1995-96	1.25	1.35	0.71	1.42
1996-97	1.44	1.49	0.84	0.81
1997-98	1.48	1.81	1.11	0.58
1998-99	1.26	1.85	1.29	0.42
1999-00	1.19	1.79	1.25	0.30
2000-01	1.18	1.55	1.22	0.20
2001-02	1.12	1.34	135	0.12
2002-03	1.15	1.25	1.47	0.86
2003-04	1.17	1.09	1.37	0.75

APPENDIX XLVIII

Liquidity ratio (Passenger Cars and Multiutility Vehicles)

Year	*Hindustan Motors Ltd.*	*Mahindra and Mahindra Ltd.*	*Maruthi Udyog Ltd.*	*Daewoo Motors India Ltd.*
1991-92	1.06	15.69	1.16	0.99
1992-93	0.97	01.15	1.03	1.28
1993-94	1.15	1.43	0.65	1.14
1994-95	0.98	1.24	0.52	6.07
1995-96	0.91	0.94	0.32	0.49
1996-97	1.16	1.31	0.65	2.24
1997-98	1.10	1.53	0.74	1.86
1998-99	0.08	1.60	1.14	1.24
1999-00	0.84	1.27	0.72	0.67
2000-01	0.90	1.25	1.09	1.71
2001-02	0.91	1.06	0.98	0.44
2002-03	0.76	0.91	1.55	1.08
2003-04	0.68	0.62	1.03	1.26

APPENDIX XLIX
Interest coverage ratio (Passenger Cars and Multiutility Vehicles)

Year	*Hindustan Motors Ltd.*	*Mahindra and Mahindra Ltd.*	*Maruthi Udyog Ltd.*	*Daewoo Motors India Ltd.*
1991-92	0.30	0.82	1.30	-0.10
1992-93	0.46	1.32	1.49	-0.03
1993-94	1.32	2.70	2.49	0.19
1994-95	1.47	5.01	2.68	0.33
1995-96	2.04	6.91	5.86	2.84
1996-97	1.80	5.08	11.50	1.10
1997-98	1.83	3.68	20.01	-11.72
1998-99	0.66	2.84	16.87	-0.92
1999-00	0.42	3.48	7.40	-0.01
2000-01	-0.19	2.14	-2.55	-0.51
2001-02	0.11	1.84	2.54	-1.46
2002-03	0.26	2.70	5.79	-1.16
2003-04	-0.81	6.70	19.82	-0.86

APPENDIX L
Debt -equity ratio (Passenger Cars and Multiutility Vehicles)

Year	*Hindustan Motors Ltd.*	*Mahindra and Mahindra Ltd.*	*Maruthi Udyog Ltd.*	*Daewoo Motors India Ltd.*
1991-92	3.46	9.04	1.58	6.37
1992-93	4.34	9.05	1.58	17.07
1993-94	3.06	10.12	1.24	11.82
1994-95	1.94	13.03	0.80	3.61
1995-96	1.46	17.48	0.43	1.79
1996-97	1.34	19.18	0.15	2.77
1997-98	1.50	10.89	0.05	3.61
1998-99	1.99	7.26	0.04	4.59
1999-00	2.85	8.16	0.12	5.38
2000-01	2.57	7.82	0.30	6.89
2001-02	1.95	6.15	0.33	14.87
2002-03	2.38	7.64	0.19	4.36
2003-04	3.73	12.70	0.11	5.14

APPENDIX LI

Fixed assets to net worth ratio (Passenger Cars and Multiutility Vehicles)

Year	*Hindustan Motors Ltd.*	*Mahindra and Mahindra Ltd.*	*Maruthi Udyog Ltd.*	*Daewoo Motors India Ltd.*
1991-92	3.05	2.42	1.62	17.51
1992-93	3.49	2.10	1.84	14.19
1993-94	2.55	0.99	2.32	8.02
1994-95	2.30	0.79	1.82	0.66
1995-96	2.05	0.71	1.52	1.46
1996-97	1.89	0.99	1.09	0.30
1997-98	1.80	1.03	0.86	0.45
1998-99	3.06	1.09	0.91	5.99
1999-00	4.58	0.91	1.22	7.14
2000-01	3.40	1.06	1.50	10.56
2001-02	4.37	1.38	1.69	61.79
2002-03	5.10	1.59	1.50	4.68
2003-04	10.78	1.43	1.28	3.96

APPENDIX LII
Current ratio (Two and Three Wheelers)

Year	*Bajaj Auto Ltd.*	*LML Ltd.*	*Maharastra Scooters Ltd.*	*TVS Motors India Ltd.*	*Kinetic Motors Company Ltd.*
1991-92	1.10	0.91	0.78	0.70	1.42
1992-93	1.31	0.88	1.12	0.75	1.56
1993-94	1.36	0.96	1.20	0.89	1.91
1994-95	1.58	1.00	1.00	1.18	1.71
1995-96	1.56	1.03	1.09	1.17	1.38
1996-97	1.39	1.07	1.10	1.25	1.24
1997-98	1.40	-	0.99	1.60	1.22
1998-99	1.41	1.20	0.98	1.55	1.23
1999-00	1.34	1.28	1.00	1.46	1.28
2000-01	1.32	1.15	1.05	1.40	1.35
2001-02	1.19	1.01	1.04	1.18	1.33
2002-03	1.02	0.94	0.91	0.94	1.56
2003-04	0.92	-	0.91	0.79	1.48

(Contd.)

(Contd. Appendix-LII)

Year	*Hero Honda Motors Ltd.*	*Kinetic Engineering Ltd.*	*Majestic Auto Ltd.*	*Scooters India Ltd.*
1991-92	1.04	1.61	0.87	-
1992-93	1.31	1.54	0.93	-
1993-94	1.28	1.41	0.92	0.97
1994-95	1.03	1.36	1.10	0.32
1995-96	0.90	1.32	1.10	0.23
1996-97	0.89	1.34	0.96	0.43
1997-98	1.06	1.50	1.00	1.50
1998-99	1.02	1.59	0.97	1.65
1999-00	0.89	1.55	0.82	1.96
2000-01	0.86	1.57	0.74	2.35
2001-02	0.65	1.48	0.69	2.44
2002-03	0.47	1.26	0.68	4.84
2003-04	0.39	1.07	0.81	4.33

APPENDIX LIII
Liquidity ratio (Two and Three Wheelers)

Year	*Bajaj Auto Ltd.*	*LML Ltd.*	*Maharastra Scooters Ltd.*	*TVS Motors India Ltd.*	*Kinetic Motors Company Ltd.*
1991-92	0.83	0.70	1.70	0.48	0.76
1992-93	1.02	0.76	2.90	0.55	1.02
1993-94	1.11	0.77	2.56	0.66	0.99
1994-95	1.40	0.76	2.41	0.76	0.86
1995-96	1.18	0.74	3.25	0.68	0.75
1996-97	1.14	0.80	2.65	1.04	1.37
1997-98	1.25	-	2.30	1.58	1.38
1998-99	1.32	1.08	2.33	1.08	0.78
1999-00	1.21	0.88	2.76	1.09	0.95
2000-01	1.23	0.63	1.96	1.07	0.79
2001-02	1.09	0.59	1.76	0.90	1.32
2002-03	1.00	0.47	1.71	0.57	1.71
2003-04	0.80	-	0.90	0.05	1.36

(Contd.)

(Contd. Appendix-LIII)

Year	*Hero Honda Motors Ltd.*	*Kinetic Engineering Ltd.*	*Majestic Auto Ltd.*	*Scooters India Ltd.*
1991-92	0.48	1.84	-	-
1992-93	0.66	2.97	-	-
1993-94	0.91	2.49	-	-
1994-95	0.70	2.21	-	-
1995-96	0.40	1.84	-	-
1996-97	0.59	2.07	-	-
1997-98	0.64	2.56	-	1.24
1998-99	0.73	2.75	1.02	1.30
1999-00	0.54	2.92	0.83	1.86
2000-01	0.47	2.72	0.83	1.78
2001-02	0.49	4.32	0.66	1.87
2002-03	0.57	3.54	0.64	2.26
2003-04	0.40	1.93	1.11	1.92

APPENDIX LIV

Interest coverage ratio (Two and Three Wheelers)

Year	Bajaj Auto Ltd.	LML Ltd.	Maharastra Scooters Ltd.	TVS Motors India Ltd.	Kinetic Motors Company Ltd.
1991-92	3.52	-0.14	288.86	1.29	2.11
1992-93	4.72	0.76	7.53	1.38	1.14
1993-94	18.24	2.45	16.80	3.29	4.42
1994-95	39.78	3.09	14.99	8.26	6.63
1995-96	60.39	2.42	19.59	13.59	6.84
1996-97	92.36	3.00	83.62	16.11	2.04
1997-98	82.33	-	679.00	6.08	1.31
1998-99	163.36	2.30	332.57	6.28	1.84
1999-00	214.25	1.26	194.35	6.36	5.14
2000-01	45.97	-0.15	4.70	4.56	7.03
2001-02	176.39	-0.58	47.71	5.59	5.84
2002-03	704.80	-0.16	164.50	18.90	1.26
2003-04	1022.34	-	-27.50	21.83	-3.27

(Contd.)

(Contd. Appendix-LIV)

Year	*Hero Honda Motors Ltd.*	*Kinetic Engineering Ltd.*	*Majestic Auto Ltd.*	*Scooters India Ltd.*
1991-92	3.36	2.71	1.31	-
1992-93	2.99	2.93	2.27	-
1993-94	3.12	3.48	3.12	-0.6
1994-95	5.33	3.79	2.24	-0.04
1995-96	8.13	7.04	1.74	0
1996-97	8.44	3.55	0.98	5.54
1997-98	14.85	4.27	0.43	9.94
1998-99	29.74	1.75	1.08	4.55
1999-00	61.43	2.30	0.74	6.87
2000-01	149.99	2.83	0.66	9.76
2001-02	460.85	1.79	-0.74	7.17
2002-03	512.31	0.94	-1.45	3.91
2003-04	139.91	-2.15	3.37	5.72

APPENDIX LV
Debt-equity ratio (Two and Three Wheelers)

Year	*Bajaj Auto Ltd.*	*LML Ltd.*	*Maharastra Scooters Ltd.*	*TVS Motors India Ltd.*	*Kinetic Motors Company Ltd.*
1991-92	0.65	4.38	0.08	3.38	1.48
1992-93	0.52	20.17	0.04	2.37	0.87
1993-94	0.43	4.92	0.02	1.59	0.35
1994-95	0.26	1.83	0.03	0.78	0.15
1995-96	0.16	1.78	0.05	0.45	0.34
1996-97	0.13	2.04	0.06	0.44	0.86
1997-98	0.12	-	0.06	0.64	1.33
1998-99	0.13	2.06	0.06	0.86	1.18
1999-00	0.14	1.56	0.07	0.67	0.72
2000-01	0.17	1.43	0.06	0.66	0.43
2001-02	0.21	2.32	0.06	0.59	0.54
2002-03	0.24	5.24	0.06	0.39	0.85
2003-04	0.27	-	0.05	0.24	1.05

(Contd.)

(*Contd. Appendix-LV*)

Year	*Hero Honda Motors Ltd.*	*Kinetic Engineering Ltd.*	*Majestic Auto Ltd.*	*Scooters India Ltd.*
1991-92	1.49	0.80	0.00	0.00
1992-93	1.27	0.90	0.00	0.00
1993-94	1.03	0.84	5.23	0.00
1994-95	0.70	0.60	1.30	0.00
1995-96	0.57	0.47	1.07	0.00
1996-97	0.67	0.50	1.49	0.00
1997-98	0.55	0.65	1.71	1.48
1998-99	0.35	0.92	1.60	0.70
1999-00	0.19	1.09	1.55	0.64
2000-01	0.11	1.09	1.33	0.65
2001-02	0.14	1.43	1.52	0.69
2002-03	0.16	1.71	3.12	0.22
2003-04	0.15	2.10	2.99	0.20

APPENDIX LVI

Fixed assets to Networth ratio (Two and Three Wheelers)

Year	Bajaj Auto Ltd.	LML Ltd.	Maharastra Scooters Ltd.	TVS Motors India Ltd.	Kinetic Motors Company Ltd.
1991-92	2.02	-19.63	0.16	1.03	2.13
1992-93	2.00	-16.89	0.15	1.05	1.13
1993-94	1.61	05.30	0.13	1.06	0.98
1994-95	0.85	02.64	0.12	1.78	0.99
1995-96	0.84	02.78	0.13	1.61	1.05
1996-97	0.76	03.71	0.16	1.47	1.49
1997-98	0.74	-	0.17	1.34	1.72
1998-99	0.64	03.24	0.20	1.90	1.77
1999-00	0.64	02.83	0.19	1.27	1.54
2000-01	0.94	04.10	0.21	1.73	1.40
2001-02	0.89	09.87	0.20	2.08	1.44
2002-03	0.81	-	0.19	1.91	1.45
2003-04	0.73	-6.56	0.18	2.02	2.13

(Contd.)

(Contd. Appendix-LVI)

Year	*Hero Honda Motors Ltd.*	*Kinetic Engineering Ltd.*	*Majestic Auto Ltd.*	*Scooters India Ltd.*
1991-92	2.33	2.49	-	-
1992-93	1.98	2.35	-	-
1993-94	1.86	2.17	-	-
1994-95	1.77	1.95	-	-
1995-96	1.50	2.00	-	-
1996-97	1.95	1.95	-	-
1997-98	1.44	1.81	-	1.24
1998-99	1.28	1.76	02.63	1.06
1999-00	1.13	1.70	03.51	0.88
2000-01	1.01	1.65	02.83	0.82
2001-02	1.04	2.08	06.56	0.83
2002-03	0.91	2.18	50.10	0.17
2003-04	0.81	3.88	1.96	0.70

APPENDIX LVII
Altman Z Score of Ashok Leyland Ltd.

Year	X_1	X_2	X_3	X_4	X_5	Z Score
1991 - 92	44.2	7.8	10.7	5.7	1.35	2.38
1992 - 93	61.6	9.0	9.5	13.5	1.05	2.31
1993 - 94	44.6	8.4	10.2	14.6	1.21	2.29
1994 - 95	57.7	9.4	9.3	20.1	0.99	2.24
1995 - 96	58.7	11.3	12.1	13.4	1.07	2.41
1996 - 97	60.4	11.6	13.0	10.1	1.11	2.49
1997 - 98	59.4	9.3	8.2	-9.5	1.14	2.20
1998 - 99	50.8	8.4	8.6	12.4	1.02	2.10
1999 - 00	49.2	8.5	10.9	12.3	1.28	2.30
2000 - 01	48.7	8.7	11.1	12.7	1.27	2.42
2001 - 02	41.3	9.1	12.9	13.4	1.40	2.53
2002 - 03	34.6	8.5	15.8	16.6	1.86	3.01
2003 - 04	29.7	8.6	22.8	23.8	2.62	3.99

X_1 -Working capital to total assets; X_2 - Net operating profit to net sales
X_3- Earnings before interest and taxes to total assets
X_4- Market value of equity to book value of debt; X_5 -Sales to total assets
Source: Computed.

APPENDIX LVIII
Altman Z Score of Tata Motors Ltd.

Year	X_1	X_2	X_3	X_4	X_5	Z Score
1991 - 92	50.1	11.5	11.0	11.2	2.91	4.09
1992 – 93	50.1	8.3	11.2	8.7	1.34	2.48
1993 - 94	44.3	8.6	14.1	9.1	1.64	2.81
1994 - 95	32.3	11.3	25.3	11.8	2.24	3.53
1995 - 96	26.3	12.1	26.3	18.9	2.16	3.62
1996 - 97	41.3	12.8	21.8	10.1	1.70	3.15
1997 - 98	34.3	10.2	11.3	7.7	1.10	2.07
1998 - 99	21.5	8.3	8.3	7.4	0.99	1.68
1999 - 00	13.2	6.3	9.2	8.5	1.46	2.06
2000 - 01	2.70	-0.1	-0.2	8.5	1.48	1.56
2001 - 02	2.10	3.5	6.4	13.9	1.82	2.19
2002 - 03	-15.3	7.7	20.4	21.5	2.63	3.36
2003 - 04	-30.6	9.8	31.0	28.0	3.14	3.59

X_1 -Working capital to total assets; X_2 - Net operating profit to net sales
X_3- Earnings before interest and taxes to total assets
X_4- Market value of equity to book value of debt; X_5 -Sales to total assets
Source: Computed.

APPENDIX LIX
Altman Z Score of Bajaj Tempo Ltd.

Year	X_1	X_2	X_3	X_4	X_5	Z Score
1991 - 92	63.2	8.7	23.5	13.4	2.69	4.42
1992 - 93	57.3	4.7	17.1	20.4	2.57	3.01
1993 - 94	51.5	5.4	29.1	13.38	2.30	4.03
1994 - 95	56.0	5.5	25.9	28.7	2.64	3.41
1995 - 96	36.7	9.2	33.2	18.8	6.60	5.37
1996 - 97	37.0	4.5	13.1	19.1	2.87	3.92
1997 - 98	85.5	3.0	7.5	17.1	2.48	3.90
1998 - 99	44.9	-3.0	7.7	18.7	2.55	3.41
1999 - 00	46.6	-0.2	0.9	14.1	3.08	3.75
2000 - 01	51.7	-0.3	0.9	13.3	2.94	3.67
2001 - 02	44.7	2.2	7.8	17.8	3.52	4.45
2002 - 03	52.5	4.9	20.7	21.5	3.14	4.65
2003 - 04	51.6	6.7	29.9	22.5	2.45	4.28

X_1 -Working capital to total assets; X_2 - Net operating profit to net sales
X_3- Earnings before interest and taxes to total assets
X_4- Market value of equity to book value of debt; X_5 -Sales to total assets
Source: Computed.

APPENDIX LX

Altman Z Score of Eicher Motors Ltd.

Year	X_1	X_2	X_3	X_4	X_5	*Z Score*
1991 - 92	56.0	4.9	13.1	29.8	2.99	4.34
1992 - 93	52.3	0.3	1.0	24.6	2.51	3.32
1993 - 94	44.3	3.1	8.6	50.4	2.66	3.82
1994 - 95	48.9	8.5	25.8	44.9	3.00	4.82
1995 - 96	52.5	8.2	26.5	45.5	3.21	5.01
1996 - 97	56.8	6.8	22.7	39.7	3.33	5.09
1997 - 98	42.6	4.5	14.7	59.7	3.26	4.67
1998 - 99	37.1	5.5	16.9	56.1	3.05	4.47
1999 - 00	29.0	6.4	22.9	55.9	3.54	5.07
2000 - 01	19.6	6.6	25.1	56.3	3.77	5.26
2001 - 02	-18.0	6.6	31.3	48.4	4.72	5.91
2002 - 03	-21.9	9.0	49.6	76.5	3.50	5.97
2003 - 04	11.8	5.2	21.8	10.2	4.18	5.17

X_1 -Working capital to total assets; X_2 - Net operating profit to net sales
X_3- Earnings before interest and taxes to total assets
X_4- Market value of equity to book value of debt; X_5 -Sales to total assets
Source: Computed.

APPENDIX LXI

Altman Z Score of Swaraj Mazda Ltd.

Year	X_1	X_2	X_3	X_4	X_5	Z Score
1991 - 92	9.2	-2.8	-15.7	65.9	5.48	5.42
1992 - 93	-3.9	-2.4	-17.0	55.9	7.00	6.69
1993 - 94	-47.8	0.1	1.70	60.5	5.91	5.75
1994 - 95	30.4	2.6	21.6	40.2	0.12	1.48
1995 - 96	60.7	6.3	37.4	33.2	5.85	8.09
1996 - 97	73.4	6.1	23.5	23.7	3.82	5.70
1997 - 98	62.7	7.0	33.0	41.9	0.21	2.40
1998 - 99	71.1	5.1	17.5	33.6	3.41	4.84
1999 - 00	70.5	3.5	18.0	38.3	5.01	6.72
2000 - 01	69.0	4.5	25.4	33.8	5.57	7.41
2001 - 02	70.5	4.8	28.5	36.8	5.85	7.92
2002 - 03	42.5	6.1	35.0	36.4	5.16	7.12
2003 - 04	62.2	6.2	30.8	9.5	5.30	7.18

X_1 -Working capital to total assets; X_2 - Net operating profit to net sales
X_3- Earnings before interest and taxes to total assets
X_4- Market value of equity to book value of debt; X_5 -Sales to total assets
Source: Computed.

APPENDIX LXII
Altman Z Score of Hidustan Motors Ltd.

Year	X_1	X_2	X_3	X_4	X_5	Z Score
1991 - 92	34.90	5.60	7.04	14.98	1.26	2.08
1992 – 93	35.16	3.70	5.26	19.86	1.42	2.19
1993 - 94	37.48	8.35	14.29	31.00	1.71	2.93
1994 - 95	35.99	8.52	16.85	36.20	1.98	3.30
1995 - 96	35.72	8.26	18.93	37.04	2.29	3.68
1996 - 97	43.34	8.00	16.51	31.79	2.07	3.44
1997 - 98	37.39	8.21	14.33	23.79	1.75	2.33
1998 - 99	34.98	3.74	6.55	18.26	1.75	2.55
1999 - 00	35.59	2.53	5.81	17.64	2.29	3.05
2000 - 01	30.16	4.82	13.51	41.63	2.80	3.92
2001 - 02	25.72	0.53	1.23	45.20	2.30	2.93
2002 - 03	28.26	1.33	0.27	42.36	2.04	2.66
2003 - 04	18.31	-5.20	10.08	43.19	1.94	2.68

X_1 -Working capital to total assets; X_2 - Net operating profit to net sales
X_3- Earnings before interest and taxes to total assets
X_4- Market value of equity to book value of debt; X_5 -Sales to total assets
Source: Computed.

APPENDIX LXIII
Altman Z Score of Mahindra and Mahindra Ltd.

Year	X_1	X_2	X_3	X_4	X_5	Z Score
1991 - 92	44.92	7.28	12.21	4.87	1.68	2.75
1992 - 93	46.40	6.01	12.88	8.14	2.14	3.25
1993 - 94	48.00	8.43	14.71	11.49	1.74	2.99
1994 - 95	40.25	11.13	20.17	14.82	1.81	3.20
1995 - 96	27.09	12.09	28.75	26.94	2.11	3.71
1996 - 97	32.03	11.73	19.58	9.90	1.67	2.92
1997 - 98	36.10	11.46	17.27	7.74	1.51	2.72
1998 - 99	33.52	10.73	15.04	7.05	1.40	2.49
1999 - 00	27.02	11.44	17.47	11.58	1.44	2.57
2000 - 01	26.40	5.64	8.10	9.74	1.44	3.75
2001 - 02	18.87	5.00	6.83	8.42	1.37	1.94
2002 - 03	12.79	7.03	11.72	10.18	1.67	2.37
2003 - 04	0.30	8.84	20.64	15.90	2.34	3.27

X_1 -Working capital to total assets; X_2 . Net operating profit to net sales
X_3- Earnings before interest and taxes to total assets
X_4- Market value of equity to book value of debt; X_5 -Sales to total assets
Source: Computed.

APPENDIX LXIV
Altman Z Score of Maruthi Udyog Ltd.

Year	X_1	X_2	X_3	X_4	X_5	Z Score
1991 - 92	44.78	6.72	18.47	29.92	2.75	4.17
1992 – 93	38.80	5.20	12.84	25.10	2.47	3.52
1993 - 94	11.14	8.15	26.82	30.36	3.29	5.82
1994 - 95	60.01	11.44	44.70	31.18	3.19	4.60
1995 - 96	50.02	12.26	58.33	42.66	4.76	6.45
1996 - 97	7.94	11.54	55.22	155.22	3.78	6.79
1997 - 98	9.42	12.65	46.63	158.22	2.69	5.47
1998 - 99	29.56	10.71	30.96	136.81	2.89	5.23
1999 - 00	17.57	4.78	18.07	24.23	2.74	3.76
2000 - 01	26.65	2.16	-5.23	11.89	2.42	3.01
2001 - 02	19.88	2.15	6.02	20.17	2.80	3.39
2002 - 03	37.64	3.72	9.66	31.69	2.59	3.97
2003 - 04	12.53	7.22	21.02	46.33	2.91	4.13

X_1 -Working capital to total assets; X_2 - Net operating profit to net sales
X_3- Earnings before interest and taxes to total assets
X_4- Market value of equity to book value of debt; X_5 -Sales to total assets
Source: Computed.

APPENDIX LXV

Altman Z Score of Daewoo Motors India Ltd.

Year	X_1	X_2	X_3	X_4	X_5	*Z Score*
1991 - 92	41.97	-1.14	1.59	23.54	1.39	2.07
1992 - 93	53.29	-0.44	-0.47	38.73	1.07	1.92
1993 - 94	52.53	2.66	3.69	64.04	1.39	2.56
1994 - 95	81.65	3.28	0.92	24.08	0.28	1.48
1995 - 96	7.40	12.82	30.81	72.16	2.40	4.12
1996 - 97	23.60	4.53	1.29	20.09	0.28	0.79
1997 - 98	15.19	-0.99	-0.10	16.69	0.10	0.37
1998 - 99	10.38	-5.29	-0.45	13.87	0.09	0.21
1999 - 00	3.78	-0.07	-0.02	15.14	0.32	0.45
2000 - 01	7.49	-5.80	-1.70	14.54	0.29	0.33
2001 - 02	1.65	-3.44	-0.26	14.16	0.08	0.13
2002 - 03	2.52	-2.96	-0.16	16.12	0.12	0.20
2003 - 04	1.86	-2.46	-0.92	14.18	0.26	0.30

X_1 -Working capital to total assets; X_2 - Net operating profit to net sales
X_3- Earnings before interest and taxes to total assets
X_4- Market value of equity to book value of debt; X_5 -Sales to total assets
Source: Computed.

APPENDIX LXVI
Altman Z Score of Baja Auto Ltd.

Year	X_1	X_2	X_3	X_4	X_5	*Z Score*
1991 - 92	29.79	9.65	21.21	17.89	2.20	3.41
1992 – 93	33.25	10.02	23.11	22.89	2.31	3.75
1993 - 94	29.32	17.41	40.08	18.42	2.30	4.33
1994 - 95	39.07	21.46	36.19	39.66	1.69	3.89
1995 - 96	23.09	22.28	37.53	38.81	1.68	3.74
1996 - 97	19.02	21.68	34.68	37.21	1.60	3.41
1997 - 98	23.13	22.08	29.35	46.24	1.33	3.16
1998 - 99	21.96	21.63	25.01	34.14	1.16	2.76
1999 - 00	17.10	22.35	22.38	24.09	1.00	1.74
2000 - 01	18.74	8.24	9.46	19.70	1.15	1.19
2001 - 02	9.64	17.07	20.34	16.16	1.19	2.31
2002 - 03	5.25	16.53	19.34	12.04	1.17	2.17
2003 - 04	-5.81	17.65	20.45	10.06	1.16	2.07

X_1 -Working capital to total assets; X_2 - Net operating profit to net sales
X_3- Earnings before interest and taxes to total assets
X_4- Market value of equity to book value of debt; X_5 -Sales to total assets
Source: Computed.

APPENDIX LXVII
Altman Z Score of LML Ltd.

Year	X_1	X_2	X_3	X_4	X_5	*Z Score*
1991 - 92	1.81	-2.04	-5.46	45.08	2.68	2.76
1992 - 93	10.73	7.24	24.42	45.18	3.37	4.67
1993 - 94	25.20	12.21	43.32	57.88	3.55	5.71
1994 - 95	30.96	8.90	29.25	42.65	3.29	5.00
1995 - 96	24.08	6.03	16.47	27.09	2.73	3.81
1996 - 97	23.15	6.45	17.46	21.08	2.71	3.78
1997 - 98	20.15	5.40	18.20	20.19	2.61	
1998 - 99	37.28	7.64	26.16	16.50	3.42	4.93
1999 - 00	26.54	4.61	9.72	20.73	2.11	2.94
2000 - 01	19.82	-0.85	-1.62	19.75	1.90	2.19
2001 - 02	10.65	-4.67	-8.55	17.67	1.83	1.71
2002 - 03	-0.87	-0.76	-2.99	15.31	3.95	3.92
2003 - 04	15.21	-0.56	-1.21	13.21	3.10	3.31

X_1 -Working capital to total assets; X_2 - Net operating profit to net sales
X_3- Earnings before interest and taxes to total assets
X_4- Market value of equity to book value of debt; X_5 -Sales to total assets
Source: Computed.

APPENDIX LXVIII
Altman Z Score of Maharastra Scooter Ltd.

Year	X_1	X_2	X_3	X_4	X_5	*Z Score*
1991 - 92	-7.48	0.05	0.12	133.10	2.14	2.85
1992 – 93	41.19	1.87	4.25	143.81	2.27	3.78
1993 - 94	9.10	0.82	1.81	143.81	2.21	3.24
1994 - 95	-4.31	0.77	1.51	128.89	1.95	2.73
1995 - 96	28.73	0.55	1.77	115.35	2.12	3.22
1996 - 97	5.15	0.10	0.24	67.49	2.30	2.77
1997 - 98	2.36	0.01	0.02	176.66	2.01	3.01
1998 - 99	4.26	0.02	0.05	107.52	2.06	2.76
1999 - 00	5.48	0.05	0.10	110.22	1.82	2.55
2000 - 01	6.98	0.14	0.18	149.41	1.25	2.24
2001 - 02	-0.57	0.06	0.04	109.06	0.70	1.35
2002 - 03	-3.07	0.03	0.01	119.43	0.36	1.04
2003 - 04	-2.77	0.05	0.01	135.11	0.22	0.91

X_1 -Working capital to total assets; X_2 - Net operating profit to net sales
X_3- Earnings before interest and taxes to total assets
X_4- Market value of equity to book value of debt; X_5 -Sales to total assets
Source: Computed.

APPENDIX LXIX

Altman Z Score of TVS Motors India Ltd.

Year	X_1	X_2	X_3	X_4	X_5	*Z Score*
1991 - 92	-14.15	8.44	28.57	62.47	3.39	4.65
1992 - 93	-7.20	7.44	27.02	66.07	3.63	4.93
1993 - 94	11.72	9.54	42.14	64.76	4.42	6.47
1994 - 95	30.13	10.29	50.53	79.96	4.91	7.56
1995 - 96	10.94	10.61	56.79	69.35	5.35	7.91
1996 - 97	28.96	11.01	48.18	37.82	4.38	6.69
1997 - 98	34.41	11.89	37.69	16.46	3.17	5.09
1998 - 99	17.15	9.55	26.21	10.01	2.74	4.00
1999 - 00	20.29	10.60	31.04	10.91	2.93	4.41
2000 - 01	23.68	5.75	17.72	9.87	3.08	4.09
2001 - 02	22.47	4.54	20.14	13.84	4.44	5.72
2002 - 03	1.30	6.83	38.98	18.95	5.71	7.22
2003 - 04	-4.12	6.90	33.01	19.96	4.79	6.14

X_1 -Working capital to total assets; X_2 - Net operating profit to net sales
X_3- Earnings before interest and taxes to total assets
X_4- Market value of equity to book value of debt; X_5 -Sales to total assets
Source: Computed.

APPENDIX LXX

Altman Z Score of Kinetic Motor Company Ltd.

Year	X_1	X_2	X_3	X_4	X_5	*Z Score*
1991 - 92	44.08	3.27	16.12	48.22	4.93	6.61
1992 – 93	56.11	2.24	7.59	88.63	3.38	4.86
1993 - 94	51.56	5.19	22.62	276.47	4.36	7.45
1994 - 95	50.18	4.32	17.15	257.09	3.97	6.74
1995 - 96	58.16	2.84	13.76	68.64	4.85	6.45
1996 - 97	55.12	2.48	8.62	29.14	3.48	4.63
1997 - 98	54.91	2.92	9.58	23.70	3.31	4.46
1998 - 99	44.67	3.62	13.66	37.32	3.78	5.03
1999 - 00	142.88	7.35	33.22	48.86	4.52	7.72
2000 - 01	38.67	6.96	33.64	70.04	4.83	6.92
2001 - 02	59.18	7.27	21.92	29.00	3.02	4.73
2002 - 03	67.23	2.24	5.08	22.01	2.27	3.41
2003 - 04	51.59	-9.369	-19.28	25.07	2.05	2.05

X_1 -Working capital to total assets; X_2 - Net operating profit to net sales
X_3- Earnings before interest and taxes to total assets
X_4- Market value of equity to book value of debt; X_5 -Sales to total assets
Source: Computed.

APPENDIX LXXI
Altman Z Score of Hero Honda Motors Ltd.

Year	X_1	X_2	X_3	X_4	X_5	Z Score
1991 - 92	20.31	7.99	24.23	31.66	3.03	4.37
1992 - 93	26.55	7.79	20.67	25.34	2.65	3.91
1993 - 94	13.73	6.90	21.94	30.17	3.17	4.33
1994 - 95	5.33	7.60	30.09	45.13	3.96	5.39
1995 - 96	6.76	7.57	31.94	37.31	4.22	5.68
1996 - 97	1.75	9.62	31.16	19.18	3.23	4.53
1997 - 98	11.98	10.25	40.40	22.73	3.90	5.65
1998 - 99	-4.71	12.04	47.02	45.60	4.54	6.47
1999 - 00	-9.28	12.87	58.49	78.18	3.33	4.06
2000 - 01	-9.85	11.97	56.18	60.08	4.69	6.95
2001 - 02	-44.68	15.58	87.87	34.30	3.64	6.42
2002 - 03	-64.62	17.37	89.11	29.74	4.13	6.72
2003 - 04	-57.18	18.42	81.78	22.86	4.44	6.84

X_1 -Working capital to total assets; X_2 - Net operating profit to net sales
X_3- Earnings before interest and taxes to total assets
X_4- Market value of equity to book value of debt; X_5 -Sales to total assets
Source: Computed.

APPENDIX LXXII

Altman Z Score of Kinetic Enginering Ltd.

Year	X_1	X_2	X_3	X_4	X_5	Z Score
1991 - 92	41.05	9.83	9.83	10.08	1.86	2.87
1992 – 93	48.64	10.85	10.85	9.31	1.70	2.85
1993 - 94	47.88	10.00	10.00	10.45	1.55	2.66
1994 - 95	43.71	10.23	10.23	17.56	1.94	3.05
1995 - 96	37.86	9.92	9.92	13.05	2.13	2.51
1996 - 97	37.20	9.57	9.57	10.36	1.95	2.91
1997 - 98	46.20	9.10	9.10	6.01	1.61	2.63
1998 - 99	36.81	9.07	9.07	3.95	1.49	2.38
1999 - 00	42.12	10.77	10.77	3.32	1.31	2.34
2000 - 01	44.58	9.39	13.35	3.07	1.42	2.54
2001 - 02	52.25	7.09	11.17	1.85	1.07	2.17
2002 - 03	49.46	6.02	5.27	2.05	0.88	1.74
2003 - 04	37.70	-17.57	-15.38	1.98	0.88	0.59

X_1 -Working capital to total assets; X_2 - Net operating profit to net sales
X_3- Earnings before interest and taxes to total assets
X_4- Market value of equity to book value of debt; X_5 -Sales to total assets
Source: Computed.

APPENDIX LXXIII
Altman Z Score of Majestic Auto Ltd.

Year	X_1	X_2	X_3	X_4	X_5	*Z Score*
1991 - 92	-	-	-	-	-	-
1992 - 93	-	-	-	-	-	-
1993 - 94	-	-	-	-	-	-
1994 - 95	-	-	-	-	-	-
1995 - 96	-	-	-	-	-	-
1996 - 97	-	-	-	-	-	-
1997 - 98	-	-	-	-	-	-
1998 - 99	17.45	6.61	13.04	14.76	1.97	2.79
1999 - 00	10.05	3.54	6.66	14.04	1.88	2.35
2000 - 01	4..91	3.27	6.46	47.45	1.98	2.58
2001 - 02	1.41	4.22	-6.42	34.48	1.52	1.47
2002 - 03	-9.82	-7.72	-15.60	32.55	2.02	1.47
2003 - 04	22.17	6.56	17.90	31.24	2.73	3.86

X_1 -Working capital to total assets; X_2 - Net operating profit to net sales
X_3- Earnings before interest and taxes to total assets
X_4- Market value of equity to book value of debt; X_5 -Sales to total assets
Source: Computed.

APPENDIX LXXIV
Altman Z Score of Scooters India Ltd.

Year	X_1	X_2	X_3	X_4	X_5	*Z Score*
1991 - 92	-	-	-	-	-	-
1992 – 93	-	-	-	-	-	-
1993 - 94	-	-	-	-	-	-
1994 - 95	-	-	-	-	-	-
1995 - 96	-	-	-	-	-	-
1996 - 97	-	-	-	-	-	-
1997 - 98	84.60	10.34	31.04	219.18	3.00	6.50
1998 - 99	85.72	6.54	15.00	172.03	2.29	4.94
1999 - 00	86.49	5.74	11.99	169.74	2.09	4.62
2000 - 01	86.18	5.09	7.34	125.24	1.44	3.54
2001 - 02	86.82	2.58	4.14	123.46	1.60	3.55
2002 - 03	27.30	3.01	1.66	148.14	0.55	1.86
2003 - 04	77.37	2.61	4.87	157.59	1.86	3.93

X_1 -Working capital to total assets; X_2 - Net operating profit to net sales
X_3- Earnings before interest and taxes to total assets
X_4- Market value of equity to book value of debt; X_5 -Sales to total assets
Source: Computed.

APPENDIX LXXV

Economic Value Added (Automobile Industry)

(Rs.in crores)

Year	*Commercial Vehicles*	*Passenger Cars and Multiutility Vehicles*	*Two and Three Wheelers*	*Industry Average*
1991-92	99.92	121.67	69.59	97.06
1992-93	-112.11	-79.78	-19.95	-70.61
1993-94	133.99	143.72	50.90	109.54
1994-95	126.49	152.87	50.86	110.07
1995-96	212.51	244.97	69.92	175.80
1996-97	139.48	106.06	50.48	98.67
1997-98	248.13	326.25	114.87	229.75
1998-99	-162.52	-214.68	-19.58	-132.26
1999-00	430.63	626.20	289.33	448.72
2000-01	102.24	45.90	139.15	95.76
2001-02	57.01	225.05	213.33	165.13
2002-03	-352.87	-1040.32	256.30	-378.96
2003-04	135.45	17.04	103.36	85.28

APPENDIX LXXVI

Economic Value Added (Commercial Vehicle)

(Rs. in crores)

Year	*Ashok Leyland Ltd.*	*Tata Motors Ltd.*	*Bajaj Tempo Ltd.*	*Eicher Motors Ltd.*	*Swaraj Mazda Ltd.*
1991-92	193.33	272.29	30.84	5.63	-2.47
1992-93	-200.47	-343.86	-14.37	-1.62	-0.25
1993-94	178.07	467.12	20.79	4.06	-0.08
1994-95	121.34	477.77	13.21	15.63	4.52
1995-96	226.19	777.68	28.86	18.21	11.60
1996-97	244.25	433.04	-4.88	14.28	10.71
1997-98	249.12	961.36	11.12	8.58	10.46
1998-99	134.05	-900.70	-53.81	3.33	4.54
1999-00	250.08	1888.03	-14.84	22.81	7.08
2000-01	283.39	199.99	-4.04	23.00	8.85
2001-02	222.16	25.98	1.59	22.82	12.48
2002-03	129.23	-1937.03	30.78	5.21	7.43
2003-04	234.91	360.56	24.88	38.26	18.62

APPENDIX LXXVII

Economic Value Added (Passenger Cars and Multiutility Vehicles)

(Rs.in crores)

Year	*Hindustan Motors Ltd.*	*Mahindra and Mahindra Ltd.*	*Maruthi Udyog Ltd.*	*Daewoo Motors India Ltd.*
1991-92	98.51	122.47	266.56	-0.86
1992-93	-82.42	-77.17	-158.32	-1.21
1993-94	120.30	195.48	256.63	2.45
1994-95	78.29	125.50	414.49	-6.80
1995-96	116.58	216.76	584.49	62.03
1996-97	47.50	113.71	311.83	-48.81
1997-98	134.10	423.90	834.13	-87.12
1998-99	-66.55	-178.50	-452.34	-161.33
1999-00	138.27	961.95	1419.86	-15.29
2000-01	6.58	307.59	-39.45	-91.12
2001-02	68.64	395.52	621.12	-185.09
2002-03	-167.24	-1040.02	-2852.98	-101.02
2003-04	-44.35	139.67	30.86	-58.01

APPENDIX LXXVIII
Economic Value Added (Two and Three Wheelers)

(Rs.in crores)

Year	*Baja Auto Ltd.*	*LML Ltd.*	*Maharastra Scooters Ltd.*	*TVS Motors India Ltd.*	*Kinetic Motor Company Ltd.*	*Hero Honda Motors Ltd.*	*Kinetic Engineering Ltd.*	*Majestic Auto Ltd.*	*Scooters India Ltd.*
1991-92	242.82	256.28	36.69	22.44	9.14	2.31	12.78	28.41	15.46
1992-93	-175.98	130.25	-29.20	0.15	-7.98	-5.59	-4.96	-49.00	-37.27
1993-94	231.55	123.90	21.97	31.50	6.57	28.46	9.09	5.45	-0.38
1994-95	278.45	110.86	9.65	39.35	4.14	22.32	6.83	-5.97	-7.88
1995-96	414.44	118.75	15.66	43.23	7.01	29.46	12.15	-4.18	-7.27
1996-97	237.60	166.24	-2.29	38.87	-0.15	37.81	5.98	-15.16	-14.68
1997-98	535.21	255.71	19.08	103.30	9.10	85.38	15.03	-1.07	12.05
1998-99	-425.16	276.42	-28.90	3.07	-1.65	39.97	-1.09	-1.97	1.05
1999-00	1452.80	462.71	69.39	252.27	27.00	278.14	36.60	14.78	10.24
2000-01	422.51	401.60	7.58	112.90	19.09	254.86	23.11	6.99	3.72
2001-02	811.70	410.00	23.43	129.29	28.47	496.11	22.93	-5.47	3.55
2002-03	2223.75	290.32	135.48	-304.01	-33.18	-34.30	-38.55	-27.78	94.98
2003-04	87.48	362.97	25.14	117.14	-21.16	494.32	-40.10	6.31	-1.90

APPENDIX LXXIX

Market Value Added (Automobile Industry)

(Rs. in crores)

Year	*Commercial Vehicles*	*Passenger cars and Multiutility vehicles*	*Two and Three Wheelers*	*Industry Average*
1991-92	1418.87	3154.84	444.41	1672.71
1992-93	832.52	1701.27	239.57	924.45
1993-94	1488.06	2944.16	415.95	1616.06
1994-95	1612.74	2563.43	636.89	1604.35
1995-96	2358.51	2826.06	659.99	1948.09
1996-97	2326.51	2844.75	667.28	1946.18
1997-98	981.16	2969.40	969.11	1639.89
1998-99	329.88	3119.87	1152.12	1533.96
1999-00	652.97	3746.39	813.83	1737.73
2000-01	600.98	2547.31	882.78	1343.69
2001-02	1143.93	2465.70	1281.13	1630.25
2002-03	745.17	2810.43	1828.57	1794.72
2003-04	950.73	3710.86	2341.22	2334.27

APPENDIX LXXX
Market Value Added (Commercial Vehicle)

(Rs. in crores)

Year	Ashok Leyland Ltd.	Tata Motors Ltd.	Bajaj Tempo Ltd.	Eicher Motors Ltd.	Swaraj Mazda Ltd.
1991-92	424.31	6283.94	305.25	39.60	41.27
1992-93	464.71	3503.05	159.37	16.40	17.06
1993-94	917.28	6069.37	350.98	67.50	35.15
1994-95	1190.49	6444.12	344.69	55.50	28.90
1995-96	1233.30	10112.67	356.93	57.96	30.18
1996-97	611.30	10700.65	282.64	12.44	25.53
1997-98	328.25	4334.61	184.20	29.20	29.55
1998-99	1027.56	295.41	228.25	55.56	42.64
1999-00	511.40	2345.58	340.08	39.90	27.89
2000-01	676.77	2054.88	219.67	31.74	21.88
2001-02	1047.77	4359.15	122.03	128.56	62.12
2002-03	2137.17	727.81	371.03	317.30	172.52
2003-04	2468.99	1206.66	340.97	443.52	293.49

APPENDIX LXXXI
Market Value Added (Passenger Cars and Multiutility Vehicles)

(Rs. in crores)

Year	Hindustan Motors Ltd.	Mahindra and Mahindra Ltd.	Maruthi Udyog Ltd.	Daewoo Motors India Ltd.
1991-92	110.63	384.56	12099.24	24.92
1992-93	47.31	367.86	6377.44	12.48
1993-94	181.07	880.37	10654.64	60.57
1994-95	142.11	841.78	9175.90	94.04
1995-96	150.23	1575.30	9478.58	100.11
1996-97	43.35	1685.95	9461.12	188.56
1997-98	-8.39	928.68	10979.28	-21.98
1998-99	9.49	1785.92	10544.05	140.00
1999-00	-28.47	926.04	14144.72	-56.74
2000-01	-84.34	417.72	10156.94	-301.09
2001-02	-23.38	462.88	9771.41	-348.11
2002-03	664.39	1465.79	9361.00	-249.46
2003-04	101.59	2643.29	12219.21	-120.64

APPENDIX LXXXII
Market Value Added (Two and Three Wheelers)

(Rs. in crores)

Year	*Baja Auto Ltd.*	*LML Ltd.*	*Maharastra scooters Ltd.*	*TVS Motors India Ltd.*	*Kinetic Motors Company Ltd.*
1991-92	2951.28	105.47	71.83	349.27	130.04
1992-93	1586.69	78.10	35.56	175.10	93.36
1993-94	2598.31	234.04	62.67	305.15	171.23
1994-95	4731.38	167.32	53.29	260.11	145.69
1995-96	4887.86	187.27	55.22	269.35	150.93
1996-97	4552.39	274.17	46.47	268.88	146.01
1997-98	6777.89	343.08	64.08	315.08	64.07
1998-99	5365.98	190.83	54.10	301.92	41.25
1999-00	3180.98	84.12	27.96	411.64	51.53
2000-01	3180.98	40.16	17.10	331.72	36.80
2001-02	4697.99	114.74	70.24	1021.94	43.85
2002-03	7714.77	150.58	120.15	1778.70	33.80
2003-04	9212.27	124.08	156.58	1800.73	38.19

(Contd.)

(Contd. Appendix-LXXXII)

Year	Hero Honda Motors Ltd.	Kinetic Engineering Ltd.	Majest Auto Ltd.	Scooters India Ltd.
1991-92	264.47	88.51	74.99	-36.17
1992-93	133.27	45.78	34.84	-26.60
1993-94	231.39	94.75	64.86	-18.84
1994-95	246.58	94.72	54.8	-21.53
1995-96	255.52	98.17	56.61	-21.00
1996-97	655.81	57.37	21.68	-17.27
1997-98	1117.02	34.87	17.16	-11.28
1998-99	4352.66	32.47	14.86	14.97
1999-00	3533.07	25.33	6.42	3.38
2000-01	4312.72	24.42	8.78	-7.64
2001-02	5531.69	29.30	17.20	3.20
2002-03	6633.43	31.11	24.62	-0.30
2003-04	9662.88	24.24	39.32	12.68

Light Commercial Vehicles

Demand: Past and Future	
Year	**No**
1990 - 91	56
1991 - 92	54
1992 - 93	57
1993 - 94	81
1994 - 95	100
1995 - 96	137
1996 - 97	91
1997 - 98	71
1998 - 99	62
1999 - 00	68
2000 - 01	71
2001 - 02	73
2002 - 03	75
2003 - 04	78
2004 - 05	81
2005 - 06	85
2006 - 07	90
2011 - 12	115

Market Growth Rates	
Year	**Growth Rates (%)**
1990-91 - 1996-97	8.4
1996-97 - 2001-02	- 4.3
2001-02 - 2006-07	4.3
2006-07 - 2011-12	5.0

Sensitivity Coefficient	11.6%

Strategic Alliances	
Company	**Collaboration**
Ashok Leyland	IVECO, Italy
Bajaj Tempo	Mercedez Benz, Germany
Eicher	Mitsubishi, Japan
M&M	Nissan Motor Co., Japan
Swaraj Mazda	Mazda Motor Co., Japan

Market Structure	
Market Segmentation	
Segment	**Share(%)**
North	18
East	9
West	33
South	40

Lead Players	
Company	**Share (%)**
Telco	52
Eicher Motors	17
Swaraj Mazda	13
M&M	12
Bajaj Tempo	6
Ashok Leyland	1

Leading Brands
Dyna Clipper, Camter, Traveller, Chital, Matador, Cabking, Standard, Swaraj Mazda

Passenger Cars

Demand: Past and Future	
Year	No.
1990-91	182
1991-92	166
1992-93	163
1993-94	207
1994-95	264
1995-96	375
1996-97	448
1997-98	448
1998-99	435
1999-00	662
2000-01	616
2001-02	678
2002-03	745
2003-04	827
2004-05	918
2005-06	1028
2006-07	1150
2011-12	2000

Market Growth Rates	
Year	Growth Rates(%)
1990-91-1996-97	16.2
1996-97-2001-02	8.6
2001-02-2006-07	11.1
2006-07-2011 -12	12.0

Sensitivity Coefficient	11.7%

Lead Players	
Company	Share (%)
Maruti Udyog	61.0
Hyundai Motor	16.0
Telco	10.6
Hindustan Motors	3.0
Ford India	2.6
Fiat India	2.5
Deawoo Motors	1.8
Honda Siel	1.8
General Motors	1.5
Mercedez Benz	0.3

Market Structure	
Market Segmentation	
Segment	Share (%)
North	43.0
East	8.0
West	26.0
South	23.0
Over Rs 1.0 mn	0.8
Rs 5,01,000 to Rs 1.0 mn	3.2
Rs 3,01,000 to Rs 5,00,000	49
Under Rs 3,00,000	47

Strategic Alliances	
Company	Collaboration
Hind. Motors	Mitsubishi, Japan
MUL	Suzuki, Japan
Honda Siel	Honda Motor Japan

Leading Brands
Maruti 800, Esteem, Omni, Lancer, Opel Astra, Opel Corsa, Mrecedez, E&S class, Uno, Ford, Ikon, Siera, Wagon R, Baleno, Alto, Zen, Altura, Opel Swing, Opel Astra Club, Indica, Sonata, Accord, Accent, Santro, Honda city, Matiz, Nexia, Palio, Versa

Multiutility Vehicles

Demand: Past and Future	
Year	No.
1990-91	37
1991-92	32
1992-93	38
1993-94	49
1994-95	51
1995-96	68
1996-97	137
1997-98	137
1998-99	115
1999-00	128
2000-01	131
2001-02	140
2002-03	150
2003-04	162
2004-05	175
2005-06	190
2006-07	208
2011-12	335

Market Growth Rates	
Year	Growth Rates(%)
1990-91-1996-97	24.4
1996-97-2001-02	0.4
2001-02-2006-07	8.2
2006-07-2011 -12	10.0

Sensitivity Coefficient	5.8%

Product Variation	
Type	Share (%)
Petrol	7
Diesel	93

Market Structure	
Market Segmentation	
Segment	Share (%)
North	36
East	11
West	33
South	20

Lead Players	
Company	Share (%)
Mahindra and Mahindra	46
Toyota Kirloskar	24
TELCO	19
Maruti Udyog	4
Baja Tempo	4
Hindustan Motors	3

Strategic Alliances	
Company	Collaboration
Maruti	Suzuki Motors, Japan
M&M	Willys Overland Corp. USA Mitsubishi, Japan
Toyota Kirloskar	Toyota Motor Co. Japan

Leading Brands
Voyager, trax, Quadro, Qualis, Armada, Gypsy, Sumo, Pick Up, Safari, Bolero, Marshal, Sierra, Indo, Gurkha

Two and Three Wheelers

Demand : Past and Future	
Year	No.
1990-91	1.82
1991-92	1.60
1992-93	1.50
1993-94	1.75
1994-95	2.19
1995-96	2.86
1996-97	2.98
1997-98	3.07
1998-99	3.37
1999-00	3.78
2000-01	3.83
2001-02	4.06
2002-03	4.30
2003-04	4.60
2004-05	4.92
2005-06	5.31
2006-07	5.73
2011-12	8.50

Market Growth Rates	
Year	Growth Rates (%)
1990-91-1996-97	8.6
1996-97-2001-02	6.4
2001-02-2006-07	7.1
2006-07-2011 -12	8.2

Sensitivity Coefficient 6.2%

Lead Players	
Company	Share (%)
Total Segment	
Hero Honda	33.0
Baja Auto	26.0
TVS Suzuki	20.0
LML	4.0
Kinetic Motors	3.0
Yamaha	5.0
Majestic Auto	2.0
Royal Enfield	0.5
Honda Motors	1.0
Maharashatra Scooters	1.5
Kinetic Egg.	4.0
4-Stroke	
Hero Honda	72.0
Bajaj Auto	22.0
Yamaha	4.0
Kinetic	2.0

Market Structure

Market Segmentation	
Segment	Share (%)
North	32
East	9
West	27
South	32

Product Variation	
Type	Share (%)
Scooters	22.3
Motorcycles	66.1
Mopeds	11.6

Leading Brands
Bajaj, Super, Chetak, Classic, Bravo, Legend, Yamaha, Stride, LML, Vespa, Kawasaki Bajaj, Hero Honda, Kinetic-Honda, Bullet 350, Shogun, Samurai, Caliber, Fiero

Market Share of Selected Sectors of Indian Automobile Industry (2003-04)

Category	*Percentage*
Commercial Vehicles	03
Passenger Vehicles	12
Two Wheelers	81
Three Wheelers	04
Total	**100**

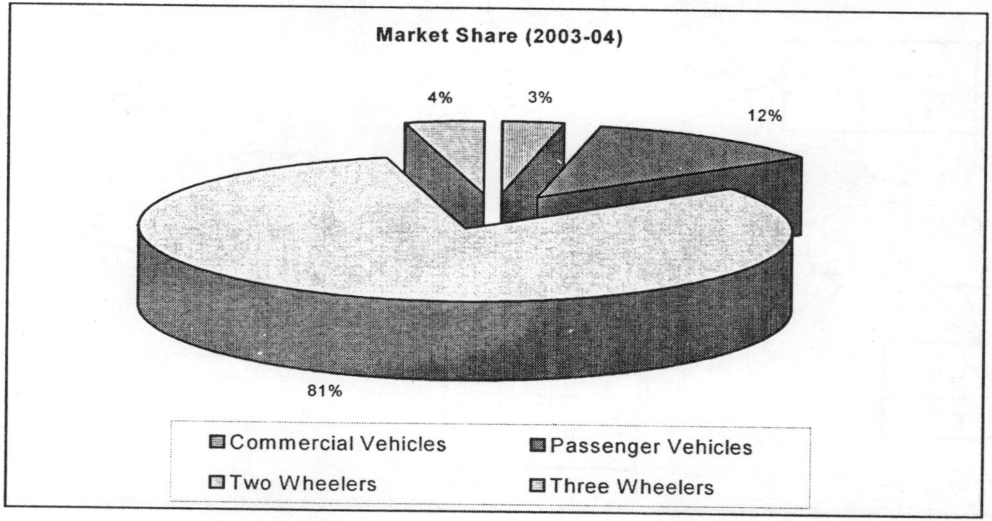

Spatial Segmentation of Automobile Demand in India

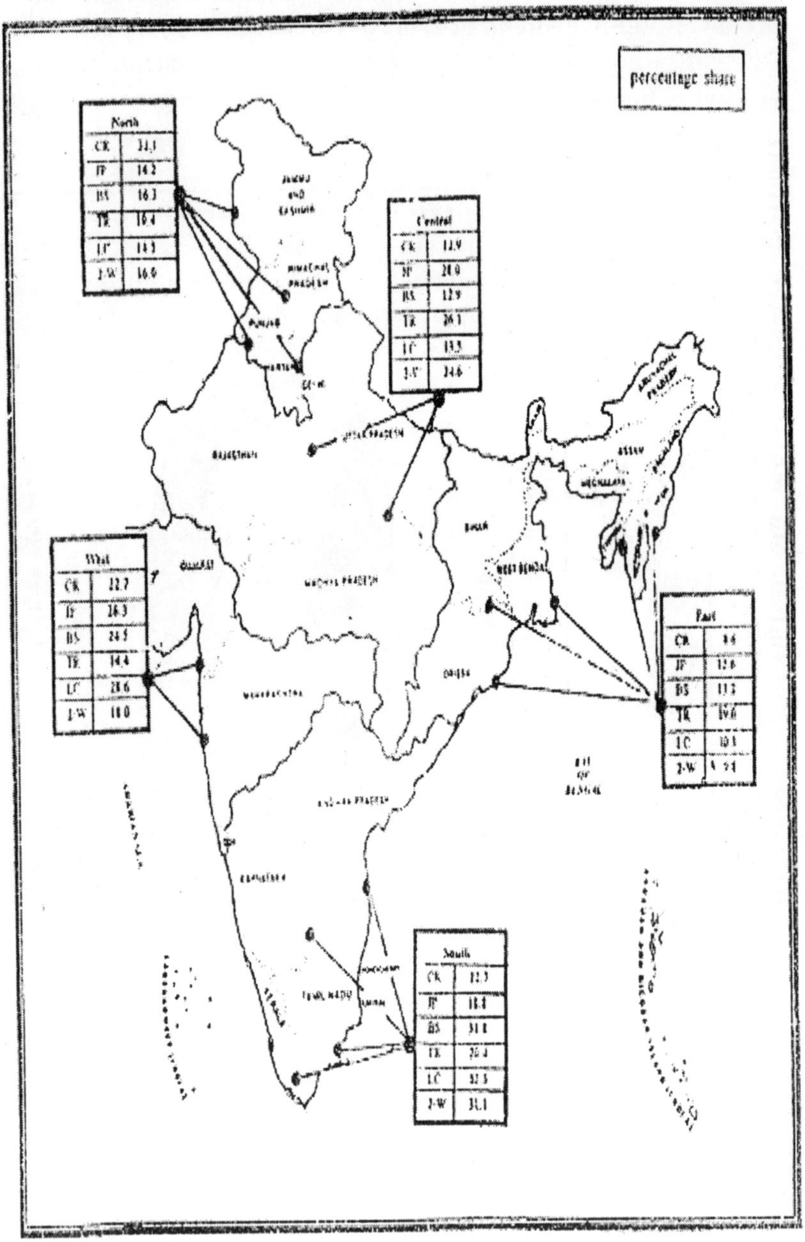

Uttar Pradesh includes Uttrakhand, Bihar includes Jharkhand; Madhya Pradesh includes Chattisgarh CR; Cars; BS: Buses; TR: Trucks; 2-W: 2-Wheelers; LC: Light Commercial Vehicles; JP: Jeeps

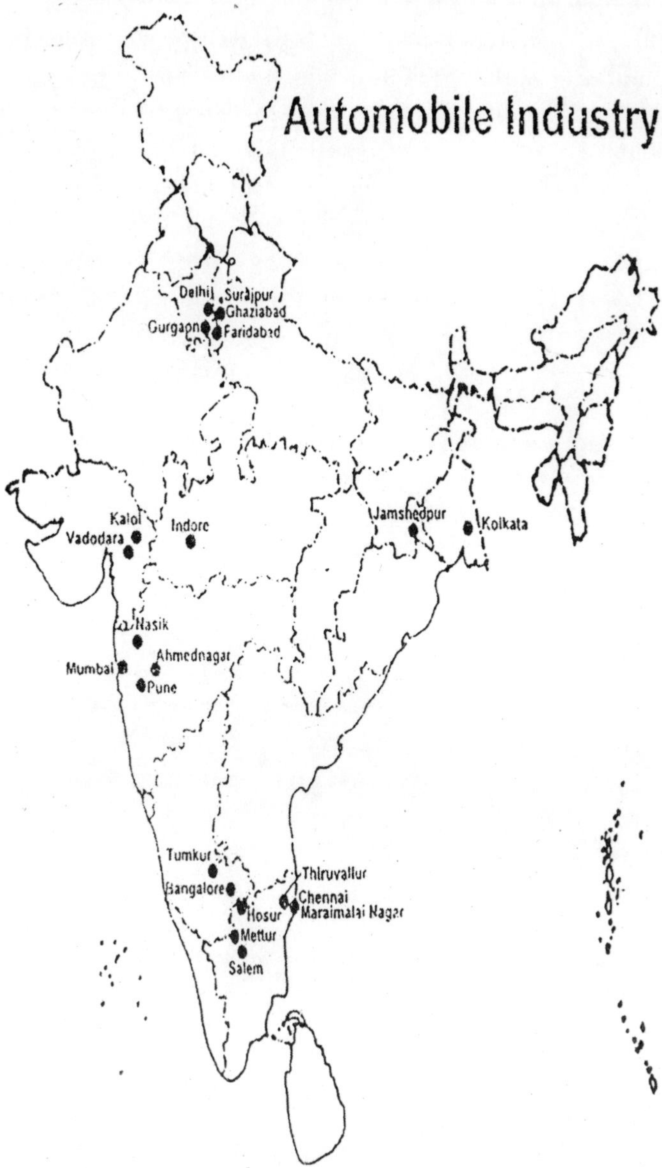
Automobile Industry
Delhi
Surajpur
Ghaziabad
Gurgaon
Faridabad
Kalol
Vadodara
Indore
Jamshedpur
Kolkata
Nasik
Ahmednagar
Mumbai
Pune
Tumkur
Bangalore
Hosur
Mettur
Salem
Thiruvallur
Chennai
Maraimalai Nagar

Bibliography

Books

Agarwal, A.N. Corporate Performance Evaluation, (Jaipur: Pointer Publisher, 1991) 66.

Agarwal, N.K. Management of Working Capital (New Delhi: Steeling Publishers Private Limited, 1983).

Agarwal, N.P. Analysis of Financial Statements: A case study of Aluminium Industry in India (New Delhi : National Publishing House,1981).

Anthony, R.N. and Reece J.S. Management Accounting- Principles (Home wood, Illinois, Richard D.Irwin, Inc., 1975) 245.

Argenti John. Corporate collapse-the causes and symptoms (New York: McGraw Hill 1976) 91.

Aziz, A. Performance Appraisal-Accounting and Quantitative Approaches (Jaipur: Pointer Publishers, 2003) 22.

Borck, Horace R.et al. Financial Accounting-Principles and Applications, 5th ed. (New York : Mc Graw Hill Book Company,1986).

Bradley, J.P. Administrative Financial Management (New York: Holt Rinechart and Winston, Inc., 1968) 173.

Das Mohapatra, A.K. Corporate Financial Management (New Delhi: Discovery Publishing House, 1999).

Duck R.E.V. and Jervis, F.R.J. Management Accounting (George G. Harrap & Company, 1964) 98.

ENO Transportation Foundation Inc., (Lansdowne : Transportation in America, VA, 1996).

Govindan Rao, D. and Mohana Rao, P. Impact of working capital on profitability in cement industry-A correlation analysis (New Delhi: Deep and Deep Publishers, 1999).

Gupta, S. P. Statistical Methods (New Delhi : Sultan Chand & Sons, 1996).

Guthman, H.G. and H.E. Dougall. Corporate Financial Policy (New Delhi : Prentic Hall, 1982) 61.

Howard and Upton. Introduction to Business Finance (New York: McGraw Hill, 1961)150.

Hunt, Willian and Donaldson. Basic Business Finance (Illinois : Richard D. Jrwinm, 1965).

Jagannath Panda and Sradhananda Das. Corporate Financial Structure (Jaipur: RBSA Publishers, 2005).

James C. Van Horne. Fundamentals of Financial Management (New Delhi: Prentice Hall, 1981)155.

John Sizer. An insight into the Management Accounting (London: Pitman, 1979)170.

Joshi, N.C. Management- Concept and Analysis (New Delhi: Vivek Publishing Co., 1977) 50.

Khan, M.Y and Jain, P.K. Financial Management (New Delhi : Tata McGraw-Hill Publishing Co., Ltd., 1996)139.

Lata Arun Rede. Profitability Trends and Business Cycle (New Delhi: Discovery Publishing House, 1998).

Lawrence, J. Gitman. Principles of Management Finance (New York: Herper & Row Publishers, 1982) 204.

Mc Taggart, James et al. The Value Imperative (New York: Published by Free Press, 1994) 4-6.

Panda, J. Paltnaik, L.M. Corporate Profitability (India: RBSA Publishers, 2005).

Pandey, I.M. Financial Management (New Delhi: Vikas Publishing House Private Ltd., 1996) 449.

Parmar, S.J. Financial Efficiency Modern Methods, Tools and Techniques (Jaipur: Raj Book Enterprises, 2004).

Pillai, R.S. N. and Bahavathi. Management Accounting, (New Delhi: S.Chand and Company Ltd).

Ralph Kennedy and Steward. Y. Financial Statements-Forms, Analysis and Interpretation , 5th ed. (Illinois; Richard D. Irwin Inc, 1968) 215-216.

Ralph, D. Kennedy, and M.Stewart. Financial Statement (Home Wood III; Richard D. Irwin, Inc, 1968) 404.

Richard M.S. Wilson and Gerard Metugh. Financial Analysis: A managerial introduction (London: Cassell Educational Limited, 1987) 5.

Sanjay J. Bhayani. Practical Financial Statements Analysis (Jaipur:Raj Book Enterprises, 2004).

Satyanarayana, J. State Government Enterprises in Andhra Pradesh: An Overview, in Rao Y. Saraswathy (eds.), Public Enterprises (A State Level Perspective), (Delhi: B.R. Publishing Corporation, 1986).

See Penerose, E.T. The Theory of Growth of Firm, (London: Basil Black Well, 1980) 25-36.

Sherlekar, S.A Industrial. Organisation and Management (Bombay: Himalya Publishing House, 1998) 375.

Slavin. A, et al. Basic Accounting for Management and Financial Control (New York : Holt, Rinshart and Winsron, Inc, 1968) 173.

Vijayakumar, A. Working Capital Management: A Comparative Study (New Delhi: Northen Book Centre, 2004).

Vijayakumar, A. Financial appraisal of Salem Co-operative Sugar Mills Ltd., Mohanur, in the book Research studies in Commerce and Management (Delhi: Classical Publishing Company, 2002) 51-65.

Vijayakumar, A. Research Studies in Commerce and Management (New Delhi : Classical Publishing Company, 2002).

Vishnu Kanta Purohit. Profitability in Indian Industries (New Delhi: Gayatri Publications, 1998).

Walker and Boughn. Financial planning and policy (Harper International student Edition Reprint, 1984) 151.

Waston J.F and. Brigham E.F. Managerial Finance, 6th ed.(Illinois: The Dryden Press, Hinsdale, 1978) 148.

Westons J.F., Eugen F. Brigham. Essentials of Managerial Finance, 9th ed. (Illinois: The Dryden Press).

Yorston, R.K. et al. Advanced Accounting, 3rd ed. (The Law Book Co., of Australia Private Ltd., 1993) 134.

Articles

Agarwal, R.N. (1999). Profitability and Growth in Indian Automobile Manufacturing Industry, Indian Economic Review, Vol. 26, No.1, pp. 81.

Aggarwal, N and Singla, S.K. (2001). How to develop a single index for financial performance, Indian Management, Vol .12, No.5, pp. 59-62.

Amit Mallick and Debasish Sur, (1998). Working Capital and Profitability: A Case Study in Interrelation, The Management Accountant, pp.805-809.

Anand, et al (1999). Economic Value Added: Business performance measure of shareholder value, The Management Accountant, pp.351-356.

Bacidore, J.M, Boquist, J.A, Miboum, T.T, Thakor, A.V. (1997). The Search for the Best Financial Performance Measure, Financial Analysts Journal, pp.11-20.

Banerjee and Ashok, (1997). Economic Value Added (EVA): a better performance measure, The Management Accountant, pp.86-88.

Banerjee and Ashok, (2000). Linkage between Economic Value Added and Market Value : An Analysis, Vikalpa, Vol. 25, No. 3, pp. 23-36.

Bao, B.H. and Bao, D.H., (1999). The Association between firm Value and Economic Value Added, Indian Accounting Review, Vol.3, No. 2, pp. 161-64.

Bardia, S.C. (2002). Economic Value Added: Overall Consideration, Economic Challenger, pp.1-7.

Bevar, W.R. (1966). Financial ratios as prediction of failure, Journal of Accounting Research, pp.71-110.

Bhanu, V. (2005). Merged Companies-their profitability performance, Indian Journal of Accounting, Vol. XXXV (2), pp.19-38.

Bhata and Dayal Bhat Nagar, (2003). Economic Value Added for comparison among companies of different industries, The ICFAI Journal of Applied Finance, No. 3, Vol. XXII, pp. 36-42.

Bothwell, Cooley and Hall (1982). A New View of Market Structure-Performance Debate, The Journal of Industrial Economics and Statistics, Vol. 64, pp. 635-645.

Burkette, G. Hedley, T.(1997). The truth about economic value added, The CPA Journal, No.7, p.46(4).

Chalam, G.V. and Dakshinamurthy, D. (1985). Performance of Public Enterprises in India: Impact of Heavy External Financing, Public Enterprises, Vol. 6, No. 2, pp.16-20.

Chandrasekaran, N. (1993). Determinants of profitability in Cement Industry, Decision, Vol. 20, No. 4, pp. 235-244.

Chattopadhayay, P. (1989). Central Government Enterprises: An Eighteen Years Profile, Facts for You, Vol. 10, No. 9, pp.11-19.

Cleveland and Frederick, W. (1993). Profitability, Uncertainty and Firm Size, Small Business Economics, Vol. 5, pp. 87-100.

Conyon, N. and Machin, S. (1991). The Determinants of Profit Margins in U.K.Manufacturing, The Journal of Economics, Vol. 34, No. 4, pp. 369-382.

Costigan, M.H. and Lovata Linda, (2002). Empirical Analysis Adopters of Economic Value Added, Management Accounting Research, Vol. 13, No. 2, pp. 40-46.

Dabasish Sur, (2001). Liquidity Management: An overview of four companies in Indian Power Sector, The Management Accountant, pp. 407-412.

Dabasish Sur, Joydeep Biswas and Prasenjit Ganguly, (2001). Liquidity Management in Indian Private Sector Enterprises-A case study of Indian Primary Aluminum industry, Indian Journal of Accounting, Vol. XXXII, pp. 8-14.

Debashish Rei and Debashish Sur, (2001). Profitability Analysis of Indian Food Products Industry: A case study of Cadbury India Ltd, The Management Accountant, Vol. 36, No. 6, pp. 407-412.

Deepak Chawola (1986). An empirical analysis of the profitability of the Indian man-made fibres industry, Decision, pp. 106-115.

Dodd, James, L, Chen, Shimine, (1997). EVA: A new panacea?, Business and Economic Review, Vol. 42, pp. 26-28.

Edwin I. Altman (1968). Financial Ratios-Discriminate Analysis and prediction of corporate bankruptcy, Journal of Finance, Vol. 9, pp. 589-609.

Ethiraj and Govindaraj (1998). The EVA feather in the market cap, The Economic Times, p. 1.

Ferri, Michael, G., and Jones, Wesley H. (1979). Determination of Financial Structure: A New Methodological Approach, The Journal of Finance, Vol. XXXIV, No. 3, pp. 631-344.

Gangadhar, V. (1982). Cement Industry-Some Aspects of Profitability, The Management Accountant, p. 477.

George Paul (1985). Financial performance of Diversified Companies in India: A comparative study of diversified and non-diversified companies, Vikalpa, Vol. 10, No. 2, pp. 179-188.

Glancey, K. (1998). Determinants of growth and profitability in small entrepreneurial firms, International Journal of Entrepreneurial Behaviour and Research, Vol. 4, No. 1, pp. 18-27.

Grant, J. (1996). Foundation of EVA for investment managers: Just in time, EVA, Journal of Financial Management, Vol. 23, No. 1, p. 41(8).

Gupta, L.O. (1979). Financial ratios as forwarding predicators of sickness, ICICI, Bombay, pp. 65-69.

Hall, M. and Weiss, L. (1967). Firm size and profitability, Review of Economics and Statistics, Vol. 49, pp. 319-331.

Harihar, T.S. (1999). EVA prorating Myths, Chartered Finance Analyst, pp. 8-9.

Jagan Mohan Rao, P. (1993). Financial Appraisal of Indian Automotive Tyre Industry, Finance India, Vol. VII, No. 3, pp. 683-685.

Jani Shweta (2003). Godrej Retools for Value, Business Standard, p. 6.

Juliet D'Souza and William Megginson, L. (1999). Financial and operating performance of privatized firms during the 1990s, The Journal of Finance, Vol. LIV, No. 4, pp. 1397-1434.

Kallu Rao, P. (1993). Inter Company Financial Analysis of Tea Industry - Retrospect and Prospect, Finance India, Vol. VII, No. 3, pp. 587-602.

Key Sengupta, (1998). An empirical exploration of the performance of Fertilizers Industry in India: An econometric analysis, Artha Vijnana, Vol. XL, No. 3, pp. 252-262.

Khustrokhan, H.R, (2002). Tata Tea Ropes in Stern Stewart & Company to Better EVA, Business Standard, p. 7.

KPMG-BS. (1998). Corporate India: An Economic Value Scoreboard, The Strategy, pp. 22-25.

Krishnaveni, (1991). Profitability and growth in Indian Automobile manufacturing industry, Indian of Economic Growth, Vol. 26, pp. 81-97.

Kuldip Kaur, (1998). Size, Growth and Profitability of Firms in India- an Empirical Investigation, Finance India, Vol. XII, No. 2, pp. 455-457.

Luber, R. B. (1996). Who are the real wealth creators. Fortune, pp. 2-3.

Mangala, Deepa and Joura Simpy, (2002). Linkage between Economic Value Added and Market Value: An Analysis in Indian context, Indian Management Studies Journal, pp. 55-56.

Mansur A. Mulla, (2002). Use of 'Z' score analysis for evaluation of financial health of textile mills-A case study, Abhigyan, Vol. XIX, No. 4, pp. 37-40.

Marcos A.M.Lima and Marcelo Resende, (2004). Profit margins and business cycles in the Brazilian industry: a panel data study, Taylor and Francis Journal in Applied Economics, pp. 923-930.

Mishra, R.K. (1988). Performance Evaluation of Public Enterprises in India, Journal of Institute of Public Enterprises, Vol. 6, No. 2, pp. 3-23.

Mohammed Rafiqul Islam (2000). Profitability of Fertilizer Industry in Bangladesh, The Management Accountant, pp. 338-345.

Nagarajan Burthwal (1990). Profitability and Structure: A Firm Level Study of Indian Pharmaceutical Industry, The Indian Economic Journal, No. 2, Vol. 38, pp. 70-84.

Nakicenovic, N.(1991). Diffusion of Pervasive System: A case of Transport Infrastructures, Technological Forecasting and Social Change, p. 39.

Ochsner (1995). Welcome to the new world of economic value added, Compensation and Benefits, Vol. 27, No. 2, p. 30(3).

Ohlson, S. (1980). Financial ratios and the prediction of bankruptcy, Journal of Accounting Research, pp. 109-131.

Pai V.S, Vadivel.V and Kamala K.H. (Dec 1995). Diversified companies and financial performance: A study, Finance India, Vol. IX, No. 4, pp. 977-988.

Pandey, I.M. (1980). Concept of Earning Power, Accounting Journal, Vol. W, p. 46.

Pant, L.W. (1991). An Investigation of Industry and Firm Structural characteristics in Corporate Turnaround, Journal of Management Studies, Vol. 28, No.12, pp. 623-643.

Parasuram, N.R. (2000). Economic Value Added: Its Computation and Impact on Selected Banking Companies, The ICFAI Journal of Applied Finance, Vol. 6, No. 4, pp. 171-178.

Putnam and Bulford (1997). EVA Analysis predicts tough time in US markets, Global Investor, pp. 42-44.

Raghunatha Reddy, D. and Padma, S. (2005). Pre and Post Merger financial performance of selected companies, Indian Journal of Accounting, Vol. XXXV (2), pp. 29-38.

Raghunathan V. and Prabina Das (1999). Corporate Performance: Post- Liberalization, The ICFAI Journal of Applied Finance, Vol. 5, No. 2, pp. 6-29.

Raj S. Dhankar (1998). A new look at the criteria of performance measurement for business enterprises in India-A study of public sector undertakings, Finance India, Vol. II, No. 1, pp. 17-28.

Rajeswari, (2000). Liquidity Management of Tamil Nadu Cement Corporation Ltd, Alangulam- A Case Study, The Management Accountant, Vol. II, No. 2, pp. 377-378.

Rao, M.P. (1985). Impact of Debt Equity Ratio on Profitability-An Exploratory Study of Engineering Industry, Lok Udyog, Vol. 19 (5), pp. 29-34.

RBI Bulletin (1995). Financial performance of private corporate business sector, Finance India, Vol. IX, No. 4, pp. 901-908.

RBI Corporate Studies Division, (2003). Performance of corporate business sector during the first half of 2002-2003, Finance India, Vol. XVII, No. 3, pp. 987-1002.

Remmers, L., Stonetill, A., Wright, R., and Beakhusen, T., Industry and size as Debt-ratio determinants in manufactuirng internationally, Financial Managmenet, Vol. III, Spring, pp. 2975.

Remmers, Lee, Stonenill, Arthur, Wright, Richard and Bekhuisen, (1974). Industry and size as Debt Ratio Determinants in Manufacturing Internationally, Financial Management, pp. 24-32.

Rosario G. Manasan, Junaita Amatong and Gil Beltran, (1988). The public enterprise sector in the Philippines: economic contribution and performance: 1975-1984, Public Enterprise, Vol. 8, No. 4, pp. 339-351.

Rutledge, J. (1993), De-jargoning EVA, Forbes, Vol. 152, No. 10, p. 148(1).

Sanjay J. and Bhayani (2006). A study on sales trend and cost structure of Indian Cement Industry, The Management Accountant, Vol. 41, No. 1, pp. 66-72.

Sankar, T.L. Mishra, R.K. and Nandagopal, R.N. (1990). State Level Public Enterprises in India: An Overview, Economic and Political Weekly, Bombay, pp.1-37.

Santimoy Patra (2005). Liquidity Vs. Profitability, Indian Journal of Accounting, Vol. XXXV(2), pp. 39-43.

Sastry, K.S. (1994). Uses of 'Z' score of selective privatization marrtioused note, Indian Journal of Finance and Research, New Delhi. pp. 85-88.

Scott, David F. and Martin, John, D. (1975). Industry influence on Financial structure, Financial Management, Vol. 4, Spring, pp. 67-75.

Scott, David, F. (1972). Evidence on the importance of Financial Structure, Financial Management, Summer, pp. 45-50.

Sidhu H.S. and Gurpreet Bhatia, (1998). Factors Affecting in Indian Textile Industry, The Indian Economic Journal, pp. 137-143.

Sidhu, H.S. and Bhatia G. (1993). Factors affecting profitability in Indian Textile Industry, The Indian Economic Journal, Vol. 41, No. 2, pp. 137-143.

Soumyendra Kishore Dutta, (1999). An Analysis of Profitability trend in the Indian Cotton Mill Industry, Asian Economic Review, Vol. 41, No. 2, pp. 294-307.

Stern and Joel (1990). One way to build value in your firm, Executive compensation, Financial Executive, pp. 51-54.

Steward, G. and Bennet (1994). EVATM Fact and Fantasy, Journal of Applied Corporate Finance, pp. 71-84.

Sudarsana Reddy, G. (2003). Financial Performance of Paper industry in A.P, Finance India, Vol. XVII, No. 3, pp. 1027-1033.

Thampy, A. and Beheli, R. (2001). Economic Value Added in Banks, The ICFAI Journal of Applied Finance, Vol. 7, No. 1, pp. 180-189.

Thenmozhie, M. (1999). Economic value added as a measure of corporate performance, The Indian Journal of Commerce, Vol. 52, No. 4, pp. 72-85.

Tully and Shawn, (1997). Adding value, Business Today, pp. 68-73.

Vijayakumar A. and Kadirvel S. (2003). Determinants of profitability in Indian Public Sector Manufacturing Industries –An Econometric Analysis, The Journal of Institute of Public Enterprises, Vol. 26, pp. 1-2.

Vijayakumar, A and Kadirvel, S. (2003). Profitability and Size of the firm in Indian Minerals and Metals industry, The Management Accountant, pp. 816-821.

Vijayakumar, A. (1996). Assessment of Corporate Liquidity-A Discriminant Analysis approach, The Management Accountant, Vol. 31, No. 8, pp. 589-591.

Vijayakumar, A. (1998). Determinants of profitability, Management Accountant, Vol. X, No. 4, pp. 925-932.

VijayaKumar, A. (2002). Determinants of Profitability-A Firm Level study of the Sugar Industry of Tamil Nadu, The Management Accountant, pp. 458-465.

Vijayakumar, A. and Venkatachalam, A. (1995). Working Capital and Profitability-An Empirical Analysis, The Management Accountant, Vol. 15, No. 3, pp. 748-750.

Whittington, G. (1980). The Profitability and Size of United Kingdom Companies 1960-1964, The Journal of Industrial Economics, Vol. 28, pp. 335-342.

Zuobao Wei, Oscar Varela, Juliet D'Souza and Kabir Hassan.M. (2003). The financial and operating performance of China's newly privatized firms, Financial Management, Vol. 32, No. 2, pp. 107-126.

Working Papers

Derek Bosworth and Joanne Loundes, (2002). The Dynamic Performance of Australian Enterprises, Working paper No.

03/2002, Melbourne Institute of Applied Economic and Social Research, The University of Melbourne.

Etebari, A. (1987). Financial ratio criteria: A hypothesis and empirical test, University of New Harcshrie, Working paper, pp. 27-32.

Jack Glen, Kevin Lee and Ajit Singh, (2004). Corporate profitability and the dynamics of competition in emerging markets. A time services analysis, ESRC Center for Business Research, Working paper No. 248/2004 University of Cambridge.

James Ted McDonald, (1997). The Determinants of Firm Profitability in Australian Manufacturing, Melbourne Institute of Applied Economic and Social Research, Working paper No. 17/97, The University of Melbourne.

Joanne Loundes, (1998). Performance of Australian Government Trading Enterprises: An overview, Working paper No. 22/98, Melbourne Institute of Applied Economic and Social Research, The University of Melbourne.

Joanne Loundes, (2001). The Financial Performance of Australian Government Trading Enterprises pre-and post–reform, Melbourne Institute of Applied Economic and Social Research, Working paper No:5./2001, The University of Melbourne,

Laurent Weill, (2004). Leverage and corporate performance-9 frontier efficiency, University Robert Schuman, instituted detudes politiques, 47 avenue de la Foret-Noire, 67082 Strasbourg cedex, France. e-mail: Laurent. Weill @ urs.G-strasbg.fr.

Mark Rogers, (2001). The Effect of Diversification on Firm Performance, Melbourne Institute of Applied Economic and Social Research, Working paper No. 02, The University of Melbourne,

Petia Topalova, (2004). Overview of the Indian corporate sector: 1989-2002, IMF working paper No: wp/04/64, Asia and Pacific Department, pp.1-41.

Ram Kumar Kakani, Biswatosh Saha and Reddy V.N. (2003). Determinants of financial performance of Indian corporate sector in the post- liberalization era; An exploratory study, NSE Research Initiative, Paper No: 5, National Stock Exchange of India Limited, pp. 1-38.

Riceman, S.S. and Cahan, S.F. (2002). "Do Managers Perform Better under EVA Bonus Schemes", Social Science Research Network Electronic Paper Collection, at http://oaoers.ssrb.cin.

Rupa Rege Nitsure and Mathew Joseph, (1999). "Liberalisation and the Behavior of Indian Industry" ABAS International Conference on "Globalisation and Emerging Economics" at Barcelona, Spain, No.14.

Simon Feeny and Mark Rogers, (1998). Profitability in Australian Enterprises, Melbourne Institute of Applied Economic and Social Research, Working paper No: 21/98, The University of Melbourne.

Simon Feeny and Mark Rogers, (1999). Market Share, Concentration and Diversification in Firm Profitability, Melbourne Institute of Applied Economic and Social Research, Working paper No: 20, The University of Melbourne.

Simon Feeny, (2000). Determinants of profitability: an empirical investigation using Australian tax entities, Melbourne Institute of Applied Economic and Social Research, The University of Melbourne.

Singh, A., and Hamid J. "Corporate financial structure in Developing Countries", IFC technical paper, No.1 The World Bank, Washington, D.C.

Unpublished thesis

Asha Jain, (1981). Price- Cost Margin in Indian Manufacturing Industries: An Econometric Analysis, Ph.D thesis, IIT, Kanpur.

Kadirvelu, S. (2002). Profitability Analysis of Selected Indian Public Sector Manufacturing Enterprises- before and after Liberalisation, Unpublished thesis, Bharathiar University, Coimbatore.

Krishnaveni, M. (2004). Performance Appraisal of an Indian Chemical Industry after Liberalisation (199192 to 2001-02),Unpublished thesis, Bharathiar University, Coimbatore.

Kulshreshtha, R.S. (1973). Profitability in India's Steel Industry-During the decade 1960-70 (A thesis submitted for the degree of Ph.D., Dept. of E.A.F.M. University of Rajashthan), p. 83.

Maninder S. Sarkaia, Shergil U.S. (2004). Market Structure and Financial Performance-An Indian Evidence with Enhanced

Controls, Ph.D Thesis Submitted to the Guru Nanak Dev University.

Wolfgang Aussenegg and Ranko Jelic, (2002). Operating performance of privatized companies in transition economies- the case of Poland, Hungary and the Czech republic, Research abstract, source: www.ssrn.com.

Reports

- Annual Reports of the Indian Automobile Industry
- Basic statistics relating to Indian Economy, Center for Monitoring Indian Economy, Mumbai, Sep 1994.
- Government of India, Annual Survey of Industries (Series), Central Statistical Organization.
- Kothari's Industrial Directory of India
- RBI Bulletin, RBI, Mumbai.
- UNIDO (1996). Industrial Development : Global Report.

Select on-line Newspapers

- Business Line
- Business Standard
- Business-Standard.com
- Deccan Chronicle
- DeccanHerald.com
- ExpressIndia.com
- Financial Express
- Hindustan Times Online
- India Today
- IndiaDaily.com
- IndiaDirect.com
- IndiaExpress.com
- IndiaInfoline.com
- IndiaPress.org
- NewsIndia-Times.com
- PatrikaOnline.com
- The Economic Times
- The Hindu
- The Times of India

Select Business Magazines

- Banking and Finance-Bi-monthly magazine on banking & finance.
- Business Barons-Bi-monthly business magazine.
- Business Today-A fortnightly business magazine.
- Business Weekly News-International weekly business reports.
- Capital Market-A business magazine focused on the stock market.
- Dhan-An online business and financial news magazine
- Domex Information-Fortnightly industrial and business bulletin.
- Fortune-A financial magazine from pathfinder
- India Investors-Weekly newsletter on stock markets.
- India Times-Online business magazine
- Industrial Economist-Online business magazine
- Industrial Magazine Online-Industry news, events, press releases, etc.

Select Search Engines and Websites

- http://did.nic.in
- http://finmin.nic.in
- http://www.altavista.com
- http://www.bisnetindia.com
- http://www.bseindia.com
- http://www.cmie.org
- http://www.economictimes.com
- http://www.gadnet.com/india.html
- http://www.indiainfoline.com
- http://www.indiamart.com/assocham
- http://www.indianindustry.com
- http://www.indiastat.com
- http://www.indiatimes.com
- http://www.india-yp.com
- http://www.indous.org
- http://www.nic.in
- http://www.nic.in/bicp/
- http://www.nic.in/delnet
- http://www.nic.in/icar

- http://www.nic.in/lawmin/
- http://www.nsdl.com
- http://www.nseindia.com
- http://www.rbi.org.in
- http://www.rediff.com
- http://www.sebi.com
- http://www.usibc.com
- http://www.yahoo.com

C

E

Index

K

L

M